Fodor's
Turkey

D0724370

PRAISE FOR FODOR'S GUIDES

"Fodor's guides . . . are an admirable blend of the cultural and the practical."
—The Washington Post

"Researched by people chosen because they live or have lived in the country, well-written, and with good historical sections . . . Obligatory reading for millions of tourists."
—The Independent, *London*

"Usable, sophisticated restaurant coverage, with an emphasis on good value."
—*Andy Birsh,* Gourmet *restaurant columnist, quoted by Gannett News Service*

"Packed with dependable information."
—Atlanta Journal Constitution

"Fodor's always delivers high quality . . . thoughtfully presented . . . thorough."
—Houston Post

"Valuable because of their comprehensiveness."
—Minneapolis Star-Tribune

Fodor's Travel Publications, Inc.
New York • Toronto • London • Sydney • Auckland

Fodor's Turkey

Editor: Nancy van Itallie
Contributors: Stephen Amsterdam, Fionn Davenport, Echo Garrett, Gareth Jenkins, Laura Kidder, Bevin McLaughlin, Rebecca Morris, Virginia O'Brien, Mary Ellen Schultz, Aaron Sugarman, Meltem Türköz
Art Director: Fabrizio La Rocca
Cartographer: David Lindroth
Illustrator: Karl Tanner
Cover Photograph: Peter Guttman

Design: Vignelli Associates

Contents

Foreword   *vi*

Highlights   *viii*

Fodor's Choice   *x*

Introduction   *xviii*

1 Essential Information   *1*

Before You Go *2*

Government Information Offices *2*
Tours and Packages *2*
When to Go *3*
Festivals and Seasonal Events *5*
What to Pack *6*
Getting Money from Home *8*
Turkish Currency *8*
What It Will Cost *8*
Long-Distance Calling *9*
Passports and Visas *9*
Customs and Duties *10*
Traveling with Cameras, Camcorders, and Laptops *11*
Language *12*
Staying Healthy *12*
Insurance *13*
Car Rentals *14*
Student and Youth Travel *15*
Traveling with Children *16*
Hints for Women Traveling Solo *17*
Hints for Travelers with Disabilities *18*
Hints for Older Travelers *19*
Hints for Gay and Lesbian Travelers *19*
Further Reading *20*

Arriving and Departing *20*

From North America by Plane *20*
From the United Kingdom by Plane, Train, and Car *22*

Staying in Turkey *23*

Getting Around *23*
Telephones *25*
Mail *26*
Tipping *26*
Opening and Closing Times *26*
Shopping *26*
Sports and the Outdoors *27*
Beaches *28*
Dining *28*

Lodging *31*
Credit Cards *32*

Great Itineraries *32*

The Aegean *32*
The Mediterranean Coast *32*
Central Anatolia *33*
Black Sea Highlights *33*
Adventuring in the East *34*

2 Portraits of Turkey *37*

Turkey at a Glance: A Chronology *38*
"The Art of the Kilim," by Alastair Hull and
Nicholas Barnard *42*

3 Istanbul *50*

4 Bursa, İznik, and Termal *91*

5 The Aegean Coast *103*

6 The Mediterranean Coast *146*

7 Ankara and Central Anatolia *181*

8 The Black Sea Coast *213*

9 The Far East *229*

Turkish Vocabulary *245*

Index *250*

Maps

Turkey *xiii*
Europe *xiv–xv*
World Time Zones *xvi–xvii*
Istanbul: Tours 1–4 *58–59*
Topkapı Palace *60*
Tour 5: The Bosporus *70*
Istanbul Dining and Lodging *78–79*
Sea of Marmara *95*
Aegean Coast *108–109*
İzmir *118*
Selçuk and Ephesus *125*
Western Mediterranean Coast *151*
Eastern Mediterranean Coast *152*
Antalya *163*

Central Anatolia *186–187*
Ankara *188*
Black Sea Coast *217*
Lake Van and the East *234–235*

Foreword

While every care has been taken to ensure the accuracy of the information in this guide, the passage of time will always bring change and, consequently, the publisher cannot accept responsibility for errors that may occur.

All prices and opening times quoted here are based on information supplied to us at press time. Hours and admission fees may change, however, and the prudent traveler will avoid inconvenience by calling ahead.

Fodor's wants to hear about your travel experiences, both pleasant and unpleasant. When a hotel or restaurant fails to live up to its billing, let us know, and we will investigate the complaint and revise our entries where the facts warrant it.

Send your letters to the editors of Fodor's Travel Publications, 201 E. 50th Street, New York, NY 10022.

Highlights and Fodor's Choice

Highlights

*By Pidgeon
O'Brien*

*Updated by
Meltem
Türköz*

Turkey's tourism industry experienced a slump in the summer of 1994, when **bombs** planted in popular tourist resorts by Kurdish guerillas claimed the lives of tourists and locals alike—and frightened off many potential visitors. By July, most hotels had about 10% to 15% occupancy and had reduced rates considerably. Visitors to Sultanahmet in Istanbul had a hard time finding trash bins, which were removed to avoid the planting of bombs.

Mrs. Tansu Ciller, a young, attractive, ambitious economics professor, was elected as the country's first **female prime minister** in June 1993 with the center right True Path Party ticket. Within a year, however, her popularity had dwindled as inflation rocketed and the economy went into a period of serious crisis.

The victory of the pro-Islamic Welfare Party in the March **local elections** set off debates about whether Turkey would be the next Iran or Algeria. The pro-Islamic party rallied much of the support lost by parties in power and was victorious in municipal elections throughout Anatolia, in Istanbul, and even in Ankara. By summer 1994, the new mayors had made their contempt for the arts very clear. While Istanbul's mayor, Recep Tayyip Erdogan, said the city theaters were a waste of money that could go elsewhere, Ankara's mayor Melih Gokcek started by pulling down statues he considered obscene.

On a more positive note, Turkey's attempts to regain ancient objects and **treasures** originally found on its soil proved fruitful. In 1993 the Lydian treasures, also called the Treasures of Croesus, were obtained from the Metropolitan Museum in New York and are now on exhibit at Ankara's Museum of Anatolian Civilizations. Sarcophagi and other ancient objects are making their way back to their places of origin, as a new precedent is set, according to which archaeological artifacts belong in the country in which they were originally found.

Istanbul's Bosporus strait was the site of a major **tanker** and freighter collision in March 1994. The collision sent the tanker up in massive flames, killing more than 30 crew members and spilling tons of crude oil into the waters. The environmental effects were as serious as the political ramifications. Under the Montreux Convention, the straits are international waters, but the potentially disastrous increase in tanker traffic, especially since the collapse of the Soviet Union, has the Istanbul public and the Turkish government up in arms. A new Bosporus Regulation drawn up by Turkey, but disputed by Russia, went into effect in July. The regulation strongly urges ships carrying potentially lethal cargo to engage pilot boats for the passage through the sometimes dodgy strait, and makes it mandatory for the navigators of these ships to notify Turkish officials before their passage.

Construction continues on a **rail project** to link Istanbul and Ankara, with part of the route passing through a new tunnel under the Bosporus. The train is projected to reach speeds exceeding 200 kilometers per hour (120 miles per hour); the trip currently takes 8 to 11 hours.

The enormous **Atatürk Dam,** slated for completion in 2005, and several related water projects will irrigate some 48,000 kilometers (30,000 miles) of formerly arid land, an area the size of Holland, Belgium, and Luxembourg combined. Initial stages of the project have already helped Turkey produce a bumper crop of wheat and other agricultural products. This has helped the nation build relations with Azerbaijan and other neighbors by supplying them with wheat and grain. The dam has had one unexpected side effect: Archaeologists are digging like mad to excavate regions that will be flooded. As a result exciting finds have been unusually frequent; most of them turn up at the Museum of Anatolian Civilizations in Ankara.

In 1993 a new link in the **Hyatt Regency** chain opened in Istanbul. The large, pink hotel is designed in a modern style reminiscent of Ottoman splendor. Plush, patterned carpeting and comfortable velvet chairs dominate the interior, with a backdrop of Turkish patterns.

The U.S. State Department continues to warn American tourists about **instability in the southeastern portion of the country.** Kurdish nationalists are campaigning for an independent homeland, and terrorists in the region have attacked the "personnel and property of organizations with official and commercial ties to the United States" in the past. For an up-to-date report on the situation, call the state-department hotline, at 202/647–5225.

Fodor's Choice

No two people will agree on what makes a perfect vacation, but it's fun and helpful to know what others think. We hope you'll have a chance to experience some of Fodor's Choices yourself while visiting Turkey. For more information about each entry, refer to the appropriate chapters within this guidebook.

Classical Sites

Aegean	Aphrodisias
	Ephesus
	Mountaintop ruins at Pergamum
	Priene
Mediterranean	Cnidos
	Mountain aerie at Termessos
	Preserved theater at Aspendos

Ottoman Sites

Bursa	Yeşil Cami
Istanbul	Dolmabahçe Palace
	Sokollu Mehmet Paşa Cami
	Sultan Ahmet Cami
	Topkapı Saray
	Türk Ve Islâm Eserlerı Müsezi, in an Ottoman palace

Byzantine Sites

Istanbul	Fourteenth-century mosaics and frescoes in the Church of the Holy Savior in Chora
	Hagia Sophia
	Süleymaniye Cami
	Yerebatan Saray

Other Monuments

Aegean	Çanakkale
Black Sea	Panoramic Monastery of the Virgin, at Sumela
Central Anatolia	Göreme Valley's Kaymaklı, a Cappadocian underground city
	Mevlana Türbesi, Konya
Far East	Ani

Fortress city of Diyarbakır

Mediterranean Dalyan's cliff tombs

Museums

Ankara Ankara Anadolu Medeniyetleri Müzesi

Black Sea Coast Byzantine frescoes and mosaics in Hagia Sophia, now a Trabzon museum

Istanbul Arkeoloji Müzesi

Mediterranean Hatay Müzesi, Antakya, for its Roman mosaics

Beaches

Aegean Akçay's long Gulf of Edremit strand

Gümüşlük, rimming half-submerged ruins on a bay

Black Sea Strand at Akçakoca, dominated by a ruined Genoese castle

Mediterranean İztuzu, between the sea and a freshwater lagoon near Dalyan

Ölü Deniz's pebble-and-sand beaches, around a lagoon

Patara

Villages and Towns

Aegean Ayvalık, for 19th-century Greek-style architecture

Black Sea Coast Historic Amasya, hemmed in by sheer rock walls

Medieval Kastamonu

Safranbolu, with its wattle-and-daub houses

Mediterranean Kaş, a seaside resort

Keci Buku, surrounded by mountains

Hotels

Aegean Kismet, Kuşadası (*$$$*)

Assos Kervansaray, Assos (*$$*)

Herodot Pansiyon, Bodrum (*$*)

Bursa Çelik Palas (*$$$$*)

Anatolia Hotel Alfina, carved from volcanic rock, Ürgüp (*$–$$*)

Istanbul Çırağan Palace (*$$$$*)

Ayasofia Pansiyons (*$$$*)

Pera Palace (*$$$*)

Yeşil Ev (*$$$*)

Hıdiv Kasrı (*$$*)

Restaurants

Aegean	Canlı Balık, Ayvalık (*$$*)
Ankara	Zenger Paşa Konaği (*$$*)
Istanbul	Urcan (*$$$*)
	Borsa Lokantasi (*$$*)
	Dört Mevsim (*$$*)
	Hacı Salih (*$*)
Mediterranean	Hisar, Antalya (*$–$$*)

Special Experiences

	Negotiating for kilims while sipping apple tea (anywhere)
Aegean	Soaking in the hot springs at Pamukkale
Bursa, Termal	A bath in the Baroque Valide Baths, Termal
	Shopping in the 16th-century atmosphere of Bursa's Bedestan
Istanbul	Exploring the Grand Bazaar
	Sunset from Çamlica, Asian Istanbul's highest hill
	View from the Galata Bridge, especially at sunset
Mediterranean	Cruise in a traditional wood *gulet*
	Swimming in a private cove beneath a Crusader castle, in the blue Gulf of Kekova

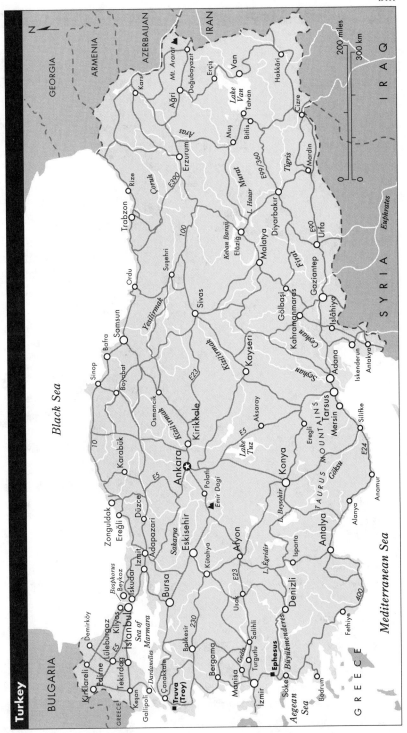

Europe

World Time Zones

Numbers below vertical bands relate each zone to Greenwich Mean Time (0 hrs.).
Local times frequently differ from these general indications,
as indicated by light-face numbers on map.

Algiers, **29**	Berlin, **34**	Delhi, **48**	Istanbul, **40**
Anchorage, **3**	Bogotá, **19**	Denver, **8**	Jerusalem, **42**
Athens, **41**	Budapest, **37**	Djakarta, **53**	Johannesburg, **44**
Auckland, **1**	Buenos Aires, **24**	Dublin, **26**	Lima, **20**
Baghdad, **46**	Caracas, **22**	Edmonton, **7**	Lisbon, **28**
Bangkok, **50**	Chicago, **9**	Hong Kong, **56**	London (Greenwich), **27**
Beijing, **54**	Copenhagen, **33**	Honolulu, **2**	Los Angeles, **6**
	Dallas, **10**		Madrid, **38**
			Manila, **57**

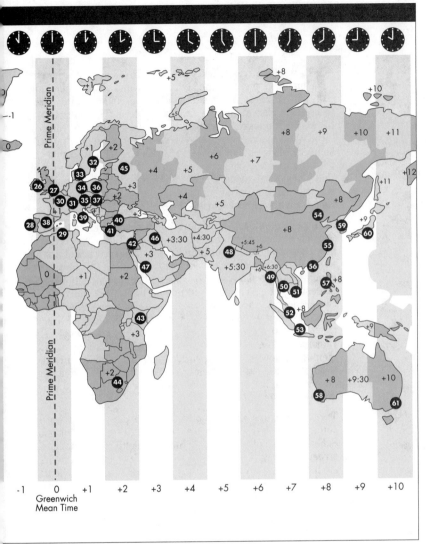

Mecca, **47**
Mexico City, **12**
Miami, **18**
Montréal, **15**
Moscow, **45**
Nairobi, **43**
New Orleans, **11**
New York City, **16**

Ottawa, **14**
Paris, **30**
Perth, **58**
Reykjavík, **25**
Rio de Janeiro, **23**
Rome, **39**
Saigon (Ho Chi Minh City), **51**

San Francisco, **5**
Santiago, **21**
Seoul, **59**
Shanghai, **55**
Singapore, **52**
Stockholm, **32**
Sydney, **61**
Tokyo, **60**

Toronto, **13**
Vancouver, **4**
Vienna, **35**
Warsaw, **36**
Washington, D.C., **17**
Yangon, **49**
Zürich, **31**

Introduction

By Rebecca Morris

To Western eyes, Turkey is exotic. Its domed mosques with minarets piercing the sky, its crowded bazaars piled high with carpets and gleaming of copper and gold, its palaces and sultans' harems are the rich stuff of fable. The muezzin's call to prayer startles our ears five times a day, and the syllables uttered by native men and scarved women are like nothing we've heard before—not one single word. This legendary strangeness both compels and confuses travelers. It also masks the reality that Turkey is a modern country, rapidly industrializing, constantly changing, growing too fast, and clamoring for recognition as a 20th-century European power.

Such strong contrasts are daily life for urban Turks, who maneuver between the ancient and modern as deftly as they cross the new Bosporus Bridge between Europe and Asia. Istanbul, they will tell you, is the world's only city that spans two continents, which makes it something of a metaphor for the nation whose largest city it is. The constant pull between East and West, between modern and traditional, creates an underlying tension that often erupts to confound Turkish society and politics. Although Turkey has been a secular democracy since 1923, Islam remains a strong force; 99% of the population is Muslim. Religious tradition prevails in rural areas, where women cling to head scarves and some are still veiled. In major Turkish cities, however, conflicting lifestyles are tolerated, and you find religious tokenism and devotion side by side.

Turkish matrons wearing baggy harem pants stride by chic young women in short skirts and boys with Western jeans. Schoolchildren of both sexes in neat black uniforms run along a street carrying books and accost you with newly learned English. "Hello," they call shyly. "Michael Jackson," they shout. In a fish restaurant along the Bosporus, male and female university students share a table and order *mezes*, the requisite Turkish hors d'oeuvres. They are drinking wine and the anise-flavored liqueur known as *raki*. On a rural bus, a woman in a flowered head scarf holds up her rosy-cheeked baby for you to admire. You mime back that he's a fine boy, and she beams a proud smile. Someday he'll wear his own school uniform—what will he think of his mother's old-fashioned clothes then? On a steep road to the Aegean, cars whiz past dignified old men leading donkeys; on sandy beaches below, tourists sunbathe in bikinis or go topless. You seek shade in a quiet Istanbul garden at noon to eat a sandwich and spot rows of men's black shoes outside a mosque. When the men finally exit in their stocking feet, all wear dark business suits and some carry briefcases. A Turk leaves his friend with the universal good-bye: "Allaha ismarladik" (I put myself in the hands of God). "Gule, gule" (Go smiling), the friend replies.

Bridging the old and the new, East and West, has made the Turks a unique people. They occupy the sites of some of the oldest cities in history; their towns and villages have risen atop the strata of great warring civilizations. Therefore, Turks walk proudly, but always a bit guardedly. They are independent, extremely courteous, and industrious. They also have an inbred instinct for survival, and that same instinct has shown them the opportunities to be had from the recent boom in tourism. In major cities, resorts, and villages near archaeological sites, everyone is an entrepreneur. No one begs; everyone—from street urchins offering shoeshines to old men hawking cucumbers by the Bosporus ferries—has something to sell you. Cold, peeled cucumbers sprinkled with salt are delicious on a hot summer day.

Urban Turkey is bursting at its seams as the countryside pours into the cities in yet another replay of the Industrial Revolution. The population of Istanbul has soared from 700,000 inhabitants in 1923 to almost 7.4 million in 1990; that of İzmir, the Aegean port that's the nation's third-largest city, increased by nearly 40% a year in the 1980s. The immense effort of metropolitan areas to accommodate such staggering growth has resulted in crowding, overbuilding, and gridlock. Air pollution is a real urban plague, especially in winter, due to the sooty lignite coal still used for heating. Electricity is expensive and at times unreliable, as is water. In Istanbul, the water supply often goes off for short periods in summer to relieve droughts. Better hotels now have their own water depots in readiness for cutoffs. Such private solutions to Istanbul's water problem have historical antecedents in the underground cisterns of the old city. Among all of Istanbul's eerie wonders, the shadowy subterranean reservoir called Yerebatan Saray (Sunken Palace) is a prize: Where else in the world can you descend into a 6th-century waterworks with dramatic illumination and classical music?

While the country has struggled with rapid industrialization, it has also benefited from it. Growth and prosperity have spurred the preservation of landmarks, the restoration of fine historic districts, and the creation of handsome new parks. Turkey tolerates no Western-style drug problem and enforces stringent drug laws. These laws apply to you, and it's foolhardy to transgress them.

If you come here, the Turk reasons, you must need a carpet. A sizable segment of the economy is based on this assumption, and there are thousands of rug sellers. Accept directions from a too-willing stranger and you may find yourself at a rug shop. Inside, everyone is charming and it's hard to escape. First you are invited to sit and offered tea. Before you can demur, a lad is sent off to fetch fragrant apple tea. Meanwhile, carpets are rapidly lifted off piles by other Turks and spread before you, one after the other. Everyone scans your expression, quick to catch the slightest glimmer of desire. The tea arrives, in small, hot glasses and smelling sweet, and is handed around to make you feel beholden. It works; you feel beholden. Carpets continue to unroll before your eyes, and it's impossible to resist the rich colors and lavish patterns, the sheer variety and beauty of them. Before you know it, you own a rug. But you must bargain: A well-managed negotiation raises everyone's esteem.

The glory of local handwoven carpets led, long ago, to strictures against shoes in mosques. Today there's a powerful odor of feet in Turkish mosques, which surely must be blamed on modern footwear. You can bet that the age of Süleyman the Magnificent did not reek of old Nikes. The mortification of going barefoot often so disconcerts Westerners that they fail to admire the floating domes of the Süleymaniye mosque or discover the dazzling floral tiles of the Rüstem Paşa. To the unconverted, mosques, like churches, require a little study, and Turkey presents unparalleled opportunities. Some Islamic countries won't let Westerners enter mosques.

Turkish cuisine provides another satisfying diversion. The country is a major food producer, and for Turks, meals are no occasion to rush. When dining out, they start with a wide variety of mezes, which can stretch into endless servings. Main dishes consist chiefly of fish, grilled meat, stews, or kebabs. The alcoholic beverages of choice are raki and local wine. (One less-than-devout Turk explained his drinking despite Islamic strictures against alcohol this way: "Tonight, we drink. Tomorrow, Allah forgives.") The universal nonalcoholic drink is tea, served in tiny tulip-shaped glasses. Coffee is more expensive and formal, and ends a meal. Neither is regarded as a mere pick-me-up. Teahouses are where Turks sit with friends, sipping, talking— and, of course, smoking. Turks smoke cigarettes all the time and everywhere. They do not regard them as threats to their health, or yours. Even foreign airplanes flying Turks get quite hazy. In rural areas, teahouses are strictly male preserves, the center of village life. The picturesque bubbling *nargile* (water pipes) can still be seen in teahouses, but the more portable cigarette rules.

Should you get lost in Turkey, you will not lack for help. Men and boys are everywhere, offering to set you straight, to guide you, or just to sell you something. Turkey has a population of 60 million, and though the country enjoyed one of the world's highest economic growth rates during the 1980s, inflation averaged nearly 50% and unemployment still runs at some 20%. More than half of the population are under 20 years of age and waiting their turn. Turkey's strong army siphons some of the excess; a 16-month military stint is compulsory for males. But thousands of men who once worked abroad have lost jobs as the result of European immigration bans and the Persian Gulf war. As a result, work is scarce and shared in odd ways. In tiny Selçuk, near Ephesus, a local carpet dealer, cousin to our pension owner, generously offered to have his nephew drive us to the archaeological site. "And my father will bring you back," he announced. The next morning, an eager teenager, trying out his English, dropped us at the site, and later, a courtly old man with an elaborate mustache rolled up in an old blue car: "Merhaba!" (Hello), he called to us. I don't know if any of these people were actually related, although rural kinship is flexible, but I expect that each, including our pension owner, got a cut of the very reasonable price we paid for a kilim. The trip was still a bargain—not only in money, but because we were sick of buses and the deal made us family, too. In Turkey, anyone who helps bring in a customer receives a cut, and it spreads the work around.

The sheer distances and geographic variety of the country, especially in Anatolia, Turkey's Asian homeland, are daunting to natives and tourists alike. Leaving Istanbul and its Byzantine churches and Ottoman palaces, you travel backward through civilizations. All roads bisect various epochs, with wonderful anachronisms and surprises en route. Modern signposts point to ancient cities: the gleaming white-marble ruins of Pergamum, fabled Troy, and Bursa, the old Ottoman capital. Beyond the Aegean port of İzmir lie the ruins of Ephesus, Priene, Didyma, Miletus, Aphrodisias—ancient Greek towns handed back and forth by vanquishing Greeks and Persians, conquered by Alexander the Great, occupied by Rome, visited by the early Christians, abandoned under the Ottomans, and miraculously, still here. Along the turquoise seacoast, long, sandy beaches stretch from the Aegean to the Mediterranean, interrupted by old port villages—Kuşadası, Bodrum (ancient Halicarnassus), Marmaris, Antalya—all reincarnated as modern resorts. The most astonishing surprises lie inland, through vast agricultural tracts of cotton and grain—Pamukkale, festooned with chalky thermal pools, and farther north, Konya, home of the whirling dervishes. Also landlocked is the ancient Hittite land of Cappadocia, whose strange volcanic peaks are pocked by Byzantine cave churches and honeycombed with labyrinthine underground dwellings. Some of these troglodyte villages were inhabited well into this century.

Ankara, Turkey's secular capital, in the center of the country, is militantly modern. It is also a national shrine to Mustafa Kemal Atatürk (1881–1938), who saved Turkey from dismemberment after World War I and founded the republic, turning it westward, away from Islam. His is the very first face you see as you change currency, and it will become very familiar; his likeness is everywhere. Thanks to Atatürk, street signs are no longer in Arabic letters, reason enough for Westerners to join the nationwide moment of silence that commemorates his death every November 10 at exactly 9:05 AM. The recent spate of mosque-building in Turkey, financed by the Saudis, must keep Atatürk fairly spinning in his secular *türbe* (tomb).

From Ankara you can travel north, along the green belt of the Black Sea coast with its tobacco, tea plantations, and forests, to mountainous Trabzon, near the Caucasus border. Trabzon is still what it has been since antiquity: a fabled and wealthy trading city. Despite modern concrete buildings, it preserves some fine Byzantine churches and their mosaics, evocative old architecture, and wonderful views. In stark contrast, if you head east from Ankara, distances grow great and towns and villages are separated by miles of brown rolling steppes, crossed by caravan routes in ancient times.

Southeast, along the Euphrates and Tigris rivers, Turkey is building a series of dams and hydroelectric plants that will increase generating power by 70% and turn 30,000 square miles of semiarid land into a breadbasket for the Middle East. This granary would be larger than Holland, Luxembourg, and Belgium combined. The completed Atatürk Dam is among the world's largest. Bulldozers bite at the heels of archaeologists, who race against time to save ancient and prehistoric monuments. Many notable sites are scheduled to be flooded soon, and electricity, development, and television will reach Anatolian hamlets little changed since biblical times.

The one region of the country that requires travelers take special care is in the far southeast, along the Syrian and Iraqi borders. In the aftermath of the Gulf crisis, the U.S. State Department issued an advisory warning Americans to be cautious when visiting this area. The danger arises not from crime but over the thorny issue of Kurdish separatism. The homeland of Turkey's Kurds, the border country is teeming with refugees. Turkey gave asylum to Iraqi Kurds fleeing Saddam Hussein's poison-gas attacks in 1988, and many thousands more fled here after the Persian Gulf hostilities ended. As a result, the region is strained. Turkey regards its Kurds, estimated at nearly one-fifth of the population, as citizens with equal rights and responsibilities. Many hold high government and military posts. Others, however, persist in their own language and are militant for nationhood. Separatist guerrillas operating around the Syrian border have plagued both Turks and Kurds, and the Turkish government has on occasion responded violently. As the region is difficult to travel in and offers few tourist amenities, it falls outside the focus of this book.

What about the future? Turkey has a challenging agenda. It is determined to prosper and claim its place among the modern states of Europe. Turkey applied for full membership in the European Union in 1987 but has been refused on a variety of grounds, including virulent objections from rival Greece (an EU member). Turks, who have suffered from bad press in the West ever since the Crusades, argue that the EU has focused on its problems while ignoring the country's economic miracle, its wide resources, and its astonishing progress. Nonetheless, Turkey has taken steps to spur EU acceptance. In 1991 the government instituted an ambitious program of constitutional and economic reforms, stressing free enterprise, higher education, jobs, social services, new freedoms for minority Kurds, and human-rights initiatives.

Even without the access to European markets that EU membership promises, the rewards of Turkey's free market have brought telephone service as well as access to color TV and reruns of "Dallas" to every village. Shops are piled with consumer goods, and credit cards are accepted in major towns.

1 Essential Information

Before You Go

Government Information Offices

In the United States
Turkish Culture and Information Office (821 United Nations Plaza, New York, NY 10017, tel. 212/687–2194, fax 212/599–7568; 1717 Massachusetts Ave. NW, Washington, DC 20036, tel. 202/429–9844 or 202/429–9409, fax 202/429–5649).

In the United Kingdom
Turkish Tourist Office (170 Piccadilly, London W1V 9DD, tel. 0171/734–8681).

U.S. Government Travel Briefings
The U.S. Department of State's **Overseas Citizens Emergency Center** (Room 4811, Washington, DC 20520; enclose S.A.S.E.) issues Consular Information Sheets, which cover crime, security, political climate, and health risks as well as embassy locations, entry requirements, currency regulations, and other routine matters. For the latest information, stop in at any U.S. passport office, consulate, or embassy; call the interactive hot line (tel. 202/647–5225; fax 202/647–3000); or, with your PC's modem, tap into the Bureau of Consular Affairs' computer bulletin board (tel. 202/647–9225).

Tours and Packages

Although you will have to march to the beat of a tour guide's drum rather than your own, a package tour is likely to save you money on airfare, hotels, and ground transportation. For the more experienced or adventurous traveler, there are special-interest tours and independent packages.

When considering a tour, read the fine print in the brochure and expect only what it specifies. Be sure to find out exactly what expenses are included (particularly tips, taxes and service charges, side trips, additional meals, and entertainment); ratings of facilities in all hotels on the itinerary; and, if you are traveling alone, the cost of a single supplement. Note whether any of the arrangements are subject to change and check the operator's policy regarding cancellations, complaints, and trip-interruption insurance. Most tour operators ask that you book through travel agents—there is no additional charge for doing so.

Fully Escorted Tours
Look into the upscale **Abercrombie & Kent International Tours** (1520 Kensington Rd., Oak Brook, IL 60521 (tel. 800/323–7308 or 703/954–2944); or try **Aim Travel** (2445 18th St., NW, Washington, DC 20009, tel. 202/387–0246); **Ara Tours** (Box 275, Palm Desert, CA 92261, tel. 310/553–3113 or 800/544–7596); **Geeta Tours & Travels** (1245 W. Jarvis Ave., Chicago, IL 60626, tel. 312/262–4959); **Globus** (5301 S. Federal Cir., Littleton, CO 80123, tel. 303/797–2800 or 800/221–0090) or its more budget-minded sister company, **Cosmos Tourama; Golden Horn Travel** (Box 207, Annapolis, MD 21401, tel. 410/757–8005 or 800/772–7009); **Insight International Tours** (745 Atlantic Ave., Suite 720, Boston, MA 02111, tel. 617/482–2000 or 800/582–8380); **Pacha Tours** (1650 Broadway, Suite 316, New York, NY 10036, tel. 212/764–4080 or 800/722–4288); **Persepolis Tours** (501 5th Ave., New York, NY 10027, tel. 212/972–1333 or 800/666–1119); **Smolka Tours** (Box 856, Frederick, MD 21705, tel. 301/695–3661 or 800/722–0057); **Topkapi** (640 S. Federal St., Suite 706, Chicago, IL 60605, tel. 312/939–3194); **Troy Tours** (16151 W. Century Blvd., Suite 1118, Los Angeles, CA 90015, tel. 310/417–3460 or 800/748–6878); or **Tursem Tours** (420 Madison Ave., New York, NY 10017, tel. 800/223–9169; 212/935–9210 in NY).

| Special-Interest Archaeology and History | Good bets include **Archaeological Tours** (30 E. 42nd St., Suite 1202, New York, NY 10017, tel. 212/986–3054), led by noted scholars; **Heredot Travel** (7 South Knoll Rd., Suite 4, Mill Valley, CA 94941, tel. 415/381–4031); and **Turtle Tours** (Box 1147, Carefree, AZ 85377, tel. 602/488–3688, fax 602/488–3406). |

Crafts, Culture and Folk Art Try **Cultural Folk Tours International** (9939 Hibert St., Suite 207, San Diego, CA 92131, tel. 619/566–5951 or 800/935–8875) or **The Texas Connection** (217 Arden Grove, San Antonio, TX 78215, tel. 210/225–6294).

Cruising **Gadabout Tours** (700 E. Tahquitz Canyon Way, Palm Springs, CA 92262, tel. 619/325–5556 or 800/952–5068) combines calls in Greek and Turkish ports on a 16-day cruise. **Remote Odysseys Worldwide** (Box 579, Coeur d'Alene, ID 83814, tel. 208/765–0841 or 800/451–6034) and **Swan Hellenic/Esplanade Tours** (581 Boylston St., Boston, MA 02116, tel. 617/266–7465 or 800/426–5492) range from wilderness coves to harbors famed in antiquity. **Zeus Tours & Yacht Cruises** (566 7th Ave., New York, NY 10018, tel. 212/221–0006 or 800/447–5667) explore Turkey's coast and islands.

Environmental **Earthwatch** (680 Mount Auburn St., Watertown, MA 02272, tel. 617/926–8000) recruits volunteers to serve in its EarthCorps as short-term assistants to scientists on research expeditions.

Outdoors and Adventure **Mountain Travel Sobek** (6420 Fairmount Ave., El Cerrito, CA 94530, tel. 510/527–8100 or 800/227–2384) arranges hiking and rafting tours. **Overseas Adventure Travel** (349 Broadway, Cambridge, MA 02139, tel. 617/876–0533 or 800/221–0814) combines hiking and sailing. **Wilderness Travel** (801 Allston Way, Berkeley, CA 94710, tel. 510/548–0420 or 800/247–6700) and **Wildland Adventures** (3516 N.E. 155th, Seattle, WA 98155, tel. 206/365–0686 or 800/345–4453) offer sailing, trekking, and climbing.

Religious-Heritage **Destination Turkey** (11521 Davis St., Moreno Valley, CA 92557, tel. 909/247–8074 or 800/653–3249) tours biblical Anatolia. **Isram Tours & Travel** (630 3rd Ave., New York, NY 10017, tel. 212/661–1193 or 800/223–7460) and **Newport International Travel** (3355 Via Lido, Suite D, Newport Beach, CA 92663, tel. 714/673–2500 or 800/345–8444) both trace the Sephardic journey to freedom. **Prime Travel** (14 N. Spruce St., Ramsey, NJ 07446, tel. 201/825–1600 or 800/344–3962), **Topkapi** (*see* Fully Escorted Tours, *above*), and **Trafalgar Tours** (11 E. 26th St., Suite 1301, New York, NY 10010, tel. 800/223–7406; 212/689–8977 in NY) trace the footsteps of Saint Paul.

When to Go

Climate Most tourists visit between April and the end of October. July and August are the busiest months (and the warmest). April through June, and September and October offer more temperate weather, smaller crowds, and somewhat lower hotel prices.

Istanbul tends to be hot in summer, cold in winter. The Mediterranean and Aegean coasts have mild winters and hot summers; you can swim along either coast from late April into October. The Black Sea coast is mild and damp, with a rainfall of 90 inches per year. Central and eastern Anatolia can be extremely cold in winter, and its roads and mountain passes closed by snow; summers bring hot, dry weather, with cool evenings.

Climate The following are the average daily maximum and minimum temperatures for major cities in Turkey.

Ankara	Jan.	40F	4C	May	74F	23C	Sept.	79F	26C
		25	− 4		49	9		52	11
	Feb.	43F	6C	June	79F	26C	Oct.	70F	21C
		27	− 3		54	12		45	7
	Mar.	52F	11C	July	86F	30C	Nov.	58F	14C
		31	− 1		59	15		38	3
	Apr.	63F	17C	Aug.	88F	31C	Dec.	43F	6C
		40	4		59	15		29	− 2
Antalya	Jan.	59F	15C	May	79F	26C	Sept.	88F	31C
		43	6		61	16		67	19
	Feb.	61F	16C	June	86F	30C	Oct.	81F	27C
		45	7		67	19		59	15
	Mar.	65F	18C	July	94F	34C	Nov.	72F	22C
		47	8		74	23		52	11
	Apr.	70F	21C	Aug.	92F	33C	Dec.	63F	17C
		52	11		72	22		47	8
Istanbul	Jan.	46F	8C	May	69F	21C	Sept.	76F	24C
		37	3		53	12		61	16
	Feb.	47F	9C	June	77F	25C	Oct.	68F	20C
		36	2		60	16		55	13
	Mar.	51F	11C	July	82F	28C	Nov.	59F	15C
		38	3		65	18		48	9
	Apr.	60F	16C	Aug.	82F	28C	Dec.	51F	11C
		45	7		66	19		41	5
İzmir	Jan.	49F	9C	May	74F	23C	Sept.	81F	27C
		36	2		54	12		58	14
	Feb.	50F	10C	June	83F	28C	Oct.	72F	22C
		36	2		59	15		52	11
	Mar.	56F	13C	July	88F	31C	Nov.	63F	17C
		38	3		63	17		47	8
	Apr.	67F	19C	Aug.	88F	31C	Dec.	52F	11C
		45	7		63	17		40	4
Trabzon	Jan.	50F	10C	May	67F	19C	Sept.	74F	23C
		40	4		56	13		63	17
	Feb.	50F	10C	June	74F	23C	Oct.	70F	21C
		40	4		63	17		58	14
	Mar.	52F	11C	July	79F	26C	Nov.	61F	16C
		40	4		67	19		52	11
	Apr.	58F	14C	Aug.	79F	26C	Dec.	54F	12C
		47	8		68	20		43	6

Information Sources For current weather conditions and forecasts for cities in the United States and abroad, plus the local time and helpful travel tips, call the **Weather Channel Connection** (tel. 900/932–8437; 95¢ per minute) from a Touch-Tone phone.

Public Holidays January 1 (New Year's Day), February 4 (beginning of Ramadan Holy Month), March 3–5 (Seker Bayrami, marking the end of Ramadan), April 23 (National Independence Day), May 19 (Atatürk's Commemoration Day, celebrating his birthday), May 1–4 (Kurban Bayrami, an important religious holiday, honoring Abraham's willingness to sacrifice his son to God), August 30 (Zafer Bayrami, or

Victory Day, commemorating Turkish victories over Greek forces in 1922, during Turkey's War of Independence), October 29 (Cumhuriyet Bayrami, or Republic Day, celebrating Atatürk's proclamation of the Turkish republic in 1923), November 10 (the anniversary of Atatürk's death, commemorated most notably by a nationwide moment of silence at 9:05 AM). Please bear in mind that Muslim religious holidays are based on the lunar calendar and will shift about 10 days backwards each year. The dates given here for the Seker and Kurban holidays are for 1995.

Festivals and Seasonal Events

January **Camel wrestling,** which takes place midmonth in Selçuk, is an incredible spectacle; there are beauty pageants for the camels, parties for their handlers, and a down-and-dirty battle royal in the ancient Greek theater at Ephesus.

March or April The **Mesir Festival** in Manisa, north of İzmir, celebrates *mesir macunu* (power gum), a healing paste made from 41 spices, particularly recommended for men.

April Early April sees one of the most popular of Istanbul's annual events, the **Istanbul International Film Festival,** when the city's silver screens come alive with a multinational array of images. Late in the month, the Istanbul suburb of Emirgan, full of gardens, stages a **Tulip Festival,** and the flower beds in its park are a riot of color. Tulips take their name from the Turkish *tulbend* (turban); the flowers were originally brought from Mongolia and, their cultivation refined by the Dutch, were great favorites of the Ottoman sultans: Ahmed III staged tulip festivals in the Topkapı palace on moonlit nights, with miles of tulip-filled vases, guests dressed in regalia of harmonizing hues, and cages of canaries hanging in the trees.

May In Marmaris, the **Yacht Festival** tips its sailor cap to the international boating crowd, which gathers here before setting sail along the Aegean or Mediterranean. The **Ephesus Arts Festival,** held during the first full week of the month, brings theater and music to the ancient city. At the end of the month is the **Denizli-Pamukkale Festival,** notable primarily for its setting amid calcified cliffs and natural hot springs.

June The **Rose Festival** in Konya brings together gardeners from throughout the region for a floral competition. **Wrestling tournaments** are held midmonth in villages throughout the country; the most famous is in Edirne, where burly, olive-oil-coated men have been facing off annually for more than 600 years. Midmonth also marks the beginning of the **Istanbul Arts Festival,** Turkey's premier cultural event, a month-long calendar of activities at sites around the city. Toward the end of the month the castle at Izmir's resort town Cesme becomes the site for the **Cesme International Song Contest.**

July **Folk Festivals** with ethnic dances, concerts, and crafts displays take place in both Kuşadası and Bursa toward the end of the month.

August The **Assumption of the Virgin Mary** is celebrated on the 15th with a special mass at the House of the Virgin Mary near Ephesus. Also during the month, a **Drama Festival** in Troy honors the work of Homer and culminates in the selection of a new Helen of Troy. From August 20 through September 10, the amusements and cultural and commercial displays of the **İzmir International Fair** fill the central Kültür Park and most of the city's hotels.

September   The **Cappadocian Wine Festival** in Ürgüp celebrates the grape harvest with tastings in midmonth. Also in midmonth, special tours of archaeological sites are offered as part of the **Hittite Festival,** centered in Corum and offering insight into one of Asia's oldest cultures; you'll find crafts shows, concerts, and tours of Hittite sites. For four days in the middle of the month, the **International Song Contest** in Antalya brings open-air concerts to the area around the marina.

October   For the first 10 days of the month, the Oscars of the Turkish film industry are presented at the **Antalya Film Festival.**

December   The **Festival of Saint Nicholas,** held at the Church of St. Nicholas in Demre, celebrates the original Santa Claus, who was in fact a bishop here in the 4th century; there are lectures, special religious services, and a symposium for clerics and academics. The **Rites of the Whirling Dervishes,** which also takes place during the month, in Konya, is a rare and extremely popular display by this mystic order; book hotel space well in advance.

What to Pack

Clothing   Turkey is an informal country, so leave the fancy clothes at home. Men will find a jacket and tie appropriate for top restaurants in Istanbul, Ankara, and İzmir; for more modest establishments, a blazer will more than suffice. Women should avoid overly revealing outfits and short skirts. The general rule is: the smaller the town, the more casual and conservative the dress.

On the beaches along the Mediterranean, however, topless sunbathing is increasingly common—though it may well attract unwanted attention. Shorts are acceptable for hiking through ruins, but not for touring mosques. The importance of a sturdy, comfortable pair of shoes cannot be exaggerated. Istanbul's Topkapı Palace is incredibly vast, and the ruins at Ephesus and elsewhere are both vast and dusty.

Light cottons are best for summer, particularly along the coast. If you're planning excursions into the interior or north of the country, you'll need sweaters in spring or fall, all-out cold-weather gear in winter. An umbrella is advisable on the Black Sea coast.

Miscellaneous   Sunscreen and sunglasses will come in handy. Outside the bigger cities and resort areas, it's a good idea to carry some toilet paper. You'll need mosquito repellent for eating outside, from March through October; a flashlight for exploring in Cappadocia; and soap if you're staying in more moderately priced hotels.

Bring an extra pair of eyeglasses or contact lenses in your carry-on luggage. If you have a health problem that requires a prescription drug, pack enough to last the duration of the trip or have your doctor write a prescription using the drug's generic name, because brand names vary from country to country (you'll still need a prescription from a doctor in Turkey in order to get the medication from a pharmacy there). Always carry prescription drugs in their original packaging to avoid problems with customs officials. Don't pack them in luggage that you plan to check, in case your bags go astray. Pack a list of the offices that supply refunds for lost or stolen traveler's checks.

Electricity   The electrical current in Turkey is 220 volts, 50 cycles alternating current (AC); the United States runs on 110-volt, 60-cycle AC. Unlike wall outlets in the United States, which accept plugs with two flat prongs, outlets in Turkey take Continental-type plugs, with two or three round prongs.

Adapters, To use U.S.-made electrical appliances abroad, you'll need an adapt-
Converters, er plug. Unless the appliance is dual-voltage, you'll also need a con-
Transformers verter. Hotels sometimes have 110-volt outlets for low-wattage appliances marked "For Shavers Only" near the sink; don't use them for a high-wattage appliance like a hair dryer. If you're traveling with an older laptop computer, carry a transformer. New laptop computers are auto-sensing, operating equally well on 110 and 220 volts, so you need only the appropriate adapter plug. For a copy of the free brochure "Foreign Electricity Is No Deep Dark Secret," send a S.A.S.E. to adapter-converter manufacturer Franzus Company (Customer Service, Dept. B50, Murtha Industrial Park, Box 142, Beacon Falls, CT 06403, tel. 203/723–6664).

Luggage Free airline baggage allowances depend on the airline, the route,
Regulations and the class of your ticket; ask in advance. In general, on domestic flights and on international flights between the United States and foreign destinations, you are entitled to check two bags—neither exceeding 158 centimeters (62 inches) (length + width + height), or weighing more than 32 kilograms (70 pounds). A third piece may be brought aboard; its total dimensions are generally limited to less than 114 centimeters (45 inches), so it will fit easily under the seat in front of you or in the overhead compartment. In the United States the Federal Aviation Administration (FAA) gives airlines broad latitude to limit carry-on allowances and tailor them to different aircraft and operational conditions. Charges for excess, oversize, or overweight pieces vary.

If you are flying between two foreign destinations, note that baggage allowances may be determined not by piece but by weight— generally 40 kilograms (88 pounds) of luggage in first class, 30 kilograms (66 pounds) in business class, and 20 kilograms (44 pounds) in economy. If your flight between two cities abroad *connects* with your transatlantic or transpacific flight, the piece method still applies.

Safeguarding Before leaving home, itemize your bags' contents and their worth in
Your Luggage case they go astray. To minimize that risk, tag them inside and out with your name, address, and phone number. (If you use your home address, cover it so that potential thieves can't see it.) Put a copy of your itinerary inside each bag, so that you can easily be tracked. At check-in, make sure that the tag attached by baggage heandlers bears the correct three-letter code for your destination. If your bags do not arrive with you, or if you detect damage, file a written report with the airline before you leave the airport.

Traveler's Traveler's checks are preferable in metropolitan centers, although
Checks you'll need cash in rural areas and small towns. The most widely recognized are **American Express, Citicorp, Diners Club, Thomas Cook,** and **Visa,** which are sold by major commercial banks. Both American Express and Thomas Cook issue checks that can be countersigned and used by you or your traveling companion. Typically the issuing company or the bank at which you make your purchase charges 1% to 3% of the checks' face value as a fee. Some foreign banks charge as much as 20% of the face value as the fee for cashing traveler's checks in a foreign currency. Buy a few checks in small denominations to cash toward the end of your trip, so you won't be left with excess foreign currency. Record the numbers of checks as you spend them, and keep this list separate from the checks.

Currency Exchange Turkey is constantly devaluating its currency due to high inflation, so wait to change money until you arrive. And don't change all of your money; payment in American dollars can often lead to an extra discount on your purchase.

A growing number of privately operated exchange booths offer significantly better rates than hotels or banks.

Getting Money from Home

Cash Machines Many automated-teller machines (ATMs) are tied to international networks such as **Cirrus** and **Plus.** You can use your bank card at ATMs to withdraw money from an account and get cash advances on a credit-card account if your card has been programmed with a personal identification number, or PIN. Check in advance on limits on withdrawals and cash advances within specified periods. Ask whether your bank-card or credit-card PIN will need to be reprogrammed for use in the area you'll be visiting. Four digits are commonly used overseas. On cash advances you are charged interest from the day you receive the money from ATMs as well as from tellers. Although transaction fees for ATM withdrawals abroad may be higher than fees for withdrawals at home, Cirrus and Plus exchange rates are excellent, because they are based on wholesale rates only offered by major banks. They also may be referred to abroad as "a withdrawal from a credit account."

Plan ahead: Obtain ATM locations and the names of affiliated cash-machine networks before departure. For specific foreign Cirrus locations, call 800/424–7787; for foreign Plus locations, consult the Plus directory at your local bank.

Wiring Money In Turkey, your only option is **Western Union** (tel. 800/325–6000), which operates through Citibank branches in Istanbul, İzmir, Mersin, Samsun, and Trabzon. A friend at home can take either cash or a check to the nearest office or pay over the phone with a credit card. Delivery usually takes two business days, and fees are roughly 5% to 10%. There are no American Express MoneyGram agents in Turkey.

Turkish Currency

The monetary unit is the Turkish lira (TL), which comes in bank notes of 10,000; 20,000; 50,000; 100,000; and 500,000. Smaller denominations come in coins of 1,000; 2,500; and 5,000. At press time (fall 1994), the exchange rate was TL 31,250 to the U.S. dollar, TL 20,408 to the Canadian dollar, and TL 49,860 to the pound sterling.

What It Will Cost

Turkey is the least expensive of the Mediterranean countries. Although inflation hovers between 50% and 70%, frequent devaluations of the lira keep prices fairly stable against foreign currencies. Only in Istanbul do costs approach those in Europe, and then only at top establishments. In the countryside, room and board are not likely to come to much more than $50 per person per day.

Taxes The value-added tax, here called *Katma Değer Vergisi*, or KDV, is 15%. Hotels typically combine it with a service charge of 10% to 15%, and restaurants usually add a 15% service charge.

Sample Prices Coffee can range from about 30¢ to $2.50 a cup, depending on wheth-
er it's the less expensive Turkish coffee or American-style coffee and
whether it's served in a luxury hotel or a café; tea, 20¢–$2 a glass;
local beer, $1–$3; soft drinks, $1–$3; lamb shish kebab, $1.50–$7;
taxi, $1 for 1 mile (50% higher between midnight and 6 AM).

Long-Distance Calling

The country code for Turkey is 90. AT&T, MCI, and Sprint have international services that make calling home relatively affordable
and convenient and let you avoid hotel surcharges. Before you go,
call the company of your choice to learn the number you must dial in
Turkey to reach its network: **AT&T** USA Direct (tel. 800/874–4000),
MCI Call USA (tel. 800/444–4444), or **Sprint** Express (tel. 800/793–
1153). All three companies offer message delivery services to international travelers and have added debit cards so that you don't have
to fiddle with change.

Passports and Visas

If your passport is lost or stolen abroad, report the loss immediately
to the nearest embassy or consulate and to the local police. If you can
provide the consular officer with the information contained in the
passport, he or she will usually be able to issue you a new passport
promptly. For this reason, keep a photocopy of the data page of your
passport separate from your money and traveler's checks. Also
leave a photocopy with a relative or friend at home.

U.S. Citizens All U.S. citizens, even infants, need a valid passport to enter Turkey
for stays of up to 90 days. You can pick up new and renewal applica-
tion forms at any of the 13 U.S. Passport Agency offices and at some
post offices and courthouses. Although passports are usually mailed
within four weeks of your application's receipt, allow five weeks or
more from April through summer. Call the Department of State Office of Passport Services' information line (tel. 202/647–0518) for
fees, documentation requirements, and other details.

Canadian Canadian citizens need a valid passport to enter Turkey for stays of
Citizens up to 90 days. Application forms are available at 23 regional passport offices as well as post offices and travel agencies. Whether for a
first or a subsequent passport, you must apply in person. Children
under 16 may be included on a parent's passport but must have their
own to travel alone. Passports are valid for five years and are usually
mailed within two weeks of an application's receipt. For fees, documentation requirements, and other information in English or
French, call the passport office (tel. 819/994–3500 or 800/567–6868).

U.K. Citizens Citizens of the United Kingdom need a valid passport to enter Turkey for stays of up to 90 days. Applications for new and renewal passports are available from main post offices as well as at the six
passport offices, located in Belfast, Glasgow, Liverpool, London,
Newport, and Peterborough. You may apply in person at all passport offices, or by mail to all except the London office. Children under 16 may travel on an accompanying parent's passport. All
passports are valid for 10 years. Allow a month for processing.

A British Visitor's Passport is valid for holidays and some business
trips of up to three months to Turkey. It can include both partners of
a married couple. Valid for one year, it will be issued on the same day
that you apply. You must apply in person at a main post office.

Customs and Duties

On Arrival Turkish customs officials rarely look through tourists' luggage on arrival. You are allowed to bring in 400 cigarettes, 50 cigars, 200 grams of tobacco, 1½ kilograms of instant coffee, 500 grams of tea, and 2½ liters of alcohol. Register all valuable personal items in your passport at your embassy on entry. Items in the duty-free shops in Turkish airports, for international arrivals, are usually less expensive here than in European airports or in-flight.

Returning Home It cannot be emphasized strongly enough that Turkey is extremely tough on anyone attempting to export antiques without authorization or anyone caught with illegal drugs, whatever the amount.

U.S. Customs If you've been out of the country for at least 48 hours and haven't already used the exemption, or any part of it, in the past 30 days, you may bring home $400 worth of foreign goods duty-free. So can each member of your family, regardless of age; and your exemptions may be pooled, so one of you can bring in more if another brings in less. A flat 10% duty applies to the next $1,000 worth of goods; above $1,400, the rate varies with the merchandise. (If the 48-hour or 30-day limits apply, your duty-free allowance drops to $25, which may not be pooled.) Please note that these are the *general* rules, applicable to most countries, including Turkey.

Travelers 21 or older may bring back 1 liter of alcohol duty-free, provided the beverage laws of the state through which they reenter the United States allow it. In addition, 100 non-Cuban cigars and 200 cigarettes are allowed, regardless of your age. Antiques and works of art more than 100 years old are duty-free.

Gifts valued at less than $50 may be mailed to the United States duty-free, with a limit of one package per day per addressee, and do not count as part of your exemption (do not send alcohol or tobacco products or perfume valued at more than $5); mark the package "Unsolicited Gift" and write the nature of the gift and its retail value on the outside. Most reputable stores will handle the mailing for you.

For a copy of "Know Before You Go," a free brochure detailing what you may and may not bring back to the United States, rates of duty, and other pointers, contact the **U.S. Customs Service** (Box 7407, Washington, DC 20044, tel. 202/927–6724).

Canadian Customs Once per calendar year, when you've been out of Canada for at least seven days, you may bring in C$300 worth of goods duty-free. If you've been away less than seven days but more than 48 hours, the duty-free exemption drops to C$100 but can be claimed any number of times (as can a C$20 duty-free exemption for absences of 24 hours or more). You cannot combine the yearly and 48-hour exemptions, use the C$300 exemption only partially (to save the balance for a later trip), or pool exemptions with family members. Goods claimed under the C$300 exemption may follow you by mail; those claimed under the lesser exemptions must accompany you.

Alcohol and tobacco products may be included in the yearly and 48-hour exemptions but not in the 24-hour exemption. If you meet the age requirements of the province through which you reenter Canada, you may bring in, duty-free, 1.14 liters (40 imperial ounces) of wine or liquor *or* two dozen 12-ounce cans or bottles of beer or ale. If you are 16 or older, you may bring in, duty-free, 200 cigarettes, 50 cigars or cigarillos, and 400 tobacco sticks or 400 grams of manufactured tobacco. Alcohol and tobacco must accompany you on your return.

An unlimited number of gifts valued up to C$60 each may be mailed to Canada duty-free. These do not count as part of your exemption. Label the package "Unsolicited Gift—Value under $60." Alcohol and tobacco are excluded.

For more information, including details of duties on items that exceed your duty-free limit, ask the Revenue Canada Customs and Excise and Taxation Department (2265 St. Laurent Blvd. S, Ottawa, Ont., K1G 4K3, tel. 613/957–0275) for a copy of the free brochure "I Declare/Je Déclare."

U.K. Customs   From countries outside the European Union (EU), such as Turkey, you may import duty-free 200 cigarettes, 100 cigarillos, 50 cigars, or 250 grams of tobacco; 1 liter of spirits or 2 liters of fortified or sparkling wine; 2 liters of still table wine; 60 milliliters of perfume; 250 milliliters of toilet water; plus £136 worth of other goods, including gifts and souvenirs.

For further information or a copy of "A Guide for Travellers," which details standard customs procedures as well as what you may bring into the United Kingdom from abroad, contact HM Customs and Excise (Dorset House, Stamford St., London SE1 9PY, tel. 0171/928–3344).

Traveling with Cameras, Camcorders, and Laptops

Film and Cameras   If your camera is new or if you haven't used it for a while, shoot and develop a few test rolls of film before you leave. Store film in a cool, dry place—never in the car's glove compartment or on the shelf under the rear window.

Airport security X-rays generally aren't harmful to film with ISO below 400. To protect your film, carry it with you in a clear plastic bag and ask for a hand inspection. Such requests are honored at U.S. airports, usually not abroad. Don't depend on a lead-lined bag to protect film in checked luggage—the airline may increase the radiation to see what's inside. Call the Kodak Information Center (tel. 800/242–2424) for details.

Camcorders and Videotape   Before your trip, put camcorders through their paces, invest in a skylight filter to protect the lens, and check all the batteries. Most newer camcorders are equipped with batteries that can be recharged with a universal or worldwide AC adapter charger (or multivoltage converter) usable whether the voltage is 110 or 220. All that's needed is the appropriate plug.

Videotape is not damaged by X-rays, but it may be harmed by the magnetic field of a walk-through metal detector, so ask for a handcheck. Airport security personnel may ask you to turn on the camcorder to prove that it's what it appears to be, so make sure the battery is charged. Note that rather than the National Television System Committee video standard (NTSC) used in the United States and Canada, Turkey uses PAL/SECAM technology. You will not be able to view your tapes through the local TV set or view movies bought there in your home VCR. Blank tapes bought in Turkey can be used for NTSC camcorder taping, but they are pricey.

Laptops   Security X-rays do not harm hard-disk or floppy-disk storage, but you may request a hand-check, at which point you may be asked to turn on the computer to prove that it is what it appears to be. (Check your battery before departure.) Most airlines allow you to use your laptop aloft except during takeoff and landing (so as not to interfere with navigation equipment). For international travel, register your foreign-made laptop with U.S. Customs as you leave the country. If your laptop is U.S.-made, call the consulate of the country you'll be visiting to find out whether it should be registered with customs upon arrival. Before departure, find out about repair facilities at your destination, and don't forget any transformer or adapter plug you may need (*see* Electricity, *above*).

Language

In 1928, Atatürk launched sweeping language reforms that, over a period of six weeks, replaced Arabic script with the Latin-based alphabet and eliminated many difficult and obscure Arabic and Persian words from the Turkish language. The result has been dramatic: The literacy rate today is 75%, compared with 9% before the reforms.

English and German are widely spoken in hotels, restaurants, and shops in cities and resorts. In villages and remote areas, you may have a hard time finding anyone who speaks anything but Turkish, though rudimentary communications are still usually possible. Try learning a few basic Turkish words; the Turks will love you for it.

Staying Healthy

There are no serious health risks associated with travel to Turkey, although you should take precautions against malaria if you visit the far southeast. No vaccinations are required for entry. However, to avoid problems at customs, diabetics carrying needles and syringes should have a letter from their physician confirming their need for insulin injections.

For minor problems, pharmacists can be helpful, and medical services are widely available. Doctors and dentists abound in major cities and can be found in all but the smallest towns as well; many are women. There are also *hastane* (hospitals) and *klinik* (clinics). Road signs marked with an *H* point the way to the nearest hospital.

Finding a Doctor The **International Association for Medical Assistance to Travellers** (IAMAT, 417 Center St., Lewiston, NY 14092, tel. 716/754–4883; 40 Regal Rd., Guelph, Ontario N1K 1B5; 57 Voirets, 1212 Grand-Lancy, Geneva, Switzerland) publishes a worldwide directory of English-speaking physicians whose qualifications meet IAMAT standards and who have agreed to treat members for a set fee. Membership is free.

The locally published English-language *Turkish Daily News* and the bimonthly *Guide*, available at major hotels and newsstands, also offer listings of English-speaking doctors.

Assistance Companies Pretrip medical referrals, emergency evacuation or repatriation, 24-hour telephone hot lines for medical consultation, dispatch of medical personnel, relay of medical records, cash for emergencies, and other personal and legal assistance are among the services provided by several organizations specializing in medical assistance to travelers. Among them are **International SOS Assistance** (Box 11568, Philadelphia, PA 19116, tel. 215/244–1500 or 800/523–8930; Box 466, Pl. Bonaventure, Montréal, Qué. H5A 1C1, tel. 514/874–7674 or 800/363–0263), **Medex Assistance Corporation** (Box 10623, Baltimore, MD 21285, tel. 410/296–2530 or 800/874–9125), **Near Services** (450 Prairie Ave., Suite 101, Calumet City, IL 60409, tel. 708/

868–6700 or 800/654–6700), and **Travel Assistance International** (1133 15th St. NW, Suite 400, Washington, DC 20005, tel. 202/331–1609 or 800/821–2828). Because these companies will also sell you death-and-dismemberment, trip-cancellation, and other insurance coverage, there is some overlap with the travel-insurance policies discussed under Insurance, *below*.

Publications *The Safe Travel Book* by Peter Savage ($12.95, Lexington Books, 866 3rd Ave., New York, NY 10022, tel. 212/702–4771 or 800/257–5755, fax 800/562–1272) is packed with handy lists and phone numbers to make for a smooth trip. *Traveler's Medical Resource* by William W. Forgey ($19.95, ICS Books, Inc., 1 Tower Plaza, 107 E. 89th Ave., Merrillville, IN 45410, tel. 800/541–7323) is also a good, authoritative guide to care overseas.

Insurance

For U.S. Most tour operators, travel agents, and insurance agents sell spe-
Residents cialized health-and-accident, flight, trip-cancellation, and luggage insurance as well as comprehensive policies with some or all of these features. Before you make any purchase, review your existing health and homeowner policies to find out whether they cover expenses incurred while traveling.

Health-and- Specific policy provisions of supplemental health-and-accident in-
Accident surance for travelers include reimbursement for from $1,000 to
Insurance $150,000 worth of medical and/or dental expenses caused by an accident or illness during a trip. The personal-accident, or death-and-dismemberment, provision pays a lump sum to your beneficiaries if you die or to you if you lose one or more limbs or your eyesight; the lump sum awarded can range from $15,000 to $500,000. The medical-assistance provision may reimburse you for the cost of referrals, evacuation, or repatriation and other services, or it may automatically enroll you as a member of a particular medical-assistance company (*see* Assistance Companies, *above*).

Flight Often bought as a last-minute impulse at the airport, flight insur-
Insurance ance pays a lump sum when a plane crashes either to a beneficiary if the insured dies or sometimes to a surviving passenger who loses eyesight or a limb. Like most impulse buys, flight insurance is expensive and basically unnecessary. It supplements the airlines' coverage described in the limits-of-liability paragraphs on your ticket. Charging an airline ticket to a major credit card often automatically entitles you to coverage and may also embrace travel by bus, train, and ship.

Baggage In the event of loss, damage, or theft on international flights, air-
Insurance lines' liability is $20 per kilogram for checked baggage (roughly about $640 per 70-pound bag) and $400 per passenger for unchecked baggage. On domestic flights, the ceiling is $2,000 per passenger. Excess-valuation insurance can be bought directly from the airline at check-in for about $10 per $1,000 worth of coverage. However, you cannot buy it at any price for the rather extensive list of excluded items shown on your airline ticket.

Trip Insurance **Trip-cancellation-and-interruption insurance** protects you in the event you are unable to undertake or finish your trip, especially if your airline ticket, cruise, or package tour does not allow changes or cancellations. The amount of coverage you purchase should equal the cost of your trip should you, a traveling companion, or a family member fall ill, forcing you to stay home, plus the nondiscounted one-way airline ticket you would need to buy if you had to return home early. Read the fine print carefully, especially sections defining "family member" and "preexisting medical conditions." **Default or bankruptcy insurance** protects you against a supplier's failure to deliver. Such policies often do not cover default by a travel agency, tour operator, airline, or cruise line if you bought your tour and the coverage directly from the firm in question. Tours packaged by one of the 33 members of the United States Tour Operators Association (USTOA, 211 E. 51st St., Suite 12B, New York, NY 10022; tel. 212/750–7371), which requires members to maintain $1 million each in an account to reimburse clients in case of default, are likely to present the fewest difficulties.

Comprehensive Policies Companies supplying comprehensive policies with some or all of the above features include **Access America, Inc.** (Box 90315, Richmond, VA 23230, tel. 800/284–8300); **Carefree Travel Insurance** (Box 310, 120 Mineola Blvd., Mineola, NY 11501, tel. 516/294–0220 or 800/323–3149); **Near** (450 Prairie Ave., Suite 101, Calumet City, IL 60409, tel. 708/868–6700 or 800/654–6700); **Tele-Trip** (Mutual of Omaha Plaza, Box 31762, Omaha, NE 68131, tel. 800/228–9792); **The Travelers Companies** (1 Tower Sq., Hartford, CT 06183, tel. 203/277–0111 or 800/243–3174); **Travel Guard International** (1145 Clark St., Stevens Point, WI 54481, tel. 715/345–0505 or 800/826–1300); and **Wallach and Company, Inc.** (107 W. Federal St., Box 480, Middleburg, VA 22117, tel. 703/687–3166 or 800/237–6615).

U.K. Residents Most tour operators, travel agents, and insurance agents sell policies covering accident, medical expenses, personal liability, trip cancellation, and loss or theft of personal property. You can also buy an annual travel-insurance policy valid for every trip (usually of less than 90 days) you make during the year in which it's purchased. Make sure you will be covered if you have a preexisting medical condition or are pregnant.

For advice by phone or a free booklet, "Holiday Insurance," that sets out what to expect from a holiday-insurance policy and gives price guidelines, contact the **Association of British Insurers** (51 Gresham St., London EC2V 7HQ, tel. 0171/600–3333; 30 Gordon St., Glasgow G1 3PU, tel. 0141/226–3905; Scottish Providence Bldg., Donegall Sq. W, Belfast BT1 6JE, tel. 01232/249176; call for other locations).

Car Rentals

Most major car-rental companies are represented in Turkey, including **Avis** (tel. 800/331–1084, 800/879–2847 in Canada); **Budget** (tel. 800/527–0700); **Hertz** (tel. 800/654–3001, 800/263–0600 in Canada); and **National** (tel. 800/227–3876), known internationally as InterRent and Europcar. In cities, unlimited-mileage rates range from $61 per day for an economy car to $115 for a large car; weekly unlimited-mileage rates range from $385 to $542. This includes tax, which in Turkey is 23% on car rentals.

Requirements Your own driver's license is acceptable. An International Driver's Permit, available from the American or Canadian Automobile Association, is a good idea.

Extra Charges Picking up the car in one city and leaving it in another may entail substantial drop-off charges or one-way service fees. The cost of a collision or loss-damage waiver (*see below*) can be high, also. Some rental agencies will charge you extra if you return the car *before* the time specified on your contract. Ask before making unscheduled drop-offs. Be sure the rental agent agrees *in writing* to any changes in drop-off location or other items of your rental contract. Fill the tank just before you turn in the vehicle to avoid being charged for refueling at what you'll swear is the most expensive pump in town. In Turkey automatic transmissions and air-conditioning are rarities. Asking for either can significantly increase the cost of your rental.

Cutting Costs Major international companies have programs that discount their standard rates by 15% to 30% if you make the reservation before departure (anywhere from 24 hours to 14 days), rent for a minimum number of days (typically three or four), and prepay the rental.

Several companies operate as wholesalers. They do not own their own fleets but rent in bulk from those that do and offer advantageous rates to their customers. Rentals through such companies must be arranged and paid for before you leave the United States. Among them is **The Kemwel Group** (106 Calvert St., Harrison, NY 10528, tel. 914/835–5555 or 800/678–0678). You won't see these wholesalers' deals advertised; they're even better in summer, when business travel is down. Always ask whether the prices are guaranteed in U.S. dollars or foreign currency and if unlimited mileage is available. Find out about any required deposits, cancellation penalties, and drop-off charges, and confirm the cost of any required insurance coverage.

Insurance and Until recently standard rental contracts included liability coverage
Collision (for damage to public property, injury to pedestrians, and so on) and
Damage coverage for the car against fire, theft, and collision damage with a
Waiver deductible. Due to law changes in some states and rising liability costs, several car-rental agencies have reduced the type of coverage they offer. Before you rent a car, find out exactly what coverage, if any, is provided by your personal auto insurer. Don't assume that you are covered. If you do want insurance from the rental company, secondary coverage may be the only type offered. You may already have secondary coverage if you charge the rental to a credit card. Only Diner's Club (tel. 800/234–6377) provides primary coverage in the United States and worldwide.

In general if you have an accident, you are responsible for the automobile. Car-rental companies may offer a collision damage waiver (CDW), which ranges in cost from $4 to $14 a day. You should decline the CDW only if you are certain you are covered through your personal insurer or credit-card company.

Student and Youth Travel

Gençtur Tourism & Travel Agency (Yerebatan Cad. 15, Sultanahmet, Istanbul, tel. 212/520–5274) and **7 TUR Tourism** (Inönü Cad. 37/2, Gümüşsuyu, Istanbul, tel. 212/252–5921) can tell Hostelling International members (*see below*) about youth discounts and accommodations. Student residences in Ankara, Bolu, Bursa, Çanakkale, İzmir, and Istanbul also serve as youth hostels.

Travelers 26 and under can purchase an Inter-Rail pass, which allows unlimited second-class rail travel in Turkey and 19 other European countries.

Travel **Council Travel Services (CTS),** a subsidiary of the nonprofit Council
Agencies on International Educational Exchange, specializes in low-cost travel arrangements abroad for students and is the exclusive U.S. agent for several discount cards. CIEE's twice-yearly *Student Travels* magazine is available at the CTS office at CIEE headquarters

(205 E. 42nd St., 16th Floor, New York, NY 10017, tel. 212/661–1450) and in Boston (tel. 617/266–1926), Miami (tel. 305/670–9261), Los Angeles (tel. 310/208–3551), and at 43 branches in college towns nationwide (free in person, $1 by mail). **Campus Connections** (1100 E. Marlton Pike, Cherry Hill, NJ 08034, tel. 800/428–3235) specializes in discounted accommodations and airline fares for students. The **Educational Travel Centre** (438 N. Frances St., Madison, WI 53703, tel. 608/256–5551) offers low-cost domestic and international airline tickets, mostly for flights departing from Chicago, and rail passes. Other travel agencies catering to students include **TMI Student Travel** (1146 Pleasant St., Watertown, MA 02172, tel. 617/661–8187 or 800/245–3672), and **Travel Cuts** (187 College St., Toronto, Ont. M5T 1P7, tel. 416/979–2406).

Discount Cards For discounts on transportation and on museum and attractions admissions, buy the **International Student Identity Card** (ISIC) if you're a bona-fide student or the **International Youth Card** (IYC) if you're under 26. In the United States the ISIC and IYC cards cost $16 each and include basic travel accident and illness coverage and a toll-free travel assistance hot line. Apply to **CIEE** (*see* address *above*, tel. 212/661–1414; the application is in *Student Travels*). In Canada the cards are available for $15 each from **Travel Cuts** (*see above*). In the United Kingdom they cost £5 and £4 respectively at student unions and student travel companies, including Council Travel's London office (28A Poland St., London W1V 3DB, tel. 0171/437–7767).

Hostelling A **Hostelling International** (HI) membership card is the key to more than 5,000 hostels in 70 countries; the sex-segregated, dormitory-style sleeping quarters, including some for families, go for $7 to $20 a night per person. Membership is available in the United States through **Hostelling International-American Youth Hostels** (HI-AYH, 733 15th St. NW, Suite 840, Washington, DC 20005, tel. 202/783–6161), the U.S. link in the worldwide chain, and costs $25 for adults 18 to 54, $10 for those under 18, $15 for those 55 and over, and $35 for families. Volume 1 of the *AYH Guide to Budget Accommodation* lists hostels in Europe and the Mediterranean ($13.95, including postage). HI membership is available in Canada through **Hostelling International-Canada** (205 Catherine St. Suite 400, Ottawa, Ont. K2P 1C3, tel. 613/748–5638) for $26.75, and in the United Kingdom through the **Youth Hostel Association of England and Wales** (Trevelyan House, 8 St. Stephen's Hill, St. Albans, Herts. AL1 2DY, tel. 01727/855215) for £10.

Tour Operators **AESU Travel** (2 Hamill Rd., Suite 248, Baltimore, MD 21210, tel. 410/323–4416 or 800/638–7640) and **Contiki** (300 Plaza Alicante No. 900, Garden Grove, CA 92640, tel. 714/740–0808 or 800/266–8454) specialize in package tours for travelers 18 to 35.

Traveling with Children

Turkey is not the easiest place to travel with young children. There are long distances to cope with, lots of hiking around rock-strewn ruins, and few child-oriented facilities. However, restaurants are generally casual and accommodating to families, and diapers and baby food are easy to find in most towns.

Publications *Family Travel Times*, published 10 times a year by **Travel With Your Children** (TWYCH, 45 W. 18th St., New York, NY 10011, tel. 212/206–0688; annual subscription $55), covers destinations, types of vacations, and modes of travel. *Traveling with Children—And Enjoying It*, by Arlene K. Butler ($11.95 plus $3 shipping per book; Globe

Pequot Press, Box 833, 6 Business Park Rd., Old Saybrook, CT 06475, tel. 800/243–0495, or 800/962–0973 in CT) helps plan your trip with children, from toddlers to teens.

Getting There
Airfares

On international flights, the fare for infants under age 2 not occupying a seat is generally either free or 10% of the accompanying adult's fare; children ages 2 to 11 usually pay half to two-thirds of the adult fare. On domestic flights, children under 2 not occupying a seat travel free, and older children currently travel on the "lowest applicable" adult fare.

Baggage

In general, infants paying 10% of the adult fare are allowed one carry-on bag, not to exceed 32 kilograms (70 pounds) or 1.14 meters (45 inches) (length + width + height) and a collapsible stroller; check with the airline before departure, because you may be allowed less if the flight is full. The adult baggage allowance applies for children paying half or more of the adult fare.

Safety Seats

The FAA recommends the use of safety seats aloft and details approved models in the free leaflet "Child/Infant Safety Seats Recommended for Use in Aircraft" (available from the FAA, APA–200, 800 Independence Ave. SW, Washington, DC 20591, tel. 202/267–3479; Information Hot Line, tel. 800/322–7873). Airline policy varies. U.S. carriers allow FAA-approved models bearing a sticker declaring their FAA approval. Because these seats are strapped into regular passenger seats, airlines may require that a ticket be bought for an infant who would otherwise ride free. Foreign carriers may not allow infant seats, may charge the child's rather than the infant's fare for their use, or may require you to hold your baby during takeoff and landing, thus defeating the seat's purpose.

Facilities Aloft

Some airlines provide other services for children, such as children's meals and freestanding bassinets (only to those with seats at the bulkhead, where there's enough legroom). Make your request when reserving. Biennially the February issue of *Family Travel Times* details children's services on three dozen airlines ($12; *see above*). "Kids and Teens in Flight" (free from the U.S. Department of Transportation's Office of Consumer Affairs, R-25, Washington, DC 20590, tel. 202/366–2220) offers tips for children flying alone.

Lodging

In general you can't count on Turkish hotels to have cribs or cots, so be sure to request them in advance. Discounts on room rates are often available, however. **Ramada Inns** in Istanbul and Antalya allow children of any age to stay free in a room with their parents, as do the **Hiltons** in Istanbul and Ankara; the Hilton in Mersin charges $20 for rollaways.

Hints for Women Traveling Solo

While Turkey is a predominantly Muslim country, women can feel quite comfortable traveling alone. However, it's not the place for clothing that's short, tight, or bare. Longer skirts and shirts and blouses with a sleeve, however short, are what it takes here to look respectable, and a woman who looks respectable is unlikely to have experiences that will leave her thinking of Turkish men as other than warm and even courtly. As in any other country in the world, the best course is simply to walk on, if approached, and to avoid potentially troublesome situations, such as deserted neighborhoods at night. Note that in Turkey many hotels, restaurants, and other eating spots identify themselves as being for an *aile* (family) clientele, and many restaurants have special sections for women and children; depending on how comfortable you are being alone, you may or may not like these areas, away from the action—and you may prefer to take your chances in the main room (though some establishments will resist seating you there).

Hints for Travelers with Disabilities

In Turkey, many buses have special seats designated for passengers with disabilities, and some of those in larger cities "kneel" to make it easier for less-mobile travelers to board. Both the Turkish Ministry of Health and the university and city hospitals can be helpful to visitors with disabilities.

Organizations Several organizations provide travel information for people with
In the United disabilities, usually for a membership fee, and some publish news-
States letters and bulletins. Among them are the **Information Center for Individuals with Disabilities** (Fort Point Pl., 27–43 Wormwood St., Boston, MA 02210, tel. 617/727–5540 or 800/462–5015 in MA between 11 AM and 4 PM, or leave message; TTY 617/345–9743); **Mobility International USA** (Box 10767, Eugene, OR 97440, tel. and TTY 503/343–1284; fax 503/343–6812), the U.S. branch of an international organization based in Britain (*see below*) that has affiliates in 30 countries; **MossRehab Hospital Travel Information Service** (tel. 215/456–9603, TTY 215/456–9602); the **Travel Industry and Disabled Exchange** (TIDE, 5435 Donna Ave., Tarzana, CA 91356, tel. 818/344–3640, fax 818/344–0078); and **Travelin' Talk** (Box 3534, Clarksville, TN 37043, tel. 615/552–6670, fax 615/552–1182).

In the United Important information sources include the **Royal Association for**
Kingdom **Disability and Rehabilitation** (RADAR, 12 City Forum, 250 City Rd., London EC1V 8AF, tel. 0171/250–3222), which publishes travel information for people with disabilities in Britain, and **Mobility International** (228 Borough High St., London SE1 1JX, tel. 0171/403–5688), an international clearinghouse of travel information for people with disabilities.

Travel **Flying Wheels Travel** (143 W. Bridge St., Box 382, Owatonna, MN
Agencies and 55060, tel. 507/451–5005 or 800/535–6790) is a travel agency specia-
Tour lizing in domestic and worldwide cruises, tours, and independent
Operators travel itineraries for people with mobility problems. Adventurers should contact **Wilderness Inquiry** (1313 Fifth St. SE, Minneapolis, MN 55414, tel. and TTY 612/379–3858 or 800/728–0719), which orchestrates action-packed trips, such as white-water rafting, sea kayaking, and dogsledding, to bring together people who have disabilities with those who don't.

Publications Several free publications are available from the U.S. Consumer Information Center (Pueblo, CO 81009): "New Horizons for the Air Traveler with a Disability" (include Dept. 608Y in the address), a U.S. Department of Transportation booklet describing changes resulting from the 1986 Air Carrier Access Act and from the 1990 Americans with Disabilities Act, and the Airport Operators Council's *Access Travel: Airports* (Dept. 5804), which describes facilities and services for people with disabilities at more than 500 airports worldwide.

The 500-page *Travelin' Talk Directory* (*see* Organizations, *above;* $35 check or money order with a money-back guarantee) lists names and addresses of people and organizations who offer help for travelers with disabilities. Twin Peaks Press (Box 129, Vancouver, WA 98666, tel. 206/694–2462 or 800/637–2256) publishes the *Directory of Travel Agencies for the Disabled* ($19.95, plus $2 for shipping), listing more than 370 agencies worldwide.

Hints for Older Travelers

Organizations The **American Association of Retired Persons** (AARP, 601 E St. NW, Washington, DC 20049, tel. 202/434–2277) provides independent travelers who are members of the AARP (open to those age 50 or older; $8 per person or couple annually) with the Purchase Privilege Program, which offers discounts on lodging, car rentals, and sight-seeing, and arranges group tours, cruises, and apartment living through AARP Travel Experience from American Express (400 Pinnacle Way, Suite 450, Norcross, GA 30071, tel. 800/927–0111 or 800/745–4567).

Two other organizations offer discounts on lodgings, car rentals, and other travel products, along with such nontravel perks as magazines and newsletters: the **National Council of Senior Citizens** (1331 F St. NW, Washington, DC 20004, tel. 202/347–8800 (membership $12 annually) and **Mature Outlook** (6001 N. Clark St., Chicago, IL 60660, tel. 800/336–6330; $9.95 annually).

Note: For reduced rates, mention your senior-citizen status when booking hotel reservations, not when checking out. At restaurants, show your identification card before you're seated; discounts may be limited to certain menus, days, or hours. If you are renting a car, ask about promotional rates that might improve on your senior-citizen discount.

Educational The nonprofit **Elderhostel** (75 Federal St., 3rd Floor, Boston, MA
Travel 02110, tel. 617/426–7788) has offered inexpensive study programs for people 60 and older since 1975. Held at more than 1,800 educational and cultural institutions, courses cover everything from marine science to Greek myths and cowboy poetry. Participants usually attend lectures in the morning and spend the afternoon sightseeing or on field trips; they live in dormitory-type lodgings. Fees for two- to three-week international trips—including room, board, and transportation from the United States—range from $1,800 to $4,500.

Publications *The 50+ Traveler's Guidebook: Where to Go, Where to Stay, What to Do* by Anita Williams and Merrimac Dillon ($12.95, St. Martin's Press, 175 5th Ave., New York, NY 10010) is available in bookstores and offers many useful tips. "The Mature Traveler" (Box 50820, Reno, NV 89513, tel. 702/786–7419; $29.95), a monthly newsletter, contains many travel deals.

Hints for Gay and Lesbian Travelers

Organizations The **International Gay Travel Association** (Box 4974, Key West, FL 33041, tel. 800/448–8550), which has 700 members, will provide you with names of travel agents and tour operators who specialize in gay travel.

Tour Tour operator **Olympus Vacations** (8424 Santa Monica Blvd., No.
Operators and 721, West Hollywood, CA 90069; tel. 310/657–2220) offers all-gay-
Travel and-lesbian resort holidays. **Skylink Women's Travel** (746 Ashland
Agencies Ave., Santa Monica, CA 90405, tel. 310/452–0506 or 800/225–5759) handles individual travel for lesbians all over the world and conducts international and domestic group trips annually.

Publications The premiere international travel magazine for gays and lesbians is *Our World* (1104 N. Nova Rd., Suite 251, Daytona Beach, FL 32117, tel. 904/441–5367; $35 for 10 issues). "Out & About" (tel. 203/789–8518 or 800/929–2268; $49 for 10 issues, full refund if you aren't satisfied) is a 16-page monthly newsletter with extensive information on resorts, hotels, and airlines that are gay-friendly.

Further Reading

Homer's *Iliad* is still the most evocative reading on the Trojan War and the key players of Turkish antiquity. The keenest insight into the ancient ruins you will encounter on your trip comes from George Bean, author of *Aegean Turkey, Turkey Beyond the Meander, Lycian Turkey,* and *Turkey's Southern Shore.*

Mary Lee Settle provides a vision of Turkey that is both panoramic and personal in *Turkish Reflections.* The book marks Settle's return to the country that was the setting for her novel *Blood Tie,* a 1978 National Book Award winner. Dame Freya Stark, one of the most remarkable travelers of our century, chronicles her visits to Turkey in *The Journey's Echo* and *Alexander's Path.* Only a piece of Mark Twain's *Innocents Abroad* is about Turkey, but it offers a witty glimpse of the country as it used to be. Hans Christian Andersen also wrote a memorable travelogue, *A Poet's Bazaar: A Journey to Greece, Turkey and Up the Danube.* Agatha Christie's *Murder on the Orient Express* provides the proper atmosphere for a trip to Istanbul, the terminus of the noted train. The *Letters and Works of Lady Mary Wortley Montagu* is a significant and entertaining book that delightfully documents life in 19th-century Ottoman Turkey— including the much-quoted passages about the harem—through the eyes of Lady Montagu, the wife of a consul.

For an introduction to Turkish literature, track down a copy of *Anatolian Tales* or *Memed, My Hawk,* by Yaşar Kemal, one of the country's most famous modern novelists. Orhan Pamuk's *White Castle,* recently published in the United States and Great Britain, is for those who want to sample a contemporary writer with great talent and technical expertise.

Arriving and Departing

From North America by Plane

Flights are either nonstop, direct, or connecting. A **nonstop** flight requires no change of plane and makes no stops. A **direct** flight stops at least once and can involve a change of plane, although the flight number remains the same; if the first leg is late, the second waits. This is not the case with a **connecting** flight, which involves a different plane and a different flight number.

Airports and Airlines Most flights arrive at Istanbul's **Atatürk International Airport.** The few that do not terminate here go to Ankara, İzmir, Adana, Antalya, and Dalaman. Options include **Delta** (tel. 800/221–1212), **THY/ Turkish Airlines** (tel. 212/986–5050 or 800/874–8875), the Turkish national airline, and European carriers—**Air France** (tel. 800/237– 2747), **British Airways** (tel. 800/247–9297), **Lufthansa** (tel. 800/645– 3880, and **Olympic Airlines** (tel. 800/223–1226)—whose service connects through their home countries.

Flying Time to Istanbul From New York: 15 hours, including layover time in Frankfurt. From Chicago: 17 hours.

Cutting Costs The Sunday travel section of most newspapers is a good source of deals. When booking, particularly through an unfamiliar company, call the Better Business Bureau and your local or state Consumer

Protection Bureau to find out whether any complaints have been registered against the company, pay with a credit card if you can, and consider trip-cancellation and default insurance (*see* Insurance, *above*).

Promotional Airfares Less expensive fares, called promotional or discount fares, are round-trip and involve restrictions, which vary according to the route and season. You must usually buy the ticket—commonly called an APEX (advance purchase excursion) when it's for international travel—in advance (seven, 14, or 21 days are usual), although some of the major airlines have added no-frills, cheap flights to compete with new bargain airlines on certain routes.

With the major airlines the cheaper fares generally require minimum and maximum stays (for instance, over a Saturday night or at least seven and no more than 30 days). Airlines generally allow some return date changes for a $25 to $50 fee, but most low-fare tickets are nonrefundable. Only a death in the family would prompt the airline to return any of your money if you cancel a nonrefundable ticket. However, you can apply an unused nonrefundable ticket toward a new ticket, again with a small fee. The lowest fare is subject to availability, and only a small percentage of the plane's total seats will be sold at that price. Contact the U.S. Department of Transportation's Office of Consumer Affairs (I–25, Washington, DC 20590, tel. 202/366–2220) for a copy of "Fly-Rights: A guide to Air Travel in the U.S."

Consolidators Consolidators or bulk-fare operators—"bucket shops"—buy blocks of seats on scheduled flights that airlines anticipate they won't be able to sell. Consolidators pay wholesale prices, add a markup, and resell the seats to travel agents or directly to the public at prices that still undercut the airline's promotional or discount fares (higher than a charter ticket but lower than an APEX ticket, and usually without the advance-purchase restriction). Moreover, some consolidators sometimes give you your money back. Carefully read the fine print detailing penalties for changes and cancellations. If you doubt the reliability of a company, call the airline once you've made your booking and confirm that you do, indeed, have a reservation on the flight.

The biggest U.S. consolidator, C. L. Thomson Express, sells only to travel agents. Well-established consolidators selling to the public include: **UniTravel** (Box 12485, St. Louis, MO 63132, tel. 314/569–0900 or 800/325–2222) and **Travac** (989 6th Ave., New York, NY 10018, tel. 212/563–3303 or 800/872–8800).

Discount Travel Clubs Travel clubs offer members unsold space on airplanes, cruise ships, and package tours at as much as 50% below regular prices. Membership may include a regular bulletin or access to a toll-free hot line giving details of available trips departing from three or four days to several months in the future. Most also offer 50% discounts off hotel rack rates, but double check with the hotel to make sure it isn't offering a better promotional rate independent of the club. Clubs include **Discount Travel International** (114 Forrest Ave., Suite 203, Narberth, PA 19072, tel. 215/668–7184; $45 annually, single or family), **Entertainment Travel Editions** (Box 1014 Trumbull, CT 06611, tel. 800/445–4137; price, depending on destination, $25–$48), **Great American Traveler** (Box 27965, Salt Lake City, UT 84127, tel. 800/548–2812; $49.95 annually), **Moment's Notice Discount Travel Club** (425 Madison Ave., New York, NY 10017, tel. 212/486–0503; $45 annually, single or family), **Privilege Card** (3391 Peachtree Rd. NE, Suite 110, Atlanta GA 30326, tel. 404/262–0222 or 800/236–9732; domestic annual membership $49.95, international, $74.95), **Travelers Advantage** (CUC Travel Service, 49 Music Sq. W, Nashville, TN 37203, tel. 800/548–1116; $49 annually, single or family), and **Worldwide Discount Travel Club** (1674 Meridian Ave., Miami Beach, FL 33139, tel. 305/534–2082; $50 annually for family, $40 single).

Publications Both "Consumer Reports Travel Letter" (Consumers Union, Box 53629, Boulder, CO 80322, tel. 800/234–1970; $39 a year) and the newsletter "Travel Smart" (40 Beechdale Rd., Dobbs Ferry, NY 10522, tel. 800/327–3633; $37 a year) have a wealth of travel deals and tips in each monthly issue. *The Official Frequent Flyer Guidebook* by Randy Petersen (4715-C Town Center Dr., Colorado Springs, CO 80916, tel. 719/597–8899 or 800/487–8893; $14.99, plus $3 shipping and handling) yields valuable hints on getting the most for your air travel dollars, as does *Airfare Secrets Exposed*, by Sharon Tyler and Matthew Wonder (Universal Information Publishing, $16.95 in bookstores). Also helpful is *202 Tips Even the Best Business Travelers May Not Know* by Christopher McGinnis (Box 52927, Atlanta, GA 30355, tel. 404/659–2855; $10 in bookstores).

Enjoying the Flight Fly at night if you're able to sleep on a plane. Because the air aloft is dry, drink plenty of fluids while on board. Drinking alcohol contributes to jet lag, as do heavy meals. Bulkhead seats, in the front row of each cabin—usually reserved for people who have disabilities, are elderly, or are traveling with babies—offer more legroom, but trays attach awkwardly to seat armrests, and all possessions must be stowed overhead.

Smoking British Airways bans smoking, and smoking is banned on all domestic U.S. flights of less than six hours' duration; the ban also applies to domestic segments of international flights aboard U.S. and foreign carriers. On U.S. carriers flying to Turkey and other destinations abroad, a seat in a no-smoking section must be provided for every passenger who requests one, and the section must be enlarged to accommodate such passengers if necessary as long as they have complied with the airline's deadline for check-in and seat assignment. If smoking bothers you, request a seat far from the smoking section.

Non-U.S. airlines are exempt from these rules but do provide no-smoking sections, and some nations, including Canada as of July 1, 1993, have gone as far as to ban smoking on all domestic flights; other countries may ban smoking on flights of less than a specified duration. The International Civil Aviation Organization has set July 1, 1996, as the date to ban smoking aboard airlines worldwide, but the body has no power to enforce its decisions.

From the United Kingdom by Plane, Train, and Car

By Plane **British Airways** (tel. 0181/897–4000) and **THY,** the Turkish national airline (tel. 0171/499–4499), make the four-hour flight to Istanbul on a regular basis, less frequently to Ankara. Discount fares are available, both through the airlines and through consolidators.

Charters not only offer substantial savings but often fly directly to coastal resort areas such as Antalya, Dalaman, and İzmir. However, they are restrictive and you'll need to buy your ticket well in advance, typically two to four weeks. Check what's available with a good travel agent, or try **Flightfile** (tel. 0171/323–4203).

By Train If you have the time—and money—consider the still glamorous **Venice Simplon-Orient Express** (Sea Containers House, 20 Upper Ground, London SE1 9PF, tel. 0171/928–6000). The route runs from

London to Paris, Zurich, St. Anton, Innsbruck, Verona, and Venice, where you transfer to a ferry for Istanbul; the trip takes more than 32 hours. Trains that are more mundane, passing through Venice or Munich, take some 40 hours: Don't expect a romantic journey.

By Car Physically possible, but why? It's nearly 3,200 kilometers (2,000 miles), some of it over rough Bulgarian roads and through what remains of Yugoslavia. If you do try it, you'll need insurance that covers both European and Asian Turkey. Contact the **Turkish Automobile Club** in Istanbul (tel. 212/231–4631) for information.

Staying in Turkey

Getting Around

By Plane **Turkish Airlines** (THY, tel. 212/252–1106; 212/574–8200 for reservations) operates an extensive domestic network, with nine flights daily on weekdays between Istanbul and Ankara alone. In summer, many flights to coastal resorts are added. Try to arrive at the airport at least 45 minutes before takeoff because security checks can be time-consuming; checked luggage is put on trolleys and must be identified by boarding passengers before it is put on the plane, and all unidentified luggage is left behind and checked for bombs or firearms.

THY offers several standard discounts on domestic flights—10% for passengers' spouses and other family members, 50% for children 12 and under, and 90% for children under 2.

By Train The term "express train" is a misnomer in Turkey. While they exist, serving several long-distance routes, they tend to be slow. The overnight sleeper to Ankara (Yataklı Ankara Ekpres) is the most charming and convenient of the trains, with private compartments, attentive service, and a candlelit dining car. The Fatih Ekspres travels daily between Ankara and Istanbul and takes about 7½ hours. There are also train services to Pamukkale and Edirne.

Amenities Dining cars on trains between major cities have waiter service and serve surprisingly good and inexpensive food. Overnight expresses have sleeping cars and bunk beds. Cost on the Istanbul–Ankara run is $35, including tips, for example; though advance reservations are a must, cancellations are frequent, so that you can often get a space at the last minute.

Fares They're lower for trains than for buses, and round-trips cost less than two one-way tickets. Student discounts are 10% (30% from December through April). Ticket windows in railroad stations are marked "Bilgisayar Gişeleri." Post offices and authorized travel agencies also sell train tickets. Book in advance, in person, for seats on the best trains and for sleeping quarters.

By Bus Buses are much faster than trains and provide excellent, inexpensive service virtually around the clock, between all cities and towns; they're fairly comfortable and sometimes are air-conditioned. All are run by private companies, each of which has its own fixed fares for different routes and, usually more significantly, standards of comfort. Most bus companies, such as Varan, Ulusoy, Pamukkale, and Hola, working between major cities and resort areas, can be counted on for fairly comfortable air-conditioned service with meals or snacks—and even no-smoking seating. You could pay anywhere from $8 to $13 for Istanbul–Ankara, say, or $11 to $16 for Istanbul–

İzmir. Outside the major cities, however, whether you end up on a new bus or on a rattling old one is simply a matter of luck. All fares include *su* (bottled water). Tickets are sold at stands in a town's *otogar* (central bus terminal); the usual procedure is to go to the bus station and shop around. All seats are reserved. When arranging, ask to sit on the shady side; even on air-conditioned buses, the sun can feel oppressive over the course of a long trip, especially given the clouds of tobacco fumes in the air—the no-smoking movement has yet to arrive in Turkey. For greater comfort on overnight trips, buy two seats and stretch out.

For very short trips, or getting around within a city, take minibuses or a *dolmuş* (shared taxi). Both are inexpensive and comfortable.

By Car The best way to see Turkey is by car, conditions notwithstanding; there are 25,000 miles of paved and generally well-maintained highways. Archaeological and historic sites are indicated by yellow signposts.

Road Conditions Signposts are few, lighting scarce, rural roads sometimes rough, and city traffic chaotic, and the country's accident rate is one of the highest in Europe.

In the countryside, watch out for drivers passing on a curve or on the top of a hill, and beware of peasant carts, unlit at night, and motorcycles weaving in and out of traffic while carrying entire families.

Urban streets and highways are jammed with vehicles operated by high-speed lunatics and drivers who constantly blast their horns. In Istanbul, it's safer and faster to drive on the modern highways. Avoid the many small one-way streets—you never know when someone is going to barrel down one of them in the wrong direction. Better yet, leave your car in a garage and use public transportation or take taxis. Parking is another problem in the cities and larger towns.

Rules of the Road In general, Turkish driving conforms to Mediterranean customs, with driving on the right and passing on the left.

Gasoline Mobil, Shell, British Petroleum, and two Turkish oil companies, Petrol Ofisi and Türkpetrol, operate stations here. Those on the main highways stay open around the clock, others from 6 AM to 10 PM.

Breakdowns A road rescue service is available on some highways; before you embark on a journey, ask your hotel how to contact it in case of an emergency. Turkish mechanics in the villages will usually manage to get you going again, at least until you reach a city, where you can have full repairs made. In urban areas, entire streets are given over to car-repair shops run by teams of experts—one specializes in radiators, another in electrical fittings, another in steering columns.

Prices are not high, but it's good to give a small tip to the person who has made your repairs. If you don't wait for the work to be done, take all car documents with you when you leave the shop. The **Türkiye Turing Ve Otomobil Kurumu** (TTOK, or Touring and Automobile Club; Şişli Halâskar Gazi Cad. 364, Istanbul, tel. 212/231–4631) has information about driving in Turkey and does repairs.

By Boat The Turks have long been a seafaring people and boats remain a vital cog in the national transportation system. In some regions, particularly the Black Sea and greater Istanbul area, ferries are the most efficient means of getting around. On the Aegean and Mediterranean coasts, the pace is slower and boats are mostly used for leisurely sightseeing. **Turkish Maritime Lines** operates both car-ferry and cruise ships from Istanbul; cruises last a day to a week, and ships are comfortable, rather like moderate-class Turkish hotels— definitely not the *QEII*.

Cruises Turkish Maritime Lines cruises are in great demand, so make your reservations well in advance, either through the head office (Rıhtım Cad. 1, Karaköy, tel. 212/249–9222) or through **Sunquest Holidays Ltd.** in London (Alsine House, Aldine St., London W12 8AW, England, tel. 0181/800–5455).

Ferries Turkish Maritime Lines' Black Sea ferry sails from June through September from the Karaköy dock in Istanbul to Samsun and Trabzon on Mondays. The 40-hour one-way Istanbul–Trabzon trip costs about $30 for a reclining seat, $38 to $94 for private cabins, plus $50 for cars. On board you'll encounter tourists and locals alike.

The Istanbul–İzmir car ferry down the Aegean coast departs every Friday year-round. The 19-hour one-way trip costs from $38 for a pullman seat to $122 for a cabin berth, plus $40 for a car.

Telephones

Most pay phones are yellow, push-button models, although a few older, operator-controlled telephones are still in use. Directions in English and other languages are posted in phone booths.

Country Code The country code for Turkey, which you'll need when dialing from abroad, is 90.

Local and Intercity Calls All public phones use *jetons* (tokens), available in 2,500 TL and 10,000 TL denominations; they can be purchased at post offices and street booths. More and more also accept debit-type telephone cards, available at post offices and hotels, in denominations of 30 (60,000 TL), 60 (110,000 TL), and 100 (160,000 TL) usage units; buy a 60 or 100 for long-distance calls within Turkey, a 30 for local usage.

To make a local call, deposit a 2,500 TL token, wait until the light at the top of the phone goes off, and then dial the number.

As of 1994, all telephone numbers in Turkey have seven-digit local numbers preceded by a three-digit city code. Intercity lines are reached by dialing 0 before the area code and number. In Istanbul, European and Asian Istanbul have been assigned separate area codes: The new code for European Istanbul (for numbers beginning with 2, 5, or 6) is 212, while that for Asian Istanbul (numbers beginning with 3 or 4) is 216.

To call long-distance within Turkey, dial 131 if you need operator assistance; otherwise dial 0, then dial the city code and number.

International Calls Hotels in Turkey, as elsewhere, levy hefty service charges on all international calls. So you're better off calling from a phone booth and using jetons or phone cards in the 100 denomination. Or use calling cards for AT&T (access number 0080012277) or MCI (0080011177).

To call from a public phone, dial 00, then dial the country code, area or city code, and the number. You can use 10,000 TL jetons—you may need several, but you won't get change. Expect to pay $3–$5 per minute.

Operators and Information Telephone operators seldom speak English. If you need international dialing codes and assistance, or phone books, go to the nearest post office.

Mail

Post offices are painted bright yellow and have PTT (Post, Telegraph and Telephone) signs on the front. The central POs in larger cities are open Monday through Saturday from 8 AM to 9 PM, Sunday from 9 to 7. Smaller ones are open Monday through Saturday between 8:30 and 5.

Postal Rates Rates are frequently adjusted to keep pace with inflation, but the cost of sending a letter or postcard remains nominal. Shipping a 10-pound rug home via surface mail will cost about $25 and take from two to six months.

Receiving Mail If you're uncertain where you'll be staying, have mail sent to Post Restante, Merkez Postanezi (central post office) in the town of your choice.

Tipping

In restaurants, a 10% to 15% charge is added to the bill in all but inexpensive, fast-food spots. However, since this money does not necessarily find its way to your waiter, leave an additional 10% on the table. In top establishments, waiters expect tips of 10% to 15% in addition to the service charge. While it's acceptable to include the tip on your bill in restaurants that accept credit cards, a small tip in cash is much appreciated. Hotel porters expect about $2. Taxi drivers are becoming used to foreigners giving them something; round off the fare to the nearest 5,000 TL. At Turkish baths, the staff that attends you expects to share a tip of 30% to 35% of the bill. Don't worry about missing them—they'll be lined up expectantly on your departure.

Opening and Closing Times

Banks are open weekdays from 8:30 until noon and from 1:30 until 5. **Mosques** are generally open to the public except during *namaz* (prayer hours), which last 30 to 40 minutes and are observed five times a day. These times are based on the position of the sun, so they vary throughout the seasons but are generally around sunrise (between 5 and 7), at lunchtime (around noon or 1, when the sun is directly overhead), in the afternoon (around 3 or 4), at sunset (usually between 5 and 7), and at bedtime (at 9 or 10). **Museums** are generally open Tuesday through Sunday from 9:30 until 4:30 and closed on Monday. **Palaces** are open the same hours but are closed Thursday. **Shops and bazaars** are usually open Monday through Saturday from 9:30 to 1 and from 2 to 7, and closed all day on Sunday and for an hour between 1 and 2 on other days. However, in resort areas, shops may stay open until 9 PM and all day Sunday.

Shopping

The best part of shopping in Turkey is visiting the *bedestans* (bazaars), all brimming with copper and brassware, handpainted ceramics, carved alabaster and onyx, fabrics, richly colored carpets, as well as lots of tourist junk. Part of the pleasure of roaming through the bazaars is having a free glass of *çay* (tea), which vendors will offer you whether you're a serious shopper or are just browsing.

Bargaining Outside the bazaars, prices are often fixed, though in resort areas many shopkeepers will bargain if you ask for a better price. But in bazaars, the operative word is "bargain." More social ritual than battle of wills, it can be great fun once you get the hang of it. As a rule of thumb, offer about 60% of the asking price and be prepared to go up to about 70% to 75%. It's both bad manners and bad business to grossly underbid or to start bargaining if you're not serious about buying.

Tax Refunds Value-added tax is nearly always included in quoted prices. Certain shops are authorized to refund the tax (ask). If the VAT is refunded is less than 50,000 TL, you can obtain it from a bank outside customs boundaries where the dealer has an account (again, ask). Otherwise, within a month of leaving Turkey, mail the stamped invoice back to the dealer, and he will mail you a check—in theory if not always in practice.

Rugs Persistent salesmen and affordable prices make it hard to leave Turkey without flat-woven **kilims** or other rugs. No matter what you've planned, sooner or later you'll end up in the cool of a carpet shop listening to a sales rap. Patterns and colors vary by region (*see* Chapter 2). The best prices and the best selection are in smaller villages. You may pay twice as much in Istanbul, particularly for older rugs, and you won't find the selection or the quality—shops here seem to cater to a package-tour crowd. Salesmen will insist they can't lower the price, but they virtually always do. Be prepared, however, to leave; and never indicate how much you like something.

Other Local Specialties Made of a light, porous stone found only in Turkey, **meerschaum pipes** are prized among pipe smokers for their cool smoke; look for a centered hole and even walls. You can also buy **tiles** and **porcelain,** though modern work doesn't compare with older stuff. Another good deal is **jewelry,** because you pay by weight and not for design—but watch out for tin and alloys masquerading as silver. Turkey is also known for its **leather goods,** but check workmanship; in general, you're better to stick with merchandise off the rack and steer clear of made-to-order goods. The stylish **baggy trousers** you've seen on MTV or in the fashion magazines are called *şalvar* here and are a long-standing tradition.

Beware of **antiques.** When dealing with pieces purported to be more than 100 years old, chances are you will end up with an expensive fake, which is just as well since it's illegal to export the real thing without a government permit. If what you covet is less than 100 years old, snap it up.

Sports and the Outdoors

Boating and Sailing Boating the Aegean or Mediterranean coast opens up otherwise inaccessible sights and bypasses the bumps and bustle of travel by road. This way, you slip past islands into narrow inlets and moor off the shore of untrammeled ruins.

Bodrum and **Marmaris** are the home ports to an extensive and popular array of boats, from sleek, modern yachts, which can be chartered bare or with crew, to traditional wooden gulets, always chartered with crew. It is usually cheaper and more reliable to deal directly with the local agencies than to get on the wrong end of a long chain of foreign-agency commissions. Yacht agencies are listed with the Turkish Culture and Information office in New York; in Turkey, Marmaris has a particularly helpful tourist office (tel. 252/412–1035) that can be called on for advice on chartering gulets.

Camping As pansiyons are cheap and plentiful and official campgrounds few, Turks themselves seldom camp out. So the predominant clientele in the well-equipped campgrounds in the Kervansaray-Mocamp chain, located nationwide in a handful of popular tourist areas, are Europeans, hippies, and international budget travelers, who enjoy these properties' electricity, running water, and the occasional swimming pool; the operating season is from April or May through October. For specific camping information contact the local tourist board listed in the city and regional chapters.

Hiking Turkey has perfectly lovely national parks with sweeping vistas on high grassy plateaus: Uludağ, near Bursa; Kovada Gölü, near Isparta, off the E24 toward Konha; and Güllük Däg, at Termessos; and Yedigöller, "Seven Lakes," north of Bolu on the E5. Yet what makes Turkey exceptional for hikers are its ancient cities. Ruins lie up and down the Aegean and Mediterranean coasts; some (Termessos, Pergamum) are atop cliffs, some (Patara, Phaselis) along beaches. At many smaller sites, you will find few—if any—other visitors. Just follow the yellow signs that mark archaeological sites, both major and obscure.

Skiing Turkey's mountains are not terribly high, and its ski resorts are old-fashioned and not terribly well-developed. Still, skiing is a possibility for those with a yen to experience yet another side of Turkey. Among the resorts, Uludağ, outside of Bursa, is the most sophisticated; Erzurum's Palandoken, in the far east, is perhaps its most challenging. When the weather is right, usually in March or April, you can ski at Sakhkent near Antalya, and then head south toward the beaches nearby for a swim.

Beaches

Turkey's best beaches are arrayed along the **Mediterranean** coast. And they are truly spectacular. From Bodrum, as you head east, top choices include those on Sedir Island; Iztuzu Beach near Dalyan, a sweeping strand around a lagoon; the Gemiler Island beaches; the placid, deep blue bay of Ölü Deniz; Patara, with its endless stretch of dazzling white sand; the private coves along the Kekova Sound; the strand among the Roman ruins at Phaselis; Ulas Beach near Alanya; and numerous unnamed coves and inlets along the route.

Beaches along the **Aegean** are pleasant enough, if not as spectacular. The most popular are, from south to north, Altınkum, Samsun Dağı National Park, Sarımsaklı near Ayvalık, and those along the Gulf of Edremit. Here the sand is still fine and white, but the beaches are shorter and more heavily used.

Dining

Cuisine Turkey is not just a geographic bridge between Europe, Asia, and the Middle East; it is a gastronomic one as well. Its cuisine reflects the long history of a people who emigrated from the borders of China to a land mass known as Asia Minor, and built an empire that encompassed Arabic, Greek, and European lands.

Though given scant public attention in the West, Turkish cuisine rivals French, according to many. It is healthful, full of vegetables, grains, fresh fish, and seemingly infinite varieties of lamb. Fish and meat are typically served grilled or roasted. The core group of seasonings is unique: garlic, sage, oregano, cumin, mint, dill, lemon, and yogurt, always more yogurt. Turkish yogurt is significantly tastier than domestic versions, and many travelers swear it helps keep their stomachs calm and stable while on the road.

This guide makes frequent references to "traditional Turkish cuisine." Here's what to expect.

Mezes   *Mezes* (appetizers), which start the meal, are often brought to your table on a tray. Standard offerings among these cold appetizers include *patlıcan salatası* (roasted eggplant purée flavored with garlic and lemon), *haydari* (a thick yogurt dip made with garlic and dill), *dolma* (stuffed grape leaves, peppers or mussels), *ezme* (a spicy paste of minced green pepper, onion, parsley, and tomato paste), *kızartma* (deep-fried eggplant, zucchini, or green pepper served with fresh yogurt), seafood salads usually made with octopus, shrimp, or mussels, *cacık* (a garlicky cold yogurt "soup" with shredded cucumber, mint, or dill), *barbunya pilaki* (kidney beans cooked with tomatoes and onions with olive oil), and *imam bayıldı* (slow-roasted baby eggplant topped with olive oil–fried onions and tomatoes and seasoned with garlic). One taste of it and you'll understand how it got its name—"the imam fainted with delight." Inevitably there will be other dishes based on eggplant, usually called *patlıcan* by the Turks—perhaps *begendi* (eggplant purée rich with butter, milk, and flour, served hot with meat dishes). Hot appetizers, usually called *ara sıcak*, include *börek* (a deep-fried or oven-baked pastry filled with cheese or meat), *kalamar* (deep-fried calamari served with a special sauce), and *midye tava* (deep-fried mussels). Individual restaurants have their personal variations on these dishes.

Kebabs   Kebabs, available almost any place you stop to eat, come in many guises. Although the meat of choice for Turks is lamb, some kebabs are made with beef or chicken. *Adana kebabs* are spicy, ground lamb patties arranged on a layer of sautéed pita bread, topped with a zippy yogurt-and-garlic sauce. *Bursa kebabs* are sliced grilled lamb, smothered in tomato sauce, butter, and yogurt. *Şiş kebabs* are the traditional skewered cubes of lamb, usually interspersed with peppers and onions. *Köfte kebabs* are meatballs made from minced lamb mixed with rice, bulgur, or bread crumbs, then threaded onto skewers.

Fish and Meat   Fresh fish, often a main course, is commonly served grilled and drizzled with olive oil and lemon. You will find *alabalık* (trout), *barbunya* (red mullet), *kalkan* (turbot), *kefal* (gray mullet), *kılıç* (swordfish, sometimes served as a kebab), *levrek* (sea bass), *lüfer* (bluefish), and *palamut* (bonito). In the meat department, there is *manti*, a sort of Turkish ravioli made with garlicky yogurt with a touch of mint. Grilled quail is most common inland; it's often marinated in tomatoes, yogurt, olive oil, and cinnamon. *Karışık ızgara*, a mixed grill, usually combines tender chicken breast, beef, a lamb chop, and spicy lamb patties, all served with rice pilaf and vegetables. *Tandır kebap*, lamb cooked in a pit, is a typically Anatolian dish.

Desserts   Desserts are sweet and sticky. You'll encounter several varieties of *baklava* (phyllo pastry with honey and chopped nuts) and *burma kadayıf* (shredded wheat in honey or syrup). Also popular are puddings, made of yogurt and eggs, or sweet rice, or milk and rice flour.

Breakfast   Usually taken in your hotel, breakfast typically consists of white goat cheese, sliced tomatoes, and olives, with a side order of toast; the menu varies little, whether you stay in a simple *pansiyon* (bed-and-breakfast) or an upscale hotel. Yogurt with honey and fresh fruit is usually available as well. If you don't see it, just ask.

Types of Restaurants   As in France, restaurants are carefully categorized. The simplest establishments, Turkey's fast-food joints, are *kebabcis* and *pidecis*. The former specialize in kebabs—marinated cubes of meat (typically lamb), usually grilled and cooked with vegetables on a skewer. The latter serves *pides*, a pizza-like snack made of flat bread topped with butter, cheese, egg, or ground lamb, and baked in a wood-fired oven. Often these eateries are little more than counters, where you belly up to the bar for instant gratification; on occasion they attain luncheonette status.

Lokantas are Turkey's bistros, unpretentious neighborhood spots that make up the vast majority of Turkish restaurants. In smaller cities, there may well be three or four in a row, each with simple wooden chairs and tables, paper napkins, maybe a tourist-board poster on the wall. In towns, villages, and any city with a harbor, many lokantas are open-air, the better to take in the waterfront and sky, or surrounded by trellises hung with flowers. As for food, you can take your pick: All serve the same traditional dishes, competently prepared, if without much distinction. Often you serve yourself, cafeteria-style, from big display cases full of hot and cold dishes—a relief if you don't speak Turkish. If there is no menu, it is because the chef only serves what is fresh, and that changes from day to day.

In the more upscale *restoran* (translated, like lokanta, as restaurant), you can expect tablecloths, menus, even a wine list, and dishes drawn from the richer, "palace" cuisine of Turkish royalty, often with Continental touches. Reservations, usually unnecessary elsewhere, are a good idea here. The best restorans are in Istanbul and Ankara, though others are scattered about the country.

Wine, Beer, and Spirits Alcohol is readily available and widely consumed, despite Turkey's predominantly Muslim culture. Among the perfectly acceptable, inexpensive local wines, the best are Villa Doluca and Kavaklidere, available in *beyaz* (white) and *kirmizi* (red). The most popular local beer is Efes Pilsen, your basic American-type pilsener. The national drink is *raki*, a relative of the Greek ouzo, made from grapes and aniseed. Turks mix it with water or ice and sip it throughout their meal or serve it as an aperitif.

Mealtimes Lunch is generally served from noon to 3, dinner from 7 to 10. You can find restaurants or cafés open virtually any time of the day or night in cities; in villages, getting a meal at odd hours can be a problem. Breakfast starts early, typically by 7 AM.

Dress Except for at restaurants classified as $$$$, where jacket and tie are usually appropriate, you can get by in jeans and sneakers, and men don't need a jacket.

Precautions Tap water is heavily chlorinated and supposedly safe to drink in cities and resorts. It's best to play it safe, however, and stick to *maden suyu* (bottled, sparkling mineral water) or *maden sodası* (carbonated mineral water), which are better-tasting and inexpensive.

Ratings Prices are per person and include an appetizer, main course, and dessert but not wine and gratuities. A service charge of 10% to 15% is added to the bill; waiters expect another 10%. Best bets are indicated by a star ★.

Category	Major Cities	Other Areas
$$$$	over $40	over $30
$$$	$25–$40	$20–$30
$$	$12–$25	$10–$20
$	under $12	under $10

Lodging

Accommodations range from the international luxury chain hotels in Istanbul, Ankara, and İzmir to charming inns occupying historic Ottoman mansions and caravansaries to comfortable, family-run *pansiyons* (guest houses) in the countryside. Plan ahead for the peak summer season, when resort hotels are often booked solid by tour companies.

Asking to see the room in advance is accepted practice. It will probably be much more basic than the well-decorated reception area. Check for noise, especially if the room faces a street or is anywhere near a nightclub or disco, and look for such amenities as window screens and mosquito coils—small, flat disks that, when lighted, emit an unscented vapor that keeps biting insects away. If the room is not to your liking, look for another place to stay.

Hotels and Motels
Hotels are officially classified in Turkey as HL (luxury), H1 to H5 (first- to fifth-class); motels, M1 to M2 (first- to second-class); and P, *pansiyons* (guest houses). However, these classifications can be misleading because they're based on the quantity of facilities rather than the quality of the service and decor, and the lack of restaurant or lounge automatically relegates the establishment to the bottom of the ratings. In practice, a lower-grade hotel may actually be far more charming and comfortable than one with a higher rating.

The major Western chains are represented by Hilton, Sheraton, and the occasional Ramada and Hyatt. All tend to be in the higher price ranges.

The standard Turkish hotel room that you will encounter endlessly throughout the country is clean, with bare walls, low wood-frame beds (usually singles or twins), and industrial carpeting or kilims on the floor. However, the less expensive properties will probably offer plumbing and furnishings that leave much to be desired. If you want a double bed as at home, go to a more expensive property, either Turkish or Western.

In addition, there are many local establishments that are licensed but not included in the official ratings list. You can obtain their names from local tourist offices.

Pansiyons
Outside the cities and resort areas, these small, family-run places will be your most common option. They range from charming, old homes decorated in antiques to tiny, utilitarian rooms done in K-Mart moderne. As a rule, they are inexpensive and scrupulously clean. Private baths are common, though they are rudimentary—stall showers, toilets with sensitive plumbing. A simple breakfast is typically included.

Apartment and Villa Rentals
If you want a home base that's roomy enough for a family and comes with cooking facilities, a furnished rental may be the solution. It's generally cost-wise, too, although not always—some rentals are luxury properties (economical only when your party is large). **Villas International** (605 Market St., Suite 510, San Francisco, CA 94105, tel. 415/281–0910 or 800/221–2260) has rentals in Turkey.

Ratings
Prices are for two people in a double room, including VAT and service charge. Best bets are indicated by a star ★.

Category	Major Cities	Other Areas
$$$$	over $200	over $150
$$$	$100–$200	$100–$150
$$	$60–$100	$50–$100
$	under $60	under $50

Credit Cards

The following abbreviations have been used: AE, American Express; DC, Diners Club; MC, MasterCard; V, Visa. Be sure to confirm credit-card acceptance at check-in.

Great Itineraries

The Aegean

The Aegean region contains many of Turkey's most spectacular archaeological sites, from the sprawling, incredibly intact ancient city of Ephesus to the spectacular mountaintop ruins at Pergamum. In between, there's sun and swimming in the placid blue Aegean.

Duration 8–10 days

Getting Around Çanakkale is 332 kilometers (205 miles) southwest of Istanbul. A car is the best way to do this trip, as it allows infinitely more freedom and access to smaller, less visited sites. You can drive via Eceabat on the European side of the country (hot, bare, but historically interesting, as the site of ancient Thrace) or via Bursa on the Asian side (where you can see İznik and Bursa).
By Car

By Bus This tour can be done by bus, as all the major cities and archaeological sites have frequent and inexpensive connecting service.

The Main Route **One night:** Çanakkale. See the Gallipoli memorials.

One night: Assos, stopping en route at the ruins of Troy and Behramkale.

One night: Ayvalık: Tour the old Greek city and Greek island of Ali Bey. Take a beach break.

One or two nights: İzmir or Foça, with a stop en route at Pergamum. Tour İzmir.

Two nights: Kuşadası via Selçuk and Ephesus. The next day, visit the ruins of Priene, Miletus, and Didiyma. Return to Kuşadası.

One night: Pammukale. Visit Aphrodisias and Hieropolis.

One or two nights: Bodrum. See its crusader castle.

The Mediterranean Coast

Turkey's Mediterranean coast is less developed and a bit wilder than the Aegean. There are wonderful ruins here as well: the windswept remains of ancient Cnidos, the unusual cliff tombs of Dalyan, the mountain aerie of Termessos.

Duration 8–10 days

Getting Around **By Car** A car allows the most freedom and allows you to visit smaller, more remote sites. To get to the area, you can fly from Istanbul to Dalaman Airport, 100 kilometers (62 miles) east of Marmaris. From the Aegean coast, simply continue east on Route 330 at Bodrum to Marmaris.

By Bus There is frequent and inexpensive service to all the major cities and archaeological sites.

The Main Route **Two nights:** Bodrum. Explore the ruins of Cnidos and the resort town of Datça.

One night: Dalyan. Visit Lake Köyceğiz, the ruins of Kaunos, and the fine beach at Dalyan.

One night: Fethiye. Visit the ruins of Xanthos and Letoön; take a sail on the Göcek Gulf. Relax at magnificent Patara beach.

One or two nights: Kale. Explore the unspoiled villages of the Kekova Sound.

One night: Kaş or Kalkan. Relax in either of these pleasant seaside resorts, then see the Church of St. Nicholas at Demre.

One or two nights: To Antalya via the ruin-strewn beach at Phaselis. Explore Antalya's old harbor and bazaar. Set out for the spectacular ruins of Termessos the next day.

One night: Side. Visit the ruins of Perge and Aspendos en route, then relax on the broad beaches of Side. (From here you can continue east or return to Antalya, where you can take connecting flights to another region of the country.)

Central Anatolia

This trip offers an incredible change of pace from the coasts. This is where you will find Ankara, the capital of modern Turkey, and scenery ranging from the pastoral plains surrounding Ankara to the bizarre, almost lunar landscape of the Göreme Valley. This was also the center of the Hittite civilization, one of the oldest in the world.

Duration 5–6 days

Getting Around **By Car** Ankara is a short flight, or a long drive, from Istanbul. Once you are there, a car offers the most flexibility, allowing you to go at your own pace and do some exploring off the beaten track.

By Bus Here, as throughout Turkey, there are good bus connections to all the towns you'll want to visit.

The Main Route **Two nights:** Ankara. See Turkey's capital and its superb Museum of Anatolian Civilizations. The following day, visit Hattuşaş, the ancient capital of the Hittites, and the archaeological site at Alacahöyük.

Two nights: Kayseri. Explore the incredible Göreme Valley and the underground cities at Kaymaklı and Derinkuyu.

One or two nights: Konya. Tour this historic Seljuk city and see the museum of the whirling dervishes.

Black Sea Highlights

The Black Sea coast is lush and verdant, edged by the dark waters on one side and towering mountains inland. This is rich agricultural country, noted for its tea, tobacco, hazelnuts, and cherries—and for Byzantine churches and hidden monasteries.

Duration 5–7 days

Getting This is the most pleasant way to go. Roads are incredibly scenic but
Around demanding, so don't try to cover too much ground at one time. From
By Car Istanbul, drive to Şile (it's 70 kilometers, or 43 miles) and start at
the western end of the coast, or fly to Erzurum at the far eastern end
and rent a car there. Another option is to drive north from Ankara to
Amasya and then on to Samsun. The following itinerary will start in
the west.

By Bus As there are connections to all sites on the itinerary below, it's also
possible to make this trip by bus.

The Main **One night:** Lake Abant, Safranbolu, or Kastamonu. After a long
Route drive from Istanbul, or a much shorter drive from Ankara, take a
rest at the wooded lake or at the unspoiled historic towns of
Safranbolu and Kastamonu.

One night: Amasya. See the old mosques and modern museum in this
historic provincial capital hemmed in by sheer rock walls.

One night: Samsun or Ünye. Drive the coast, breeze through the
pleasant small towns of Ordu and Gıresun, and rest for the night in
the big city (Samsun) or the tiny coastal town (Ünye).

One or two nights: Trabzon. See the fine museum and other sights of
this ancient Byzantine city, and visit the Rize tea plantations. Stop
at the Sumela Monastery.

One or two nights: Erzurum. Make a side trip to the windswept ruins
of Kars and Ani.

Adventuring in the East

In 1994 the U.S. State Department and the British Government dis-
couraged visitors from traveling to this region. It's best to play it
safe and check any travel advisories before setting out.

This truly off-the-beaten-track itinerary leads through wild mountain gorges and past Mt. Ararat (the likely home of Noah's Ark), the
massive fortress city of Diyarbakır, and the incredible, colossal statues atop Nemrut Dağı. Accommodations are generally basic, but
the sights are unlike any you'll see elsewhere.

Duration six–eight days

Getting The easiest way to get to Erzurum, the starting point, is by air from
Around Istanbul, though you can also drive there from Ankara or Trabzon.
By Car From there, you'll have the most freedom if you travel by car.

By Bus Shuttle buses to Nemrut Dağı depart well before dawn—so while
it's possible to do this itinerary by bus, there are some drawbacks.
Then again, since some of the roads are difficult, you might prefer to
leave the driving to someone else if you are not particularly adventurous at the wheel.

The Main **One or two nights:** Erzurum. Take a day trip to Kars and visit the
Route ruins of Ani.

One night: Doğubeyazt. See biblical Mt. Ararat and the Ishak Paşa
Palace.

Two nights: Van. Visit Van Castle at sunset and explore Akdamar
Island, the ruins of the Urartrian civilization, and the Van museum.

One or two nights: Diyarbakır. Tour the vast medieval walls. Consider a day trip to ancient Mardin, a city by the Syrian border, if you have the time.

One night: Kâhta. Visit Nemrut Daği and its colossal statues. From here you can head due west to Cappadocia and Ankara, or southwest to Antalya and the Mediterranean coast.

2 Portraits of Turkey

Turkey at a Glance: A Chronology

ca 9000 BC First agrarian settlements in the world are established in southern Turkey and northern Iraq

6500–5650 BC Catalhoyuk flourishes: the largest early agricultural community yet discovered and the oldest known site with religious buildings

2371–2316 BC Reign of King Sargon of Akkad, whose empire reached from **Mesopotamia** to the southern parts of Anatolia (Asia Minor), the area that is now Turkey.

ca 2200–1200 BC Indo-European invaders include the **Hittites,** who establish an empire in Anatolia, pushing out the Mesopotamians.

1296 BC Hittites defeat the Egyptian pharaoh **Ramses** II, at the battle of Kadesh, halting Egypt's northern advance and strengthening their hold over Anatolia.

ca 1200 BC New waves of invaders break up the Hittite empire.

1184 BC The traditional date for the end of the legendary Trojan War, the accounts of which are believed to be based on a real conflict.

ca 1000 BC West coast of Asia Minor settled by Aeolians, Dorians, and Ionians from Greece.

ca 657 BC Foundation of **Byzantium** by Megarian colonists from Greece, led, according to legend, by Byzas, after whom the city was named.

559–529 BC Reign of **Cyrus** the Great, the founder of the Persian empire, who subdues the Greek cities of Asia Minor, defeats the **Lydian** king, Croesus, reputedly the richest man in the world, and unifies Asia Minor under his rule.

334 BC **Alexander the Great** conquers Asia Minor, ending Persian domination and extending his empire to the borders of India

323 BC Alexander the Great's sudden death creates a power vacuum and his vast empire disintegrates into a number of petty kingdoms.

190 BC The Seleucid monarch **Antiochus III,** defeated by the Romans at the battle of Magnesia, cedes his territory west of the Taurus mountains to Rome.

133 BC **Rome** consolidates its military and diplomatic gains in the region by creating the province of Asia Minor.

AD 284–305 Reign of the emperor **Diocletian,** who divides the Roman Empire into eastern and western administrative branches and shifts the focus of power eastward by establishing Nicomedia (Izmit) as a secondary, eastern capital.

325 The Ecumenical **Council of Nicaea** (Iznik), the first attempt to establish an orthodox Christian doctrine.

330 The emperor Constantine establishes Christianity as the state religion and moves the capital of the Roman Empire from Rome to the town of Byzantium, which is greatly enlarged and renamed **Constantinople** ("City of Constantine").

527–563 Reign of **Justinian I.** The Byzantine empire reaches its military and cultural apogee. Hagia Sophia is rebuilt and rebuilt again.

674–678	Arab invaders sweep through the Byzantine Empire and lay siege to Constantinople before being repulsed.
1037	The **Seljuk Turks,** nomad tribes from central Asia recently converted to Islam, create their first state in the Middle East.
1071	The Byzantine Emperor Romanos IV is defeated by the Seljuk sultan Alp Arslan at the battle of Manzikert (Malazgirt), opening Anatolia to Turkish settlement.
1081–1118	Reign of emperor **Alexios I Commenus,** who successfully deals with the threats of Venetians and Crusaders. His daughter Anna chronicles the history of the time in the *Alexiad.*
1204	Constantinople is sacked by the **Fourth Crusade,** the Byzantine emperor expelled, and a Latin Empire of Constantinople established.
1243	The Seljuk sultan is defeated by Genghis Khan's Golden Horde at Kosedag and the Seljuk empire disintegrates into petty states.
1261	The Byzantine emperor Michael Palaeologus is restored to a greatly weakened throne.
1300	Traditional date of the foundation of the **Ottoman Empire** at Bursa under **Osman I** (1258–1326). Over the next century Osman and his sons conquer much of Anatolia and southeastern Europe.
1402	The Mongol leader Tamerlane (Timur) defeats the Ottoman emperor Bayezit near Ankara, leading to a decade of civil war among his sons.
1453	Constantinople, the rump of the once mighty Byzantine Empire, falls to the Ottoman sultan Mehmet II.
1462	Mehmet II begins building a new palace at Topkapı.
1520–1566	Reign of **Suleyman the Magnificent,** under whom the Ottoman Empire stretches from Iraq to Algeria. Ottoman culture reaches new heights, epitomized by the magnificent buildings of the architect Sinan.
1571	The defeat of the Ottoman fleet at **Lepanto** by an alliance of European states dents the legend of Turkish invulnerability.
1609	Work begins on the building of the Blue Mosque in Constantinople.
1683	The failure of the Ottoman siege of **Vienna** marks the high point of Turkish expansion into Europe and the beginning of a decline. Over the next century most of eastern Europe is detached from the empire.
1774	The Treaty of Kuchuk Kainarji (Küçük Kaynarca) brings the Ottoman Empire under the influence of Catherine the Great's Russia, and the Eastern Question is posed for the first time: who will get the Ottoman lands when the empire falls?
1807	Sultan Selim II is overthrown by the Janissaries, the Ottoman praetorian guard, whose influence has grown to dominate the imperial court.
1826	The sultan Mahmut II (1808–1839) massacres the Janissaries in the Hippodrome and attempts to introduce reforms, including compulsory male education; but the empire continues to disintegrate under the forces of nationalism.
1853–1855	The **Crimean War.** Britain and France support "the sick man of Europe" in a bid to prevent Russian expansion into the Mediterranean. Florence Nightingale nurses the sick and wounded at Scutari (Uskudar).

1876–1909 Reign of sultan Abdul Hamid II, who begins as a constitutionally minded liberal and ends as a despot.

1877–1878 The Western powers come to the aid of the Ottomans after they are defeated in another **Russo-Turkish** war; but most of the empire's territory in Europe is lost.

1889 Birth of **Mustafa Kemal**

1908 The "Young Turk revolution" compels Abdul Hamid to grant a new representative constitution.

1909 Abdul Hamid reneges on his reforms and is deposed by the Young Turks, who replace him with his brother, Mehmet V, the first constitutional sultan.

1911–1913 The disastrous **Balkan Wars** discredit the liberal movement and a military government takes power under Enver Pasha.

1914–1918 Enver Pasha's decision to enter World War I on the side of the Central Powers precipitates the final collapse of the Ottoman Empire. Despite repulsing an Allied landing at **Gallipoli**, the Turkish armed forces are resoundingly defeated, and the Ottomans are forced to accept humiliating peace terms, including the occupation of Constantinople.

1919–1922 Greek forces invade Western Anatolia and are finally defeated by General Mustafa Kemal, the hero of the Turkish resistance at Gallipoli.

1922 The Mudanya Armistice recognizes the territorial integrity of Anatolia. Under the leadership of Mustafa Kemal, the sultanate is abolished and Mehmet VI, the last sultan, goes into exile.

1923 October 29: the **Turkish Republic** is proclaimed, with Ankara as its capital and Mustafa Kemal as its first president and leader of the sole political party, the Republican People's Party.

1924–34 Mustafa Kemal, soon to be renamed Atatürk ("Father of Turks"), introduces sweeping reforms, including: the abolition of the Caliphate; the secularization of the legal system; the banning of the fez and veil; the enfranchisement of women; the introduction of a Latin alphabet and calendar; and the introduction of surnames.

1930 Name Istanbul officially adopted.

1938 Ataturk dies.

1939–45 Turkey remains neutral throughout most of World War II, only declaring war on Germany in the final months in order to secure a seat at the new United Nations, of which she becomes a founding member.

1950 Other parties are allowed to stand in the general elections and **Adnan Menderes** is elected prime minister as leader of the Justice Party. But the transition to multi-party democracy proves problematic as mounting civil unrest prompts three military coups over the next 30 years.

1974 Turkey invades **Cyprus** in the wake of a failed, Greek-sponsored military coup, resulting in the island's partition.

1980 The republic's third military coup brings Chief of Staff **Kenan Evren** to power. Turgut Ozal, a U.S.-educated engineer, takes control of the economy and introduces radical, Western-oriented, free market reforms.

1983 **Turgut Ozal** is elected prime minister in the first post-coup elections.

1987 Turkey applies for full membership of the European Union.

1993 **Tansu Ciller** is appointed as Turkey's first female prime minister, succeeding Suleyman Demirel, who replaces the late Turgut Ozal as president.

1994 **Kurdish Separatists** set off bombs in Istanbul and continue their struggle against government forces in the southeast. Preliminary negotiation for a customs union with the EU begin. Local elections bring **pro-Islamic militants** to power in Istanbul, Ankara, and other cities in Anatolia.

The Art of the Kilim

By Alastair
Hull and
Nicholas
Barnard

Alastair
Hull is a
collector,
expert, and
dealer in
kilims.
Nicholas
Barnard is a
writer and
organizer of
original
tribal-art
exhibits.

What are kilims? The word *kilim* simply means a flat-woven rug, or a rug without a knotted pile. There are many variations used in different languages: *gelim* in Iran, *kelim* in Afghanistan, *kylym* in Ukraine, *palas* in the Caucasus, *bsath* in Syria and Lebanon, *chilim* in Romania and kilim, again, in Turkey, Poland, Hungary, and Serbia. Moreover, flat weaving is found in some form all over the world, from the Great Plains of North America to Scandinavia and Indonesia. At times there is only a structural similarity in what is produced, but the disciplines imposed by the materials and techniques often result in strikingly similar designs and compositions.

Until recently the kilim has been considered the poor relation of the Oriental knotted carpet by collectors and traders alike. For generations this view has prevailed, and the majority of books on rugs dismiss the kilim in a few sentences as an inferior and simple tribal product. In the last two decades, however, there has been an explosion of interest in the decorative, utilitarian, and collectible qualities of these remarkable objects. Today, kilims captivate an ever-widening audience throughout the Western world. And Anatolia is leading the kilim-producing world in both the quality and quantity of the modern production.

Kilims have been an essential piece of decorative, practical, and portable furniture for the peoples of the Middle East and Asia for a very long time. Together with jewelry, clothing, tent furnishings, and animal trappings, kilims have helped to form the identity of a village or nomadic tribal group. They were made for use on the floors and walls of tents, houses, and mosques and as animal covers and bags. Most kilims were made for family and personal use, although some villages and towns became famous in the 17th and 18th centuries for their fine commercial production, and remain so today. Family wealth was stored up in kilims, knotted rugs, precious metals, and animals, and at times of famine or crisis any of these possessions could be bartered for grain or be exchanged into local currency for use in the nearest market town.

Kilims have always played a central role in the family as part of the dowry or bride price. Then, as now, marriage involved much more than the union of two people. The girl, betrothed at an early age, became an instrument of liaison between families, to the mutual commercial, financial, and political benefit of all parties concerned. The joint wealth of the two families was consolidated with rugs, jewelry, and other items; the dowry also consisted of animals and grazing, water, and irrigation rights. The young girl, learning alongside her mother and other members of her family, made her own dowry of kilims and textiles as a labor of love. Each piece embodies the inheritance of family traditions and tribal folklore. The position and status of a family were directly related to the quality and quantity of the bride's dowry, and this explains to some extent why the kilim has in the past had so much effort, craftsmanship, and creativity lavished upon it with no prospect of financial gain from the marketplace or bazaar.

In the late 19th and early 20th centuries, tribal groups began to lose their cohesion in the face of commercial and government pressures. Once tribes became sedentary and had to survive by trade and barter, they copied whichever designs were fashionable and salable. Marriages between tribes became more common, increasing the intermingling of often totally different cultures and confusing the heritage of traditional arts. These changes were often accompanied by a decline in craftsmanship, but the fusion of clans and tribes of fundamentally different origins has sometimes resulted in exquisite and unusual kilims, which have appeared on the market during the last 30 years.

Workshop production of kilims in villages usually indicates a nomadic tribe that has settled, in ancient or modern times, continuing to weave for domestic, and latterly for commercial, reasons. Present-day Turkey has become the center for the village and workshop production of kilims for export and trade; orders are placed by telex, and many designs and colors are inspired by Western interior designers. Chemical dyes are used, and yet it is interesting to see the reemergence of the rich, glowing colors of natural dyes, matched with ancient and often long-forgotten motifs and symbols, to satisfy an ever-growing demand for more-traditional kilims.

The reasons for making kilims have changed greatly in recent years. Utility and religious and cultural significance have largely been replaced by profit and commerce. By looking at many different kilims, old and new, from many different areas, one can begin to appreciate those that seem to be original and not mass produced. These are the genuine article—kilims that retain their true ethnic identity, woven without compromise and with a craftsmanship that reflects love and heritage in their making.

Until the 20th century many tribes were utterly self-sufficient in their weaving, a situation unknown in Europe since the Middle Ages. The source of the wool or animal hair, the streams to soak the fleeces, the plants and compounds for dyeing, and the timber to make the frame for the loom were all found within tribal boundaries, whether the tribes were nomadic or seminomadic. Kilims from different geographical, and hence tribal, areas show startling variations in color and texture, and this is in part due to the very specific localized sources of these basic raw materials.

Throughout central Asia the dominant source of yarn has always been the domesticated sheep, of which there are three types: fat-tailed, long-tailed, and fat-rumped. Fat-tailed sheep are found throughout Asia; their tails can develop to an enormous size—30 or 40 pounds. Long-tailed sheep are found on the southern borders of Afghanistan and fat-rumped sheep in Turkestan, a tribal area of central Asia. The quality of wool from all sheep depends entirely on climate and pasture, and the wool from the fat-tailed sheep is famous for its hard, coarse, and long staple, which gives a lustrous shine with excellent dye-taking qualities. Unlike flocks in the more developed world, where breeding has produced fleeces of uniform color, sheep are found throughout Asia that are brown, black, white, and a misty red, all in one flock, and sometimes all on one animal.

Camels, goats, and horses also provide a source for yarn. Goat hair is used for its strength and its attractive, high sheen. The warps of saddle and donkey bags, animal covers, and some of the kilims of central Asia are made of goat hair or of goat hair and sheep's wool combined. The sides of the kilims, the selvages, are often of goat hair. Camel hair is used for both the weft and warp in kilims, to rich and subtle effect, especially when it is left undyed. Horse hair from the mane and tail is often tied in tassels on bags, and, like goat hair, it gives added strength in binding and finishing a kilim.

White cotton has always been used by certain tribes and is becoming increasingly popular as a way of highlighting designs and patterns. Unlike white wool, cotton does not turn cream or ivory in color with age. Its structural qualities are also much valued. Since the turn of this century, cotton has tended to replace wool in the warps of Anatolian kilims. This is a good indication of how commercial zeal can influence traditional practice. Previously, there was no alternative to wool or local materials, and a weaver would never have parted with cash for cotton to weave into a kilim that she was not intending to sell for profit. Cotton-and-wool mixtures are found in 19th-century kilims, and the spinning of the materials together results in a fine yarn that is strong yet supple.

A distinctive feature of kilim weaving is that individual color sections are completed before the weaver moves on to other areas of the rug. This is in total contrast to knotted-pile carpets, where the weaver works straight across the carpet in horizontal lines of knots, using many different colors in close succession. The kilim weaver will work on one block of color, laying perhaps 20 wefts before beating them down with a comb and moving on to the adjacent color.

Traditional nomadic weavers were unable to carry large quantities of prepared wool with them and so would use whatever color and texture of wool came to hand each time the portable loom was set up. Because of this, the exact colors that the weaver had planned for the design could not always be found, and the kilim became an endlessly shifting colorscape.

Until the mid-19th century only colored dyes from animal, vegetable, and mineral sources were known, and there were thriving industries associated with the cropping and mining of the raw materials throughout Asia. In towns and villages, yarn would be taken to professional dyers, and naturally dyed yarn could be bought in the markets. All kilims made before the 1850s were, therefore, naturally dyed, a process that has continued until very recently. Nomadic or seminomadic peoples, making kilims for their own use, sometimes had access to natural dyestuffs—substances that grew wild amongst their grazing animals—and so the women would collect herbs, flowers, and roots for their own special color recipes. The migratory life only allowed for the carriage of small quantities of dyed wool, made up a batch at a time, and this is one explanation for the natural variations in color found in the older kilims.

A whole spectrum of natural colors can be obtained from the flowers, fruit, vegetables, and insects—even the earth—in kilim-producing areas. All natural dyes (with the exception of yellow) retain their colors extraordinarily well, but they do begin to fade naturally after about 50 years and will run if not well fixed. The positive aspect of this is that a kilim will mellow beautifully over the years if traditionally made with natural dyes.

In the late 19th century, weavers began experimenting with chemical dyes, achieving, at times, only limited success. However, with chemical dyes, weavers had a complete and relatively easy choice of colors, free from the limitations, and the natural aesthetic integrity, of the natural sources available to them in their homelands. Vivid oranges and yellows that had been so difficult to fix in the past were now readily available. The use of chemical dyes spread rapidly, spawning village industries and reaching even the least accessible and most self-sufficient weavers of all, the nomadic tribeswomen.

Kilims produced in the first flush of this new craze display a rather startling use of many different, not always harmonious colors, and until recently some chemical dyes, such as aniline and acid-base dyes, corroded the wool, faded quickly, and would not withstand washing with detergents. But chemical dyes do not always result in clashing color effects, or poor durability. In the last 30 years chrome-mordanted colors have been developed that are indistinguishable, when used well, from natural dyes. Ironically, it is in these same 30 years that the natural-dye lobby among consumers and collectors in the West has met with some success. Classes of instruction in the art of natural dyeing and a price premium for kilims with vegetable dyes have ensured a contemporary revival in traditional techniques among the kilim producers of Anatolia.

There is no representation of the Deity in Islam, either in the form of the written word or through the depiction of people (man being made in God's image). In Islamic art some figurative forms, human and animal, are permitted, but in many cases it is considered disrespectful to walk over them, thus precluding their use in knotted rugs and kilims. For the tribal weavers, however, connections with their natural environment, with their animals, and with their family groups are very strong and deeply rooted and will override religious taboo. So, although recognizable objects are depicted in their rugs, they will never be seen to form part of a complete, pseudorealistic picture.

Two factors other than religion influence the designs that a weaver will choose for her kilim. One is the discipline of the weaving techniques themselves, which produce mostly abstract patterns; the other is the natural environment in which the weaver lives and from which she will adapt motifs to represent lakes, rivers, flowers, petals, trees, and leaves, or domestic animals (sheep, goats, and camels), wild animals, and insects (snakes, scorpions, and spiders). She will incorporate images from her own household, such as a kettle, teapot, ewer, comb, beater, or lamp, as well as, more recently, objects of Western influence, including cars and bikes and even helicopters and automatic rifles.

Perhaps the most familiar motif used on kilims is the Tree of Life, which, to the weaver, could represent equally well the presence of water in desert lands, or the family, with the trunk as the father and the branches as the children. Another genuinely symbolic motif is the talismanic evil eye, or *nazarlik*, used to deflect evil and to balance the adverse effects on the kilim of other motifs, such as the spider or scorpion.

On many modern kilims, made in the last 30 years or so, ancient motifs have been misrepresented or given a new twist because the weaver has not been aware of the origins of the design she is using. Modern weavers often work from "cartoons" or pictures of old rugs, re-creating them for an enthusiastic Western market. Original motifs will be modified in this process to suit a pre-ordained shape or weaving technique, and so the evolution of the ancient design continues under modern conditions.

Yet the roots of tribal traditions are deep within the mind of the weaver. An English textile-designer friend traveled to Anatolia recently with a design for a kilim that was totally divorced from traditional uses of color as dictated by the weaving methods. His major difficulty was finding a weaver who could understand this totally alien and new composition. Why were certain colors appearing where they were, and why were certain shapes, unrelated to traditional methods, being used? Here was a pattern that departed from the inbuilt and centuries-old methods. The weavers may be able to absorb small design changes within a basically traditional format, but it would be impossible for them to change their whole style of expression, even temporarily. Pattern for them makes no sense unless it is an integral part of the whole woven composition.

Until recently there were, generally speaking, three clear-cut categories from which to choose when buying a kilim: there were antique flat-weaves made over 100 years ago, before the influences of export trade began to be felt; there were old kilims, made in this century, some of whose compositions clearly display the blending of different tribal and regional traditions; and there were modern, largely commercially produced kilims, woven in village workshops, often to orders from retailers in the

West and often much removed from their local, traditional techniques and patterning.

Over the past five years, however, a fourth category has developed—the new facsimiles being produced in Anatolia. These are completely traditional in style and form and are made largely as a response to the increasing Western demand for authentic, quality weavings. Many have been specially commissioned by Western dealers, and most are made for export. Various grades are available, determined by the quality of the weaving—from coarse to very fine—and by the complexity of patterning in the overall composition. Most of these kilims are chemically dyed, and those that do make use of vegetable and natural dyes enjoy a considerable premium in price.

The safest purchase in terms of financial investment is, without doubt, an antique kilim. But it is dangerous to assume that a kilim is rare or excellently designed and constructed simply because it is old; there have always been good weavers and bad weavers, weaving good, bad, and indifferent kilims. Anyone interested in buying an antique kilim should take time to examine as many old and antique rugs as possible and should talk to a knowledgeable, trustworthy dealer to get a clear idea of which rugs are considered important and collectible.

Collectibility is not determined by the vagaries of fashion. A rug is collectible if it is rare or unusual and if it is very well woven; these are unchanging qualities, and one may assume that such a rug will increase in value as an investment. Antique kilims are invariably the most expensive to buy, both in the West and in their country of origin; ironically, there is often a much better choice in Europe and North America, in terms of price and kilim type, than there is in Anatolia or central Asia.

Very fine antique kilims are obviously too expensive for many people, but large numbers of old, traditional weavings can be found to suit most budgets. Old kilims are not yet considered a financial investment in themselves and should really be valued for their decorative and practical qualities on a personal level. Until about 30 years ago, few kilims were produced for commercial gain, and so traditional kilim shapes and compositions were made, and weaving techniques practiced, as they had been for generations. Antique kilims are now very difficult to find in their countries of origin, and the same will soon be true of traditional old kilims. Their increasing rarity will doubtless be reflected in their rising values.

Of the modern production, it is safe to assume that the finest facsimiles of antique weaving and dyeing techniques will become the investments of the future, and the highest-quality naturally dyed Anatolian replicas will definitely improve and mellow with age and use.

In Anatolia, kilims can be recognized by their tribe and area of origin to within a group of villages or even a single village. Many distinctive kilims of the 19th century can be attributed to the to the area around **Bergama and Balikesir,** in western Anatolia, now one of the last strongholds of the Yoruk peoples. Most of the antique Balikesir kilims are patterned with an interlocking grid of blue on a red ground, with dazzling results. More recent Balikesir kilims are varied in design, often decorated with medallions of different sizes on a plain ground, with simple side and end borders or skirts.

It is unusual to find kilims from Anatolia with any area left undecorated, and those from the **Manastir** region are therefore easy to recognize. The kilims have very strong and simple compositions, usually on a tomato-red or black ground with a plain central field decorated with very few designs. The *mihrab*, the ceremonial mosque archway, is represented in Manastir kilims by a distinct, floating line rather than by a pattern.

The village of **Mut** lies south of the Taurus mountains, another region of the seminomadic Yoruk pastoralists. The kilims from this area are often found with dark warps of goat hair or brown wool. Brightly colored medallions are set against a red ground, usually a pair of designs in a mirror image.

Aydin is a town near the Aegean coast and is a productive source of kilims, often woven in two halves and joined together. As with most western Anatolian kilims, the Aydin examples are brightly colored with small patterns.

The town of **Konya** lies at the south and center of a most prolific weaving area, that of west-central Anatolia, once known as Karaman. Konya kilims are made wholly of wool and are often large, woven in two or three pieces, with a predominantly white or cream background color into which is woven a strong central series of oval medallions.

The kilims of the central area of Anatolia around **Kayserı** are very loosely woven, and the older examples have a silky and flat texture. Modern Kayserı kilims are generally red and black, fading to pinks and grays.

Maylatya is in Kurdish country and gives its name to the numerous kilims that are produced in the area by both Kurds and Turkic peoples. Woven in two pieces with warps of white wool, the kilims are usually long, relatively narrow, and difficult to make. Commonly, three central medallions are split by the central joint, at times most irregularly, and the white sections of the composition are given brilliance by the use of white cotton yarn. Some of the longest Anatolian kilims are found in the Malatya area. Known as band kilims, they can exceed 15 feet in length; and each of the two sections is often, and most unusually for Anatolia, a complete composition in itself. They are sometimes cut and sold as runners. Predominant colors are red and blue with striking white bands.

Woven by Kurds, most **Sivas** kilims, and indeed most of the kilims made anywhere east of here, are prayer mats in muted colors with a strong single and central mihrab motif. All are made in one piece, and the mihrab is bordered by three narrow bands full of floral designs.

Prayer rugs from around **Bayburt** and **Erzurum** are woven in predominantly yellow or ocher colors with tiered central mihrabs surrounded by stylized floral designs, especially carnations. Many of the kilims have their year of weaving woven into the design. Just east of this area is the village of **Bardiz,** where most of the Karabagh or modern Bessarabian kilims are made. The Kurdish weavers are excellent copyists and have been producing these large floral-pattern kilims since the 1920s, using European tapestry designs such as those from Aubusson and Savonnerie in France. Curiously, these were themselves derived from the original Ottoman floral kilims of the 17th century—a full circle of design ideas.

The remote and mountainous district of eastern Anatolia around **Van** has maintained many clans of seminomadic Kurds, largely undisturbed for thousands of years. The kilims are, unusually, square and are generally in two pieces; many examples bear a resemblance to the kilims of northwest Persia and the Caucasus, made by other Kurdish groups. Kilims from Van are well made with good-quality wool and will last for many years.

The kilims from the **Kars** area, close by the Russian border, are typical of most Kurdish work—either long narrow strips or small prayer rugs. Thick, dark wool warps give a ribbed effect, and, in general, colors are browns, pinks, and oranges.

The area of European Turkey known as **Thrace** is thought to be the region of origin for many distinctive kilims. The typical composition is simple, often the Tree of Life in its many forms, surrounded by a floral border with animal and leaf motifs. Those from around the town of Sarkoy are of the finest quality.

When seeking out kilims, do not assume that those bought in Turkey will be cheaper than those for sale in the West. A rug bought in an Istanbul bazaar may often be just as expensive as in London or New York, if not more so. And do beware of the hidden costs and regulations governing a sale for personal export. These include shipping, packing, and handling charges, as well as export and import tax. All these expenses add up and can mean that the overall cost is considerably more than you at first calculate. But for the memories and stories associated with the purchase of a kilim in a bazaar—the haggling, the playacting, and the gallons of sweet tea consumed before the deal is struck—there is no substitute.

3 Istanbul

Walking through Old Stamboul can be overwhelming. To the right, as you stroll up Kabasakal Sokak, are the Baths of Roxelana, ambitious wife of Süleyman the Magnificent. To the left are the workshops of traditional craftspeople—a courtyard surrounded on all sides by a low-slung building of honey-colored stone, filled with tiny shops housing bookbinders, joiners, calligraphers, paper makers. Beyond the baths, a well-worn obelisk in a grassy, rectangular open space marks the site of the ancient Roman hippodrome, on the far side of which, directly opposite the imposing Blue Mosque, stands the 16th-century palace of Ibrahim Paşa, Süleyman's grand vizir, or prime minister. Now a superb museum, this was once the finest private residence in Istanbul. Alas for Ibrahim, Roxelana coveted the vizir's lovely palace (not to mention the power it represented) and convinced her husband to have him murdered in his sleep so she could possess it. Turn right and you are face to face with Hagia Sophia, the Church of the Holy Wisdom, which dates from AD 532. In its day it was the greatest church in all Christendom, with a dome so monumental that worshipers believed it to be suspended from heaven by a chain. Continue walking for a block or so and you pass Justinian's other church, Hagia Eirene, Hagia Sophia on a smaller scale. Then you come to the outer gate of Topkapı Palace, a sprawling city unto itself that once employed 50,000 people and stood for centuries as the home of the Ottoman sultans and one of the world's great treasure houses.

It is a truly astounding commingling of history, art, and architecture. And yet it is only appropriate in a city that stood at the center of the world for more than a thousand years. Though it is often remarked that Turkey straddles Europe and Asia, it is, of course, really Istanbul that does the straddling: The vast bulk of the country resides comfortably on the Asian side. European Istanbul is separated from its Asian suburbs by the Bosporus, the narrow channel that connects the Black Sea, north of the city, to the Sea of Marmara, to the south. (From there it is only a short sail to that superhighway of the ancient world, the Aegean.) The European side of Istanbul is itself divided by a body of water, the Golden Horn, an 8-kilometer-long (5-mile-long) inlet that separates Old Stamboul, also called Old Istanbul, from the New Town, known as Beyoğlu. It is across the Golden Horn that the Byzantines once positioned an enormous chain, in hopes of protecting their capital city from naval attack. The tactic worked for a time but ultimately failed, after the young Ottoman sultan Mehmet II (ruled 1451–81) had his ships dragged overland from the Bosporus and dropped in behind the chains.

It was, of course, more than a mere accident of geography that destined Istanbul for greatness. Much of the city's character and fame was created by the sheer force of will of four men. At Constantinople in AD 330, Constantine the Great founded a "New Rome" that would survive long after the Roman Empire had crumbled in the West. Under the Byzantine emperor Justinian (ruled 527–65), Constantine's capital flourished. It was Justinian who ordered the construction of the magnificent Hagia Sophia in 532, on the site of a church originally built for Constantine. This awe-inspiring architectural wonder, which still dominates the city's skyline, spawned untold imitators: Its form is copied by many mosques in Istanbul and elsewhere in Turkey, most notably the Blue Mosque, which sits across the square like a massive bookend.

Mehmet II, known as Fatih (the Conqueror) is the man responsible for the fact that those Hagia Sophia clones are mosques and not churches. It was Mehmet who marched into a long-neglected, nearly ruined Constantinople in 1453, rebuilt it, and renamed it Istanbul. In 1468, after settling in, he began a summer palace on the picturesque hill at the tip of the city where the Golden Horn meets the Bosporus. That hideaway grew into the fabulous Topkapı Palace. The palace's first full-time resident was Süleyman I the Magnificent (ruled 1520–1566), who led the Ottoman Empire to its highest achievements in art and architecture, literature and law. Süleyman made the decision to commission the brilliant architect Sinan (1489–1587) to design buildings that are now recognized as some of Islam's finest mosques, Istanbul's grand Süleymaniye and intimate Sokollu Mehmet Paşa among them.

The monuments built by these titans, or in their honor, dominate and define the city and lead the traveler into the arms of the past at every turn. But Istanbul has its modern side, too, with all the concomitant traffic jams, air pollution, and overdevelopment, and brash concrete and glass hotels creeping up behind its historic old palaces. Day and night, Istanbul has a schizophrenic air. At dawn, when the muezzin's call to prayer rebounds from ancient minarets, a few hearty revelers make their way home from the nightclubs and bars while other residents kneel on their prayer rugs, facing Mecca. Women in jeans, business suits, or elegant designer outfits pass others wearing long skirts and head coverings. Donkey-drawn carts vie with old Chevrolets and Pontiacs and shiny Toyotas and BMWs for dominance of the noisy, narrow streets. And the seductive Oriental bazaar competes with Western boutiques for the time and attention of both tourists and locals: The props may be new, but the song of the shopkeeper and ritual haggling are as old as the city itself.

How to get your bearings in such an unpredictable place? Head for the Galata Bridge, which spans the mouth of the Haliç (Golden Horn). You stand on a new drawbridge, stronger and wider than its weary predecessor, an old pontoon bridge that was dismantled and moved in 1993. Look to the north and you will see the New Town, modern Beyoğlu, with Taksim Square at its center. From the square, high-rise hotels and smart shops radiate out on all sides. Beyond Beyoğlu, the fashionable suburbs of Arnavutköy, Bebek, Yeniköy, Tarabya, and Sarıyer line the European side of the Bosporus. Look southeast, across the Bosporus, and you can see the Asian suburbs of Kadıköy and Üsküdar. To the south lies the old walled city of Stamboul, also called Sultanahmet (after the sultan who built the Blue Mosque), with Hagıa Sophia and Topkapı Palace at its heart. Turn to look up the Golden Horn and you should be able to make out three more bridges, the Atatürk, favored by cabdrivers hoping to avoid the Galata, the Old Galata Bridge, now reconstructed to serve traffic between Haskoy and Balat toward the inland tip of the Golden Horn, and the Fatih, out at the city's northwestern edge. Galata Bridge is a good orientation point for another reason: Filled with peddlers selling everything from pistachio nuts and spices to curly-toed slippers fancy enough for a sultan, it offers a compelling slice of Istanbul's frenetic street life. Fishermen grill their catches on coal braziers and tempt hungry passersby while motorists slowed by the activity blast their horns constantly, usually to no avail.

Frankly, those who like their monuments preserved in a pristine state will be sorely disappointed in this noisy and chaotic city. Yet the Turks seem to take the mayhem in good spirits, and you should, too. On the twisty, crowded old city streets, there is an infectious energy, a pulse of life that inspires. See the sites, dodge the cars, eat heartily. Like strong Turkish coffee, Istanbul has its grit but is bracing and filled with rich, rarefied flavor.

Essential Information

Important Addresses and Numbers

Tourist Information The **Turkish Ministry of Tourism** maintains tourist information offices at Atatürk Airport (tel. 212/663–6363), the Hilton Hotel (tel. 212/233–0592), the International Maritime Passenger Terminal at Karaköy Square (tel. 212/249–5776), in the Sultanahmet district (Divan Yolu Cad. 3, tel. 212/518–1802), and in the Beyoğlu district (Mesrutiyet Cad. 57, tel. 212/243–2928). Hours are usually from 9 until 5, sometimes with an hour closed around noon.

Embassies **U.S.** (Meşrutiyet Cad. 147, Tepebaşı, Beyoğlu, tel. 212/251–3602). **Canada** (Büyükdere Cad. 107/3, Bengün Han, Gayrettepe, tel. 212/272–5174). **U.K.** (Meşrutiyet Cad. 34, Tepebaşı, Beyoğlu, tel. 212/252–6436).

Emergencies **Tourism police** (tel. 212/527–4503). **Ambulance** (tel. 112; International Hospital Ambulance, tel. 212/663–3000). **Hospitals** (American Hospital, Güzelbahçe Sok. 20, Nişantaşı, tel. 212/231–4050); International Hospital (Yesilyurt, tel. 212/663–3000); German Hospital (Siraseviler Cad. 119, Taksim, tel. 212/293–2150); these are good sources for an English-speaking doctor. **24-hour pharmacies** (tel. 111); there's one in every neighborhood, and all Istanbul pharmacies post the name and address of the nearest pharmacy open around the clock. **Taksim** (Istiklal Cad. 17, tel. 212/244–3195) is centrally located in the Taksim district.

English-Language Bookstores The most complete stock is at **Redhouse,** near the Grand Bazaar, the retail outlet of a Turkish English-language publisher founded by missionaries during Ottoman days (Riza Paşa Yokuşu 60, Sultanahmet, tel. 212/627–8100). Others include the **Dünya** (Narlıbahçe Sokak 15, Cağaloğlu, tel. 212/512–0190 and Istiklâl Caddesi 469, Beyoğlu, tel. 212/249–1006) bookshops, which have books and magazines in English and branches at the Conrad, Hilton, Hyatt, and Swissotel; **ABC Bookstore** (Istiklâl Caddesi, 461, Beyoğlu, tel. 212/249–2414); and **Net,** publishers of tourism guides (Yerebatan Cad. 16/3, Sultanahmet, tel. 212/620–8406).

Travel Agencies Most are along Cumhuriyet Caddesi, off Taksim Square, in the hotel area: **American Express** (Hilton Hotel, Cumhuriyet Cad., Harbiye, tel. 212/241–0248 or 212/241–0249), **Intra** (Halâskârgazi Cad. 111, Harbiye, tel. 212/247–8174), **Setur** (Cumhuriyet Cad. 107, Harbiye, tel. 212/230–0336), and **Vitur** (Cumhuriyet Cad. 269, Harbiye, tel. 212/230–0896).

Arriving and Departing by Plane

Airports and Airlines All international and domestic flights arrive at Istanbul's **Atatürk Airport** (information tel. 212/663–6400). The main airlines flying into the airport include **Delta** (tel. 800/221–1212); **Air France** (tel. 800/237–2747), **British Airways** (tel. 800/247–9297), and **Lufthansa** (tel. 800/645–3880), as well as **THY** (Turkish Airlines, tel. 212/986–5050), the Turkish national airline.

Between the Airport and City Center Shuttle buses make the 30- to 40-minute trip from the airport's international and domestic terminals to the THY terminal in downtown Istanbul, at Şişhane Square, near the Galata Tower (tel. 212/ 245–4208 or 212/245–4238); buses to the airport depart from here every hour from 6 AM until 11 PM and as demand warrants after that. Allow at least 45 minutes for the bus ride in this direction, and plan to be at the airport two hours before international flights to allow for the time-consuming security and check-in procedures. Taxis charge about $15 to Taksim Square and $11 to Sultanahmet Square (between the Blue Mosque and Hagia Sophia).

Arriving and Departing by Car, Train, and Bus

By Car The E6 runs between Istanbul and central Anatolia to the east. The busy and often hair-raising E5 (also called Londra Asfaltı) leads from Edirne in northern Turkey to the west of Istanbul, to Atatürk Airport and on through the city walls at Cannon Gate; the neighborhood by the gate is called Topkapı, though it is nowhere near Topkapı Palace. Alternatives to E5 when leaving the city, numerous car ferries ply the Sea of Marmara from the Kabataş docks, or there's an overnight ferry to İzmir from the Eminönü docks.

By Train Trains from Europe and the west arrive at **Sirkeci Station** (tel. 212/ 527–0051) in Old Stamboul, near the Galata Bridge. Trains from Anatolia and the east come into **Haydarpaşa Station** (tel. 216/336–0475) on the Asian side.

By Bus Buses arrive at the Esenler Otogar (tel. 212/658–0505), outside the city near Bayrampasa. This terminal, which replaced the chaotic Topkapı Terminal in 1994, is accessible by the also new and efficient **Hizli Tren** (Rapid Train) system, which leaves from Aksaray. A few buses from Anatolia arrive at Harem Terminal, on the Asian side of the Bosporus (tel. 216/333–3763). Most bus companies will have minibus services from the bus terminals to the area around Taksim Square and Aksaray, which is close to many hotels. The other option is private **taxis,** which cost about $12 from Esenler Terminal to Taksim or Sultanahmet and about $10 from the Harem terminal. Customers also pay the Bosporus bridge toll when crossing from Asia to Europe, or vice versa.

Getting Around

The best way to get around all the magnificent monuments in Old Stamboul is to walk. They're within easy strolling distance of one another, along streets filled with peddlers, shoeshine boys, children at play, and craftspeople at work. The setting shifts frequently, from narrow, cobbled streets to wide, tree-lined boulevards.

To get to other areas, you can take a bus or one of the many ferries that steam between the Asian and European continents. Dolmuşes and private taxis are plentiful, inexpensive, and more comfortable than city buses. There's no subway system, but there is the Tünel, a tiny underground train that's handy for getting up the steep hill from Karaköy (the neighborhood on the Beyoğlu side of the Galata Bridge) to the bottom of İstiklal Caddesi, Beyoğlu's main street. It runs every 10 minutes and costs about 25¢.

By Bus   The city's red-and-beige buses are crowded and slow, but they are useful for getting around and inexpensive, at about 50¢ per ride. The route name and number are posted on the front of each of vehicle; curbside signboards list routes and itineraries. Buy tickets before boarding; they're available individually and in books of 10 at newsstands around the city, and, for a few cents above face value, can also be purchased from shoeshine boys and the men sitting on wooden crates at most bus stops. Two or three London-style double-deckers operate between Sultanahmet and Emirgan on the Bosporus, and Taksim and Bostanci on the Asian side. Unlike the older city buses, these are clean and offer a panoramic ride. A bus attendant collects fares ($1).

By Dolmuş   These shared taxis, many of them classic American cars from the '50s, run along various routes. Like taxi stands, dolmuş stands are marked by signs, and you can sometimes hail them on the street. The destination is shown on either a roof sign or a card in the front window. Dolmuş stands are placed at regular intervals, and the vehicles wait for customers to climb in; tell the driver where you want to get off when you get in, and he will stop when he gets there. Though the savings over a private taxi are significant, the quarters can sometimes be a little too close for comfort.

By Taxi   Taxis are metered and inexpensive. Some drivers do not speak English and may not know every street, so write down the name of the one you want and those nearby, and the name of the neighborhood you're visiting. Although tipping is not automatic, it is customary to round off the fare to the nearest 5000 TL. Avoid taxi drivers who choose roundabout routes for more money by having your hotel's attendant, or a Turkish speaker, talk to the driver before you get in.

By Boat   You would expect a sprawling city surrounded by water to be well served by ferries, and Istanbul does not disappoint. The main docks are at Eminönü, on the Old Stamboul side of the Galata Bridge; Karaköy on the other side of the bridge; Kabataş, near Dolmabahçe Palace; and, across the Bosporus on the Asian shore, at Üsküdar and Kadiköy. Commuter ferries of various sizes crisscross between these points day and night, and, like New York's Staten Island Ferry, provide a wonderful view of the city at a most reasonable price (usually $1 or less round-trip). One of the most practical and speedy innovations on Istanbul's waterways has been the seabuses (*deniz otobüsü*), which are large and powerful catamarans painted blue, red, and white, operating to and from Kabatas, Bostanci, Princes' Islands, Yalova, and Bakırkoy. The interiors are air conditioned and are reminiscent of a large aircraft. Schedules are available at docks marked Deniz Otobüsü Terminali.

Traveling farther afield, some boats head north up the Bosporus toward the Black Sea. These make for a highly worthwhile excursion, as they stop at six towns on the European side and three on the Asian side on the way up to the castle of Anadolu Kavağı, on the Asian side; here, the ship turns around and retraces its route back to Istanbul. The Anadolu Kavağı boat, which makes all the stops and is best for sightseeing, leaves year-round from the Eminönü Docks, Pier 5, next to the Galata Bridge on the Old Istanbul side, at 10:30 AM and 1:30 PM with two extra trips on weekdays and four extra trips on Sunday from April through August. Unless you speak Turkish, have your hotel call for boat schedules, as English is rarely spoken at the docks. The round-trip fare is $6; the ride each way lasts one hour and 45 minutes. You can disembark at any of the stops and pick up a later boat, or return by taxi, dolmus, or bus for about the same cost.

Guided Tours

Guided tours are arranged through travel agencies, and their offerings are all pretty similar, though names may change. "Classical Tours" take in Hagia Sophia, the Museum of Turkish and Islamic Arts, the Hippodrome, the Yerebatan Saray (Sunken Palace), and the Blue Mosque in their half-day versions ($25); the Topkapı Palace, the Süleymaniye Cami (Mosque of Süleyman), the Grand or perhaps the Egyptian Bazaar, and lunch in addition to the above sights in their full-day version ($50; $60–$80 by private car). "Bosporus Tours" usually include lunch at Sarıyer and visits to the Dolmabahçe and Beylerbeyi palaces. A "Night Tour" ($50) includes dinner, drinks, and a show at either the Kervansaray or the Galata Tower nightclub.

Exploring Istanbul

Ironically, Istanbul's Asian side is filled with sprawling, Western-style suburbs, and its European side is a maze of mosques, opulent palaces, and crowded Oriental bazaars. The five tours below focus on the European side, making occasional forays across the water.

Begin in the heart of Old Stamboul, on the southern side of the Golden Horn, where you will find the richest concentration of history in the city; Tour 1 takes in Topkapı Palace, the city's fine Archaeological Museum, Hagia Sophia and the Blue Mosque, and the beautiful Sokollu Mehmet Paşa Cami. Tour 2 picks up where the first leaves off, at the Grand Bazaar, and covers the neighborhoods between the market and the Galata Bridge, with visits to several smaller markets and some fine, famous old mosques. In Tour 3, you cross the Galata Bridge and make your way along İstiklal Caddesi to Taksim Square in Beyoğlu, taking in ornate, turn-of-the-century embassies, old movie palaces, and fashionable shops. In Tour 4, you make your way north along the Bosporus, stopping at four spectacular, latter-day palaces of the Ottoman sultans. Lush Yıldız Park provides a peaceful resting stop along the way. Your final tour takes in the outer suburbs on both sides of the Bosporus, and their imposing castles, their beautiful rows of the Ottoman wood-frame houses known as *yalı* among the Turks, and their good seafood restaurants, some of the best in the region.

Highlights for First-Time Visitors

Arkeoloji Müzesi, Tour 1
Blue Mosque, Tour 1
Çamlıca, Off the Beaten Track
Dolmabahçe Palace, Tour 4
Egyptian Bazaar, Tour 2
Galata Bridge, Tour 3
Grand Bazaar, Tour 2
Kariye Museum, Off the Beaten Track
Hagia Sophia, Tour 1
Süleymaniye Cami, Tour 2
Topkapı Palace, Tour 1
Türk Ve Islâm Eserleri Müzesi, Tour 1
Yerebatan Saray, Tour 1

Tour 1: Old Stamboul

Numbers in the margin correspond to points of interest on the Istanbul: Tours 1–4 map.

This tour doesn't cover a great deal of physical distance, but it can be exhausting, for it spans vast epochs of history and contains an incredible concentration of art and architecture. The best way to get around is on foot.

❶ Istanbul's number-one attraction is the **Topkapı Saray** (Topkapı Palace) on Seraglio Point, where the Bosporus meets the Golden Horn. The vast palace was the residence of sultans and their harems until 1868, when Sultan Abdül Mecit I (ruled 1839–61) moved to the European-style Dolmabahçe Palace farther up the Bosporus. Plan on spending several hours and go early, before the bus-tour crowds pour in; gates open at 9 AM. If you go by taxi, be sure to tell the driver you want the Topkapı Saray in Sultanahmet, or you could end up at the Topkapı bus terminal on the outskirts of town.

Sultan Mehmet II built the first palace during the 1450s, shortly after his conquest of Constantinople. Over the centuries, sultan after sultan added ever more elaborate architectural frills and fantasies, until the palace had acquired four courtyards and quarters for some 5,000 full-time residents, many of them concubines and eunuchs. The initial approach to the palace does little to evoke the many tales of intrigue, bloodshed, and drama attached to the structure. The first entrance or Imperial Gate, leads to the **Court of the Janissaries,** also known as the First Courtyard, an area the size of a football field that now serves as a parking lot. As you walk ahead to the ticket office, look to your left, where you will see the **Aya Irini** (Church of St. Irene). This unadorned redbrick building, now used for concerts, dates back to the earliest days of Byzantium. The lane leading down the hill just past the church leads to the Archaeological Museum (*see below*).

Formed in the 14th century as the sultan's corps of elite guards, the Janissaries were recruited as young boys from Ottoman-controlled territories in the Balkans, taught Turkish, and instructed in Islam. Though theoretically the sultan's vassals, these professional soldiers quickly became a power in their own right, and more than once their protests—traditionally expressed by overturning their soup kettles—were followed by the murder of the reigning sultan. During the rule of Sultan Mahmut II (ruled 1808–39), the tables were finally turned and the Janissaries were massacred in what has come to be known as the Auspicious Event.

Next to the ticket office is the **Bab-ı-Selam** (Gate of Salutation), built in 1524 by Süleyman the Magnificent, who was the only person allowed to pass through it on horseback; others had to dismount and enter on foot. Prisoners were kept in the towers on either side before their execution next to the nearby fountain. It is once you pass this gate that you begin to get an idea of the grandeur of the palace.

The **Second Courtyard,** just slightly smaller than the first, is planted with rose gardens and ornamental trees, and filled with a series of ornate *köşks*, pavilions once used for both the business of state and more mundane matters, like feeding the hordes of servants. To the right are the palace's immense kitchens, which now display one of the world's best collections of Chinese porcelains including 10th-century T'ang, Yuan celadon, and Ming blue-and-white pieces dating from the 18th century, when the Chinese produced pieces to order for the palace. Straight ahead is the **Divan-ı-Humayun** (Assembly Room of the Council of State), once presided over by the

Ali Paşa/Nuruosmaniye Mosques, **10**

Arkeoloji Müzesi, **2**

Beyazıt Mosque, **11**

Blue Mosque, **4**

Çırağan Palace, **25**

Dolmabahçe Mosque, **23**

Egyptian Bazaar, **16**

Eminönü, **14**

Galata Bridge, **17**

Galata Tower, **19**

Galatsaray Square, **21**

Grand (Covered) Bazaar, **9**

Hagia Sophia, **3**

Hippodrome, **5**

Ibrahim Paşa Palace/Museum of Turkish and Islamic Arts, **6**

Istanbul University, **12**

Naval Museum, **24**

Rüstem Paşa Cami, **15**

Sokollu Mehmet Paşa Cami, **7**

Süleymaniye Cami, **13**

Taksim Square, **22**

Topkapı Saray, **1**

Tünel Square, **20**

Voyvoda Caddesi, **18**

Yerebatan Saray, **8**

Yıldız Park, **26**

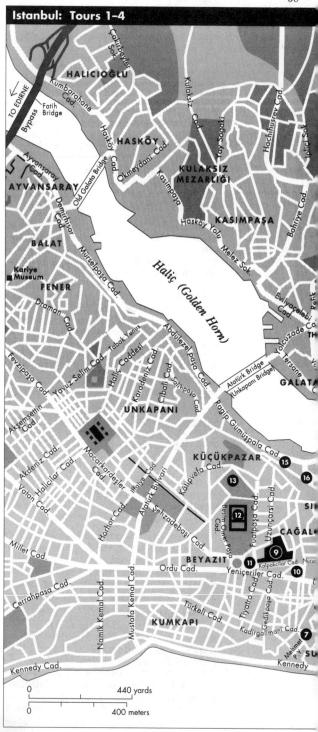

Istanbul: Tours 1–4

0   440 yards
0   400 meters

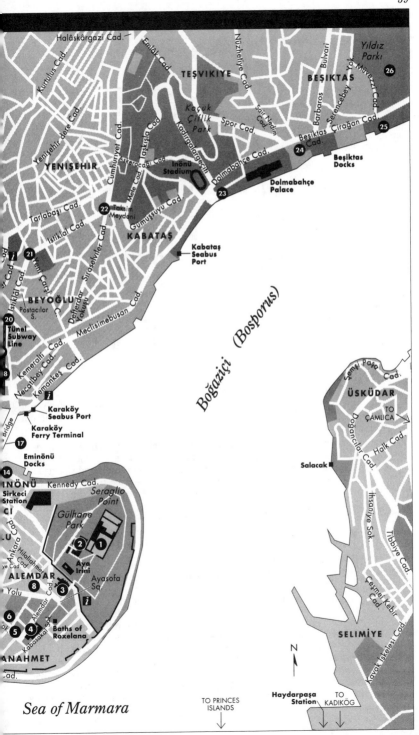

Halâskârgazi Cad.

TEŞVIKIYE

BEŞIKTAS

Yıldız
Parkı

26

Küçük
Çiftlik
Park

Spor Cad.

BEŞIKTAS

25

YENİŞEHIR

Inönü
Stadium

24

Beşiktaş
Docks

Tarlabaşı Cad.

İstiklal Cad.

22

Taksim
Meydanı

23

Dolmabahçe
Palace

KABATAŞ

Kabataş
Seabus
Port

21

BEYOĞLU

Postacılar
S.

Boğaziçi (Bosporus)

20

Tünel
Subway
Line

8

ÜSKÜDAR

TO
ÇAMLICA

Karaköy
Seabus Port

Karaköy
Ferry Terminal

17

Salacak

Eminönü
Docks

14

NÖNÜ

Kennedy Cad.

Seraglio
Point

Sirkeci
Station

CI

Gülhane
Park

LU

2

1

ALEMDAR

Aya
Irini

8

3

Ayasofia
Sa.

Yolu

6

5

4

Baths of
Roxelana

ANAHMET

SELIMIYE

Sea of Marmara

N

TO PRINCES
ISLANDS

Haydarpaşa
Station

TO
KADIKÖG

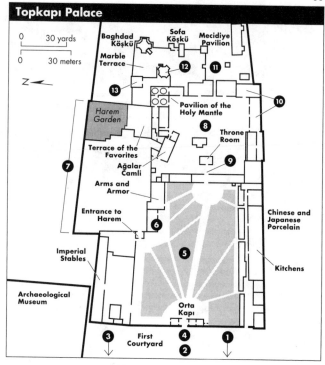

Imperial Gate, **1**
Court of the Janissaries, **2**
Ava Irini, **3**
Bab-i-Selam, **4**
Second Courtyard, **5**
Divan-i-Humayun, **6**
Harem, **7**
Third Courtyard, **8**
Bab-i-Saadet, **9**
Treasure, **10**
Fourth Courtyard, **11**
Erivan Köşk, **12**
Sünnet Odaski, **13**

grand vizir. When the mood struck him, the sultan would sit behind a latticed window, hidden by a curtain so no one would know when he was listening, although occasionally he would pull the curtain aside to comment.

One of the most popular sections of Topkapı is the **Harem,** a maze of 400 halls, terraces, rooms, wings, and apartments grouped around the sultan's private quarters to the west of the Second Courtyard. Only 40 rooms, meticulously restored, are open to the public (and only on tours, which leave every half hour and cost $1). But they give you an idea of both the opulence and the regimentation of harem life. Only a few qualified for presentation to the sultan; even then, not all walked the Golden Way, by which the favorite of the night entered the sultan's private quarters. The first areas you see, which housed the palace eunuchs and about 200 lesser concubines, resemble a monastery; the tiny cubicles are as cramped and uncomfortable as the Harem's main rooms are large and opulent. In this splendid complex, which you see as you penetrate the Harem, private apartments around a shared courtyard housed the chief wives (Islamic law permitted up to four); the Valide Sultan (Queen Mother), the absolute ruler of the Harem, had quite a bit of space as well as her own courtyard and marble bath. The sultan's private rooms are a riot of brocades, murals, colored marble, wildly ornate furniture, gold leaf, and fine carving. Fountains, also much in evidence, were not only decorative; they made it hard to eavesdrop on royal conversations. All told, it is a memorable, worthy backdrop to the rise and fall of princes and pretenders. You exit the Harem into the somewhat smaller **Third Courtyard.**

To see it to best advantage, make your way to its main gate, the **Bab-ı-Saadet** (Gate of Felicity), then exit and reenter. Shaded by regal old trees, the Third Courtyard is dotted by some of the most ornate of the palace's pavilions. Foreign ambassadors once groveled just past the gate in the **Arz Odası** (Audience Chamber), but access to the courtyard was highly restricted, in part because it housed the **Treasury,** four rooms filled with jewels, including two uncut emeralds, each weighing about 8 pounds, that once hung from the ceiling. Here, too, are the dazzling emerald dagger used in the movie *Topkapi* and the 84-carat Spoonmaker diamond that, according to legend, was found by a pauper and traded for three wooden spoons. Not surprisingly, this is one of the most popular sections of the palace, and it can get quite crowded. Also within this courtyard you can view a collection of thousands of Turkish and Persian miniatures, relics of the prophet Mohammed, and the rich costumes of the Imperial Wardrobe. Imperial fashion (male, of course) evolves slowly in the magnificent display of sultans' robes from the first to the last ruler. Some robes are bloodstained and torn from assassins' daggers, garments stiff with gold and silver thread, tooled leather, gold, silver, and jewels.

Time Out Just past the Treasury, on the right side of the courtyard, are steps leading to the 19th-century Rococo-style Mecidiye Pavilion, also known as the Köşk of Sultan Abdül Mecit I (ruled 1839–61), for whom it was built. It now houses the **Konyalı Restaurant** (tel. 212/ 513–9696), which serves traditional Turkish dishes (albeit with that mass-produced flavor) and has a magnificent view of the Golden Horn. On a terrace below is an outdoor café with an even better view. Go early to beat the tour-group crush. The restaurant and the café are open for lunch only.

The **Fourth Courtyard,** the last, contains small, elegant summer houses, mosques, fountains, and reflecting pools, scattered amid the gardens. Here you will find the cruciform **Rivan Köşk,** built by Murat IV in 1636 to commemorate a military victory. In another pavilion, the **Iftariye** (Golden Cage), the closest relatives of the reigning sultan lived in strict confinement under what amounted to house arrest, ostensibly to help keep the peace, although it meant that heirs had no opportunity to prepare themselves for the formidable task of ruling a great empire. The custom began during the 1800s, superseding an older practice of murdering all possible rivals to the throne. Just off the open terrace with the wishing well is the lavishly tiled **Sünnet Odası** (Circumcision Room), where little princes would be taken for ritual circumcision during their ninth or tenth year (not happily, one suspects). *Topkapı Palace, Gülhane Park, near Sultanahmet Sq., tel. 212/512–0480. Admission: $2.50. Open Wed.– Mon. 9:30–5:30.*

Return to the First Courtyard, and you can follow the signs leading down the hill to three important museums. (This can be done another day!) The **Arkeoloji Müzesi** (Archaeological Museum) houses a fine collection of Greek and Roman antiquities, including pieces from Ephesus and Troy and a magnificent tomb believed to belong to Alexander the Great. As most of the pieces have been removed from archaeological sites of Turkey's ancient cities you will encounter later, touring the museum will help you visualize what belongs in their various gaps and empty niches. Outside the museum is a small garden planted with bits of statuary and tombstones. The **Eski Şark Eserleri Müzesi** (Museum of the Ancient Orient) is something of a disappointment, despite its Sumerian, Babylonian, and Hittite treasures. The place needs a fresh coat of paint, the displays are unimaginative, and the descriptions of what you see are terse at best. The **Çinili Kösk** (Tiled Pavilion) has ceramics from the early Seljuk and Ottoman empires and some exquisite tiles from İznik, which produced perhaps the finest ceramics in the world during the 17th and 18th centuries. Covered in a bright profusion of colored tiles, the building itself is part of the exhibit. *Gülhane Park, adjacent to Topkapı Palace, tel. 212/520–7742. Admission to all 3 museums: $1.50. Open Tues.–Sun. 9:30–4:30 (Tiled Pavilion 9:30–noon).*

❸ Just outside the walls of Topkapı Palace is **Hagia Sophia** (Ayasofya in Turkish; Church of the Holy Wisdom); it is perhaps the greatest work of Byzantine architecture. Built of ivory from Asia, marble from Egypt, and columns from the ruins of Ephesus, it took 10,000 men six years to complete. Its magnificent dome, the world's largest until St. Peter's Basilica was built in Rome 1,000 years later, was considered nothing short of miraculous by the faithful. Though some were afraid to enter lest the whole thing come crashing down, others argued that it was conclusive proof that God was on their side. Nothing like it had ever been attempted before—new architectural rules had to be made up as the builders went along. As the cathedral of Constantinople, Hagia Sophia was Christendom's most important church for 900 years. It survived earthquakes, looting crusaders, and other disasters until 1453, when the city fell to Mehmet the Conqueror. The church was then converted into a mosque, and its four minarets were added by succeeding sultans. Amazingly, the church's mosaics were not destroyed. Instead, they were plastered over in the 16th century at the behest of Süleyman the Magnificent (ruled 1520–66), who felt they were inappropriate for a mosque. In 1936, Atatürk made Hagia Sophia into a museum. Shortly thereafter, American archaeologists discovered the mosaics, which were restored and are now on display. Above where the altar would have been is a giant portrait of a somber Virgin Mary with the infant Jesus, and alongside are severe-looking depictions of archangels Michael and Gabriel. Ascend to the gallery above (worth the hike!) and you will find the best of the remaining mosaics, executed in the 13th century. There is a group with Emperor John Comnenus, the Empress Zoe and her husband (actually, her third husband; his face was added atop his predecessor's), and Jesus with Mary, and another of John the Baptist. According to legend, the marble and brass **Sacred Column** in the north aisle of the mosque "weeps water" that can work miracles. It's so popular that, over the centuries, believers have worn a hole through the column with their constant caresses. Today, visitors of many faiths stick their fingers in the hole and make a wish; nobody will mind if you do as well. *Ayasofya Sq., tel. 212/522–1750. Admission: $4.50. Open Tues.–Sun. 9:30–4:30.*

❹ Across from Hagia Sophia is the **Blue Mosque,** officially called Sultan Ahmet Cami—as grand and beautiful a monument to Islam as Hagia Sophia is to Christendom. It is a massive structure, studded with mini- and semidomes and surrounded by six minarets. This number briefly tied it with the Elharam Mosque in Mecca, until Sultan Ahmet I (ruled 1603–17) was forced to send his architect down to the Holy City to build a seventh minaret and reestablish Elharam's eminence. Press through the throng of touts and trinket sellers, and enter the mosque at the side entrance that faces Hagia Sophia. You must remove your shoes and leave them at the entrance. Immodest clothing is not allowed, but an attendant at the door will lend you a robe if he feels you are not dressed appropriately.

It is only after you enter that you understand why this is called the Blue Mosque. Its interior is decorated by some 20,000 or so exquisite, shimmering blue İznik tiles, interspersed with 260 stained-glass windows; an airy arabesque pattern is painted on the ceiling. After the dark corners and stern, sour faces of the Byzantine mosaics in Hagia Sophia, this light-filled mosque is positively cheery. Architect Mehmet Aga, known as Sedefkar (Worker of Mother-of-Pearl), spent eight years getting the mosque just right, beginning in 1609. His goal, set by Sultan Ahmet, was to surpass Justinian's masterpiece—completed nearly 1,100 years earlier—and many believe he succeeded. *Sultanahmet Sq., no phone. Admission free. Open daily 9–5.*

The **Hünkar Kasri** (Carpet and Kilim Museums), a good place to prepare yourself for the inevitable duel with a modern-day carpet dealer, are in the mosque's stone-vaulted cellars and upstairs at the end of a stone ramp, where the sultans rested before and after their prayers. Here, rugs are treated as works of art and displayed in a suitably grand setting. *Adjacent to Blue Mosque, tel. 212/528–5332. Admission: $1.50 adults, 25¢ students. Open Tues.–Sat. 8:30–5.*

❺ The **Hippodrome,** a long park directly in front of the Blue Mosque, was once a Roman stadium with 100,000 seats and the focal point for public entertainment, including chariot races and circuses. It was also the site of riots and public executions. This was once an elaborately decorated space, embellished with a life-size sculpture of four horses cast in bronze. That piece was taken by the Venetians and now adorns the entrance to the cathedral San Marco. All that remains on the grassy open space today are an **Egyptian Obelisk** from the 15th century BC; the stumpy bronze **Serpentine Column,** nabbed from the Temple of Apollo at Delphi in Greece, which portrayed three intertwined snakes until the snake heads were lopped off in the 18th century; and the **Column of Constantinos,** an obelisk of rough-cut limestone that was sheathed in bronze until the time of the Crusades, when the metal was probably melted down to make weapons. You'll also encounter thousands of peddlers selling postcards, nuts, and souvenirs.

❻ On the western side of the Hippodrome is the **Ibrahim Paşa Palace** (circa 1524), the grandiose residence of the son-in-law and grand vizir of Süleyman the Magnificent. The striated stone mansion was outfitted by Süleyman to be the finest private residence in Istanbul, but Ibrahim Paşa didn't have long to enjoy it: He was executed when he became too powerful for the liking of Süleyman's power-crazed wife Roxelana. The palace now houses the **Türk Ve Islâm Eserleri Müzesi** (Museum of Turkish and Islamic Arts), which offers a superb insight into the lifestyles of Turks of every level of society, from the 8th century to the present. Collections include everything from an authentic nomad tent to a re-created Ottoman living room from a house in Bursa. *Şifahane Sok., on Hippodrome across from Blue Mosque, tel. 212/522–1858. Admission: $2.50. Open Tues.–Sun. 9:30–5.*

Continue southwest of the Hippodrome down Mehmet Paşa Yokuşu ❼ and look for the **Sokollu Mehmet Paşa Cami** (Mosque of Mehmet Paşa) at Özbekler Sokak. This small mosque, built in 1571, is generally regarded as one of the most beautifully realized projects of the master architect Sinan, who designed more than 350 other buildings and monuments under the direction of Süleyman the Magnificent. Rather than dazzle with size, this mosque integrates all its parts into a harmonious whole, from the courtyard and porticoes outside to the delicately carved *mimber* (pulpit) and well-preserved İznik tiles set off by pure white walls and stained-glass windows done in a floral motif inside. *Mehmet Paşa Cad. at Özbekler Sok., no phone.*

Walk back along the length of the Hippodrome and cross the busy main road, Divan Yolu. Turn left onto Hilaliahmer Caddesi. On your left is the **Yerebatan Saray** (Sunken Palace), also known as the Basilica Cistern, the most impressive part of an underground network of waterways created at the behest of Emperor Constantine in the 3rd century and expanded by Justinian in the 6th century. The cistern was always kept full as a precaution against long sieges. Today it is an oddly atmospheric space, with 336 marble columns rising 26 feet to support Byzantine arches and domes. Piped-in classical music accompanies the sound of endlessly dripping water. *Yerebatan Cad. at Divan Yolu, tel. 212/522–1259. Admission: $1. Open daily 9–5.*

Time Out If you need a break and want a real treat, spend an hour in a Turkish bath. One of the best is **Cağaloğlu Hamamı** (Hilaliahmer Cad., tel. 212/522–2424), in a magnificent 18th-century building near Hagia Sophia. You get a cubicle to strip down in—and a towel to cover up with—and are then escorted into a steamy, marble-clad temple to cleanliness. There are hot and cold taps for washing (and self-service baths cost just $5); an extra $10 buys you that time-honored, punishing yet relaxing pummeling known as Turkish massage. These baths are open daily from 8 AM until 7 PM for women, and from 7 AM until 9 PM for men.

Tour 2: The Grand Bazaar to Eminönü

There is plenty of Old Stamboul to see outside the walls of Topkapı. This tour makes its way through several markets, takes in two of Istanbul's most beautiful mosques, and ends at the Galata Bridge, positioning you to take on the New Town in Tour 3.

The best way to do the **Grand Bazaar** (Kapalı Çarşı)—a 15-minute walk or 5-minute taxi ride northwest of the Hippodrome—is to take a deep breath and plunge on in. This early version of a shopping mall, also known as the covered Bazaar, consists of a maze of 65 winding, covered streets crammed with 4,000 tiny shops, cafés, and restaurants. Originally built by Mehmet II (the Conqueror) in the 1450s, it was ravaged in modern times by two fires, one in 1954 that virtually destroyed it, and a smaller one in 1974. In both cases, the bazaar was quickly rebuilt in something resembling the original style, with arched passageways and brass-and-tile fountains at regular intervals.

In 1994 the covered bazaar was the site of two bomb blasts, in which several people were injured and two died. The outlawed Kurdistan Workers Party (PKK), which has been at war with the Turkish government since 1983 demanding an independent Kurdish state, claimed responsibility for the explosions. It is not clear whether these incidents are isolated or slated to become a regular part of the PKK's effort to sabotage the tourism industry in Turkey.

In one sense, it's a shopper's paradise, filled with thousands of different items, including fabrics, clothing, brass candelabra, furniture, and jewelry. But be warned: There is also a fair share of junk tailored for the tourist trade. A separate section for antiques at the very center of the bazaar, called the Bedestan, is definitely worth checking out. Outside the western gate to the bazaar, through a doorway, is the Sahaflar Çarşısı, the Old Book Bazaar, where you can buy new editions and antique volumes in Turkish and other languages. *Yeniçeriler Cad. and Fuatpaşa Cad. Admission free. Open Apr.-Oct., Mon.-Sat. 8:30—7; Nov.-Mar., Mon.-Sat. 8:30-6:30.*

⑩ The two mosques just to the east of the bazaar are the **Ali Paşa** and **Nuruosmaniye** (Light of Osman). The smaller Ali Paşa was built in 1497. Nuruosmaniye, built in the 18th century, is an example of Turkish Baroque, a much more ornamental style than that seen in earlier mosques. On the other side of the bazaar, across Fuatpaşa

⑪ Caddesi, is the **Beyazıt Mosque,** which dates from 1504 and is the oldest of the Ottoman imperial mosques still standing in the city. And no, your eyes do not deceive you; this domed mosque, too, was inspired by Hagia Sophia.

⑫ Follow Fuatpaşa Caddesi up to the grounds of **Istanbul University,** which has a magnificent gateway facing Beyazıt Square. The campus, with its long greens and giant plane trees, originally served as the Ottoman War Ministry, which helps explain the grandiose, martial style of the portal and main buildings. In the garden stands the white marble 200-foot **Beyazıt Tower,** the tallest structure in Old Stamboul, built in 1823 by Mahmut II (ruled 1808–39) as a fire watch station.

⑬ Follow Besim Omer Paşa Caddesi, the western border of the university, to the 16th-century **Süleymaniye Cami** (Mosque of Süleyman). This is the grandest and most famous creation of its designer, Sinan, and it houses his tomb as well as that of his patron, Süleyman the Magnificent. With the elegant simplicity of Hagia Sophia, its massive dome is supported by four square columns and arches, and exterior walls buttress smaller domes on either side. The result is a soaring space and the impression that the dome is held up principally by divine cooperation. Though this is the city's largest mosque, its decor is significantly less ornate and more spiritual in tenor than that of other imperial mosques. Do note the lovely İznik tiles in the *mihrab* (prayer niche). *Süleymaniye Cad., near Istanbul University's north gate, no phone. Open daily.*

⑭ Head down the hill toward the Golden Horn and the neighborhood known as **Eminönü,** a transportation hub built around the Galata Bridge and the big ferry docks adjacent. As you approach the Egyp-

⑮ tian Bazaar, look for Hasırcılar Caddesi and the **Rüstem Paşa Cami.** This small, often overlooked mosque, built in the 1550s for Süleyman's grand vizir, is another Sinan masterpiece. Unassuming from the outside, it is decorated inside with dazzling İznik tiles in a striking array of colors and patterns. *Hasırcılar Cad., south of Eminönü Cad., no phone. Open daily.*

⑯ Continue along Hasırcılar Caddesi to the **Mısır Çarşısı** (Egyptian Bazaar), also known as the Spice Market. It was built in the 17th century to generate rental income to pay for the upkeep of the **Yeni Cami** (New Mosque) next door. Once a vast pharmacy filled with burlap bags overflowing with herbs and spices used for folk remedies, the bazaar today is chockablock with bags full of fruit, nuts, and royal jelly from the beehives of the Aegean coast, as well as white sacks spilling over with culinary spices. Though only a fraction of the size of the Grand Bazaar, it is still lively and colorful. The Yeni Cami, which dates from the 17th century, on the other hand, is inferior in design and decor to other mosques you've seen; you can give it a pass if your time is short. *Hamidiye Cad., across from Galata Bridge, no phone. Egyptian Bazaar: Open Mon.-Sat. 8–7.*

Time Out   **The Pandeli** (Mısır Çarşısı, tel. 212/522–5534), up two flights of stairs over the arched gateway to Egyptian Bazaar, is a frenetic old-

Istanbul restaurant serving typical Turkish fare for lunch in a decor of incredible tiles. Servings here are not what they used to be, but it remains a charming place for a break.

Tour 3: Galata to Taksim

This tour takes you into the heart of the New Town, where the first thing you will learn is that "new" is a relative term. Much of what you will see dates from the 19th century—except for the shops and imported American movies, which are strictly 20th-century!

⑰ Cross over the new **Galata Bridge,** stopping to take in one of the world's great city views as you go: In Old Stamboul, behind you as you cross the bridge, the landmarks include Topkapı Palace and the domes and minarets of Hagia Sophia and the Blue Mosque, and the Süleymaniye and Yeni mosques. Ferries chug out on the Bosporus, and the Galata Tower rises high on the Beyoğlu side of the Golden Horn. The new drawbridge you will be standing on opened in 1993, when it replaced the old pontoon bridge that had been around since 1910, the days when horse, ox, or mule-drawn carriages rattled across it for a fee. In 1994, the old bridge underwent repairs and face-lifts and was moved up toward the Golden Horn's tip to connect Balat and Haskoy.

⑱ Just to your left as you leave the north end of the bridge is a minor point of curiosity, **Voyvoda Caddesi.** This nondescript commercial street is named after the 15th-century warrior Voyvode of Transylvania, better known as Vlad the Impaler, or Count Dracula. The Turks claim to have captured the bloodthirsty character and buried the corpse somewhere under this street. The Romanians, however, have a different story, and another tomb, near Bucharest.

⑲ The area's most prominent landmark is the **Galata Tower,** built by the Genoese as part of their fortifications in 1349, when they controlled this side of the Golden Horn. In this century, the rocket-shape tower served as a fire lookout until 1960. Today it houses a restaurant and nightclub (*see* Nightclubs in Arts and Nightlife, *below*), and a viewing tower that is open by day. There is an elevator. *Büyük Hendek Cad., 212/245–1160. Admission: $1. Open daily 9–8.*

The neighborhood around the tower was a thriving Italian settlement both before and after the fall of Constantinople. In 1492, when the Spanish Inquisition drove the Sephardic Jews from Spain and Portugal, many of the refugees settled here. For centuries after, there was a large Jewish population in Galata. Although most of them have moved to residential areas, they retain their traditions. Today, 16 active synagogues, one of which dates from the Byzantine period, serve a Jewish community of 25,000. The Neve Shalom synagogue, on Büyük Hendek Sokak near the Galata Tower, was where 22 Sabbath worshippers were shot by Arabic-speaking gunmen in September 1986. A visit to the now high-security location requires a show of identification. Some older Turkish Jews still speak a dialect of medieval Spanish called Ladino or Judeo-Espanol.

⑳ Continue up the hill to **Tünel Square,** the northern terminus of the city's mini-underground—the other stop is Karaköy, at the bottom of the hill. This is the start of **İstiklal Caddesi** (Independence Street), the main thoroughfare of European Istanbul, once known as the Grand Rue de Pera. Various embassies in ornate turn-of-the-century buildings and slowly decaying 19th-century apartments still line the route, along with bookstores, fashion boutiques, kebab shops, and movie theaters. To avoid the uphill walk, you can take the trolley running along İstiklal every 10 minutes or so all the way to Taksim Square; the fare is about 50¢.

Otherwise, walk uphill, past the **Swedish Consulate,** and then take a right on Postacilar Sokak, which brings you into a quiet, tree-shaded square bordered by the elegant old French and Italian consulates, a spot little changed in more than 100 years. Return to İstiklal. Peek into the courtyard behind the shop at No. 331, where you will find the 18th-century church of **San Antonio di Padua,** one of the city's best-known functioning Roman Catholic churches.

㉑ İstiklal takes a bend at **Galatsaray Square.** The impressive building behind the massive iron gates is a high school, established in 1868 and for a time the most prestigious in the Ottoman Empire, where French was the language of choice. Across the street, at No. 51, is the entrance to the **Çiçek Pasaji** (Flower Arcade), a lively warren of flower stalls, tiny restaurants, and bars, where street musicians often entertain. Curmudgeons swear that the passage is a pale shadow of its former self—its original neo-Baroque home collapsed with a thundering crash one night in 1978 and its redone facade and interior have the feel of a historic reproduction—but you can still get a feel for it at its bohemian best. Behind the Flower Market is the **Balık Pazarı** (Fish Market), a bustling labyrinth of stands peddling fish, fruits, vegetables, and spices—with a couple of pastry shops thrown in—that makes for great street theater. *Open Mon.–Sat. during daylight.*

At the end of the Fish Market, at Meşrutiyet Caddesi, is the **Üç Horan Armenian Church,** an unexpected sight, with its crosses and haloed Christs, in Moslem Istanbul. Return to İstiklal.

㉒ At the top of İstiklal is **Taksim Square,** the not particularly handsome center of New Town, especially since municipal subway digging turned its belly into a deep concrete crevasse. It's basically a chaotic traffic circle with a bit of grass and a *Monument to the Republic and Independence* featuring Atatürk and his revolutionary cohorts. Around the square are Istanbul's main concert hall, **Atatürk Kültür Merkezi** (Atatürk Cultural Center), the high-rise Marmara Hotel, and, set back a bit in a grassy promenade, the 23-story Sheraton Hotel.

On the main street headed north from the square, Cumhuriyet Caddesi, you will find shops that sell carpets and leather goods, the entrances to the Sheraton, Hyatt, Divan, and Hilton hotels, several travel agencies and airline ticket offices, and a few nightclubs. Cumhuriyet turns into Haláskârgazi Caddesi, and when this street meets Rumeli Caddesi, you enter the city's high-fashion district, where Turkey's top designers sell their wares.

Tour 4: Three Palaces

This outing takes you north along the Bosporus for a look at the later palaces of the Ottoman sultans. It's a bit of a hike from Taksim Square, so you might want to take a cab, dolmuş, or bus, at least as far as the Dolmabahçe Palace. The tour ends in the cool green forest of Yıldız Park.

㉓ If you're walking from Taksim Square, take Gümüssuyu Caddesi all the way down the hill to the Bosporus. The **Dolmabahçe Mosque,** founded in 1853 by the mother of Sultan Abdül Mecit, will be on your right. To the left is an ornate **Clock Tower** and the gateway to **Dolmabahçe Palace.** The palace was also built in 1853 and was the residence of the last sultans of the Ottoman Empire. After the establishment of the modern republic in 1923, it became the home of Atatürk, who died here in 1938. The name, which means "filled-in garden," predates the palace; Sultan Ahmet I (ruled 1603–17) had a little cove filled in and an imperial garden planted here in the 17th century.

The palace, floodlit at night, is an extraordinary mixture of Hindu, Turkish, and European styles of architecture and interior design. Abdül Mecit, a sybaritic man whose free-spending lifestyle (his main distinction) eventually bankrupted his empire, intended the structure to be a symbol of Turkey's march away from its Oriental past and toward the European mainstream. He gave his Armenian architect, Balian, complete freedom and an unlimited budget. His only demand was that the palace "surpass any other palace of any other potentate anywhere in the world." The result was a riot of Rococo—marble, vast mirrors, stately towers, and formal gardens along a facade stretching nearly ½ kilometer (⅓ mile). His bed was solid silver; the tub and basins in his marble-paved bathroom were carved of transparent alabaster. Europe's royalty contributed to the splendor: Queen Victoria sent a chandelier weighing 4½ tons, Czar Nicholas I of Russia provided polar-bear rugs. The result is as gaudy and showy as a palace should be, all gilt and crystal and silk, and every bit as garish as Versailles. You must join a guided tour, which takes about 80 minutes. *Gümüşsuyu Cad., tel. 212/261–0225. Admission: $3. Open Apr.–Oct., Tues., Wed., and Fri.–Sun. 9–4; Nov.–Mar., Tues., Wed., and Fri.–Sun. 9–3.*

㉔ Exiting the palace, walk east along Beşiktas Caddesi. The **Naval Museum** (Deniz Müzesi) contains some impressive memorabilia of what was, after all, the 16th century's leading sea power. The flashiest displays are the sultan's barges, the long, slim boats that served as the primary mode of royal transportation for several hundred years. There is also a collection of cannons, including a massive, 23-ton blaster built for Sultan Selim the Grim, and an early Ottoman map of the New World cribbed from Columbus, dating from 1513. *Beşiktaş Cad., tel. 212/261–0040. Admission: $1. Open Wed.–Sun. 9:30–12:30, 1:30–5:00.*

㉕ Continue past the Beşiktaş ferry docks; the street becomes Çırağan Caddesi. A short walk brings you to the former **Çırağan Palace,** now the city's most luxurious hotel. Abdül Mecit's brother and successor, Sultan Abdül Aziz (ruled 1861–76), built the palace in 1863. That the palace is about a third the size of Dolmabahçe, and much less ornate, says a good deal about the declining state of the Ottoman Empire's coffers after Abdül Mecit's 22-year spending spree. A vacuous 230-pound hulk of a man, Abdül Aziz was as extravagant as his brother; having begun his reign by ordering an 8-foot-long bed wide enough to accommodate himself and a concubine, he was soon attempting to emulate the splendors he had seen on travels in England and France. Today the recently restored grounds, with their splendid swimming pool at the edge of the Bosporus, are worth a look, and the hotel bar offers a plush, cool respite with a view.

㉖ **Yıldız Park** is directly above Çırağan Palace. Its wooded slopes once formed part of the great forest that covered the European shore of the Bosporus from the Golden Horn to the Black Sea. During the reign of Abdül Aziz, the park was his private garden, and the women of the harem would occasionally be allowed to visit. First the gardeners would be removed, then the eunuchs would lead the women across the wooden bridge from the palace and along the avenue to the upper gardens. There, secluded from prying eyes, they would sit in the shade or wander through the acacias, maples, and cypresses, filling their baskets with flowers and figs. *Çırağan Cad., tel. 212/ 261–8288. Admission: 25¢ pedestrians, $1 cars. Open daily 9–6.*

At the top of the park, Sultan Abdül Hamit II (ruled 1876–1909) built yet another palace, **Yıldız.** Visiting dignitaries from Kaiser Wilhelm to Charles de Gaulle and Margaret Thatcher have all stayed in its graceful Chalet away from the bustle of the city. It is often blissfully empty of tourists, which makes a visit all the more pleasurable. Forgotten is the political turmoil of the era: The last rulers of the once-great Ottoman Empire were all deposed: free-spending Abdül Aziz; his unfortunate nephew, Murad (who, having spent most of his life in the Harem, isolated in the Cage, was none too sound of mind); and Abdül Hamid himself, who distinguished himself as the last despot of the Ottoman Empire. *Tel. 212/261–8288. Admission: $1. Open Tues.–Sun. 9–4.*

Time Out The **Malta Pavilion** (tel. 212/260–0454), an ornate, late 19th century gem within tranquil Yıldız Park, serves tea, lunch, and cocktails daily until 7 PM.

Tour 5: The Bosporus

Numbers in the margin correspond to points of interest on the Tour 5: The Bosporus map.

There are good roads along both the Asian and the European shores, but the most pleasant way to explore the Bosporus is by ferry from the Eminönü docks in the old town (*see* Getting Around in Essential Information, *above*). The ferry zigzags from shore to shore as it makes its way down the waterway and back, and you can hop off wherever you like. Along the way, you will see wooded hills, villages large and small, modern and old-fashioned, and the old wooden summer homes called *yalıs* (waterside houses) that were built for the city's wealthier residents in the Ottoman era. When looking at ferry schedules, remember that *Rumeli* refers to the European side, *Anadolu* to the Asian.

The trip affords a splendid view of the Golden Horn and, soon after, of Dolmabahçe Palace. The graceful **Bosporus Bridge,** completed in 1973, in time for the 50th anniversary of the Turkish Republic, is Europe's longest suspension bridge and the first to connect Europe and Asia. The **Ortaköy Mosque,** underneath the Bosporus Bridge on the European side, dates from the 1850s. It is a rather odd structure, with Corinthian columns out front and decorative Arabic calligraphy done by Sultan Abdül Mecit inside.

㉗ Just past the bridge on the Asian side is the **Beylerbeyi Palace.** Built for Sultan Abdül Aziz in 1865, it is a mini Dolmabahçe, filled with marble and marquetry and gold-encrusted furniture. The central hall has an attractive white marble fountain and a stairway wide enough for a regiment. You must join a tour to see the palace. *On main shore rd., n. of Bosporus Bridge; ferries from Eminönü stop in front; no phone. Admission: $3. Open Tues., Wed., and Fri.–Sun. 9:30–4:30.*

Back on the European side is a pretty little village called **Arnavutköy,** with a row of 19th-century wooden houses at the water's edge, followed by **Bebek,** a fashionable suburb with good restaurants and a jazz club or two. Just before the second Bosporus bridge are two fortresses, **Rumeli Hisarı** (Thracian Castle) and

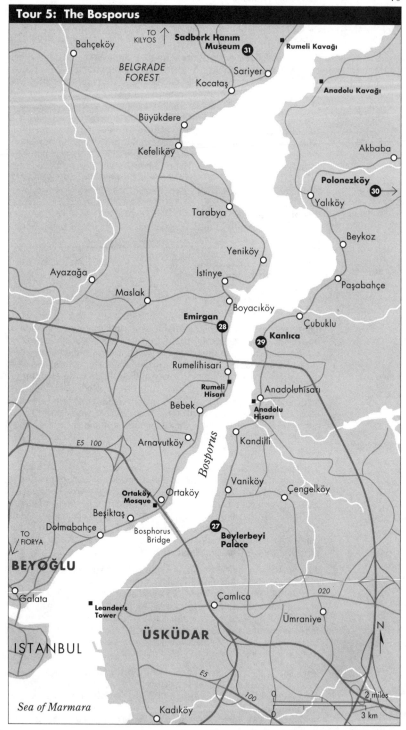

Tour 5: The Bosporus

TO
KILYOS

Bahçeköy

Sadberk Hanım Museum **31**

■ **Rumeli Kavağı**

BELGRADE FOREST

Sarıyer

Kocataş

■ **Anadolu Kavağı**

Büyükdere

Akbaba

Kefeliköy

Polonezköy **30**→

Yalıköy

Tarabya

Beykoz

Yeniköy

Ayazağa

İstinye

Paşabahçe

Maslak

Boyacıköy

Emirgan **28**

Çubuklu

Kanlıca **29**

Rumelihisarı ■

Rumeli Hisarı

Anadoluhisarı

Bebek

■ **Anadolu Hisarı**

E5 100

Arnavutköy

Kandilli

Bosporus

Vaniköy

Çengelköy

Ortaköy Mosque ■ Ortaköy

Beşiktaş

Dolmabahçe

Bosphorus Bridge

27

Beylerbeyi Palace

TO
FIORYA

BEYOĞLU

Galata

■ **Leander's Tower**

Çamlıca

020

Ümraniye

ÜSKÜDAR

N

ISTANBUL

E5

100

0   2 miles
0   3 km

Sea of Marmara

Kadıköy

Anadolu Hisarı (Anatolian Castle). Sultan Beyazıt I built Anadolu Hisar on the Asian, or Anatolian, side in 1393 to cut off Constantinople's access to the Black Sea. Rumeli Hisar was built by Mehmet the Conqueror in 1452, a year before his siege of Constantinople finally succeeded. The crenellated walls and round towers of the fortresses are popular with photographers, though what you see from the water is about all there is to see. In the summer, Rumeli Hisar is sometimes used for Shakespeare performances (usually in Turkish) and music and folk dancing. *Rumeli Hisar admission: $1. Open Tues.–Sun. 9:30–5.*

㉘ Emirgan, a village on the European side, was named after a 17th-century Persian prince who was presented with a palace here by Sultan Murat IV (ruled 1623–40). The woods above it stand in one of the city's most charming parks, with flower gardens and a number of restored Ottoman pavilions—ornate, almost Victorian-style villas and conservatories—converted into cafés.

The oldest surviving yalı, Saffet Paşa Yalısı, can be seen across the **㉙** water at **Kanlıca,** a quaint row of 19th-century wooden villas painted white. From here, you can take a taxi to the **Hidiv Kasrı** (Palace of the Khedive), a delightful Art Nouveau structure that has been restored and opened as a restaurant and hotel (*see* Dining *and* Lodging, *below*). "Khedive" was the title of Egypt's rulers during Ottoman times. The Ottomans had managed to retain control of this longtime fiefdom after a coup by granting power to the upstart, one Muhammed Ali, whose descendants continued to rule while paying tribute to the empire.

From Pasabahçe on the Asian side, you can take a taxi to **㉚ Polonezköy,** a small village where, oddly enough, you can dine on hearty Polish food. The area was settled in the 1840s by Poles fleeing Russian invaders. Today it is populated by their descendants, who have opened guest houses, butcher shops, and restaurants. Wealthier Istanbulites have summer villas here, and you can rent a horse in the village square and ride, as they do, through the woods that surround the town. In the fall, you can walk through the woods and handpick chestnuts.

Back on the European side, pleasant stops include **Yeniköy;** the fashionable resort area of **Tarabya;** and **Sarıyer,** a typical Bosporus fishing village with a tree-lined waterfront, several good fish **㉛** restaurants, and the surprising **Sadberk Hanım Museum,** named for the deceased wife of billionaire businessman Vehbi Koç and occupying an attractive old waterfront mansion. Though small, the museum has an enviable collection of very high-quality pieces. Half is dedicated to Islamic and Turkish arts (from İznik tiles to Ottoman embroidery and calligraphy), and half to Anatolian archaeology (Hittite pottery and cuneiform tablets). *Piyasa Cad. 27–29, tel. 212/ 242–3813. Admission: $1. Open summer, Thurs.–Tues. 10:30–6; winter, Thurs.–Tues. 10–5.*

Rumeli Kavaği and **Anadolu Kavaği,** respectively, are the ferry's final stops. They are small and quaint fishing villages known for their seafood restaurants. Anadolu Kavagi, the more northern village, is particularly fun; it has sidewalk sellers offering deep-fried mussels and wickedly sweet waffles. A short walk up a hill behind town takes you to the castle, a perfect spot for watching sunsets and for a bird's-eye view of the Bosporus entrance to the Black Sea. You can get off the ferry at these spots and catch a later one back to Sariyer, or Eminönü. Check the schedule board at the ferry docks.

Istanbul for Free

Entrance to any of the city's mosques is always free, as is the view from Galata Bridge at sunset. The city's parks—Yıldız, Gülhane (by the Archaeological Museum), Emirgân, and Belgrade Forest (near the village of Kilyos, about an hour north of the city on the European side of the Bosporus)—are either free or open to visitors at a nominal admission, and they offer neatly tended flower gardens, cool shade, Bosporus views, and eminently reasonable teahouses. The panoramic view of the Bosporus, Golden Horn, and Marmara Sea from the Çamlica Hill on the Asian side is breathtaking and priceless, but comes for free. The Flower Arcade, off İstiklal Caddesi, is street theater at its best. If you ask a carpet seller to teach you about rugs, you will get a free cup of tea and a wide-ranging discourse on any number of subjects; of course, you don't *have* to buy. During the summer, a free sound-and-light extravaganza, with music, illuminates Hagia Sophia and the Blue Mosque. Pick up a schedule of shows in English at the tourist information kiosk in the Hippodrome.

What to See and Do with Children

With its hectic pace, traffic jams, and often irritatingly polluted air, Istanbul is not a particularly easy city for families with young children. Still, there are some options: the mummies at the Archaeological Museum, a ferry ride across the Bosporus, and the Topkapı Palace, with its swords and shining armor. The bright colors and trinkets of the Grand Bazaar will certainly please children; whether parents will be equally pleased is another question.

Off the Beaten Track

The **Kariye Museum** is often passed over because of its inconvenient location at the western edge of the city, near the remnants of the city's Byzantine walls. The museum occupies what was once the **Church of the Holy Savior in Chora,** first built in the 5th century under the aegis of Justinian and rebuilt several times since. But you come to see not the architecture but the dazzling 14th-century mosaics and frescoes depicting biblical scenes from Adam to the life of Christ; they are considered to be among the finest Byzantine works in the world. The historic Ottoman buildings around the museum have been restored as well, and there is a tea shop with light fare served on the lovely garden terrace. Just west of the Chora are the **Constantinian Walls,** built by Emperor Theodosius II in AD 413. The massive walls, several stories high and 10 to 20 feet thick in some spots, protected Constantinople from onslaught after onslaught of Huns, Bulgarians, Russians, Arabs, Goths, and Turks. The walls were breached only twice: by the crusaders in the 1200s and Mehmet the Conqueror in 1453. *1 block n. of Fevzipaşa Cad., by Edirne Gate in city's outer walls, tel. 212/523–3009. Admission: $1.50. Open Wed.–Mon. 9:30–4:30.*

The best views of the Istanbul skyline at sunset are from **Çamlica,** the highest hill on the Asian side of the city. The area near Kısıklı Square and the Üsküdar ferry dock has several pavilions where you can order tea and sit on cushions at low brass tables, as well as outdoor booths where you can buy pancakes with honey, corn on the cob, and other snacks. At the **Çamlica Café** (Sefatepsesi, tel. 216/335–3301), one of several restaurants on the hill, you can dine by candlelight after the sun has set, served by waiters in traditional garb.

Another great hill for watching sunsets is **Salacak,** also on the Asian side, opposite Leander's Tower. You can reach it by ferry from Eminönü to Üsküdar; then it's a 10-minute walk past the open-air cafés and yalis that line the waterfront. Fish, typically grilled, is clearly the order of the day in eating spots at the water's edge. One popular restaurant on the wharf, with an excellent view of the city's minaret-studded skyline, is **Huzur** (İskele Cad. 20, tel. 216/333–3157).

Shopping

Shopping Districts

The **Grand Bazaar** (*see* Exploring Istanbul, *above*) is a neighborhood unto itself and a treasure trove of all things Turkish—carpets, brass, copper, jewelry, textiles, and leather goods. The fashions are not bad either—not quite up to Italian style, but dramatically less expensive. **Nuruosmaniye Caddesi,** one of the major streets leading to the bazaar, is filled with some of Istanbul's most stylish shops, with an emphasis on fine carpets, jewelry and made-in-Turkey fashions.

The New Town has several main areas for shopping. **İstiklal Caddesi** has everything from stores that sell old books and Levis to the Vakko department store (İstiklal Cad. 123 and other locations; tel. 212/251–4092 for information), a somewhat less stylish, Turkish version of Saks Fifth Avenue. The high-fashion district centers on **Halâskârgazi Caddesi** and **Rumeli Caddesi,** a bit north of İstiklal Caddesi, where you will find the best efforts of Turkish fashion designers. Two streets in the Kadiköy area of New Town that offer a variety of suburban shopping options are **Bağdat** and **Bahariye Caddeleri.** The **Ataköy Shopping and Tourism Center,** a large shopping mall near the airport, has stores selling Levis and Benetton merchandise, and a McDonald's. **Akmerkez,** in the posher Etiler district, is a large and luxurious shopping mall, selling internationally recognized trademarks such as Ralph Lauren and Villeroy and Boch, and containing a movie theater and cafés.

Markets

Don't miss the **Egyptian Bazaar,** also known as the Spice Market (*see* Tour 2 in Exploring Istanbul, *above*). **Balıkpazarı** (Fish Market) sells, despite its name, anything connected with food, from picnic supplies to exotic spices and teas; it's in Beyoğlu Caddesi, off İstiklal Caddesi. A flea market is held in **Beyazıt Square,** near the Grand Bazaar, every Sunday. **Sahaflar Çarşışı** is home to a bustling book market, with old and new editions; most are in Turkish, but English and other languages are represented. Also on Sunday, you'll find a traditional crafts market, with street entertainment, along the Bosporus at **Ortaköy.**

Specialty Stores

Antiques These are a surprisingly rare commodity in this antique land, perhaps because the government, to ensure that Turkish culture is not sold off to richer nations, has made it difficult to export antiques. **Sofa** (Nuruosmaniye Cad. 42; also at the new Swissôtel), an exception, stocks a fascinating collection of old maps and prints, original İznik and Kütahya ceramics, vintage jewelry, and assorted other treasures. The friendly and informative **Ory & Ady** (Serifagu Sok. 7–8, in the Bedestan section of the Grand Bazaar) specializes in Ottoman miniatures, illustrations, and prints. **Çığır Kitabevi** (Sahaflar Çarşışı 17) has an impressive collection of old books, many with lovely illustrations. Though there is a law against removing antiquities from the country, you may buy and export pieces that are less than 100 years old.

Carpets and Kilims There are carpet shops at nearly every turn, and all stock a variety of rugs at a variety of prices. Some of the better ones include **Adnan Hassan** (Halicilar Cad. 90), **Celletin Senghor** (in the Grand Bazaar), **Ensar** (Arasta Bazaar 109), **Al-Dor** (Faruk Ayanoglu Cad. 5–8), and the shops along Nuruosmaniye Caddesi, particularly **Çinar** at No. 6. Each shop has slightly different pieces, so you will have to look at several to get a feel for the market. On the other hand, there's nothing wrong with buying from the first shop you go into if you find something you love. For best buys, look outside Istanbul.

Clothing **Angel Leather** (Nuruosmaniye Cad. 67) has kidskin suede and leather in skirts and jackets; the best of Turkish leather is on par with Italian leather, quality-wise, though the designs are not as stylish. **Sube** (Arasta Bazaar 131) sells handmade kilim slippers with leather soles and kilim boots for a fraction of their price in New York City. Turkish designer **Zeki Triko** sells his own bathing suits, completely up-to-date, at his eponymous boutiques (Valikonagi Cad.). **Vakko** (*see above*) is Turkey's leading department store, with fashions for men, women, and children; and more fashionable **Beymen's** (Halâskârgazi Cad. 230) is Istanbul's version of Bloomingdale's. **Beymen's Club** (Rumeli Cad. 81) is more casual, somewhat Polo in style.

Jewelry Specialties include amber necklaces and ethnic Turkish silver jewelry threaded with coral and lapis lazuli. **Venus** (Kalpakcilar Cad. 160) and **Georges Basoglu** (Cevahir Bedestan 36–37) have distinctive and original pieces. **Nasit** (Arasta Bazaar 111) often has vintage silver as well as new. **Urart** (Abdi Ipekçi Cad. 181) sells chic interpretations of ancient Anatolian designs.

Sports and Fitness

Participant Sports

Golf Istanbul is not a noted golfing destination; you won't find Sawgrass or Pebble Beach, but the courses are perfectly fine if you need a fix. Itinerant players are welcomed at the **Golf Club** (Büyükdere Cad., Ayazağa, tel. 212/264–0742) and the Kemer Golf & Country Club (Kemerburgaz in the Belgrade Forest, 25 minutes from Istanbul, tel. 212/239–7913), which has a nine-hole course.

Health and Fitness Clubs The best of these are at the big hotels, particularly the **Swissôtel, Çirağan Palace, Hilton,** and **Conrad Istanbul International** (*see* Lodging, *below*).

Hiking and Jogging If walking the city's Byzantine streets leaves you wanting more exercise, try one of its parks. The wooded slopes of **Yıldız Park,** just north of the Çirağan Palace, are blissfully uncrowded. **Belgrade Forest** has enticing wooded paths, **Emirgân Park** is noted for its flower gardens and Bosporus views, and **Gülhane Park** is conveniently located, right alongside Topkapı Palace. If you like to rough it,

Alternatif Turizm (Bağdat Caddesi 36/8, Kızıltoprak, tel. 216/345–6650) organizes hiking trips to sites near Istanbul, as well as treks to Mt. Palandoken (Erzurum) and Mt. Erciyes (Kayseri).

Spectator Sports

Soccer is the main event here, and Turkish Division One is the country's Major Leagues. Matches take place from September through May at **Inönü Stadium** and **Ali Sami Yen Stadium.** You can get tickets at the stadium or ask at your hotel for help. Basketball, wrestling, and other indoor sports are held at the **Lutfi Kırdar Sports Hall.**

Beaches

The European shore of the Sea of Marmara is muddy and unpleasant, the Bosporus is famous for its dangerously strong currents, and either way, the water is pretty cold. Stick with the hotel pool.

If you must, the best bet is probably to make the hour-long drive to the area's best beach, at **Kilyos** on the Black Sea. Avoid the municipal beaches at Florya, a suburb on the European side, where bacteria have dangerously contaminated the waters. In fact, limit your contact to gazing. But don't worry: If you're heading to the Aegean or Mediterranean coast, there's plenty of splendid swimming ahead.

Turkish Baths

When you're ready for a steam and brisk massage at a Turkish bath, try the historic **Cağaloğlu Hamamı** (Yerebatan Cad., tel. 212/522–2424), where Florence Nightingale and Kaiser Wilhelm II have soaked, or the **Galatasaray Hamam** (Suterazi Sok. 24, tel. 212/244–1412). Both are several hundred years old, with marble steam rooms and a generally upscale Turkish clientele. (Turks of lesser means head for plainer, less costly baths.) Here you'll pay $5 if you go the self-service route, $10–$15 with a massage.

Dining

Istanbul has a wide range of restaurants, and prices to match. Dining rooms in most of the major hotels serve rather bland international cuisine. It's far more rewarding to eat in Turkish restaurants. Beer, wine, and sometimes cocktails are widely available despite Moslem proscriptions against alcohol. Dress is casual unless otherwise noted. For details and price-category definitions, *see* Staying in Turkey, in Chapter 1, Essential Information.

Highly recommended restaurants are indicated by a star ★.

$$$$ **Club 29.** Seafood is the thing to order at this chic restaurant, which serves the in crowd in spring, fall, and winter in a suburb called Etiler and in summer on the Asian side of the Bosporus. The Etiler location is all silver and crystal and candlelight; the Asian premises recall a Roman villa, except for the view of the yachts bobbing in the harbor. After midnight, discotheques get going upstairs in both locations, and the action goes until 2 AM. The place can be pretty dead when the weather gets cold. *Nispetiye Cad. 29, Etiler, tel. 1/265–2925 in spring, fall, and winter; Paşabahçe Yolu, Çubuklu, tel. 1/322–3888. Reservations required. Jacket advised. AE, DC, MC, V. No lunch.*

$$$$ Körfez. Call ahead and this restaurant in the picturesque Asian village of Kanlıca will ferry you across the Bosporus from Rumeli Hisar to your table. The decor is nautical, and the seafood fresh, superbly cooked to order, and innovative— for example, flying-fish chowder, shrimp in béchamel sauce, and sea bass cooked in salt. *Körfez Cad. 78, Kanlıca, tel. 216/332–0108. Reservations advised. AE, DC, MC, V. Closed Mon.*

$$$$ Reşat Paşa Konağı. In this pink and white turn-of-the-century Turkish gingerbread-style villa delicious Ottoman and Turkish dishes are served in a chic and ornate atmosphere. Although it is a little out of the way on the Asian side, it's well worth the trip, which you can make with a taxi driver instructed by your hotel. Order à la carte and sample such dishes as the mixed seafood cooked in a clay pot, or let the waiter tempt you with the *Paşa Sofrası*, a fixed menu including 20 cold and hot appetizers, shish kebab as a main course, and lemon helva for dessert, all accompanied by unlimited domestic drinks. A band plays traditional Turkish music (*Fasil*) on weekends. *Kozyatağı Mahallesi, Sinan Ercan Cad. 34/1, Erenkoy, tel. 216/361–3411. Reservations advised. AE, DC, V.*

$$$$ Tuğra. In the historic Çırağan Palace, this spacious and luxurious restaurant serves the most delectable of long-lost and savored Ottoman recipes, including stuffed blue fish and Circassian chicken. Cookbooks from the Ottoman palace were used to re-create some of the dishes. But that's not all. The Bosporus view is flanked by the palace's marble columns, and ornate glass chandeliers hover above, all to make you feel like your own version of royalty. *Çırağan Cad. 84, tel. 212/258–3377. Reservations advised. AE, DC, MC, V.*

$$$$ Ziya. Power lunchers and Turkish yuppies patronize this spot, located in a white, two-story mansion with a lovely garden, for its international cuisine, elegant modern decor, and see-and-be-seen atmosphere. The crepes with caviar and smoked sturgeon are not cheap, but you would pay a lot more in Paris or New York. *Mualim Naci Cad. 109, Ortaköy, tel. 1/261–6005. Reservations advised. AE, DC, MC, V.*

$$$ Cemal Balik. Roaming musicians, boisterous conversation, and menus offering a wide variety of fish dishes are the attractions at the many excellent restaurants in the Kumkapı area. At this one try the pickled fish appetizer and the grilled fish kebabs. *Capariz Sok. 27, tel. 1/527–2288. Reservations not necessary. DC, MC, V.*

$$$ Divan. The Divan is a rare exception to the rule that suggests avoiding hotel restaurants. The menu offers a thoughtful blend of Turkish and French cuisine, the surroundings are elegant, and the service is excellent. *Cumhuriyet Cad. 2, Beyoğlu, tel. 212/231–4100. Reservations advised. Jacket and tie advised. AE, DC, MC.*

$$$ Gelik. This restaurant in a two-story l9th-century villa is usually packed, often with people who want to savor its delicious specialty: all types of meat roasted in deep cooking wells to produce unusual, rich stews. *Sahilyolu 68–70, tel. 212/560–7284. Reservations advised. AE, DC, MC, V.*

$$$ Sarniç. The setting deep down in an old Roman cistern is highly unusual. Candlelight reflects off the arched stone walls of yellow brick, and a massive fireplace provides warmth in chilly weather. The service is fairly formal, and the fare is a mix of Turkish and Continental, ranging from duck à l'orange to *döner kebab* (lamb grilled on a spit). *Sogukçesme Sok., Sultanahmet, tel. 212/512–4291. Reservations advised. AE, V.*

$$$ Urcan. ★ This is one of the city's very best. Photographs taken at the restaurant of internationally known celebrities and politicians meet you as you enter. The theme is heavily nautical, with fishing nets and gear on the ceiling and trophy fish on the walls, and the menu offers an astounding variety of seafood—some of which you will see still swimming in tanks by the entrance—in preparations ranging from simple grills to rich cream sauces. The atmosphere is charged by diners having a good time. *Sarıyer Pier, Sarıyer, tel. 212/242-0367. Reservations advised. AE, MC, V.*

$$ Borsa Lokantasi. This unpretentious spot serves some of the best
★ food in the city. The baked lamb in eggplant puree and the stuffed artichokes are highly recommended. But expect plain wood chairs and tables, paper napkins, and a crowd of hungry Turks. *Yalıköşkü Cad., Yalıköşkü Han 60-62, Eminönü, tel. 212/522-4173. Halâskârgazi Cad. 90-1, Osmanbey, tel. 212/232-4200. Reservations advised. AE, DC, MC, V. No credit cards at Eminönü. No dinner. Closed Sun.*

$$ Dört Mevsim. Located in a handsome Victorian building on New
★ Town's main drag, Dört Mevsim is noted for its blend of Turkish and French cuisine and for its owners, Gay and Musa, the Anglo-Turkish couple who opened it in 1965. On any given day, you'll find them in the kitchen overseeing the preparation of such delights as shrimp in cognac sauce and baked marinated lamb. The setting is woody Victorian, with soft lighting and lace curtains on the window. *İstiklal Cad. 509, Beyoğlu, tel. 212/245-8941. Reservations advised. DC, MC, V. Closed Sun.*

$$ Dunya. This restaurant is right on the Bosporus in the city's Bohemian quarter, Ortaköy. As wonderful as the view—which includes the Bosporus Bridge, the Ortaköy mosque, and many a passing boat—is, the food, which includes fresh and delicious appetizers such as eggplant or octopus salad, and grilled *cipura* (bream) is even better. Ask for a table on the terrace as close to the water as possible. *Salhane Sok. 10 Ortaköy, tel. 212/258-6385. Reservations advised. No credit cards.*

$$ Fırat. At this hopping Kumkapı fish house, you barely have time to settle yourself in your chair before the food starts coming at you: salads, a savory baked liver dish, shrimp with garlic. In addition to the usual grilled presentation, fish here is baked in a light cream or tomato-based sauce to great effect. Just point at what you want, but try to pass on a round or two to save room for dessert. *Çakmaktaş Sok. 11, Kumkapı, tel. 212/517-2308. Reservations not necessary. No credit cards.*

$$ Hanedan. The emphasis is on kebabs, all kinds, all excellent, and the mezes—tabouli, hummus, and the flaky pastries known as *böreks*— are much tastier than elsewhere. Crisp white linens set off the cool, dark decor of the dining room. Tables by the front windows offer the advantage of a view of the lively Beşiktaş ferry terminal. *Çiğdem Sok. 27, Beşiktaş, tel. 212/260-4854. Reservations advised. AE, MC, V.*

$$ Hidiv Kasrı. A string trio often plays at mealtimes in this restored palace on the Asian shore of the Bosporus. The food is refined but traditional: kebabs, lamb chops, fish, and eggplant in various guises. Inside, the decor is sumptuous Art Nouveau; a spacious terrace above the fragrant gardens provides seating in summer. The palace is up a long, windy road from the town square, so you'll need a car or taxi to get here. *Hidiv Kasrı, Çubuklu, tel. 216/331-2651. Reservations advised. Jacket and tie advised. MC, V.*

$$ Kaptan. Long rows of tables, a low ceiling, and a prowlike front terrace make you feel almost as if you're dining on a boat at this crowded, animated fish restaurant in one of the many suburbs along the Bosporus. The view could be better—the water is on the other side of the main road—but the experience rewards the taxi ride out nonetheless. Try the tasty *kılıç* (swordfish) kebab or the grilled

Dining

Borsa Lokantasi, **19**
Cemal Balik, **9**
Club 29, **4**
Divan, **30**
Dört Mevsim, **20**
Dunya, **40**
Fırat, **10**
Gelik, **8**
Hacı Salih, **28**
Hacıbaba, **27**
Hanedan, **35**
Hidiv Kasrı, **1**
Kaptan, **2**
Körfez, **3**
Osmancık, **21**
Rejans, **26**
Resat Paşa Konağı, **41**
Sarniç, **18**
Tuğra, **36**
Urcan, **39**
Yakup, **22**
Yeşil Ev, **15**
Ziya, **38**

Lodging

Ayasofia Pansiyons, **17**
Barut Guesthouse, **11**
Berk Guest House, **16**
Büyük Londra, **25**
Büyük Tarabya, **5**
Çırağan Palace, **37**
Conrad İstanbul, **34**
Divan, **30**
Hidiv Kasrı, **1**
Hilton Hotel, **32**
Hotel Empress
Zoe, **14**
Hotel Nomade, **13**
Hotel Zürich, **7**
Hyatt Regency, **31**
Ibrahim Paşa Oteli, **12**
Merit Antique
Hotel, **6**
Oriental Hotel, **29**
Pera Palace, **23**
Richmond Hotel, **24**
Swissôtel Istanbul, **33**
Yeşil Ev, **15**

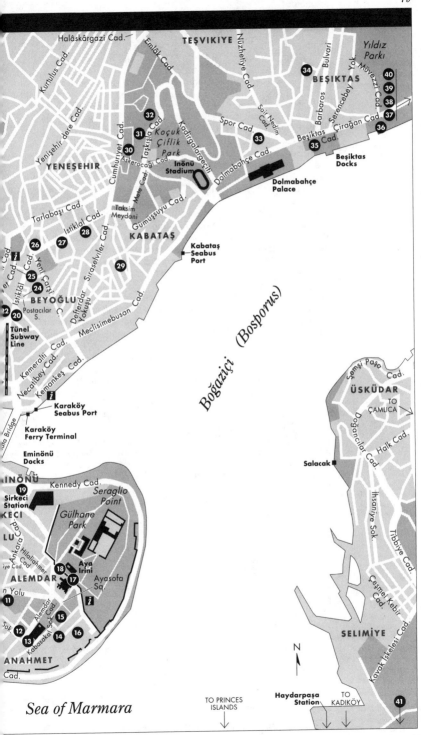

kalkan (turbot). *Birinci Cad. 5, Arnavutköy, tel. 212/265–8487. Reservations advised. No credit cards.*

$$ Osmancık. This is a Turkish restaurant on the 23rd floor of the Pullman Etap Hotel with a 360-degree view of the Bosporus, the Golden Horn, and the rest of Istanbul. The fixed menu includes starters such as *Osmancik Boregi* (cheese-filled pastries topped with a yogurt sauce) and grills, and all you want to drink from domestic liquors. Entertainment, which starts after 9 PM, comes in the form of *fasil* (traditional Turkish music), followed by a belly dancer. *Meşrutiyet Caddesi, Tepebası, tel. 212/251–5074. Reservations advised; make sure to ask for a table by a window. AE, DC, MC, V.*

$$ Yeşil Ev. The peaceful, marble-paved terrace by a cool garden here is a good choice for alfresco dining. The food is Turkish with a Continental overtone: cold duck salad, seafood casserole, mixed grill. *Kabasakal Sok., Sultanahmet, tel. 212/528–6764. Reservations advised. AE, V.*

$ Hacıbaba. This is a large, cheerful place with travel posters on the wall and a shady terrace overlooking the Greek Orthodox churchyard below, a few steps in from İstiklal Caddesi. The menu runs the gamut of Turkish specialties; the lamb kebabs are good, and there are so many mezes that you may never get around to ordering a meal. *İstiklal Cad. 49, Taksim, tel. 212/244–1886. Reservations advised. AE, DC, V.*

$ Hacı Salih. This tiny, family-run restaurant has only 10 tables, so ★ you may have to line up for dinner. But the traditional Turkish fare here is worth the wait. Lamb and vegetable dishes are specialties, and while alcohol is not served, you are welcome to bring your own. *Anadolu Han 201, off Alyon Sok. (off İstiklal Cad.), tel. 212/243–4528. Reservations sometimes accepted. No credit cards. BYOB. No dinner. Closed Sun.*

$ Rejans. Slightly down-at-the-heels, much as mother Russia is, this restaurant oozes atmosphere; even the waiters are an eccentric bunch. The walls are half wood-paneled, half covered in peeling wallpaper. The borscht and stroganoff are sturdy and filling rather than haute. Try the chicken Kiev and sample the lemon vodka that will be plopped down on your table—you pay by the glass. *Olivo Geçidi 15, off İstiklal Cad., Galatasaray, tel. 212/244–1610. Reservations advised. AE, DC, MC, V. Closed Sun.*

$ Yakup. This cheery hole-in-the-wall is smoky and filled with locals rather than tourists, and it can get loud, especially if there is a soccer match on the television. From the stuffed peppers to the böreks and octopus salad, the mezes are several notches above average. *Asmalı Mescit Cad. 35–37, tel. 212/249–2925. Reservations not necessary. No credit cards.*

Lodging

While virtually everything you want to see in Istanbul is in the older part of town, on the European side, all the big modern hotels are mainly around Taksim Square in New Town and, increasingly, along the Bosporus, a 15- or 20-minute cab ride away. The Aksaray, Laleli, Sultanahmet, and Beyazıt areas have more modest hotels and family-run *pansiyons*, as bed-and-breakfasts are called in Turkey. The trade-off for the simpler quarters is convenience: Staying here makes it easy to go back to your hotel at midday or to change before dinner. No matter where you stay, plan ahead: Istanbul has a chronic shortage of beds. For details and price-category definitions, *see* Staying in Turkey in Chapter 1, Essential Information.

Highly recommended establishments are indicated by a star ★.

$$$$ Çırağan Palace. This newly renovated 19th-century Ottoman palace
★ is currently the city's most luxurious—and most expensive—hotel.
The setting is exceptional, right on the Bosporus and adjacent to
lush Yıldız Park; the outdoor pool is on the water's edge. The public
spaces are all done up in cool, sumptuous marble, though the rooms
are on the bland side, with gray walls and carpets; the views, over
the Bosporus or Yıldız Park, help. Be sure to specify old or new
wing; the new looks at the palace, and the old is in it. *Çırağan Cad.
84, Beşiktaş, tel. 212/258–3377, fax 212/259–6687. 312 rooms with
bath. Facilities: 2 restaurants, bar, pool, Turkish bath, health spa,
casino. AE, DC, MC, V.*

$$$$ Conrad Istanbul. This big, round, showy, 14-story tower has views
over the Bosporus and terraced gardens. The lobby has a domed
ceiling and marble staircase, and rooms all around have good views,
pastel colors, and contemporary Italian furnishings. *Barbaros Bul.
46, Beşiktaş, tel. 212/227–3000, fax 212/259–6667. 627 rooms with
bath. Facilities: 2 restaurants, 3 bars, health club, indoor and outdoor pools, 2 tennis courts, shopping arcade, business center, casino. AE, DC, MC, V.*

$$$$ Hilton Hotel. Lavishly decorated with white marble, Turkish rugs
and large brass urns, this is one of the best Hiltons in the chain.
Though built in the early 1970s, it has aged well. The extensive
grounds, filled with gardens and rosebushes, make the hotel a restful haven in a bustling city. Rooms are Hilton-standard, with plush
carpeting and pastel decor; ask for one with a view of the Bosporus.
*Cumhuriyet Cad., Harbiye, tel. 212/231–4650, fax 212/240–4165.
498 rooms with bath. Facilities: 4 restaurants, bar, pool, Turkish
bath, beauty and health spa, 3 tennis courts, 2 squash courts, shopping arcade, casino. AE, DC, MC, V.*

$$$$ Hyatt Regency. The newest addition to Istanbul's luxury hotel is a
massive but tastefully designed pink building reminiscent of Ottoman splendor. So is the interior, which has plush carpeting and
earthy tones. Rooms have views of the Bosporus and the Taksim district. *Abdi Ipekci Cad. 34/12, Macka, tel. 212/234–5272, fax 212/
231–7748. 360 rooms with bath. Facilities: 2 restaurants, café, bar,
pool, beauty salon, health club, business center, baby-sitting service. AE, DC, MC, V.*

$$$$ Swissôtel Istanbul. This bright, new hotel boasts a brilliant location
just above Dolmabahçe Palace. The building was controversial—nobody liked the idea of such a big, modern structure towering over
and contrasting with the palace below. But you'll appreciate its
views—all the way to Topkapı Palace across the Golden Horn. The
lobby, vast with high ceilings, is usually filled by the tinkling of a
piano. The occasional Swiss-village mural strikes a jarring note in
Istanbul, but service is crisp and efficient and the clientele is a real
international mix. The rooms, done in muted greens, have contemporary if undistinguished furnishings. *Bayıldım Cad. 2, Maçka, tel.
212/259–0101, fax 212/259–0105. 503 rooms with bath. Facilities: 4
restaurants, 2 bars, pool, health club, business center. AE, DC,
MC, V.*

$$$ Ayasofia Pansiyons. These guest houses are part of an imaginative
★ project undertaken by the Touring and Automobile Club (a Turkish
organization that promotes tourism and historic preservation) to re-
store a little street of 19th-century wooden houses along the outer
wall of Topkapı Palace. One of the houses has been converted into a
library and the rest into pansiyons, furnished in late Ottoman style
with Turkish carpets and kilims, brass beds, and big European ar-
moires. Front units have an incredible view of Hagia Sophia. During
the summer, tea and refreshments are served in the small, white-
trellised garden to guests and nonguests alike. *Soğukçeşme*

Sok., Sultanahmet, tel. 212/513–3660, fax 212/513–3669. 57 rooms with bath. Facilities: restaurant, café, bar, Turkish bath. AE, MC, V.

$$$ Büyük Tarabya. This summer resort, less than an hour's drive up the Bosporus from the center of Istanbul, is popular among the more affluent locals. Though it has been around for years, it is well maintained and perfectly modern, with bright white walls and plenty of cool marble. It has a private beach on a lovely bay. *Kefeliköy Cad., Tarabya, tel. 212/262–1000, fax 212/262–2260. 262 rooms with bath. Facilities: restaurant, bar, pool, health club. AE, MC, V.*

$$$ Divan. Smaller than the nearby Hilton and Sheraton, this is a quiet, modern hotel with an excellent restaurant. The staff is thoroughly professional, the rooms and public spaces quite comfortable. The lobby is done up with Turkish rugs and brass, the good-size rooms in bright peach. *Cumhuriyet Cad. 2, Şişli, tel. 212/231–4100, fax 212/248–8527. 180 rooms with bath. Facilities: restaurant, bar, tea shop. AE, DC, MC.*

$$$ Merit Antique Hotel. Formerly part of the Ramada chain, this hotel was created by combining four elegant turn-of-the-century apartment buildings. While the cream-colored rooms are generic and unimpressive, the public spaces couldn't be grander, with their arched glass canopies and reproduction furnishings in turn-of-the-century style; there's even a small stream, stocked with goldfish, running through the lobby. The only drawback is the neighborhood, on the Old Town side, which is full of cheap hotels and restaurants. *Ordu Cad. 226, Laleli, tel. 212/513–9300, fax 212/512–6390. 275 rooms with bath. Facilities: 4 restaurants, bar, pool, health club, casino. AE, MC, V.*

$$$ ★ Pera Palace. This grand hotel with a genuinely Turkish feel was built in 1892 to accommodate guests arriving on the *Orient Express* and, although modernized, has lost none of its original Victorian splendor. The elevator looks like a gilded bird cage, the main stairway is white marble, and the lobby surrounding it has 20-foot-high coral marble walls. The high-ceilinged guest rooms are similarly Belle Epoque, though furnished with reproductions. Ask to see the room where Atatürk used to stay; it has been furnished with some of his personal belongings and is maintained as a visitor attraction. *Meşrutiyet Cad. 98, Tepebaşı, tel. 212/251–4560, fax 212/251–4089. 145 rooms with bath. Facilities: restaurant, bar. AE, DC, MC, V.*

$$$ ★ Yeşil Ev (Green House). Another Touring and Automobile Club project, this one is around the corner from the Ayasofia Pansiyons, and the location is spectacular, on the edge of a small park between the Blue Mosque and Hagia Sophia. It's decorated in old-fashioned Ottoman style with lace curtains and latticed shutters; rooms have brass beds and carved wooden furniture upholstered in velvet or silk (but they're small, with smallish baths and no phones or televisions). In summer, you can dine on marble tables in a high-walled garden, and the food, traditional Turkish fare, is excellent. *Kabasakal Sok. 5, Sultanahmet, tel. 212/517–6785, fax 212/517–6780. 20 rooms with bath. Facilities: restaurant, garden. AE, V.*

$$ ★ Barut Guesthouse. Smallish rooms have plain wooden furniture in this quiet and secluded hostelry in the heart of Old Istanbul. The roof terrace overlooks the Sea of Marmara, and the lobby is filled with Turkish carpets. Owners Hikmet and Füsün Barut are well-regarded local artists who create beautiful marbled paintings and objects and run a modest gallery on the property. *Ishak Paşa Cad. 8, Sultanahmet, tel. 212/516–0357, fax 212/516–2944. 23 rooms with bath. MC, V.*

$$ Büyük Londra. Another old Victorian hotel, similar to the Pera Palace but not as grand, this six-story establishment built in the 1850s as the home of a wealthy Italian family has grown old gracefully. Rooms are small and comfortably worn, and the current layout brings to mind an old apartment building. The dark woods and velvet drapes used in the high-ceilinged lobby and dining room exude an aura of the Ottoman Victorian era. *Meşrutiyet Cad. 117, Tepebaşı, tel. 212/245–0670, fax 212/245–0671. 54 rooms with bath. Facilities: restaurant. AE, MC, V.*

$$
★ **Hıdiv Kasrı.** You'll find it well worth your while to make the 40-minute drive out of the city, along the Asian side of the Bosporus, to stay here. Built in 1900 for the *khedive (hıdiv,* in Turkish)—the Ottoman-controlled ruler in Egypt—as his summer palace *(kasrı),* it's one of Istanbul's truly special hotels, a riot of Levantine opulence. The furniture is Art Nouveau, the colonnaded central hall has a lovely marble fountain, and the curved dining room has a spectacular domed ceiling supported by white marble columns. The conservatory is now a café, and there is a salon where classical music performances are often held. *Hıdiv Kasrı, Çubuklu, tel. 216/331–2651, fax 216/322–3434. 12 rooms, some share bath. Facilities: restaurant, concert hall. AE, DC, V.*

$$ **Hotel Zürich.** This 10-story hotel is efficient, well run, and one of the choicer options in Laleli; the lobby is highly polished and the rooms bright and carpeted, with little balconies. The higher floors are quieter. *Harikzadeler Sok. 37, Laleli, tel. 212/512–2350, fax 212/526–9731. 132 rooms with bath. Facilities: restaurant, 2 bars, nightclub. MC, V.*

$$ **Ibrahim Paşa Oteli.** This exquisitely renovated old Turkish house in the historic Sultanahmet neighborhood has panoramic views of the Bosporus and Sultanahmet Square. It's the right place if you want to treat yourself. *Terzihane Sok. 5, Sultanahmet, tel. 212/518–0394 or 212/518–0395, fax 212/518–4457. 19 rooms with bath. Facilities: restaurant, bar. MC, V.*

$$ **Richmond Hotel.** Wonderfully sited on pedestrian Istiklal Caddesi and very close to the consulates, this hotel is a restored turn-of-the-century building with plush, clean rooms, some with views of the Bosporus. The sidewalk patisserie Lebon at the entrance is a remake of the original. *Istiklal Cad. 445, tel. 212/252–5460, fax 212/252–9707. 101 rooms with bath. Facilities: restaurant, cafe, meeting room, bar. AE, V.*

$ **Berk Guest House.** Güngör and Nevin Evrensel run this clean and quite comfortable pansiyon in a converted private home. There are no real public spaces to speak of, though two of the rooms have balconies overlooking a garden. *Kutlugün Sok. 27, Sultanahmet, tel. 212/516–9671, fax 212/517–7715. 7 rooms with bath. No credit cards.*

$ **Hotel Empress Zoe.** This small, unusual, and friendly hotel is conveniently near the sights in Sultanahmet. Named for the 11th-century empress who was one of the few women to rule Byzantium, it is decorated with murals and paintings in the style of that period. The rooms, accented with colorful textiles and paintings, have cool marble bathrooms. The American owner, Ann Nevans, is a wonderful help with personalized itineraries. *Akbıyık Cad., Adliye Sok. 10, Sultanahmet, tel. 212/518–2504, fax 212/518–5699. 12 rooms with bath. MC, V.*

$
★ **Hotel Nomade.** The service is personal, the beds comfortable, and the prices low at this Sultanahmet pansiyon. The building is a restored, five-story Ottoman house decorated with kilims and folk crafts. The rooms are small, and those downstairs share a bath. The roof-garden bar and terrace have incredible views of all of Sultanahmet. *Ticarethane Sok. 7, Sultanahmet, tel. 212/511–1296, fax 212/513–2404. 12 rooms, some share bath. AE, MC, V.*

$ **Oriental.** This modest hotel is conveniently located near Taksim Square and a short walk or ride away from such sights as Dolmabahçe Palace and Sultanahmet. The front rooms have superb views of the Bosporus. *Cihangir Cad. 60, Taksim, tel. 212/252–6870, fax 212/251–5321. 20 rooms with bath. Facilities: bar. AE, MC, V.*

The Arts and Nightlife

For upcoming events, reviews, and other information, pick up a copy of *The Guide,* a new and reliable bimonthly English-language publication that has listings of hotels, bars, restaurants, and events, as well as features about aspects of Istanbul life; or check the *Turkish Daily News,* the English-language newspaper.

The Arts

Istanbul entertainment ranges from the **Istanbul International Festival,** held from late June through mid-July and attracting internationally known performers, to the **Istanbul International Film Festival,** held for two weeks every April, when an international and eclectic selection of new films as well as classics is shown on the city's screens. In May, Istanbul hosts an **International Theater Festival,** which attracts major stage talent from both eastern and western European countries. It is still a matter of speculation how the new pro-Islamic municipal government will affect the quantity and quality of these types of events. Because there is no central ticket agency, ask your hotel to help you get tickets or inquire at the box office or local tourist offices.

To order tickets to the Istanbul International Festival in advance, apply to the **Istanbul Foundation for Culture and Arts** (Kültür ve Sanat Concer Vakfi, Yıldız, Beşiktaş, tel. 212/261–3294 or 212/260–9072). Performances, which include modern and classical music, ballet, opera, and theater, are given throughout the city in historic buildings, such as Hagia Eirene and Rumeli Castle. The highlight of the festival is the performance of Mozart's *Abduction from the Seraglio* at Topkapı Palace, the site that inspired the opera.

Concerts   The main concert hall is **Atatürk Kültür Merkezi,** at Taksim Square. The **Istanbul State Symphony** performs here from October through May, and ballet and dance companies year-round. Tickets are available from the box office (tel. 212/251–5600).

The **Cemal Reşit Rey Concert Hall,** in Harbiye close to the Hilton, hosts recitals, chamber and symphonic music, and modern dance performed by international talent (tel. 212/248–5392 or 212/240–5012).

The Touring and Automobile Association organizes chamber music performances at **Beyaz Köşk** (in Emirgan Park) and **Hıdiv Kasrı** (in Çubuklu), two small 19th-century palaces. For information, contact the Touring and Automobile Association (Halâskârgazi Cad. 364, Şişli, tel. 212/231–4631).

Film   There are number of renovated movie theaters on the strip of Istiklal Caddesi between Taksim and Galatasaray usually showing the latest from Hollywood, with a few current European or Turkish movies thrown in. Look for the words *Ingilizce* (English) or *Orijinal* (original language), or you will be seeing a film dubbed in Turkish. Films in languages other than English will have subtitles in Turkish. If it's film festival time, you'll find a great variety to choose from; ask for a schedule from any box office and make sure to purchase tickets in advance. Seats are reserved.

Nightlife

Bars and Lounges

With views over the Bosporus, and a top-notch restaurant next door, **Bebek Bar** (Bebek Ambassadeurs Hotel, Cevdet Paşa Cad. 113, Bebek, tel. 212/263-3000) gets the dress-up crowd. **Beyoğlu Pub** (Istiklal Cad. 140/17, Beyoglu, tel. 212/252-3842) sits off Istiklâl Caddesi in a pleasant garden and draws moviegoers and an expatriate crowd; at **Cuba Bar** (Vapur Iskelesi Sok. 20, Ortaköy, tel. 212/260-0550), in the bohemian Ortaköy district, a band dishes out Latin rhythms while the cook offers a special Cuban soup; **Memo's** (Salhane Sok. 10, Ortaköy, tel. 212/261-8304), located exquisitely on the Bosporus, hosts the showy crowd; the disco gets rolling around 11 PM. **Kulis** (Cumhuriyet Cad. 117, tel. 212/246-9345), a smoky, all-night hangout for actors and writers, offers good light-jazz piano. **Orient Express Bar** (Pera Palas Hotel, Mesrutiyet Cad. 98, tel. 212/251-4560) is hard to beat for its turn-of-the-century atmosphere; you can't help but sense the ghosts of the various kings, queens, and Hollywood stars who have passed through its doors. Local young professionals patronize **Zihni** (Bronz Sok. 1A, Teşvikiye, Maçka, tel. 212/246-9043) for lunch and for evening cocktails.

Discos

Discos get rolling by about 10 and usually keep going until 3 or 4. In addition to **Regine's** (*see* Nightclubs, *below*), **Juliana's** (Swissotel the Bosporus, Maçka, tel. 212/259-0940) is a popular disco with space-age decor. With its "Mad Max" decor, shoulder-high bursts of foam on the dance floor, and wild shows, **2019** (100 Yil Sanayi Sitesi, tel. 212/285-1896) is one of the hottest scenes in town. **Memo's** (*see above*) draws glossy types. **Discorium** (Esentepe, tel. 212/274-8410) is filled with modern-day Young Turks serious about having a good time amid flashing lights and mirror balls. **Club 29** (Paşabahçe Yolu, Çubuklu, tel. 216/322-2829), a bit classier, holds forth in a faux-Roman villa by the Bosporus on the Asian side from mid-June through September (*see* Dining, *above*). **Samdan** (Nisbetiye Cad., Etiler, tel. 212/263-4898; Piyasa Cad. 101, Büyükada, tel. 216/382-2654 in summer), which also has a fancy restaurant, is favored by fashionable Turks and the international expatriate crowd.

Nightclubs

Probably a good deal tamer than you would expect to find in the exotic East, Istanbul nightclub shows include everything from folk dancers to jugglers, acrobats, belly dancers, and singers. Recent developments in Eastern Europe and Russia have also made some of Istanbul's nightclubs famous for Russian or Romanian dancing girls. Some routines are fairly touristy (like the singer doing "New York, New York" after asking if anyone from the audience is from the States) but still fun. Typically, dinner is served after 8, and floor shows start around 10. Be aware that these are not inexpensive once you've totaled in drink, food, and cover. Reservations are a good idea; be sure to specify whether you're coming for dinner as well as the show or just for drinks.

There are several good bets. **Balim** (Kemerhatun Mah, Hamalbaşi Cad. 8, Beyoğlu, tel. 212/249-5608) has a dependable, if unspectacular, floor show, with singers and a variety of folk and belly dancers, and a more wholesome crowd than you'll find in other places. **Galata Tower** (Kuledibi, tel. 212/245-1160) is high atop New Town in a round room sheathed in windows; the ambience is strictly hotel lounge, and the Turkish dishes are only average. Comfortable, well-established **Kervansaray** (Cumhuriyet Cad. 30, tel. 212/247-1630) offers food somewhat better than at the Galata Tower and shows featuring young, energetic belly dancers. The revue at **Regine's** (Cumhuriyet Cad. 16, tel. 212/247–1630) serves up some of Istanbul's best-known belly dancers, soft-core strippers, and big dance-production numbers heavy on the costumes; an adjacent upscale disco hops until 4 AM.

At the seedy strip-tease places off İstiklal Caddesi, the goal is to get customers to pay outrageous drink prices for questionable companionship.

Excursion to the Princes Islands

The nine islands in the Sea of Marmara, about 20 kilometers (12 miles) from Sultanahmet, have proven a useful amenity for Istanbul. In the days when the city was known as Constantinople, religious undesirables sought refuge here; in the time of the sultans, the islands provided a convenient place to exile untrustworthy hangers-on. By the turn of the last century, well-heeled businessmen had staked their claim and built many of the Victorian gingerbread–style houses that lend the islands their charm. Today, they provide a leafy retreat. Restrictions on development and a ban on automobiles maintain the old-fashioned peace and quiet—transportation is by horse-drawn carriage or bicycle. Though there are no real sights and populations swell significantly on summer weekends, the Princes Islands are perfect for relaxed outings, delightful after crowded Istanbul.

Of the nine islands, only four have ferry service, and only the two largest, Heybeli and Büyükada, are of real interest. Both are hilly and wooded, and the fresh breeze is gently pine-scented. Kınalıada (from *kınalı*, "dyed with henna"), one of the other two, is tiny and pretty much treeless, with only a small monastery to see; Burgaz is a bit bigger, with a year-round population of 1,000 and three old Greek Orthodox churches, but no hotels and only stone beaches.

Arriving and Departing by Boat

Ferries ($1.50) make the trip from Sirkeci or Bostanci (Asian side) docks in half an hour to an hour, depending on where they depart. Go straight to Büyükada and catch a local ferry to Heybeli later. Ferry tickets are round-trip and are collected on return. Much quicker, though less romantic, is the seabus, departing from Kabatas near the Dolmabahce Mosque and from Bostanci seabus terminals on the Asian side. Buy tokens for the seabus at the terminal.

Getting Around

Since no cars are allowed on the islands, you'll do most of your exploring on foot. Alternatively, you can hire a horse-drawn carriage for a pleasantly lazy hour-long tour that takes in most of the significant features of either Büyükada or Heybeli ($10–$15). The other, perhaps more strenuous, but definitely fun, option, is to rent a bicycle ($2 per hour) from one of the bike shops near the clock tower on Büyükada.

To get from one island to the other, hop aboard any of the several daily ferries.

Exploring

Büyükada To the left as you leave the boat you will see a handful of restaurants with names like Monte Carlo, Capri, and Milano. They are pleasant dives, somewhat overpriced as island restaurants tend to be, and there's little difference among them.

To reach the splendid, old **Victorian houses,** walk to the clock tower and bear right. Carriages are available at the clock tower square. The carriage tour winds up hilly lanes that are lined with gardens filled with jasmine, mimosa, and imported palm trees. After all of Istanbul's mosques and palaces, the frilly, pastel houses come as something of a surprise. But it is quite easy to imagine men in panama hats and women with parasols having picnics out in the garden. You can have your buggy driver wait while you make the 20-minute hike up Yücetepe Hill to the **Greek Monastery of St. George,** where there are three chapels and a sacred fountain believed to have healing waters. As you walk up the path, you'll notice the pieces of cloth, string, and paper that visitors have tied to the bushes and trees, in hope of a wish coming true. This is a popular pilgrimage site, especially at Greek Easter, when hundreds take the hike barefoot. If you're lucky, the monastery will be serving its homemade wine. About the only other place to go is **Yörük Ali Plaj,** the public beach, on the west side of the island, an easy walk from the harbor. There is a little restaurant at the beach.

Heybeli The big building to the left of the dock, the **Deniz Kuvetler** (Turkish Naval Academy), is open to visitors except on Sunday, though there's not really much of interest to see. On the right, teahouses and cafés stretch along the waterfront. Here, too, you can take a leisurely carriage ride, stopping, if the mood strikes, at one of the island's several small, sandy, and rarely crowded beaches—the best are on the north shore at the foot of Değirmen Burnu (Windmill Point) and Değirmen Tepesi (Windmill Hill). You can rent a rowboat for a few dollars at these beaches and row out to one of the other Princes Islands across the way. You will also pass the ruined monastery of the Panaghia, founded in the 15th century. Though damaged by fires and earthquakes, the chapel and several red-tile-roofed buildings remain. Unlike at Büyükada, the carriages here do not climb the hills above the harbor, where the old mansions and gardens are. The walk, however, is none too strenuous.

Dining and Lodging

There is little difference from one restaurant to the next. The best bet is to pass by the local restaurant row, cast an eye over the premises, look at the menu, and ask to see the kitchen (a common practice throughout Turkey; often you will be shown to the kitchen before you even ask). If the place is crowded with Turks, it is usually good. The best lodging options are on Büyükada.

Splendid Hotel. For character, it's hard to beat this wooden, turn-of-the-century hotel, with its old-fashioned furniture, large rooms, and Ottoman Victorian styling. The hotel is topped by twin white domes, copies of those at the Hotel Negresco in Nice. No wonder it's hard to get a room on summer weekends unless you book ahead. *23 Nisan Cad. 71, Büyükada, tel. 216/382–6950, fax 216/382–1949. 24 rooms with bath. Facilities: restaurant, pool, disco. No credit cards. Closed Oct.–Apr. $$$*
Villa Rifat. This hotel is smaller, less ornate, and cozier than the Splendid. Its primary advantage is its small strip of private beach.

*Yılmaztürk Cad. 80, Büyükada, tel. 216/351–6068. 6 rooms with
bath. No credit cards. Closed Oct.–Apr. $$*

Excursion to Edirne

Unlike Istanbul, which every conqueror and pretender within
marching distance hoped to have as his capital, Thrace was the sort
of country that most warriors passed on through. The climate is
harsh—sizzling in summer, bitter in winter—and the landscape un-
exceptional. For the modern visitor, however, there are some wor-
thy sights, particularly Edirne, the capital of the Ottoman Empire
before the fall of Constantinople.

Edirne was founded in the 2nd century AD as Hadrianopolis by the
Roman emperor Hadrian. It has been fought over by Bulgars, cru-
saders, Turks, Greeks, and Russians through the centuries, though
once the Ottoman capital was moved to Istanbul, it became some-
thing of a picturesque backwater. Its rich collection of mosques and
monuments is relatively unspoiled by the presence of the concrete
towers so prevalent in Turkey's boomtowns. Its lanes are still cob-
bled and are shaded by the overhanging balconies of traditional Ot-
toman wooden houses.

Tourist Information

The tourist information office in Edirne is on Talat Paşa Caddesi,
near Hürriyet Meydanı (Freedom Square, tel. 284/212–1518).

Arriving and Departing by Car, Bus, and Train

By Car Edirne is about 75 kilometers (46 miles) northwest of Istanbul, via
E5.

By Bus There are frequent buses from Istanbul's Esenler Terminal. The
ride lasts four hours and costs $4.

By Train Three trains daily leave Istanbul's Sirkeci Station for the painfully
slow 6- to 10-hour trip; the cost is only about $5, so you are better off
taking the bus or driving.

Getting Around

The bus and train stations are on the outskirts of town, too far to
walk to comfortably. Take a taxi into the center, asking for Hürriyet
Meydanı. The sites within town can all be reached on foot.

Exploring Edirne

Hürriyet Meydanı, the central square, should be your starting point.
At its center stands the monument to Edirne's great passion: Two
enormous wrestlers steal the spotlight from the obligatory Atatürk
statue. Just off the north side of the square is the **Üç Şerefeli Cami**
(Mosque with Three Galleries), built between 1437 and 1447. The
galleries circle the tallest of the four minarets, which are notable for
their fine brick inlay. On the mosque grounds is the 15th-century
Sokurlu Hamam, built by Sinan and one of the country's more ele-
gant baths. It is still open to the public from about 8 in the morning
until 10 in the evening ($4 for bath, $10 with massage).

Walk east along Talat Paşa Caddesi to the **Eski Cami** (old mosque).
The mosque is well named: Completed in 1414, it is the city's oldest.

The huge-scale calligraphy illustrating quotes from the Koran and naming the prophets is exceptional in its grace and intricacy. Adjoining is the **Rüstempaşa Kervansaray,** restored and reopened as a hotel, just as it was in the 16th century. Also alongside the mosque is the 14-domed Bedestan, and one block away on Talat Paşa Caddesi, the **Ali Paşa Bazaar.** Both are more authentic than Istanbul's Grand Bazaar, as the wares sold here—coffeepots, kilims, soap shaped like fruits and vegetables, towels—are meant for locals rather than tourists.

Follow Mimar Sinan Caddesi to the **Selimiye Cami.** This, not Istanbul's Süleymaniye, is the mosque Sinan described as his masterpiece, and it is certainly one of the most beautiful buildings in Turkey. It was completed in 1575, when the architect was 85 years old. The central dome, more than 100 feet in diameter and 148 feet high, rests on eight pillars, set into the walls so as not to disturb the interior space. External buttresses help support the weight of 999 windows; legend has it that Sultan Selim thought 1,000 might be a bit greedy. The marble mimber is exquisitely carved, and the mihrab is set back in an apse adorned with exceptional İznik tiles. The *medrese* (mosque compound) houses Edirne's Türk-Islâm Eserleri Müzesi (Museum of Turkish and Islamic Art), which displays Islamic calligraphy and photos of local wrestlers, as well as collections of weapons and jewelry from ancient Thrace, folk costumes, kilims, and fine embroidery.

The other great mosque in Edirne is on the outskirts of the city, across the Tunca River. The immense **Beyazıt Cami** complex is about a 20-minute walk from Hürriyet Meydanı via the fine-hewn, six-arched Beyazıt Bridge, which dates from the 1480s, as does the mosque (you can also go via dolmuş from the square). The absence of pillars to support the mosque's large dome is remarkable, as is the marble fretwork of the mihrab. The medrese includes two schools, a mental institution, a poorhouse, and soup kitchens, and all have been restored.

Another 20-minute walk farther upstream from the mosque brings you to **Sarayiçi,** the site of Edirne's famous wrestling tournament. Usually held in June, it is the best known of those held in villages throughout the country: its burly, olive-oil-coated men have been facing off annually here for more than 600 years. Thousands of spectators turn out.

Dining

Aile Restaurant. This locally popular restaurant serves stewed meat and vegetable dishes at lunch and switches to grilled fare in the evening. On the second floor above a bank, next to the post office, it has clean, modest seating, and the food is good and fresh. *Belediye Işhanı, Kat 2, tel. 284/225–1250. Reservations not necessary. No credit cards. $*

Çatı. This restaurant serves typical but delicious Turkish dishes such as *tas kebap* (diced and stewed meat and vegetables with rice or bread) and *islim kebap* (a tender chunk of roast lamb covered with strips of eggplant). It's a clean place with views of the main square and the market. *Hürriyet Meydanı, tel. 284/225–1307. Reservations advised for groups. No credit cards. $*

Doruk. Opened in late 1993, it specializes in meat dishes and is a notch above the competition. About a mile outside the city center on a woody roadside, it has both indoor and outdoor seating. Locals go there for the *tandir kebab* (lamb baked in a clay pit). If that's too heavy for you, try the lamb or chicken *sis kebab*, or the *kasarli kofte* (meatballs stuffed with cheese). The inside of the restaurant is filled with plants and trees, while marble steps and a fountain dominate the entrance outside. *Karaağaç Yolu, (between the Bunca and the Meriç bridges), tel. 284/213–8865. Reservations advised. V. $*

Lodging

Hotel Rüstem Paşa Kervansaray. The Kervansaray was built in the 1500s, reputedly by the celebrated architect Sinan, and today is the most impressive hotel in Edirne, at least from the outside. The rooms have high ceilings and decorative fireplaces, plain furniture, and low, single beds. The building sprawls around a pleasant courtyard full of flowers and shaded by a huge çinar tree. Rooms near the nightclub are noisy. Still, the place has character. *İki Kapılı Han Cad. 57, Sabuni Mah, tel. 284/212–6119 or 284/225–2125, fax 284/212–0462. 100 rooms with bath. Facilities: restaurant, nightclub. No credit cards. $$*

Sultan Oteli. A nondescript, 1970s-ish hotel, the Sultan Oteli is efficient, clean, and well located near the main square and the tourism office. The rooms have little in the way of decor or amenities, but the restaurant is popular with Turks and visitors. *Talat Paşa Bulv. 24, tel. 284/225–1372, fax 284/225–5763. 90 rooms with shower. Facilities: restaurant. MC, V. $$*

4 Bursa, İznik, and Termal

Whether you are heading for the Aegean or for Ankara and central Anatolia, you would do well to take two or three days to explore this region near the southern shore of the Sea of Marmara. Both Bursa and İznik have reaped the rewards of rich histories, and Termal remains a particularly Turkish spa.

Bursa, one of Turkey's more prosperous cities—a pleasing mix of bustling modernity, old stone buildings, and wealthy suburbs with vintage wood-frame Ottoman villas—became the first capital of a nascent Ottoman Empire after the city was captured in 1326 by Orhan Gazi (ruled 1326–61), the empire's first sultan. It was here that Ottoman architecture bloomed, laying the foundation for more elaborate works to be found in the later capitals, Edirne and Istanbul. More than 125 mosques here are on the list kept by the Turkish Historical Monuments Commission, and their minarets make for a grand skyline. Among its residents, Bursa is proudly called Yeşil, or Green, Bursa, both for the green İznik tiles decorating some of its most famous monuments and for its parks and gardens and the national forest surrounding nearby Mt. Uludağ. Uludağ, at 8,300 feet, is also a popular ski resort.

İznik, known as Nicaea in ancient times, was put on the map in 316 BC when one of Alexander the Great's generals claimed the city. Six years later it was conquered by another general, Lysimachos, who renamed it Nikaea after his wife. In AD 325 and again in 786, Nicaea hosted international ecumenical councils, which had profound effects on the practice of Christianity. The first, in 325, condemned as heresy the proposition suggested by the Arian sect, which held that God alone was divine; the opposition Athanasian sect successfully argued that Christ was one with God and equally divine. The second council, in 786, rejected iconoclasm, or the "breaking of images," and allowed the adoration and use of icons and religious art, resolving a hotly contested issue of the day. The Seljuks made the city their capital for a brief period in the 11th century; Byzantine emperors in exile did the same in the 13th century, while Constantinople was in the hands of Crusaders. Orhan captured it in 1331. Following the Ottoman conquest of Istanbul, İznik became a center for the ceramics industry. To upgrade the quality of native work, Sultan Selim I (ruled 1512–15), known as "The Grim," imported 500 Persian potters from Tabriz after he conquered it. The government-owned kilns were soon turning out incredibly rich tiles with intricate motifs of circles, stars, and floral and geometric patterns, executed in lush turquoise, green, blue, red, and white. Despite their costliness, their popularity spread through the Islamic world. Today original İznik tiles can be found in museums in Europe and the United States, as well as in Turkey.

Termal is notable for one and only one reason—its natural hot springs. A popular spa since Roman times, the springs were used by the Ottomans, refurbished in 1900 by Sultan Abdül Hamid II, and regularly visited by Atatürk during breaks from the frenzied business of running the country in the 1920s and '30s. It maintains something of that 1930s air, and its restored baths, shady gardens, and piney woods are time-proven restoratives. There is little evidence today of Termal's ancient history, but the waters continue to attract the weary.

Essential Information

Important Addresses and Numbers

Tourist Information There are tourist offices in **Bursa** (Ulu Camii Park, Atatürk Cad. 1, tel. 224/221–2359) and **İznik** (Belediye Ishanı, 2nd Floor, Kılıçaslan Cad., tel. 266/757–1933). For information about **Termal** and its hotels, call its hotel-and-baths complex at 216/835–7413 (*see* Dining and Lodging, *below*).

Emergencies **Tourist Police** (in Bursa, tel. 224/224–1994).

Arriving and Departing by Plane

Airports and Airlines **Sönmez Holding Hava Yolları** (tel. 212/663–6838 or 212/663–6463), a domestic airline, operates two flights daily Monday–Saturday from Istanbul to Bursa. The trip takes roughly 20 minutes. You can take a shuttle bus or taxi into the city.

Arriving and Departing by Car, Boat, and Bus

By Car From Istanbul take the dreary E5, lined with factories and slowed by heavy truck traffic headed for Ankara. At İzmit take Route 130 to Yalova, a small city (population 60,000) and transportation center east of Termal; Route 575 connects Yalova and Bursa.

Better yet, take the car ferry from Kartal, just east of Üsküdar on the Asian side of Istanbul, to Yalova. The trip costs about $10 one way, but lops 140 kilometers (87 miles) off the journey. From Bursa, Route 200 runs west toward Çanakkale and the Aegean, east toward Ankara.

By Boat Seabuses and express ferries operate daily between Istanbul's Kabataş docks and Yalova. A seabus from Kabataş docks costs only about $2 and takes just under an hour; the express ferry, also $2, takes two hours. Seabuses also travel to Yalova from Kartal and Bostanci docks on the Asian side, but Kartal is difficult and time-consuming to reach by public transportation. By hydrofoil the trip takes a little more than an hour and costs about $8; by express ferry it's two hours and $2. There is a car ferry from Kartal that also accepts passengers, although the dock is difficult to reach by public transportation. Be sure to check in at least 45 minutes ahead of scheduled departure in summer, or risk not getting on.

By Bus Several buses daily make the trip from Istanbul's new bus terminal at Esenler to Yalova and Bursa, but as it can take five hours, you will probably prefer the ferry, which takes less than half the time. By bus, the trip costs about $2 one way.

Getting Around

By Car From Yalova, Termal is 12 kilometers (7½ miles) west via the road marked ÇINARCIK; Bursa is 60 kilometers (37 miles) south via Route 575; İznik is 62 kilometers (38 miles) southeast (via Route 575 south and Route 150, which loops around İznik Lake).

By Bus and Dolmuş Just off the dock in Yalova, to the left, you will find minibuses headed for İznik and Bursa, both 90 minutes and a $2 bus fare away. Make sure not to mistake the İznik bus for those headed for Izmit. Dolmuşes also wait off the docks; they cost a bit more than the bus and offer comparable comfort and speed.

Between Bursa and İznik, service is by bus (about $2) and dolmuş ($2–$5).

To get from Yalova to Termal, walk from the ferry dock straight ahead to the traffic circle with the big statue of Atatürk, turn right, and walk one block. Bus 4 (marked TAŞKÖPRÜ– TERMAL) departs from here; the fare is about 50¢ for the 20-minute ride. Minibuses get you there for slightly more.

The telephone number for the Bursa bus station is 224/254–7217.

Guided Tours

Travel agencies in Bursa arrange guided tours of Bursa and İznik: **Yöntur Turizm** (Çekirge Cad. 9, tel. 224/222–8342).

Exploring Bursa, İznik, and Termal

If you arrive by car from Istanbul, İznik is a logical place to start. Otherwise, you might take in the baths at Termal, head for İznik, then overnight in Bursa. It is possible to do Bursa from Istanbul in a day, although it will be a long and tiring one.

Highlights for First-Time Visitors

Bedestan, Tour 3
Valide and Kurşunlu baths, Tour 1
Yeşil Cami, Tour 3

Tour 1: Termal

Numbers in the margin correspond to points of interest on the Sea of Marmara map.

❶ **Termal** is a self-contained resort with two hotels, exotic gardens, and three public thermal baths on its grounds. With their rich mineral waters, the baths are the real lure. There are several ways to enjoy the spa. You can make your way through the gardens and greenery to the grand **Sultan** or somewhat less imposing **Valide** baths—the Valide being the mother of the reigning sultan in Ottoman times. Both are Ottoman institutions, with Baroque decor and hot mineral waters; you can rent your own individual cabin and soak to your heart's content in a deep, gray marble tub. The **Kurşunlu** (Lead-Roof Bath), a third option, has a large outdoor thermal pool as well as an indoor pool and sauna. The Sultan is the priciest, the others are slightly less; all have lockers where you can store your clothes and towels for use after a soak. If you stay overnight, you can also soak at either of the hotels, whose baths are open to guests only. *Sultan admission: $3.50 per person, $5 for 2. Valide admission: $2 per person for 90 min. Kurşunlu admission: $2.50 for outdoor pool, $2 for enclosed pool and sauna, $2.50 per person for private cubicle, $3.50 for 2.*

Atatürk liked Termal so much he had a house built for himself here. From the path from the Kurşunlu pool you can see **Atatürk's Cottage,** together with a white house with gingerbread trim that was used by his guests. When you're finished soaking, make a quick stop at the museum devoted to him, a plain, modern structure built in 1929. It contains little more than some heavy wood furniture but has

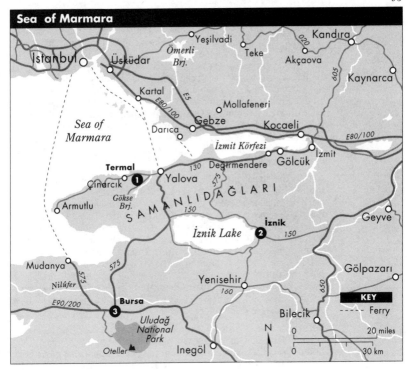

Sea of Marmara

a delightful tea garden on one side. *No phone. Admission: $1. Open during daylight hours.*

Tour 2: İznik

2 Lakeside **İznik** is rather run-down today, but it has an incredible past. It is the place where the famed İznik tiles were made, although the ceramic industry went into decline in the 18th century. It is only now making a comeback by reproducing the rich colors of the original tiles, though on a small scale and without great success so far.

Start at the center of town, at **Sancta Sophia** (Church of the Holy Wisdom). The church was built in the 6th century, during the reign of Justinian, and the primitive mosaic floor is believed to date from that time. The wall mosaics were added as part of a reconstruction in the 11th century, after an earthquake toppled the original church. There are some fine fragments of Byzantine fresco and mosaic work, including a mural of Jesus with Mary and St. John the Baptist. It was here that the great ecumenical councils of the 4th and 8th centuries were held. *Atatürk Cad. and Kılıçaslan Cad. Admission: $1. Open daily 9–noon and 2–5. If closed, ask for key at İznik Museum a few blocks away.*

Walk east along Kılıçaslan Caddesi, the town's main street, past the **Belediye Saray** (Town Hall), the tourist office, and the **Hacı Özbek Cami,** a mosque dating from 1332. The Ottoman style here is very primitive, the scale small, and ornamentation lacking compared to that of later buildings in Bursa and Istanbul.

A couple of blocks farther on, turn left on Yeşil Cami Caddesi. Here you will find the **Yeşil Cami,** known as the Green Mosque because of the color of much of its tile work. Take a mental picture of this structure, which is done in the Seljuk Turk style, to compare to later mosques in Bursa, where the Ottoman style developed later on. The Seljuk style is simpler than the Ottoman, certainly: Seljuk mosques usually have just one room under one dome and borrow Persian and Indian architectural and decorative traditions from the eastern extremities of their empire; Ottoman mosques, as exemplified by Bursa's Ulu Cami, draw on Byzantine structures such as Istanbul's Hagia Sophia. Ironically, the Green Mosque's blue and green tiles are not the original İznik work, which was damaged by various earthquakes and replaced during the last century.

Across the street is the **İznik Museum.** The building itself is rather interesting—it was built in 1388 as a soup kitchen. Such kitchens were often constructed by the wealthy near mosques to serve free food to the poor as examples of Muslim charity. Today the museum contains an array of artifacts, from Greek grave markers to Ottoman perfume bottles and İznik tiles. If you have time, ask at the museum about a visit to the Byzantine Tomb, **Yeraltı Mezar,** on the outskirts of town. Discovered in the 1960s, this 5th-century burial place of an unknown family has well-preserved painted murals of peacocks, flowers, and abstract patterns in the Byzantine style. *İznik Museum, Müze Sok., tel. 224/757–1027. Admission: $1. Open daily 9–noon and 1:30–5.*

Return to Kılıçaslan Caddesi and continue eastward to the rough stone blocks that mark the city walls and the arched, gray-stone **Lefke Kapısı,** actually a series of three sturdy, handsome gates built in honor of a visit by Hadrian in AD 120, with old inscriptions, marble reliefs, and friezes intact. You can scramble up onto the old city walls, if you like, for a good view. Thick, sturdy fortifications like these were what saved many an ancient city from ruin. Outside the gate is the city graveyard as well as Muslim tombs belonging to a nobleman named Hayrettin Paşa and lesser luminaries. The oldest is 600 years old.

Tour 3: Bursa

❸ Bursa, set along the slopes of Uludağ, suffers a bit from the sprawls. It stretches along an east–west axis, and its main street winds and changes names many times between the city center and the neighborhood known as Çekirge, several kilometers (a couple of miles) to the west. The town square, at the intersection of Atatürk Caddesi and İnönü Caddesi, is a logical starting point.

The area, officially Cumhuriyet Alanı (Republic Square) is popularly called **Heykel** (Statue), after its imposing equestrian statue of Atatürk. Head east from here (left, when facing Atatürk), turn left onto Yeşil Caddesi, and walk another few blocks. Bursa is known as Yeşil (Green) Bursa, not only because of its many trees and parks but because of its **Yeşil Cami** (Green Mosque), at the eastern end of Yeşil Caddesi, and its **Yeşil Türbe** (Green Tomb).

An incredible juxtaposition of simple form, inspired stone carving, and spectacular İznik tile work, the Yeşil Cami is widely thought to be the finest mosque in Turkey. The beauty of the mosque starts at its carved-marble entryway, where feathery patterns in the stone create a complex design. Inside is a sea of fine blue and green İznik tiles, many with exquisite floral designs. The central hall rests under two shallow domes; in the one near the entrance, an oculus sends down a beam of sunlight at midday, illuminating a fountain delicately carved from a single piece of marble. The *mihrab* (prayer niche) towers almost 50 feet, and there are intricate carvings near the top. On a level above the main doorway is the sultan's loge, lavishly decorated and tiled; if you are lucky, a caretaker will take you up to see it.

Work on the mosque began in 1421, during the reign of Mehmet I Çelebi (ruled 1413–21), known as the Gentleman. The Yeşil Türbe, directly across Yeşil Caddesi, is Mehmet's tomb, built three years later. The "green" tomb is actually covered in blue tiles, added after an earthquake damaged the originals in the 1800s. Inside, however, are an incredible abundance of original İznik tiles, including those sheathing Mehmet's immense sarcophagus. The other tombs belong to his children. *Eastern end of Yeşil Cad., opposite Yeşil Cami. Admission free. Open daily 8:30–noon and 1–5:30.*

Also part of this complex is a former theological school that now houses the **Bursa Etnoğrafya Müzesi** (Bursa Ethnographic Museum). The collection is a good one, with tile work, inlaid wood, jewelry, books and almanacs, pottery, and bits of Seljuk architectural decoration. *Yeşil Cad., on w. side of Yeşil Cami. Admission: $1. Open Tues.–Sun. 8:30–noon and 1–5:30.*

Time Out The several tea gardens on the west side of the Yeşil Mosque and Yeşil Tomb are pleasant places to have a sandwich or pastries and take in views of the city and distant plains. The two mosques in the distance, the **Emir Sultan** (1431, to the right) and **Yıldırım Beyazıt** (1391, to the left), are not worth visiting in any case, as earthquakes have damaged them inside.

Returning to Heykel, head downhill on Inönü Caddesi a few blocks, stopping just short of a small mosque set out onto the street. To the right is the **Bat Pazar.** The geese for which it was named are long gone, but this is a picturesque spot, filled with ironmongers, blacksmiths working their forges, and peddlers of various sorts working out of small, often open-air shops. You can pick up a rug here, or some handmade kitchen utensils; Bursa knives are highly regarded throughout the country. For a hint of what the city was like in earlier days, a stroll through this bazaar is highly recommended.

Cross Inönü Caddesi and walk east on Cumhuriyet Caddesi to the **Orhan Cami.** Built for Sultan Orhan in 1335, this is the first truly Ottoman mosque. Although small, it has a graceful porch and fountain. Across the street is Bursa's **City Hall.** The Turks generally favor modern, practical concrete in their civic buildings, but this one is done in dark wood timbers and has a more rustic feeling.

From here you can slip into one of the entrances to the **Bedestan** (Covered Bazaar). The bazaar was built in the 1300s by Yıldırım Beyazıt I (ruled 1389–1402), but was flattened by a massive earthquake in 1855. It has been lovingly restored, and many of the old Ottoman *hans* (markets) inside still provide the flavor of the 16th century. By and large, the bedestan is less touristy and more atmospheric than Istanbul's Grand Bazaar. Best buys include silver and gold jewelry, thick Turkish cotton towels, and silk goods.

Come out the other side of the bazaar, at Atatürk Caddesi. The striking building with its 20 domes, near the intersection with Cumhuriyet Caddesi, is the aptly named **Ulu Cami** (Grand Mosque). The mosque dates from 1396: Sultan Beyazıt had it built after vowing to build 20 mosques if he was victorious in the battle of Nicopolis in Macedonia; this one mosque with 20 domes was something of a compromise. Its interior is decorated with an elegantly understated display of fine Islamic calligraphy spelling out the names of holy disciples of Islam.

To the west, Atatürk Caddesi curves around the remains of the ancient citadel—built by the Ottomans atop Byzantine foundations—that protected the city against myriad invasions. Today there are tea gardens, small stands of trees, and other obstructions, so the walls don't look all that impressive. Instead of continuing downhill, turn left and head uphill into the neighborhood known as **Hisar** (Fortress). This is where Bursa started, like so many cities of old—within the walls of a fortress. Pınarbaşi Caddesi is the main street through this part of town; make a detour on Kale Caddesi, a particularly atmospheric block lined with wood-frame houses dating from the 17th to 19th centuries. In a small park not far from citadel walls, overlooking Cemal Nadir Caddesi, are the **tombs of Osman and Orhan,** considered founders of the Ottoman Empire. The word Ottoman derives from Osmanli, the people led by Osman. Osman—the son of a warrior chieftain named Ertuğrul Gazi, who had taken control over an area near Bursa—sought to expand the boundaries of his father's state and eventually laid seige to Bursa. But it wasn't until 1326, several years after he died, that the city fell and the Ottomans, under Orhan, claimed the victory. The tombs date from the 19th century; the originals were destroyed in an earthquake.

On Kaplıca Caddesi, a short walk west of Hisar and farther up the slope, is a neighborhood known as **Muradiye.** The **Sultan Murat II Cami** and surrounding complex were built in 1425–26, during the reign of Mehmet the Conqueror, in honor of its namesake, Mehmet's father. The mosque is unexceptional, perhaps because Mehmet's attentions were so firmly focused on Constantinople, which he would soon win. The mihrab is decorated in plain blue-and-white tiles; the exterior has some highlights of blue tile. Outside, next to the mosque in what is surely the city's most serene resting place, there is a fountain ringed by 11 tombs. Among those buried here are Murat himself, Mehmet, and Mustafa, the eldest son of Süleyman the Magnificent, who was strangled in his father's tent. The Sultan's ambitious wife, Roxelana, had persuaded her husband that Mustafa was a traitor.

Across the mosque's park is the **17th-Century House,** an old Ottoman home that is now a museum, complete with authentic period carpets and furniture. For a glimpse into another day's "Lifestyles of the Rich and Famous," take a look. *Kaplıca Cad. Admission: $1. Open Tues.–Sun. 8:30–noon and 1–5.*

Find your way down the hill to Çekirge Caddesi. Dominating the view is the refreshingly green **Kültür Park** (Culture Park). Many Turkish towns have such a park, with restaurants, tea gardens, a pond with paddleboats, a sports stadium, and a Ferris wheel. This park is quite large, stretching for about a dozen city blocks and containing Bursa's **Arkeoloji Müsezi** (archaeological museum). The museum is pleasant enough, with its Roman coins and other artifacts, but there are better in Istanbul, Ankara, and elsewhere. (The same goes for the small **Atatürk Museum,** with old-fashioned furniture and a few exhibits on the great leader's life, located across Çekirge Caddesi.) *Archaeological Museum, on s. side of park, where Cemal Nadir Cad. turns into Çekirge Cad., tel. 224/220–3695. Admission: $2. Open Tues.–Sun. 8:30–noon and 1–5:30.*

The affluent suburb called Çekirge starts here and continues west. Bursa has been a spa town since Roman times; the thermal springs run along these slopes, and many of the hotels here offer mineral baths as a much-sought-after amenity.

Bursa is also the jumping-off point for excursions to **Uludağ,** where you will find a lush national park and Turkey's most popular ski resort. To fully appreciate why the town is called Green Bursa, take the 30-minute ride up the *teleferik* (cable car) from Namazgah Caddesi to the mountain's summit for a panoramic view. You can also make the hour-long drive, taking Çekirge Caddesi west. All Uludağ resort hotels are in an area near the highest peak, called Oteller. From here you can reach wonderfully undeveloped spots for hiking during the summer, at blissfully cool temperatures. *Teleferik, tel. 224/221–3635. Fare: $8 round-trip. Park admission for cars: $2.50. Teleferik operates year-round, every 30 or 40 min. during daylight.*

Off the Beaten Track

If you're heading on to Çanakkale and the Aegean coast, consider taking a break at **Kuş Cenneti National Park,** beside Lake Kuş. There are benches and tables for picnics, a viewing tower for birdwatching, and a small information center with exhibits describing the 200 species of bird that visit the park. Take Route 200 west about 100 kilometers (62 miles); you should see signs for the park before Bandırma.

Shopping

In Bursa the **Bedestan,** the covered bazaar behind the Ulu Cami, is where the action is from 8 to 5 Monday through Saturday. As is traditional, each section is dominated by a particular trade: jewelers, silk weavers, antiques dealers. The **Koza Han** section, in a historic courtyard by the eastern entrance, is the center of the silk trade. The **Emir Han,** in the southwestern section, is another silk market and has a lovely fountain and courtyard tea garden. These hans are particularly lively in June and September, the silk harvesting months, when buyers swarm in from around the country to place orders. Bursa has been a center of the silk industry since the coming of the Ottoman sultans and remains a good place to buy silk scarves, raw-silk fabric by the yard, and other silk products.

Antiques are to be found in the small **Eski Aynalı Çarşı** section of the bazaar. Of particular note is a shop called **Karagöz,** which has a fine collection of old copper and brass, kilims, jewelry, and the translucent, vividly colored shadow-play puppets from which the store takes its name.

Sports

Uludağ, 33 kilometers (21 miles) southwest of Bursa, is Turkey's largest ski resort. It has 30 intermediate and beginner trails, with five chair lifts and six T-bars. There are ski-rental shops at the base of the mountain. Prime season is January–April, and the resort is packed on weekends.

Dining and Lodging

While restaurants in this area are not generally up to Istanbul standards, there are a number of good choices, the fanciest being those at the Çelik and Dilmen hotels. For details and price-category definitions, *see* Staying in Turkey in Chapter 1, Essential Information.

Bursa
Dining

Cumurcul. This old house converted into a restaurant in the Çekirge section of town is a local favorite. Grilled meats and fish are attentively prepared; ask the waiters to show you what's freshest. In addition to the usual cold mezes, there is a selection of hot starters, including a particularly tasty borek. *Çekirge Cad., tel. 224/235-3707. Reservations advised. AE, MC, V. $$*

Hacı Bey. Arguments never end over where to find the best Bursa kebab, but this downtown stop is always a contender. The setting is basic cafeteria-style, but the food is what counts. *Ünlü Cad., Yılmaz İş Han, tel. 224/221-6440. No reservations. No credit cards. $*

Kepabçı Iskender. Bursa is famous for the main dish served here: Iskender (or Alexander's) Kebap, skewer-grilled slivers of meat and pita bread immersed in a rich tomato sauce topped with butter and yogurt. *Ünlü Cad. 7, Heykel, tel. 224/221-4615. No reservations. No credit cards. $*

★ **Özömür Koftecisi.** *Köfte*, a rich, grilled patty of ground beef or lamb, is a regional specialty, and that's pretty much the thing to get here. The restaurant gets the nod over others thanks to its charming location in the covered market, by the Ulu Cami. *Ulucami Cad. 7, no phone. No reservations. No credit cards. $*

Selçuk. Another Kültür Park restaurant with the usual array of Turkish specialties, this one offers a shady terrace and slightly lower prices than its neighbors. *Kültür Park, tel. 224/220-9696. Reservations not necessary. No credit cards. $*

Lodging

★ **Çelik Palas.** This is quite the poshest hotel in Bursa. Its main attraction is its domed, Roman-style pool fed by hot springs; you will find your fellow guests constantly traipsing through the hallways in their robes en route. The pool, by the way, was where the late king of Libya was when he learned that Colonel Mu'ammar Qaddafi had taken over his country. The hotel has a lively 1930s design scheme, and some rooms have balconies. *Çekirge Cad. 79, tel. 224/233-3800, fax 224/236-1910. 173 rooms with bath. Facilities: restaurant, bar, nightclub, disco, thermal pool. AE, MC, V. $$$$*

Hotel Dilmen. The lobby in this fancy, modern hotel in the Çekirge section is accented by gleaming brass and stained-glass windows. Rooms, however, are simply furnished. There are the requisite thermal baths, a pleasant garden terrace and bar, and views of the valley. *1 Murat Cad. 20, tel. 224/233-9500, fax 224/235-2568. 98 rooms with bath. Facilities: restaurant, bar, thermal pool, fitness room. MC, V. $$$*

Ada Palas. The thermal pool of this hotel near the Kültür Park is inviting, and the price tag is lower than that at the nearby Çelik. Rooms are unexceptional but in good condition, thanks to a recent renovation. *1 Murat Cad. 21, tel. 224/233-3990, fax 224/236-4656. 39 rooms with bath. Facilities: thermal pool. V. $$*

Hotel Dikmen. This hotel is not to be confused with the Dilmen (*see above*). Although less grand than Çekirge hotels, the Dıkmen is conveniently located downtown. It has large, plain guest rooms, a spacious lobby, and a sunny garden with a marble fountain. It is often filled by tour groups. *Fevzi Çakmak Cad. 78, tel. 224/224-1840, fax*

224/224–1844. 53 rooms with bath. Facilities: restaurant, bar. No credit cards. $$

İznik
Dining

İznik Göl Restaurant. This lakeside eatery offers pleasant seating outdoors under orange awnings. The menu consists of the typical Turkish fare, with fresh appetizers and grills; the only difference is the local specialty: *yayın* (eel) from the lake, either fried or marinated and grilled on skewers with onions, peppers, and bay leaves. The cat that adopted the restaurant will gladly accept your leftovers. *Göl Kenarı, tel. 224/757–2448. Reservations necessary on weekends. No credit cards. $–$$*

Kırık Çatal. Open since 1964, this restaurant is run by the same people who manage the Burcum Motel. No one knows why or how it got its name, which means "broken fork." The great variety of fresh appetizers and hot main dishes, including the local eel, are served on an open-air terrace. *Göl Kenarı, tel. 224/757–1576. Reservations necessary for large groups. No credit cards. $–$$*

Lodging

Çamlık Motel. In this quiet and newly expanded lakeshore establishment, rooms are sparsely furnished and unadorned, but the garden on the lake is pleasant and doubles as a café. *Göl Kenarı, tel. 224/757–1362, fax 224/757–1631. 33 rooms with bath. No credit cards. $*

Motel Burcum. This is another lakeside hotel with sparsely furnished rooms. The loudspeakers in the adjacent café could be a bother for those who like it quiet, but the personnel is friendly and the restaurant has a diverse choice of fresh vegetable and meat dishes. *Göl Kenarı, tel. 224/757–1011. 25 rooms with bath. V. $*

Termal
Dining and Lodging
★

Turban Yalova Termal Çamlık Oteli. This pleasant hotel adjoining the baths sits on a ridge overlooking the resort's grounds and dates from Termal's modern heyday in the 1930s. It has a good Turkish restaurant and an array of modern, white-tile tubs filled with its thermal waters. Guest rooms in the back are less expensive, and in the off-season rates drop significantly. *Tel. 216/835–7410, fax 216/835–7413. 83 rooms with bath. Facilities: restaurant, thermal baths. DC, MC, V. $$*

Turban Yalova Termal Çınar Oteli. This hotel has the same ownership, management, accommodations, and phone number as the Çamlık (*see above*). It is a bit less atmospheric because it doesn't have as good a view, but it's still comfortable. Its baths have old-fashioned gray-marble tubs like those at the Sultan baths. Book here if the Çamlık is full. *Tel. 216/835–7410, fax 216/835–7413. 18 rooms with bath. Facilities: restaurant, thermal baths. DC, MC, V. $$*

Uludağ
Dining and Lodging

Although many establishments here are open only in winter, the following are open all year. Dining options in the area are pretty much limited to the hotels.

Grand Hotel Yazıcı. This slant-roof, seven-story hotel is probably the most luxurious of the resorts, with the most facilities. The rooms are pleasant, the lobby huge and showy. Your lasting impressions will probably involve acres of marble and the boisterous noise from the hotel's Greek taverna. *Oteller Mevkii, tel. 224/285–2050, fax 224/285–2048. 162 rooms with bath. Facilities: restaurant, bar, nightclub, disco, pool, fitness room, sauna, café, bank, 2 tennis courts, basketball court. MC, V. $$–$$$*

Otel Beceren. This Turkish version of the Alpine ski lodge gets the nod for service, and its chalet decor certainly makes sense in the area. The hotel is not as well equipped as the Yazıcı, however. *Oteller Mevkii, tel. 224/285–2111, fax 224/285–2119. 80 rooms with bath. Facilities: restaurant, bar, pool, sauna. No credit cards. $$–$$$*

Büyük Otel. The Büyük was the first lodge on the mountain when it was built 30 or so years ago, and despite its small rooms it remains popular. If your taste runs to the more old-fashioned, you'll prefer this low-slung property to its modern neighbors. *Oteller Mevkii, tel. 224/285–2216, fax 224/285–2220. 98 rooms with bath. Facilities: restaurant, bar, outdoor pool, disco. No credit cards. $$*

Nightlife

Bursa

The **Kervansaray Termal Hotel** (Çekirge Meydanı, tel. 224/233–9300) has a wonderful floor show, with noted local singers and belly dancers. The presentation is more traditional and less touristy than similar offerings in Istanbul, although there is no skimping on the glitz. The price tag is substantial, too—about $30 per person with dinner. The **Çelik Palas** (*see* Lodging, *above*) has a somewhat more refined lounge act.

Uludağ

The **Büyük Otel** and **Grand Hotel Yazıcı** (*see* Dining and Lodging, *above*) have lively discos. The settings are far from Studio 54–flashy, but there are usually plenty of people out for fun.

5 The Aegean Coast

Travelers, it seems, have flocked to the Aegean coast for as long as there have been travelers. In the 2nd century AD, the Greek often considered the first travel writer, Pausanias, gave a rave review to the region, known to him as Ionia—several of the most important members of the alliance of 12 ancient Greek cities known as the Ionian League were here. "The wonders of Ionia are numerous," he wrote. "The Ionian country has excellently tempered seasons, and its sanctuaries are unrivaled, the Ephesian sanctuary for its size and wealth and the Milesian sanctuary at Brandchidai [known to the Greeks as Didyma and to Turks today as Didim]. You would gasp at the Herakleion at Erythrai and Athena's Temple at Priene." Pausanias was also fond of the countryside around Ephesus, the bay near ancient Erythrai, north of Çesme, which had what he called "the healthiest sea-water baths in Ionia," and the river Meles near Smyrna, present-day İzmir, which boasted "the finest water, and a cave at its springs where they say Homer wrote his poetry."

Though not all the wonders Pausanias described are visible today, enough are left to give you a good idea of what life was like when this part of the world could fairly have been called the center of the universe. The dusty yellow road signs that point out historical sites are everywhere here: Some have yet to be excavated, while others excavated years ago are once again returning to a wild state. The riches that remain include some of the finest reconstructed Greek and Roman cities in the world, including the fabled Troy, Pergamum, Ephesus, and Aphrodisias. Great chunks of stone from these and other antique sites were carted off for use in the construction of Byzantine and later monuments; and in the 19th century, before Turkey outlawed the exportation of antiquities, some of the best finds— statues, friezes, inscriptions, and other material—were crated up and shipped off to Europe by the foreign archaeological teams. They can now be seen in institutions such as the British Museum in London and Berlin's great Pergamonmuseum.

Yet even without the great friezes and statuary, all the sites, grand and small, have more atmosphere than a Cecil B. deMille epic. In summer all are best explored early in the morning or late in the afternoon, when the heat eases up and there are smaller crowds. As for the middle of the day, you can always head for one of the fine sandy beaches that line the coast—after all, the Aegean is more than a museum of classical antiquity.

Summer's mix of constant sunshine and inviting beaches has made the area a center for hedonism as well, and there are two Club Meds and booming resort towns like Bodrum, which is called the Turkish Saint-Tropez by its boosters.

One unfortunate by-product of centuries of popularity is overdevelopment. In the rush to promote tourism, acres of coastline have been despoiled by concrete. Though some vacation developments are attractive, Mediterranean-style communities with whitewashed walls and red tile roofs, others are half-built eyesores, all concrete skeletons and gouged-out earth. Fortunately, the Turks seem to be learning from their experience with boom-and-bust cycles and have lately created several slow-growth and nondevelopment zones, in areas such as the coastline between Alexandria Troas and Behramkale, and out along the Datça peninsula. A few years back, environmentalists convinced the Turkish government to scrap plans for a hotel zone at Dalyan, just north of the point where the Aegean gives way to the Mediterranean, and create a nature preserve instead. It is a strategy that all who love Turkey applaud.

Essential Information

Important Addresses and Numbers

Tourist Information There are tourist offices in **Ayvalık** (Yat Limanı Karşısı, tel. 266/312–2222), **Bergama** (Zafer Mah. İzmir Cad. 54, tel. 232/633–1862), **Bodrum** (Eylül Meyd. 12, tel. 252/316–1091), **Çanakkale** (İskele Meyd. 67, tel. 286/217–1187), **Çesme** (İskele Meyd. 8, tel. 232/712–6653), **İzmir** (Atatürk Cad. 418, Alsancak, tel. 232/422–0207, and Gaziosmanpasa Bul. 1/C, tel. 232/484–2147), **Kuşadası** (İskele Meyd., tel. 256/614–1103), and **Selçuk** (Atatürk Mah., Agora Çarsisi 35, tel. 232/892–6328).

Consulates They're in İzmir for the **United States** (Atatürk Cad. 92, tel. 232/421–3643) and the **United Kingdom** (Mahmut Esat Bozkurt Sok. 49, tel. 232/421–1795). There's no Canadian consulate.

Emergencies **Tourist Police** (tel. 252/316–1009 in Bodrum, tel. 232/421–8652 in İzmir).

Arriving and Departing by Plane

Airports and Airlines The major airport serving the region is **Adnan Menderes Airport,** 25 kilometers (16 miles) south of İzmir; **Turkish Airlines** (THY, tel. 212/252–1106 in Istanbul) and **Istanbul Airlines** (tel. 212/509–2124 or 212/509–1641 in Istanbul) make the hour-long flight direct from Istanbul.

THY offers two other options in summer: Fly nonstop from London or Frankfurt into İzmir. Or connect through Istanbul to **Dalaman Airport** on the Mediterranean coast, near Marmaris, and drive the Aegean from south to north. Dalaman is 395 kilometers (237 miles) from İzmir.

Arriving and Departing by Car, Train, Bus, and Boat

By Car A car is a definite plus for exploring this region, since it allows you to stop at will at picturesque towns and to track down lesser-known ruins and less-crowded beaches. However, it's a long haul from Istanbul to İzmir—666 kilometers (411 miles), an exhausting seven- or eight-hour drive. If you opt to make this trip, pick up Route 200 heading west toward Çanakkale. From there, the E24 follows the coast south all the way to Kuşadası, where it turns inland toward Antalya. Route 525 continues along the coast, past Priene and Miletus; Route 330 branches off in Bodrum and connects with the main Mediterranean highways.

By Train Trains to İzmir from Istanbul take a good 10 to 12 hours. From Istanbul, you start out by taking a boat across the Sea of Marmara, and about four hours later you connect with a train at Bandırma. Take the morning, rather than night, departure if you want to enjoy the scenery of the cruise and the northern Aegean. Contact **Turkish Maritime Lines** (Rihtim Cad. 1, Karaköy, tel. 212/249–9222) in Istanbul for schedules and fares.

By Bus Buses, typically modern and air-conditioned, operate between all the towns on the itinerary and from there depart for the major archaeological sites. Typical travel times are: Istanbul to Çanakkale, six hours; Çanakkale to İzmir (via Bergama, Ayvalık, and Ayvacık), six hours; İzmir to Bodrum, 3½ hours.

By Boat From Gelibolu (Gallipoli), you can reach Çanakkale by car and pas-
From Gelibolu senger ferry across the Dardanelles, the straits dividing Europe
and Asia. Boats depart on the hour from Eceabat, near the battlefields, about 330 kilometers (200 miles) and a three- or four-hour
drive from Istanbul. The crossing takes about 30 minutes, and the
cost is $6 for a car and driver and 50¢ per additional passenger and
those without a car.

From Istanbul **Turkish Maritime Lines** (*see above*) operates passenger and car ferry
services to İzmir. Boats leave in the afternoon and arrive the next
morning, and fares range from $25 for a single seat to $110 for a suite
accommodating from two to four. In summer there is also service between İzmir and Marseille, Genoa, Venice, and Piraeus, the port for
Athens.

Getting Around

By Car Except around İzmir, where heavy and hectic traffic requires serious concentration to keep you from getting lost, the highways are
generally in good condition, the traffic fairly light, and the main attractions relatively close together. As you head south, distances are:
Çanakkale to Bergama, 245 kilometers (151 miles); Bergama to İz-
mir, 98 kilometers (60 miles); İzmir to Ephesus, 76 kilometers (47
miles); Ephesus to Bodrum, 172 kilometers (106 miles).

Car Rentals **İzmir** has Avis (tel. 232/421–1226), Budget (tel. 232/425–8012),
Europcar/National (tel. 232/425–4698), and Hertz (tel. 232/421–
7002).

By Bus Though it's slower and more restrictive than traveling by car, bus
travel is a viable option if you don't want to rent a car. It's exceptionally inexpensive, as fares are rarely more than a few dollars, and all
the towns and attractions are well served by bus. When you arrive at
the main bus station for one town, simply ask about connecting service to the next town along the line.

By Boat The Aegean coast is one of the more popular routes for the international yachting crowd—not surprisingly, since seeing the coast by
boat is so pleasant. Usually, harbors are right in the city center, and
the main archaeological sites are a cheap and easy cab ride away.
Kuşadası and Bodrum are charter centers; contact local tourist
boards or the Turkish Culture and Information Office in New York
(*see* Before You Go in Chapter 1, Essential Information) for information and listings of yacht agencies.

Guided Tours

Travel agencies in all the major towns offer tours of the historical
sites.

Ayvalık At the harbor, dozens of small tour boats offer two-hour outings
along the coast and to nearby islands (around $5, $10 including a
meal).

İzmir **Egetur Travel** (Talat Paşa Bul. 2/B, tel. 232/421–7925) is the local
American Express representative.

Kuşadası **Akdeniz Turizm** (Atatürk Bul. 26, tel. 256/614–1140) and **Toya
Turizm Seyahat Acentesi** (Atatürk Bul. 60, tel. 256/614–3344), as
well as travel agencies along Teyyare Caddesi, offer escorted tours
to Ephesus; to Priene, Miletus, and Didyma; and to Aphrodisias and
Pamukkale.

Exploring the
Aegean Coast

The following tours start in the north at Çanakkale and work their way south to Bodrum, with one detour inland to the ruins at Aphrodisias and the natural hot springs of Pamukkale.

Highlights for First-Time Visitors

Akçay's Gulf of Edremit strand, Beaches
Anzac Memorial, Gallipoli (Gelibolu), Tour 1
Aphrodisias, Tour 3
Assos, Tour 1
Ayvalık, Tour 1
Beach at Gümüşük, Beaches
Ephesus, Tour 4
Pamukkale's hot pools, Tour 3
Pergamum, Tour 1
Priene, Tour 4

Tour 1: The Northern Aegean

The northern Aegean offers rich exploring. You start at the tip of the Çanakkale peninsula and the battlefields of Gallipoli, pass through legendary Troy, detour along one of Turkey's grandest back-country drives, stop at the clifftop ruins of ancient Pergamum, and take a beach break before ending up on the outskirts of İzmir. You will need at least two overnights to cover the ground comfortably, though you could easily spend a whole week.

Numbers in the margin correspond to points of interest on the Aegean Coast map.

❶ **Çanakkale,** which marks the northernmost tip of the Aegean coast, is an agricultural center and garrison town with drab, utilitarian architecture and few frills. Yet it remains the guardian of the Dardanelles, the narrow straits that separate Europe from Asia and connect the Aegean with the Sea of Marmara. This strategic point has been fought over since the days of the Trojan War. En route to Greece, the invading armies of the Persian conqueror Xerxes used a bridge made of boats to cross the straits in 480 BC; the Spartans crushed the Athenians here in 404 BC, effectively ending the Peloponnesian War. A century later, the straits were crossed by Alexander the Great (356–323 BC, ruled 336–323) on his march from Macedonia to conquer Asia, and, in the 14th century, provided the nascent Ottoman Empire with its first access to Europe. In March and April of 1915, during World War I, the Allied Powers tried to breach Çanakkale's defenses in the infamous Gallipoli campaign, devised by the young Winston Churchill, then Lord of the Admiralty. The goal was to capture Istanbul and control the entire waterway from the Aegean to the Black Sea. After nine months and bloody fighting that left some 250,000 casualties on each side, the Allies admitted defeat and retreated, beaten by the superior strategy of Lieutenant-Colonel Mustafa Kemal—the man who would later be called Atatürk.

The ferry docks abut the town's main square, **İskele Meydanı** (Docks Square), and signs all over town direct you to the "Feribot." For an overview of the straits and a closer look at Çanakkale's military his-

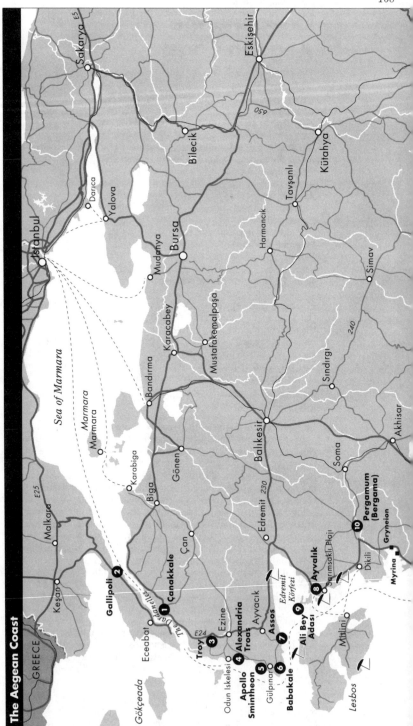

The Aegean Coast

GREECE

Keşan

Malkara

E25

Gökçeada

Eceabat

Gallipoli

2

1 Çanakkale

The Dardanelles

Odun İskelesi

Troy **3**

Ezine

E24

Alexandria Troas **4**

Apollo Smintheon

Gülpınar **5**

6

Babakale

Ayvacık

Assos **7**

Ali Bey Adası

9

Edremit Körfezi

8 Ayvalık

Sarımsaklı Plajı

Lesbos

Mitlini

Dikili

10 Pergamum (Bergama)

Gryneion

Myrina

İstanbul

Darıca

Yalova

Mudanya

Bursa

Karacabey

Karabiga

Biga

Çan

Gönen

Bandırma

Sea of Marmara

Marmara

Marmara

Bilecik

Mustafakemalpaşa

Balıkesir

Edremit

230

Sindırgı

Soma

Akhisar

Eskişehir

Kütahya

650

Tavşanlı

Harmancık

Simav

240

Sakarya E5

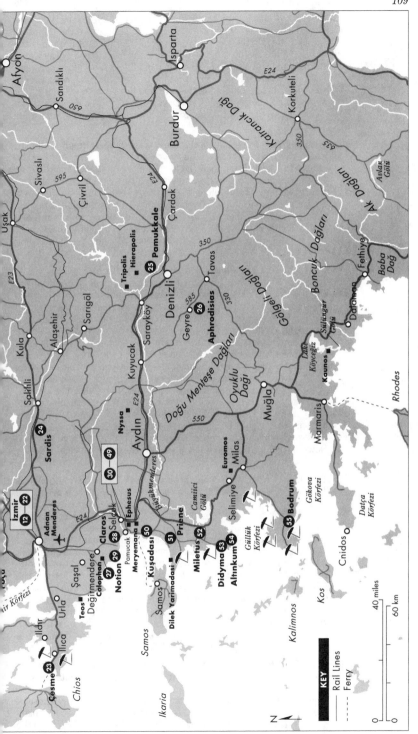

tory, head south along the waterfront promenade to the **Askeri Ve Deniz Müzesi** (Army and Navy Museum). It occupies the imposing Çanak Kale (Fortress of Çanak), built in the 15th century under the aegis of Mehmet the Conqueror. Inside the high, sturdy gray walls, there is much weaponry on display, including dozens of cannons, ancient and modern, but the real reason to come here is for the sweeping view of the mouth of the Dardanelles and the Aegean. *On waterfront, 3 blocks s. of ferry dock. Admission free. Museum open Tues.–Thurs. and Sat.–Sun. 9–noon and 1:30–5. Fortress grounds open daily until 10.*

❷ To experience something of the great tragedy of **Gallipoli** (Gelibolu, in Turkish), return to the main square and take the ferry across the straits to Eceabat and visit the 31 military cemeteries that line the former battlefields, now a war memorial; two sections mark the two major battlegrounds—along the coast between Kabatepe and Suvla Bay, and at Cape Helles. If you don't have a car, either hire a taxi for the day (about $20) or sign up for the half-day excursion from **Troy-Anzac Tours** (near the clock tower on the south side of İskele Meyd., tel. 286/217–5849 or 286/217–5867; about $15 per head, including breakfast).

From the ferry landing, it's a 20-minute drive east via the single road skirting the coast. In 1994 a major forest fire destroyed many of the trees in the region. Start with the small but poignant exhibit of photographs at Kabatepe. There are several cemeteries here, all with long, mesmerizing rows of austere white crosses. The Anzac Memorial at Lone Pine Cemetery bears the names of the Australian and New Zealand troops killed during the battle. Farther on along the same road is the French cemetery and the Turkish trenches where Atatürk's men dug themselves in. You can also look down on Sulva Bay as the Turkish defenders did and imagine the coming onslaught. At Cape Helles, there is a massive, four-pillared memorial to Turkey's own war dead, more than 50,000. When returning on the ferry to Çanakkale, look for the memorials to the two world wars carved into the cliffs on the European side. The earlier reads: "Stop, O passerby. This earth you tread unawares is where an age was lost. Bow and listen, for this quiet place is where the heart of a nation throbs."

❸ The ruins of what many scholars believe to be ancient **Troy,** known as Truva to the Turks and Ilion to the Greeks, are 32 kilometers (20 miles) southwest of Çanakkale, about 40 minutes via the E24. Although Troy was long thought to be simply an imaginary city created by the blind poet Homer in his epic *Iliad*, the site was excavated in the 1870s by Heinrich Schliemann, a minister's son and German businessman who had struck it rich in California's gold rush. While scholars scoffed, he poured his wealth into the excavations and had the last laugh: He found the remains not only of the fabled Troy but also of nine successive civilizations, one on top of the other, dating back 5,000 years (and now known among archaeologists as Troy I–IX). Subsequent excavations during the 1930s revealed 38 additional layers of settlements. A new dig by a German team, meanwhile, has revealed the footings of a late Bronze Age wall; the find enlarges the supposed Troy by fivefold.

Still, it is Homer's Troy that fascinates most. Archaeologists currently believe that the Troy of the Trojan War represents the seventh layer (1300 BC–900 BC), though no one is quite certain. Schliemann found a hoard of jewels that he believed were those of the mythological King Priam, but they have more recently been dated to the much earlier Troy II (2600 BC–2300 BC). Adding to the controversy that surrounded his discoveries even then, Schliemann smuggled the jewels out of the country and his wife was seen wearing them at fashionable social events. Schliemann later donated them to Berlin's Pergamonmuseum; they disappeared during World War II. They reappeared as recently as 1993, when Moscow announced that their State Pushkin Museum of Fine Arts housed the lost "treasure of Priam," which had disappeared during the Red Army's sack of Berlin. Although Germany, Greece, and Turkey all have pressed claims to the treasure, recent custom dictates that archaeological finds belong to the country in which they were originally found.

As Homer's story was written some 500 years after the war—generally believed to have taken place around 1250 BC—it is hard to say how much of it is history and how much is invention. Nonetheless, it makes for a romantic tale. Paris, the son of King Priam, abducted the beautiful Helen, wife of King Menelaus of Sparta, and fled with her to Troy. Menelaus enlisted the aid of his brother, King Agamemnon, and launched a thousand ships to get her back. His siege lasted 10 years and involved such ancient notables as Achilles, Hector, and the crafty Odysseus, King of Ithaca. It was Odysseus who ended the war, after ordering a huge wooden horse to be built. When it was completed, the Greeks retreated to their ships and pretended to sail away. The Trojans hauled the trophy into their walled city and celebrated their victory. Under cover of dark, the Greek ships returned, and the attackers at last gained entry to Troy, after soldiers hidden inside the horse crept out and opened the city's gates. Hence the saying "Beware of Greeks bearing gifts."

What you will see today depends on your imagination. Some find the site highly suggestive, with its remnants of massive, rough-hewn walls, paved chariot ramp, and strategic view over the coastal plains to the sea. Others consider it an unimpressive row of trenches with piles of earth and stone. Considering Troy's fame (and the difficulties involved in conquering it), the city is surprisingly small. The best-preserved features are from the Roman city, with its *bouleuterion* (assembly building), the site's most complete structure, and small theater. There is an exhibit space with little to see, really (all the good stuff has been hauled off to Istanbul and Ankara); a site plan shows you the general layout and marks the beginning of a signposted path leading to key features from several of the historic civilizations. However, labeling is cursory, so to appreciate Troy's significance fully, it's best to come prepared with a detailed history like scholar George Bean's *Aegean Turkey* (W. W. Norton, 1978) or to take a guided tour. English-speaking guides may or may not be available at the site; if you don't want to take your chances, arrange a tour in advance with a travel agent. As for the oft-debated horse, well, he's there, a giant wooden fellow stuck out near the parking area, duly entertaining to children, who climb up inside for a look around. *Follow signs from Rte. E24, no phone. Admission: $2.50. Open daily 8–7.*

Unless time is short, leave the E24 and take the scenic unnumbered coast road south 73 kilometers (45 miles) to Assos, watching for the signs to Gülpinar or Geyikli, the major towns along the route. While there is nothing particularly wrong with the E24, the coast road winds through olive groves, cotton fields, and the occasional small village, past hidden ruins, often backed by exceptional sea views. Unlike much of the rest of the Aegean region, this area is blissfully undeveloped, and herds of goats and sheep are about the only traffic you will encounter. Some of that has unfortunately begun to change.

Especially around Troy, which was a strict NATO military zone until the collapse of the Soviet Union, land developers have started to creep in. Manfred Korfmann, the archaeologist working on the Troy excavation, has proposed that the whole area should be declared a UNESCO World Cultural Heritage Zone.

About 30 kilometers (18 miles) south of Troy on the coast road, you should pass through a town called Odun Iskelesi. South of here another 5 kilometers (3 miles), signs mark the ruins of **Alexandria Troas.** Founded at Alexander the Great's behest around 330 BC, the city became a wealthy commercial center and the region's main port. At one time the city, formerly called Antigonia, surpassed Troy in its control over the traffic between the Aegean and the Sea of Marmara and was even considered as a capital for the Roman and Byzantine empires. The seaside location that won it prosperity also invited plundering by raiders, which led to its demise. Saint Paul visited twice on missionary journeys in the middle of the 1st century AD, proceeding by land to Assos at the end of the second trip. In the 16th and 17th centuries, when the city was called Eski Stamboul (old Istanbul), Ottoman architects had stones hauled from here to Istanbul for use in the building of imperial mosques, the Blue Mosque in particular. Visit today not so much to see the scanty ruins—the remnants of the city's monumental baths and its aqueduct—as for the setting, tucked away in a deserted stretch of wilderness. Shrubs and weeds cover the pottery-strewn ruins, which have patches of cultivated land between them. You can often have it all to yourself.

In the village Gülpinar, about 20 kilometers (12 miles) south of Alexandria Troas via the coast road, is a small temple to **Apollo Smintheon** dating to the 2nd century BC. Smintheus—one of the sun god's many names, meaning "killer of mice"—alludes to a problem that Teucer, the town's founder, had with mice eating his soldiers' bowstrings. The temple is just a trifle, but it has some interesting carved pillars and is surrounded by wild pomegranate trees.

You can detour, if you like, 10 kilometers (6 miles) southwest to **Babakale** at the southern tip of the Çanakkale peninsula. There is a minuscule, sleepy fishing village with a 16th-century castle above the harbor. No one is sure who built the castle, only that it was a haven for pirates until a Turkish naval officer named Mustafa Paşa routed them out in the late 18th century. Mustafa Paşa went on to build a small mosque and *hamam* (Turkish bath) in the village. Babakale is not the place to visit for monuments, which are decidedly minor, but for its wholly unspoiled flavor.

The real payoff for this excursion along the coast is Behramkale (just under 20 kilometers, or 12 miles, southeast of Gülpinar), known in ancient times as **Assos.** As you approach, the road forks, one route going up to the ancient village atop the hill and the other twisting precariously down to the tiny modern port (it's harrowing at night, so arrive before dark). The port is truly a marvel, a tiny hamlet pressed against the sheer cliff walls, transformed into a low-key yet trendy resort. There are a few small hotels, built of volcanic rock, that seem much older than they are, a fleet of fishing boats, and a small, rocky beach. The effect is charming. The crowd is an interesting mix of Turkish elite, artists, and intellectuals.

The ruins of Assos, on a site measuring about five square city blocks, lie at the top of the hill. Founded about 1000 BC by Aeolian Greeks, the city was successively ruled by Lydians, Persians, Pergamenes, Romans, and Byzantines, until Sultan Orhan Gazi (1288–1360) took it over for the Ottomans in 1330. Aristotle is said to have spent some time here in the 4th century BC, and Saint Paul stopped here en route to Miletus, where he visited church elders in about AD 55. The old stone village just under the ruins is unpretentious and little changed in the last century, though the carpet and trinket sellers have grown more aggressive of late. Abandon your car on one of the wider streets and make your way up the steep, cobbled lanes to the top of the acropolis, where you will be rewarded with a sensational view of the coastline and, in the distance, the Greek island of Lesbos, whose citizens were Assos's original settlers. The site's layout resembles Pergamum's, with the gymnasium, theater, *agora* (marketplace), and, carved into the hillside below the summit of the acropolis, the site of the **Temple of Athena** (circa 530 BC), which has splendid sea views and is being reconstructed. A more modern addition to the site is the **Murad Hüdavendigâr Mosque,** built in the late 14th century. It is very simple, a dome atop a square, with little decoration. The Greek crosses carved into the lintel over the door indicate that the Ottomans used building material from an earlier church, possibly one on the same site. Back down the slope, on the road toward the port, there is a parking area for the **necropolis** and city walls stretching 3 kilometers (2 miles). Assos was known for its sarcophagi, made of local limestone, which were shipped throughout the Greek world. Unfortunately, most of the tombs here are broken into pieces.

Heading back toward the E24 and the town of Ayvacık (19 kilometers, or 11 miles, northeast), you'll pass an old Ottoman bridge, built in the 1300s, and a pine forest near the village of Passaköy. Route E24/550 leads around the **Edremit Körfezi** (Gulf of Edremit), a pleasant stretch of olive groves, pine forests, and small beach resorts patronized more by Turks than by foreign visitors. Colorful teahouses surrounded by gardens sprawl along the shores, and good, casual seafood restaurants abound, most of them with picnic tables and benches on open terraces, serving plates heaped with oysters. The major resort areas are **Akçay,** notable for its long stretch of beach, and **Ören,** which has campgrounds nearby. Founded in 1443 BC and once known as Adramyttion, Edremit itself is one of Asia Minor's oldest settlements, though with virtually no historic remains. Today's Edremit is famous for the quality and abundance of its olives and olive oils.

8 **Ayvalık,** 131 kilometers (81 miles) south of Assos on the E24, is a delightful but rapidly growing coastal town. It first appears in Ottoman records at the late date of 1770, when an Ottoman naval hero, Gazi Hasan Paşa, was aided by the local Greek community after his ship sank nearby. Soon after, the town was granted autonomy, perhaps as a gesture of gratitude, and the Muslim population was moved to outlying villages, leaving the Greeks to prosper in the olive oil trade. In 1803, an academy was founded following Plato's instructions, with courses in Attic Greek, physics, logic, philosophy, rhetoric, and mathematics. (Unfortunately, nothing remains of the school today.) It all came to a crashing halt at the close of World War I, when the Greeks invaded Turkey and claimed the Aegean coast. The Turks ousted the Greek army in 1922, and the entire Greek community of Ayvalık was deported.

What you will see today is some of the finest 19th-century Greek-style architecture in Turkey. Unlike the typical Ottoman house (tall, narrow, and built of wood, with an overhanging bay window), Greek buildings are stone, with classic triangular pediments above a square box. The best way to explore is to turn your back to the Aegean and wander the tiny side streets leading up the hill into the heart of the old residential quarter (try Talat Paşa Caddesi and Gümrük Caddesi). Several historic churches in town have been converted into mosques: St. John's is now the **Saatli Cami** (Clock Mosque); St. George's is now the **Çinarlı Cami** (Plane Tree Mosque). The **Taxiarchis Church,** now a museum, displays a remarkable series of paintings on fish skin depicting the life of Christ. After wandering through town, take Talat Paşa Caddesi or Gümrük Caddesi back down the hill, cross Inönü Caddesi, and keep going (you will be on the spit of land behind the harbor) until you reach Mareşal Cakmak Caddesi (it's only a block or two past Inönü Caddesi). Amid several old buildings here you will find the 19th-century **French Embassy,** just behind the post office. It still carries the sign "L'Union de Paris" atop its door, a reminder of Ayvalık's importance in an earlier day.

❾ From Ayvalık, you can drive or take a boat to **Ali Bey Adası** (also known as Cunda Island). Like Ayvalık, it was once predominantly Greek, and some Greek is still spoken here. Today, it is a delightful fishing town, whose good seafood restaurants, lining the atmospheric quay, are noted for their grilled *çipura* (a local fish) and dishes made with octopus, served grilled, fried, or in a cold seafood salad, usually with oil and vinegar. The island's Greek houses are well preserved and varied, and the 19th-century **St. Nicholas Church** in the middle of town is a must-see. Though the frescoes have been defaced—the eyes of the apostles have been gouged out—there is an amusing depiction of Jonah with a whale that looks a lot like the grouper you could order for lunch. With its large cracks, caused by an earthquake in 1924, and the birds flying around its airy domes, the whole place has a ghostly air. If the church is closed, wait by the front door and someone will eventually come by to let you in.

From May through September, boats leave daily from Ayvalık for the Greek island of Lesbos (one in the morning, one in the late afternoon). The customs building and police station near Ayvalık's post office are the places to go for information. The formalities are fairly simple: You buy your ticket a day in advance and leave your passport behind, then pick up the necessary paperwork before departure. Round-trip tickets cost about $40 per person.

Before leaving Ayvalık, consider a rest on the 10-kilometer (6-mile) stretch of beach called **Sarmısaklı.** Take the main street, Atatürk Caddesi, west along the coast. The beachside resorts a few kilometers down provide a good place to stay overnight before tackling the ruins at Pergamum, 40 kilometers (24 miles) to the southeast from Ayvalık.

Time Out From Sarmısaklı, follow the signs leading up to **Şeytan Sofrası** (the Devil's Table). This summit provides the best vantage point in town, with a view of the archipelago, neighboring islands, and shimmering blue Aegean. The teahouse and bar here make this a popular destination for sunset-watching.

❿ To get to **Pergamum,** follow the signs along the E24 toward Bergama, the modern-day name of the ancient Greek-Roman site. If you're traveling by bus, be certain it is going all the way to Bergama, or you'll find yourself dropped off at the outskirts of the city, 8 kilometers (5 miles) from the main archaeological site. The attractions here are spread out over several square miles, so if you don't have a car, negotiate with a taxi driver in Bergama (you have to pass through the town anyway) to shuttle you from site to site—this shouldn't cost more than $10 or $20, depending on how long you plan to spend looking around. All told, you will probably want to spend half a day.

Pergamum was one of the ancient world's major powers, though its moment of glory was relatively brief. Led by a dynasty of maverick rulers, it rose to prominence during the 3rd and 2nd centuries BC. Impressed by the city's impregnable fortress, Lysimachus, one of Alexander the Great's generals, here stowed the booty he had accumulated while marching through Asia Minor. When Lysimachus was killed in 281 BC, Philetaerus (c. 343 BC–263 BC), the commander of Pergamum, claimed the fortune and holed himself up in the city. After defeating the horde of invading Gauls that had been sacking cities up and down the coast in 240 BC, the Pergamenes were celebrated throughout the Hellenic world as saviors. Philetaerus, who was succeeded by his nephew Eumenes I, was rumored to have been a eunuch because of an accident in childhood. The dynasty established by Philetaerus, known as the Attalids, ruled from then until 133 BC, when the mad Attalus III (circa 170 BC–133 BC) died and bequeathed the entire kingdom to Rome. By a liberal interpretation of his ambiguous bequest, his domain became the Roman Province of Asia and transformed Rome's economy with its wealth.

The city was a magnificent architectural and artistic center in its heyday—especially under the rule of Eumenes II (197 BC–159 BC), who lavished his great wealth on it. He built Pergamum's famous library, which contained 200,000 books. When it rivaled the great one in Alexandria, Egypt, the Egyptians banned the sale of papyrus to the city. Pergamum responded by developing a new paper—parchment—made from animal skins instead of reeds. This *charta pergamena* was more expensive but could be used on both sides; because it was difficult to roll, it was cut into pieces and sewn together, much like today's books. Unfortunately, nothing remains of either collection: Julius Caesar's troops burned the Alexandria library, and Mark Antony shipped all the Pergamum books to Cleopatra as a present. Four hundred years later, during wars between Arabs and Christians, these, too, went up in flames.

The most dramatic of the remains are at the **acropolis.** Signs point the way to the 6-kilometer (4-mile) road to the top, where you can park your car and buy a ticket and perhaps one of the reasonably good picture books containing site maps on sale here, then begin to explore. Broken but still mighty triple ramparts enclose the Upper Town with its temples, palaces, private houses, and gymnasia (schools). In later Roman times, the town spread out and down to the plain, where the Byzantines subsequently settled for good.

After entering the acropolis through the Royal Gate, you can follow a couple of different paths. To start at the top, pick the path to the far right, which takes you past the partially restored **Temple of Trajan,** at the summit. This is the very picture of an ancient ruin, with its burnished white marble pillars high above the valley of the Oç Kemer Çayi (Selinos River). On the terraces just below, you can see the scant remains of the **Temple of Athena** and the **Altar of Zeus;** once among the grandest monuments in the Greek world, the latter was excavated by German archaeologists who sent Berlin's Pergamon-museum every stone they found, including the frieze, 400 feet long, that vividly depicted the battle of the gods against the giants—now all that's left is the altar's flat stone foundation. The **Great Theater,** carved into the steep slope west of the terrace that holds the Temple of Athena, is another matter; it can seat some 10,000 spectators and retains its astounding acoustics. You can test them by sitting near the top and having a companion do a reading at the stage area. *Tel. 232/633–1096. Acropolis admission: $2.50. Open Apr.–Oct., daily 8:30–6:30; Nov.–Mar., daily 8:30–5.*

Back in town, stop at the **Kızıl Avlu** (Red Courtyard), named for the red bricks from which it is constructed. You will pass it on the road to and from the acropolis—it's right at the bottom of the hill. This was the last pagan temple constructed in Pergamum before Christianity was declared the state religion in the 4th century. At that time it was converted into a basilica dedicated to Saint John. The walls remain, but not the roof. Most interesting are the underground passages, where it is easy to imagine concealed pagan priests supplying the voices of "spirits" in mystic ceremonies. *Tel. 232/633–1096 at Archaeological Museum for information. Admission: $1. Open Apr.–Oct., daily 9–noon and 1–7; Nov.–Mar., daily 9–noon and 1–5.*

Continue along the road past the Red Courtyard, which becomes, in the town center, Hükümet Caddesi. The main street in modern Bergama, it is the site of Bergama's **Arkeoloji Müzesi** (Archaeological Museum), one of Turkey's better provincial museums with its substantial collection of statues, coins, and other artifacts excavated from the ancient city. *Hükümet Cad., tel. 232/633–1096. Admission: $2. Open Apr.–Oct., daily 9–noon and 1–7; Nov.–Mar., daily 9–noon and 1–5:30.*

The ancient city's final site, the well-preserved and fairly compact **Asklepieion,** is believed to be the world's first full-service health clinic. To get there, follow the main road, Hükümet Caddesi, back toward the E24; on the western edge of the city, near the tourist information office, follow the sign pointing off to the right. The site is 1½ kilometers (about 1 mile) from the tourist office or 3½ kilometers (2 miles) from the museum.

The name is a reference to Asklepios, god of medicine and recovery, whose snake and staff are now the accepted symbol of modern medicine. In the heyday of the Pergamene Asklepieion in the 2nd century AD, patients were prescribed such treatments as fasting, colonic irrigation, and running barefoot in cold weather. The nature of the treatment was generally determined by interpretation of the patient's dreams. You enter the complex at the column-lined **Holy Road,** once the main street connecting the Asklepieion to Pergamum's acropolis. Today, you follow it for about a city block into a small square and through the **propyleum,** the main gate to the temple precinct. Immediately to the right are the **Shrine of Artemis,** devoted to the Greek goddess of chastity, the moon, and hunting, and the **library,** a branch of the one atop the acropolis. Patients also received therapy accompanied by music during rites held in the intimate theater, which is now used each May for performances of the Bergama Arts Festival. Nearby is a series of pools used for mud and sacred water baths, and a subterranean passageway leading down to the sacred cellar of the **Temple of Telesphorus,** where the devout would pray themselves into a trance and record their dreams upon waking; later, the dreams would be interpreted by a resident priest. *Tel. 232/633–1096 at Archaeological Museum for information. Admission: $2.50. Open daily 8:30–5.*

Go back through Bergama, then follow the E24 and local Route 250 ⓫ south about 70 kilometers (42 miles) to **Foça,** a pleasant fishing village with good restaurants, a few cozy pansiyons–and a big Club Med nearby. Odysseus is said to have lost six of his men in the straits between Scylla and Charybdis, but these islands are rather more tame today, providing the best beaches in the area; you can hire a boat in the village for $10 or $20 for the ride out. If it's late in the day, or you just prefer staying in a small town instead of the big-city Izmir—another 70 kilometers (42 miles) farther south—Foça is a good spot to stay at overnight.

Tour 2: İzmir and Environs

Numbers in the margin correspond to points of interest on the İzmir map.

The 104 kilometers (64 miles) of coast between Bergama and **İzmir** were once thick with Greek settlements. Today only İzmir remains. Called Smyrna from the time of the Greeks until 1923, the city was a vital trading port; while often ravaged by wars and earthquakes, it also had its share of glory. There is respectable evidence that Homer was born in Old Smyrna sometime around 850 BC, and Alexander the Great favored the city with a citadel atop the city's highest hill, known today as the **Kadifekäle** (the Velvet Fortress)—the name, according to romantics if not to scholars, alludes to the resemblance of the present-day citadel's walls to rubbed velvet. Rebuilt after various mishaps and enlarged and strengthened by successive conquerors, the structure looks like a childhood fantasy of a medieval castle, with its solid stone blocks (some dating from Alexander's day), its Byzantine cisterns, and its Ottoman buttresses jutting out to support the walls. The sweeping view of the city and its harbor from the windy restored ramparts makes the citadel a good spot to orient yourself.

Smyrna became an important city under the Romans, and the restored **Agora** (market) at the foot of Kadifekäle hill, just off 816 Sokak (816 Street), was the Roman city's market. The present site is a large dusty open space surrounded by ancient columns and foundations. There are well-preserved Roman statues of Poseidon, Artemis, and Demeter in the northwest corner. To get there from Kadifekäle, exit from the fortress's main gate and take the road that descends to the left; when you see steps built into the sidewalk, turn right and go down. *Admission: $1. Open daily 8:30–5:30.*

The city fell into assorted hands after the Romans, starting with the Byzantines and Arabs. From 1097 on, Smyrna became a battlefield in the Crusades, passing back and forth between the forces of Islam and Christendom. Destroyed and restored successively by Byzantines and Seljuks, Smyrna was held by the Knights of Rhodes in 1402 when the Mongol raider Tamerlane came along, sacked it yet again, and slaughtered its inhabitants. Thirteen years later Sultan Mehmet I Çelebi incorporated it into the Ottoman Empire.

Toward the end of the 15th century, Jews driven from Spain settled in Smyrna, forming a lasting Sephardic community. By the 18th and 19th centuries, Smyrna had become a successful, sophisticated commercial port with an international flavor. Its business community included sizable Italian, Greek, Armenian, British, French, and Jewish contingents. This era came to an end with World War I, when Ottoman Turkey allied itself with Germany. In 1918, the Greek army, aided by the British and French, landed at the harbor and claimed the city. The occupation lasted until 1922, when Turkish troops under Mustafa Kemal (Atatürk) pushed the Greeks back off the coast. On September 9, 1922, he whom his people called the Gazi (war veteran) made a widely cheered entry into the liberated port. The joy of the crowds was short-lived; a fire caught everybody—civilians and soldiers, friends and foes alike—in the blaze. Fanned by the wind, it burned wooden houses like matches while hidden stores

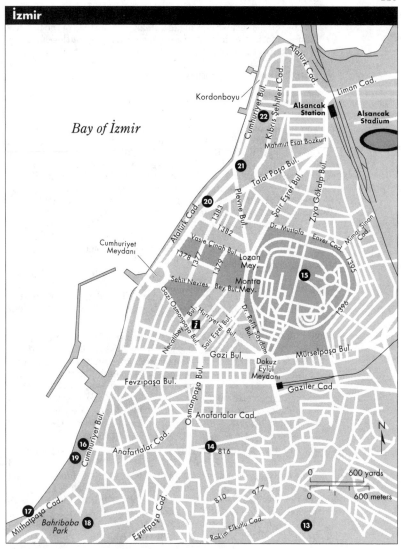

Kordonboyu

Bay of İzmir

Cumhuriyet Bul.
Atatürk Cad.
Kıbrıs Şehitleri Cad.
Liman Cad.

Alsancak Station

Alsancak Stadium

Mahmut Esat Bozkurt

22

21

Talat Paşa Bul.
Şair Eşref Bul.
Ziya Gökalp Bul.
Plevne Bul.
Dr. Mustafa
Enver Cad.
Mimar Sinan Cad.

Cumhuriyet Meydanı

Atatürk Cad.
20

1383
1382
Vasıf Çınah Bul.

1378 1377 1379
Lozan Mey.

Şehit Nevres Bey Bul.
Montra Mey.

15

1395

1396

Gazi Osmanpaşa Bul.
Necatibey Bul.
Bul. Hürriyet
Şair Eşref Bul.
Dr. Refik Saydam Bul.

i

Gazi Bul.

Dokuz Eylül Meydanı

Mürselpaşa Bul.

Fevzipaşa Bul.

Osmanpaşa Bul.

Gaziler Cad.

Anafartalar Cad.

Cumhuriyet Bul.
16
19

Anafartalar Cad.

N

14 816

Eşrefpaşa Cad.

810 977

0   600 yards

0   600 meters

17
Mithatpaşa Cad.
Bahribaba Park
18

Rakim Elkullu Cad.

13

Agora, **14**
Arkeoloji Müzesi, **18**
Atatürk Müzesi, **21**
İzmir Etnoğrafya Müzesi, **17**
Kadifekäle, **13**
Konak Square, **16**

KültürPark, **15**
NATO Southern Command Headquarters, **20**
Saat Kulesi, **19**
Selçuk Yasar Müzesi, **22**

of munitions exploded. It was, in Mustafa Kemal's own words, "the end of an era."

İzmir was quickly rebuilt—and given a Turkish name. Like the name, much of the city dates from the '20s, from its wide boulevards to the office buildings and apartment houses, painted in bright white or soft pastels. Turkey's third-largest town, with more than 2 million inhabitants, it is not particularly pretty, though it has a pleasant, palm-lined harborfront promenade and a peaceful green
⓯ park at its center, the **Kültür Park** (Culture Park). As İzmir is Turkey's second port and industrial center and ranks first in export trade, it makes sense that the city is the site of a major industrial fair, which fills area hotels during its run in the Kültürpark from late August to late September. To get here from the Agora, exit the market on the north and make a right on Anafartalar Caddesi; follow it as it curves east and north to Dokuz Eylül Meydanı (July 9 Square), which borders the park. From here, wander through the small curving lanes toward the shore.

⓰ **Konak Square,** at the water's edge, is one of the two main squares in the city (the other, Cumhuriyet Meydanı, or Republic Square, is to the north along Atatürk Caddesi). Konak marks the start of the modern-day marketplace, a maze of tiny streets filled with shops and covered stalls. Unlike Istanbul's Grand Bazaar, İzmir's is not covered. Anafartalar Caddesi is the bazaar's principal thoroughfare, but do try the smaller side streets, where you'll find a fish market (entered at Anafartalar Cad. 173–175) and minimarkets dedicated to musical instruments, songbirds, clothing, blankets, and many other treats. If you have a problem finding a particular market, just ask a vendor for directions; he or she will be glad to help. *Open Mon.–Sat. 8–8.*

A few blocks south of Konak via Cumhuriyet Bulvarı (Republic
⓱ Boulevard) are the **İzmir Etnoğrafya Müzesi** (Ethnographic Muse-
⓲ um) and the modern **Arkeoloji Müzesi** (Archaeological Museum). The former centers on folk arts and daily life, with everything from period bedrooms to a reconstruction of İzmir's first Turkish pharmacy. The Archaeological Museum contains the 2nd-century statues of Demeter and Poseidon found when the Agora was excavated, as well as an impressive collection of tombs and friezes, and the memorable, colossal statue of Roman emperor Domitian (AD 51–96, ruled 81–96). *Both in Bahribaba Parki, at Cumhuriyet Bul., tel. 232/425–4677. Admission: $2 for each site. Open daily 9–5:30.*

The most fashionable section of town is the waterfront promenade, known as the **Atatürk Caddesi** and later as **Kordonboyu** (Cordon). It starts at the museum complex and stretches north along the busy
⓳ harbor, past the 19th-century Ottoman **Saat Kulesi** (Clock Tower),
⓴ ㉑ the **NATO Southern Command Headquarters,** and a small **Atatürk Müzesi** (Atatürk Museum; Atatürk Cad., Konak 248, tel. 232/421–7026) in an old, pale yellow Levantine building. There are several good seafood restaurants along this strip, all with a few tables outside, overlooking the water. A block back from the water is the
㉒ **Selçuk Yaşar Müzesi** (Cumhuriyet Cad. 252, tel. 232/422–6532), an art gallery with an extensive collection of contemporary Turkish paintings.

Numbers in the margin correspond to points of interest on the Aegean Coast map.

When İzmirites want to get away from the city, most head west, out onto the Çesme peninsula. The drive, over Route 300 through a disappointing landscape of concrete developments and military bases, takes a bit more than an hour (only slightly more in some buses). At some points, you can see traces of an old **Roman bridge**—basically a long, thin line of dark stone blocks—running parallel to the highway, a few yards out into the sea. The last third of the drive is somewhat more attractive as the road rises through rolling hills dotted by low scrub and touches of greenery and then descends into the whitewashed village of **Çesme.**

㉓

Two historic sea battles were fought off Çesme's coast. The first, in 190 BC, ended with the defeat of Hannibal, the famed general of Carthage, at the hands of the Romans. Nearly 2,000 years later, in 1770, the Russian fleet utterly destroyed the Ottoman navy, a blow from which the empire never recovered. Things are quieter today. Inside its 14th-century **Genoese castle** is a Museum of Ottoman Arms; next door, also on Cumhuriyet Meydanı, is the 16th-century **Kanuni Kervansaray,** now a hotel and restaurant (*see* Dining and Lodging, *below*). *Castle admission: $2. Open daily 8:30–11:45 and 1–5:15.*

The several good beaches are the main event, however. About 5 kilometers (3 miles) south of town, out along Akburun (White Cape), there are a number of nice stretches, including **Pirlanta,** as well as numerous unnamed coves. The same distance north of town is the popular **Ilıca** beach.

㉔

Some 90 kilometers (56 miles) east of İzmir, about an hour's drive on the E23, is the ancient city of **Sardis,** onetime capital of the ancient country of Lydia under King Croesus (ruled 560–546 BC), who put a lot of money into building temples, the most famous of which is the Temple of Artemis. The Lydians' main claim to fame comes from their invention of minted coinage at the end of the 7th century BC. Today it is possible to see the remains of the equipment that was used to melt and shape the gold they were so skillful in extracting. In 546 BC the city came under Persian rule, when Cyrus captured Sardis but spared Croesus's life. In Byzantine times it was the site of a diocese, and in the 14th century AD was taken by the Turks. As the older city was fairly well destroyed by a major earthquake in AD 17, most of the remains date from the Roman empire, which held sway in the area until the 3rd century AD. South of the village of Sartmustafa, a sign points the way down an unpaved but passable road to the ruined **Temple of Artemis.** This massive structure, slightly bigger than Athens's Parthenon, is unfortunately not as well preserved; however, reerected columns with their fine Ionic capitals and the one wall still standing hint at the temple's former grandeur. The acropolis behind it offers splendid views, but the hike up and down can take two hours. Heading back to the highway and crossing it, pick up another dirt road—this one heading north; some 10 minutes away on foot, much less in a car, are the rest of the ruins, including the massive **gymnasium** complex. Bathers would enter through the colonnaded *palaestra* (exercise hall), continue through the row of changing rooms, and end up in the enormous *caldarium* (hot pool). The complex's ornate **Marble Court,** where you can see the remains of Byzantine-era shops, has been reconstructed, revealing a multistory facade with carved reliefs. The restored **synagogue** dates from the 4th century AD and has some intact mosaic pavements. *No phone. Admission: $1 for each site. Open daily 8:30–dusk.*

Tour 3: Inland to Aphrodisias and Pamukkale

If you have the time, do take this 232-kilometer (143-mile) detour inland about two hours due east of İzmir to the spa town of Pamukkale, highlighted in every Turkish promotional brochure. On the way back you can make a stop at Aphrodisias, one of the most extensive ruins in all of Turkey. To make the excursion comfortably, allow two days and plan on an overnight at Pamukkale. To get there, follow Route E24 south of İzmir to Selçuk, then inland almost as far as Denızli. Bus tours are easily arranged in İzmir and Kuşadası.

㉕ Pamukkale first appears as an enormous, chalky white cliff rising some 330 feet from the plains. Mineral-rich volcanic spring water cascades over basins and natural terraces, crystallizing into white curtains of solidified water seemingly suspended in air. The hot springs in the area, used today by people who believe that the water can cure rheumatism and other problems, were first visited by the ancient Romans, and you can see the remains of Roman baths among the ruins of nearby **Hierapolis,** founded early in the 2nd century BC by the king of Pergamum and now a national park. To get to Hierapolis, continue on the main road through Pamukkale village and park up by the Pamukkale Motel, or a bit farther up near the **Roman theater,** whose large capacity—15,000—indicates the popularity of the waters here. Now restored, it is once again used for performances. *Admission: $3. Open 9:30–6.*

Because the sights here are spread over about ½ kilometer (⅓ mile), prepare for some walking. Between the theater and the Pamukkale Motel are the ruins of a **Temple of Apollo** and a bulky **Byzantine church.** The monumental fountain known as the **Nymphaion,** just north of the Apollo temple, dates from the 4th century AD. Near the northern city gates, a short drive or long walk, is another indication of the town's former popularity: a vast **necropolis,** with more than a thousand cut-stone sarcophogi spilling all the way down to the base of the hill. The stone building that enclosed Hierapolis's baths is now the **Pamukkale Museum,** definitely worth a look for its display of many fine marble statues found at the site. *Tel. 258/272–2077 at tourism office for information. Museum admission: $1. Open daily 8:30–noon and 1–5:30.*

You don't have to stay in Pamukkale to take advantage of its thermal pools (the best is at the **Pamukkale Motel**)—you simply pay a guest fee. But Pamukkale is a good place to overnight, with its abundance of motels and hotels, before tackling the ruins of Aphrodisias on your way back to the coast.

After a good, restful soak, take the E24 west toward İzmir. At Kuyucak, about 55 kilometers (33 miles) from Pamukkale, turn off the E24 and head south for 35 kilometers (21 miles), following the
㉖ signs from the village of Geyre to **Aphrodisias,** the city of Aphrodite, goddess of love. Though most of what you see today dates from the 1st and 2nd centuries AD, archaeological evidence indicates that the local dedication to Aphrodite followed a long history of veneration of pre-Hellenic goddesses (such as the Anatolian mother goddess and the Babylonian Ishtar). It is a huge site, though only about half of it has been excavated so far. Aphrodisias, which was granted autonomy by the Roman Empire in the late 1st century BC, prospered as a significant center for religion, arts, and literature in the early 1st century AD. Imposing Christianity proved far more difficult than granting the pagan city autonomy, however, due to the cult of Aphrodite. One method that was used to mop up remnants of paganism was to rename the city, first Stavropolis (City of the Cross), then just Caria, which archaeologists believe is the origin of the name of the present-day village of Geyre. Excavations here have also led archaelogists to believe that this was a thriving haven for the art of sculpture, which found patrons beyond the borders of the city. The

signatures of Aphrodisian artists on statues, fragments, and bases as far away as Greece and Italy attest to this.

The beauty of Aphrodisias, one of the most attractive ruins in Turkey, is in its details. The towering Babadağ range of mountains to the east of the city offered ancient sculptors a copious supply of white and delicately veined blue-gray marble, which has been used to stunning effect in the statues you will see in the site museum, in the columns that sprout throughout—fluted, spiral, and otherwise—and in the delicate reliefs of gods and men, vines and acanthus leaves on decorative friezes.

Start your tour at the site museum, just past the ticket booth, where you can pick up a site guide and map (you'll need it, as the signage is poor). The museum's splendid collection includes several impressive statues from the site, among them one of Aphrodite herself. *Tel. 256/ 448–8004 or 256/443–5190. Museum admission: $3. Open daily 8:30–5.*

From the museum, follow the footpath to the right, which makes a circuit around the site and ends up back at the museum. The **Tetrapylon,** recently restored, is a monumental gateway with four rows of columns and some of the better decorative friezes at the site. The **Temple of Aphrodite** was originally built in the 1st century BC on the model of the great temples at Ephesus. Its gate and many of its columns are still standing; some bear inscriptions naming the donor of the column. The statue of Aphrodite that was once the temple's focal point has been moved to the museum. Next to the temple is the fine **Odeon,** an intimate, semicircular concert hall and public meeting room. Farther on is the impressive **stadium,** which once was the scene of foot races, boxing and wrestling matches, and other competitions—horse and chariot races were held in Greek cities' hippodromes. The stadium, which is one of the best preserved of its kind anywhere, could seat up to 30,000 spectators. One of the most striking sites here is the **theater,** built into the side of a small hill and still being excavated. Its 5,000 lush white marble seats are simply dazzling on a bright day. The adjacent **School of Philosophy** has a colonnaded courtyard with chambers lining both sides where teachers would work with small groups of students. *No phone. Site admission: $3. Open daily 8:30–5.*

Tour 4: The Southern Aegean

This tour will take you all the way to the end of the Aegean coast at Bodrum, perhaps Turkey's smartest seaside resort, through countryside that is incredibly rich in both ruins and scenery. Ephesus is without doubt one of the finest archaeological sites on the globe, and while less grand, the ruins of Priene, Miletus, and Didyma combine to provide an insightful trip into the ancient world. At the end of the trail is that pleasure dome, Bodrum. You will need at least three days to cover all the ground, though once you get here, you may want to stay for weeks.

The E24 is the quickest route from İzmir south to Ephesus, but if you have a mind to wander and visit a few minor sites, take the road that leads through the ancient Ionian cities of Colophon, Claros, and Notion, following the road signs to towns en route: Menderes, Şaşal, Değirmendere. There are also some good stretches of beach at the southern end of the route, just past Notion.

❷ The first site is **Colophon,** near the village of Değirmendere. The farthest inland of the Ionian cities, Colophon was prosperous in the

8th and 7th centuries BC. The fine horses and fierce cavalry it was known for were often enlisted as allies by foreign armies to finish off unending wars. The popularity of the nearby oracle at Claros, the fertility of their land, and their skill as mariners made the citizens of this city very wealthy—so wealthy that it was possible to find more than a thousand musk-scented men dressed in purple strolling through the agora. In Colophon's heyday, women musicians were paid an official salary by the government to play from dawn to dusk, while puppies were sacrificed to the Wayside Goddess of the underworld. A combination of extreme wealth and possibly decadence—and the founding of nearby Ephesus—brought about Colophon's decline. In the 3rd century, the population here were moved by Lysimachus to fill his new-walled city of Ephesus, and according to Pausanias, those who resisted were "buried left of the road to Claros." Today, there is not much to see except the remains of a wall, though excavations have uncovered streets, a stoa, and a temple dedicated to Demeter.

28 **Claros,** 7 kilometers (4 miles) farther south, was the site of a highly regarded oracle and **Temple of Apollo,** now simply standing alongside the road. Claros is mentioned in Homer's verses as the site of an important cult as far back as the 7th and 6th centuries BC. Because the location, in a low-lying valley that was probably the site of a sacred spring and wood, is subject to flooding, the temple is often buried in mud, but ongoing excavations should be clearing that. Excavations have also revealed much information about how the oracles were performed in the temple. A mazelike corridor leads you the sacred oracle chamber, where annually appointed male prophets would drink holy water and reveal prophecies through a priest and thespios, a composer of poetry, who would versify the prophet's utterings. Fragments of colossal statues of Apollo, Artemis, and Leto are scattered about, with the statue of Apollo estimated as having been 24 to 25 feet high. Inscriptions of oracles from the temple have been found as far away as southern Russia, Algeria, Sardinia, and even Great Britain. According to one source, an oracle at this temple predicted the destruction of Europe and Asia in a war over the beautiful Helen.

29 The crumbling remains of **Notion,** Colophon's port, are scattered along a clifftop a couple of kilometers, or about a mile, to the south along the same road. After Lysimachus depopulated Colophon to furnish Ephesus, Notion had a brief period of prosperity, when it was known as the New Colophon, but as Ephesus grew, Notion's population and wealth dwindled. You can make out the foundations of a temple, an agora, and a theater. Down below is a pleasant beach. An even more isolated beach, **Gümüşsu,** is a bit farther west; make a right at the "T" intersection. At **Pamucak,** a growing resort en route to Selçuk, 25 kilometers (about 15 miles) along the road heading east, the strand is busier and not as attractively sited, though still quite pleasant.

30 **Selçuk** is notable for its proximity to the magnificent ruins of **Ephesus,** 4 kilometers (2½ miles) west. The Delphi oracle led the Ionian Greeks here from their original home in central Greece in the 11th century BC by advising Androkles, the Ionian leader, that "The site of the new town will be shown . . . by a fish; follow the wild boar." According to the legend, as Androkles and his men were traveling in the vicinity of what became Ephesus, they came across some people cooking fish. Soon after, as the story goes, a fish, about to be cooked over an open fire, jumped and knocked embers into nearby brush. The fire spread, and a boar fleeing the flames was hunted down and killed at Mt. Koressos, later called Bülbül Dağ, or Mount of the Nightingale, by the Turks. And that is where the Ionians settled.

Ephesus, on the sea at the time, quickly became a powerful trading port and sacred center for the cult of Artemis. Its fame drew the attention of a series of conquerors, among them Croesus of Lydia and 6th-century BC Cyrus of Persia. After a Greek uprising against the Persians failed, Ephesus managed to stay out of trouble, often by playing up to both sides of any conflict. Perhaps because the Temple of Artemis was consumed by fire on the day Alexander the Great was born, Alexander himself aided the city in its efforts to rebuild after his rise to power. Like most Ionian cities in Asia Minor, Ephesus became a Roman city, and eventually a Christian one, though not without a struggle. In the Acts of the Apostles, Saint Luke writes at length about the popularity of the cult of Artemis, referring to the goddess by her Latin name, Diana. It was this city's silversmiths who drove Saint Paul out of Ephesus for fear that his preaching would lessen the sale of the "silver shrines for Diana," claiming, "by this craft we have our wealth." When Saint Paul addressed the town in its amphitheater, saying that "there are no gods made with hands," the local silversmiths rioted; they were "full of wrath, and cried out, saying, 'Great is Diana of the Ephesians'" (Acts XIX, 24–40). Paul is believed to have written some of his Epistles here. Saint John visited between AD 37 and AD 48, perhaps with the mother of Jesus, and again, in 95, when he is supposed to have written his Gospel here and died. In AD 431, Ephesus was the scene of the Third Ecumenical Council, during which Mary was proclaimed the Mother of God.

Like many of the other ancient cities in this region, Ephesus was doomed by the silting in its harbor. By the 6th century the port had become useless and the population had shifted to what is now Selçuk; today, Ephesus is 5 kilometers (about 3 miles) from the sea. The new city was surrounded by ramparts and a citadel built. In the year 1000, crusaders came from the West, Turks from the East. Ephesus became known as Hagios Theologos (Holy word of God) and then by the Turkish version of that name, Ayasoluk. The first Seljuk invaders were fought off in 1090, and the Byzantines held out until 1304. The town fell under the rule of the Ottoman Empire in the beginning of the 15th century.

Numbers in the margin correspond to points of interest on the Selçuk and Ephesus map.

Though Selçuk is very much on the beaten path for tourists, it has retained some charm, dominated as it is by its crenellated, gray stone Byzantine **fortress,** which, when floodlit at night, seems to float above the town. There is, however, nothing in particular to see in the fortress, so head instead to the 6th-century **Basilica of St. John** on Ayasoluk Hill (take St. Jean Sokak about two blocks up). Built by Justinian over a 2nd-century tomb generally believed to hold Saint John the Evangelist, "the disciple that Jesus loved," the basilica was once topped with 11 domes and rivaled Istanbul's Hagia Sophia in scale. Though the barrel-vaulted roof collapsed after a long-ago earthquake, the church is still an incredible sight, with its labyrinth of halls and marble courtyards. *St. Jean Sok., no phone. Admission: $2. Open daily 8–5.*

Continuing along St. Jean Sokak for several more blocks, you will reach the **Isa Bey Cami,** a mosque dating from 1375. Its jumble of architectural styles suggests a transition between Seljuk and Otto-

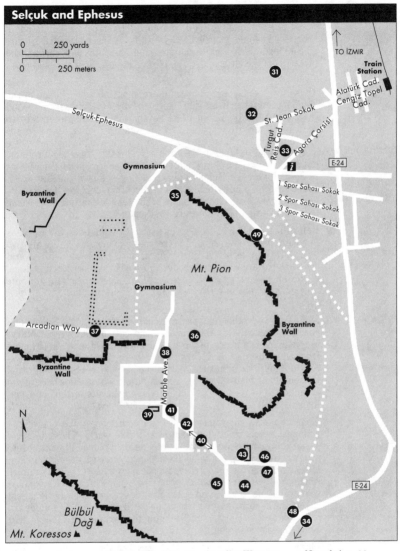

Selçuk and Ephesus

0   250 yards
0   250 meters

TO İZMIR

Train Station

Atatürk Cad.
Cengiz Topel Cad.

Selçuk-Ephesus

St. Jean Sokak

Turgut Reis Cad.

Agora Çarşısı

E-24

1 Spor Sahası Sokak
2 Spor Sahası Sokak
3 Spor Sahası Sokak

Gymnasium

Byzantine Wall

Mt. Pion

Gymnasium

Arcadian Way

Byzantine Wall

Byzantine Wall

Marble Ave.

N

Bülbül Dağ
Mt. Koressos

E-24

Basilica of St. John, **31**
İşa Bey Cami, **32**
Ephesus Museum, **33**
Meryemana, **34**
Stadium, **35**
Theater, **36**

Arcadian Way, **37**
Marble Avenue, **38**
Library of Celsus, **39**
Street of Kuretes, **40**
Brothel, **41**
Temple of Hadrian, **42**
Prytaneion, **43**

Nymphaion, **44**
Temple of
Domitian, **45**
Odeon, **46**
State Agora, **47**
Magnesian Gate, **48**
Graves of the Seven
Sleepers, **49**

man design: Like later Ottoman mosques, this has a courtyard, something not found in Seljuk mosques. The structure is built out of "borrowed" stone: marble blocks with Latin inscriptions, Corinthian columns, black granite columns from the baths at Ephesus, and pieces from the altar of the Temple of Artemis. *St. Jean Sok. Open daily 9–5.*

Those fragments, unfortunately, are about all you will see of the Temple of Artemis itself, a holy site that drew pilgrims from around the ancient world and one of its Seven Wonders. Begun in the 7th century BC, greatly expanded by the wealthy Lydian king Croesus and redone in marble in the 6th century BC, it was burned down by a disgruntled worshiper in 356 BC. Alexander the Great had it rebuilt, but it was sacked by Goths in AD 263 and later stripped for materials to build Istanbul's Hagia Sophia and Selçuk's own Basilica of St. John. Today a muddy field and a lone column drum on the Selçuk–Ephesus road are all that remain of the temple that was once some four times larger than Athens's Parthenon.

㉝ Before heading to Ephesus, make a stop at the well-laid-out **Ephesus Museum.** Along with some fine frescoes and mosaics, there are two pale white statues of Artemis. In each, she is portrayed with several rows of what are alternatively described as breasts or a belt of eggs; in either case, they symbolize fertility. *Agora Çarsisi, opposite tourist information office, tel. 5451/1010. Admission: $2.50. Open Tues.–Sun. 8:30–6.*

Saint Paul and Saint John preached in both Ephesus and Selçuk and changed the cult of Artemis into the cult of the Virgin Mary.
㉞ **Meryemana,** the House of the Virgin Mary, is 5 kilometers (3 miles) from Ephesus via the E24 from Selçuk and the road to Germencik-Aydın. This is thought to have been the place where Saint John took the mother of Jesus after the crucifixion and where some believe she ascended to heaven. Pope Paul VI visited the site in 1967 and confirmed its authenticity. *Admission: $1.50. Open daily 7:30–sunset.*

Ephesus is the showpiece of Aegean archaeology and one of the grandest reconstructed ancient sites in the world. The extensive, remarkably preserved remains are especially appealing out of season, when the place can seem like a ghost town with its shimmering, long, white marble road grooved by chariot wheels. In the summer it's packed with tourists, many of whom come off the Greek ships that cruise the Aegean and call at Kuşadası, 20 kilometers (12 miles) to the south, so go early or late in the day if possible. Site guides are available at the trinket stands ringing the parking lot; allow most of a day to see everything.

The ruins of Ephesus were rediscovered in the late 19th century, and excavations have been going on for nearly a century. As a result, the site is a pleasure to explore: Marble-paved streets take you past buildings and monuments that have been partially reconstructed, so that you half expect to see toga-clad Greeks emerging.

The road leading to the site parking lot passes a 1st-century AD
㉟ **Stadium,** where chariot and horse races were held on a track 712 feet long, and where gladiators and wild beasts met in combat before 70,000 spectators. On your left after you enter the site is the 25,000-
㊱ seat **theater,** backed by the western slope of Mt. Pion. A huge semicircle, with row upon row of curved benches, it was begun by Alexander's general Lysimachus and completed by the emperors Claudius and Trajan in the 2nd century AD. There is a fine view from the top of the steps; higher still, near the top of Mt. Pion, are vestiges of the city's Byzantine walls. The theater is used for music and

dance performances each May during the Selçuk Ephesus Festival of Culture and Art. Leading away from the theater toward the ancient
㊲ port, now a marsh, is the **Arcadian Way.** The main route to the port in ancient times, this 1,710-foot-long street was once lined with shops and covered archways. Only a long line of slender marble columns remains.

㊳ In front of the theater is **Marble Avenue.** Follow it to the beautiful,
㊴ two-story **Library of Celsus.** The courtyard of this much-photographed building is backed by wide steps that climb to the reading room, where you can still see rolls of papyrus. The library is near
㊵ Marble Avenue's intersection with the **Street of Kuretes,** a still impressive thoroughfare named for the college of priests once located there. Strategically positioned at this corner is a large house be-
㊶ lieved to have been a **brothel;** look for the floor mosaics of three women. To the right along the street are the multistoried houses of the nobility, with terraces and courtyards. To the left are public build-
㊷ ings. A block down from the brothel is the fine facade of the **Temple of Hadrian,** with four Corinthian columns and a serpent-headed hydra above the door to keep out the evil spirits; beyond is a partially restored fountain dedicated to the emperor Trajan. The street then forks and opens into a central square, which once held the
㊸ ㊹ **Prytaneion,** or town hall; the **Nymphaion,** a small temple decked
㊺ with fountains; and the **Temple of Domitian** on the south side of the square, once a vast sanctuary with a colossal statue of the emperor for whom it was named. All are now a jumble of collapsed walls and columns. Returning to the Street of Kuretes, turn right to reach the
㊻ **odeon,** an intimate semicircle with just a few rows of seats, where spectators would listen to poetry readings and music. Columns mark
㊼ ㊽ the northern edge of the **State Agora.** Beyond, the **Magnesian Gate** (also known as the Manisa Gate), at the end of the street, was the starting point for a caravan trail and a colonnaded road to the Temple of Artemis. *Site entry 4 km (2½ mi) w. of Seļuk on Selçuk–Ephesus rd., tel. 5451/1010. Admission: $1. Open daily 8–5:30.*

㊾ A 10-minute walk along an unpaved footpath from the Magnesian Gate are a small church in a field and, alongside, the **graves of the Seven Sleepers.** According to legend, seven young men of Ephesus—all good Christians—hid in a cave to avoid persecution by the Romans in the 3rd century AD. They fell into a sleep that lasted 200 years, waking only after the Byzantine Empire had made Christianity the official state religion. When they died, they were buried here, and the church that you see was built over them. The tombs in the large cemetery are largely from the Byzantine era.

Numbers in the margin correspond to points of interest on the Aegean Coast map.

㊿ **Kuşadası** exists primarily to serve the tourists making the modern-day pilgrimage to Ephesus. It's 20 kilometers (12 miles) south of Selçuk and Ephesus on the coast road, which is known, not surprisingly, as the Kuşadası road. A small fishing village as late as the 1970s, it is now a sprawling, hyperactive town packed with curio shops and a population of around 40,000. Still, Kuşadası's cheery holiday atmosphere is hugely popular with British tourists. Good hotels and restaurants are more plentiful than elsewhere along the coast; there's even a bit of nightlife. And it's the jumping-off point for the 2½-hour boat trip to the Greek island of Samos. Tickets, which should be obtained a day in advance, can be purchased at any travel agency in town (*see* Guided Tours in Essential Information, *above*); the cost is about $35 each way, and departures are at 8 and 5 daily.

A 300-year-old **caravansary** (Atatürk Bul. 1, tel. 63/614–115) is now the Club Kervansaray hotel and restaurant; and there's an old **Genoese castle** on Güvercin Adası (Pigeon Island), connected to town by a causeway off of Kadınlar Denizi, just south of the harbor. Today the site of a popular disco and several pleasant teahouses with gardens and sea views, the fortress was home to three Turkish brothers in the 16th century. These infamous pirates—Barbarossa, Oruc, and Hayrettin—pillaged the coasts of Spain and Italy and sold passengers and crews from captured ships into slavery in Algiers and Constantinople. Rather than fight them, Süleyman the Magnificent (ruled 1520–1566) hired Hayrettin as his Grand Admiral and set him loose on enemies in the Mediterranean. The strategy worked: Hayrettin won victory after victory and was heaped with honors and riches when he died at age 70 in 1546.

If you're looking for beaches, either backtrack to **Pamucak** (*see above*) or travel 33 kilometers (20 miles) south to lovely, wooded **Samsundağ National Park** (also known as **Dilek Peninsula National Park**), which has good hiking trails and several quiet stretches of sandy beach. To get there, take the coast road, marked Güzelçanlı or Devutlar, from about 10 kilometers (6 miles) south of Kuşadası. *Park admission: $2. Open Apr.–Dec.*

Taken together, the southernmost Ionian cities—Priene and Miletus—along with the holy sanctuary of Apollo at Didyma, present a rich trove of sights. Head south from Kuşadası on Route 525 and turn off onto the unnumbered road to Priene shortly after the market town of Söke; the archaeological site is 14 kilometers (9 miles) to the southwest. Signs on this same road point the way to Miletus, 21 kilometers (13 miles) farther south, and to Didyma, 20 kilometers (13 miles) beyond that. Turn off toward Yeniköy, halfway between Didyma and Miletus, to return to Kuşadası and Route 525, which proceeds south to Bodrum.

⑤ **Priene** is the most spectacularly located of all the ancient cities on the Aegean: atop a steep hill high above the flat valley of the Büyük Menderes (Maeander River). Dating from about 350 BC, the city you see today was still under construction in 334, when Alexander the Great liberated the Ionian settlements from Persian rule. At that time it was a thriving port. But as in Ephesus, the harbor silted over, commerce moved to neighboring Miletus, and the city's prosperity waned, around the 4th century BC. As a result, the Romans never rebuilt Priene, and the simpler Greek style predominates, as in few other ancient cities in Turkey. Excavated by British archaeologists in 1868–69, it's smaller than Ephesus and far less grandiose.

From the visitor parking area, the walk up to the site is fairly steep; because your routes through it are well marked, you won't need a map. After passing through the old city walls, you follow the city's original main thoroughfare; note the drainage gutters and the grooves worn into the marble paving stones by the wheels of 4th-century BC chariots. Continuing west, you come to the well-preserved **bouleterion** (council chamber) on the left. Its 10 rows of seats flanked an orchestra pit with a little altar, decorated with bulls' heads and laurel leaves, at the center. Passing through the doors on the opposite side of the council chamber takes you to the **Sacred Stoa,** a colonnaded civic center, and the northern edge of the **agora,** the marketplace. Continuing west along the broad promenade, you pass the remains of a row of **private houses,** typically two or three rooms on two floors; of the upper stories, only traces of a few stairwells remain. In the largest house, a statue of Alexander was found, a remnant that seemed to say "Alexander slept here."

A block or so farther along the main street is the **Temple of Athena.** Its design—the work of Pytheos, architect of the Mausoleum of Halicarnassus (one of the Seven Wonders of the Ancient World)—was repeatedly copied at other sites in the Greek world. It was not a place for worshipers to gather but a dwelling for the god; only priests could enter. Alexander apparently chipped in on construction costs. Earthquakes have toppled the columns; the five that have been reerected provide an evocative vision of the temple that once was, with its stunning view over the Menderes valley. A walk north and then east along the track leads to the well-preserved little **theater,** sheltered on all sides by pine trees. Enter through the stage door onto the orchestra section; note the five front-row VIP seats, carved thrones with lions' feet. If you scramble up a huge rock known as Samsun Dağı (behind the theater and to your left as you face the seats), you will find the scanty remains of a **Sanctuary of Demeter,** goddess of the harvest; a few bits of columns and tumbledown walls remain, as well as a big hole through which blood of sacrificial victims was poured to the deities of the underworld. Since few people make it up here, it is an incredibly peaceful spot, with a terrific view over Priene and the plains. Above this, should you care to go farther, are the remnants of a Hellenistic fortress. *No tel. Priene site admission: $1.50. Open daily 8:30–6.*

52 **Miletus** was one of the greatest commercial centers of the Greek world before its harbor, too, was silted over. The first settlers were Minoan Greeks from Crete, who arrived between 1400 and 1200 BC. The Ionians, who arrived 200 years later, slaughtered the male population and married the widows. The philosopher Thales was born here in the early 6th century BC; he calculated the height of the pyramids at Giza, suggested that the universe was actually a rational place despite its apparent disorder, and coined the phrase "Know thyself." An intellectual center, the city was also home to the mathematicians Anaximenes, who held that air was the single element behind the diversity of nature, and Anaximander, whose ideas anticipated the theory of evolution and the concept of the indestructibility of matter. Like the other Ionian cities, Miletus was passed from ruling empire to ruling empire—being successively governed by Alexander's generals Antigonus and Lysimachus and Pergamum's Attalids, among others. Under the Romans, who came later, the town finally regained some control over its own affairs and shared in the prosperity of the region. Saint Paul preached here before the harbor became impassable and the city had to be abandoned once and for all.

The archaeological site is sprawled out along a desolate plain. Well-marked trails make a guide or map unnecessary. The parking lot is right outside the city's most magnificent building—the **Great Theater,** a remarkably intact 25,000-seat amphitheater built by the Ionians and kept up by the Romans. Along the third to sixth rows, some inscriptions reserving seats for notables are still visible, and the vaulted passages leading to the seats have the feel of a modern sporting arena. Climb to the top of the theater for a look at the defensive walls built by the Byzantines and a view across the ancient city.

To see the rest of the ruins, follow the dirt track to the right of the theater. A stand of buildings marks what was once a broad processional avenue. The series begins with the **delphinion,** a sanctuary of Apollo; a **Seljuk hamam** added to the site in the 15th century, with pipes for hot and cold water still visible; a **stoa** (colonnaded porch) with several reerected Ionic columns; the foundations of a **Roman**

bath and **gymnasium**; and the first story of the **Nymphaion,** all that remains of the once highly ornate three-story structure, resembling the Library of Celsus at Ephesus, that distributed water to the rest of the city.

To the south, your dirt track becomes a tree-lined lane that leads to the **İlyas Bey Cami,** a mosque built in 1404 in celebration of its builder and namesake's escape from Tamerlane, the Mongol terror. The mosque is now a romantic ruin: The ceiling is cracked, dust covers the tiles, and birds roost inside. The path from the mosque back to the parking lot passes a small and underwhelming museum displaying artifacts found at the site. *No phone. Admission: ruins $1.50, museum $1.50. Open Tues.–Sun. 8:30–6.*

53 From Miletus, signs point the way to **Didyma** (Didim in Turkish) along a 20-kilometer (12-mile) road that follows the trail of the ancient Sacred Way, which once connected the city with Didyma's **Temple of Apollo.** As grand in scale as the Parthenon—measuring 623 feet by 167 feet—the temple has 124 well-preserved columns, some still supporting their architraves; its oracles rivaled those of Delphi. Started in 300 BC and under construction for five centuries, it was never actually completed, and some of the columns remain unfluted. Beneath the courtyard is a network of underground corridors where the temple priests would consult the oracle. The corridor walls would throw the oracle's voice into deep and ghostly echoes, which the priests would interpret. The tradition of seeking advice from sacred oracles probably started long before the arrival of the Greeks; in all likelihood, the Greeks converted an older Anatolian cult based at the site to their own religion. The Greek oracle had a good track record, and at the birth of Alexander the Great (356 BC) predicted that he would be victorious over the Persians, that his general Seleucus would later become king, and that Trajan would become an emperor.

The popularity of the oracle dwindled with the rise of Christianity, around AD 385, and the temple was later excavated by French and German archaeologists; its statues are long gone, hauled back to England by Sir Charles Newton in 1858. Fragments of bas-relief on display by the entrance to the site include a gigantic head of Medusa and a small statue of Poseidon and his wife, Amphitrite. *20 km (12 mi) s. of Miletus, 5 km (3 mi) n. of Altınkum, no phone. Admission: $1.50. Open daily 8:30–6.*

54 For a rest after all this history, continue another 5 kilometers (3 miles) south to **Altınkum.** The white sand beach, which stretches for a bit less than 1 kilometer (½ mile), is bordered by a row of decent seafood restaurants, all facing the water, some small hotels.

Alternatively, to return to Route 525, backtrack to Akköy and turn off for Yeniköy, halfway between Didyma and Miletus. As you head to Bodrum, there are a few attractions worth seeing if time permits. Consider a detour along **Çarnıçi Gölü** (Lake Bafa), which maintains the illusion of still being an inlet of the sea as it was in Roman times (*see* Off the Beaten Track, *below*). Along the left side of the road at Selimiye is the **Temple of Euromos,** a 2nd-century AD temple dedicated to Zeus whose rows of slender columns tower over olive trees. **Milâs,** 22 kilometers (13 miles) south, stands on the site of ancient Mylasa, the capital of the independent kingdom known as Caria around 350 BC; there's an impressive Roman gateway, locally called **Baltalı Kapı** (Gate of the Ax), and a Roman mausoleum that seems a miniature replica of the famous Mausoleum in Halicarnassus, with a pyramidal roof held by Corinthian columns. Some 18th-century Ottoman mansions line the city's riverfront.

⑤⑤ Bodrum, known as Halicarnassus in antiquity, stretches along the shore of two crescent-shaped bays and has for years been the favorite haunt of the Turkish upper classes. Today thousands of foreign visitors have joined the elite, and the area is bursting at the seams with villas, hotels, guest houses, cafés, restaurants, and discos. Comparing it to Saint-Tropez on the French Riviera, some sniff that Bodrum is spoiled. But it is still beautiful, with its gleaming, whitewashed buildings covered with bougainvillea and unfettered vistas of the sparkling bays.

Founded around 1000 BC, Halicarnassus was one of the first Greek colonies in Asia. While the northern cities of the Aegean formed the Ionian League, those farther south joined the Dorian Federation, which included Kos, Rhodes, Cnidos, Lalysos, Lindos, Camiros—and Halicarnassus. Halicarnassus reached its height under Mausolus, who ruled from 377 to 353 BC as a satrap (governor) of what was then a distant outpost of the far-flung Persian Empire. After his death, his wife (who was also his sister), Artemesia, succeeded him. Upon learning that a woman ruled Halicarnassus, Rhodes sent its fleet to seize the city, only to be promptly, and soundly, defeated. It was Artemisia who ordered the construction of the great white marble tomb that made the Seven Wonders list and gave us the word mausoleum. The **mausoleum** consisted of a solid rectangular base topped by 36 Ionic columns, surmounted by a pyramid, and crowned with a massive statue of Mausolus and Artemesia riding a chariot. Sadly, what is left of the site—which is two blocks north of the bay, indicated by signs on Neyzen Tevfik Caddesi, the shore road ringing the west bay—is not worth the price of admission. *Tel. 6141/1095. Admission: $2. Open Tues.–Sun. 8–5.*

It would be more profitable to scramble up the hill to the overgrown remnants of the ancient **theater,** due north of the mausoleum site. This is one of the few surviving pre-Hellenic theaters in Asia Minor, thus one of the oldest, and a popular place to take in a sunset. No admission is charged.

The European crusaders known as the Knights of St. John seized Bodrum the town in 1402 and dismantled the mausoleum, using many of the stones to build the **Petronion** (Castle of St. Peter), the most outstanding historic sight in modern Bodrum and one of the great showpieces of late-medieval military architecture. The castle and its beautiful gardens, anchoring the wedge of land that separates the town's two bays and visible from every part of town, look as if they belong in a fairy tale. On the ramparts, heraldry buffs might recognize prominent coats-of-arms—those of the Plantagenets, d'Aubussons, and others. The five turrets are named after the homelands of the knights, who came from England, France, Germany, Italy, and Spain. Inside is an unusual and interesting **Museum of Underwater Archaeology,** with treasures recovered from historic wrecks discovered off the Aegean coast. *Kale Cad., tel. 6141/2516. Admission, including castle and museum $3. Open Tues.–Sun. 8:30–noon and 1–5.*

Kale Caddesi, which leads from the castle into town and is known as **Cevat Şakir** north of Adliye Cami, is Bodrum's main shopping street. **Neyzen Tevfik Caddesi** runs along the west side of the bay, the marina side, and **Alim Bey Caddesi** along the other bay. The main form of recreation on these avenues is finding a table at an outdoor café, ordering up, doing some people-watching, and arguing over whether the next day's activity will be an afternoon's sail, a trip to one of the area's pristine beaches, or an adventurous excursion over rough dirt roads to some of the more obscure ancient Greek and Roman ruins that dot the peninsula.

What to See and Do with Children

Children are bound to enjoy the **Castle of St. Peter** in Bodrum; in addition to the fairy-tale design, there are usually maids and knights wandering about in medieval costume. The pools at **Pamukkale** are not only warm but have fun bits of columns and statues to swim around and explore up close. The songbird market at Konak Square in İzmir is an unusual, colorful treat.

Off the Beaten Track

Shortly before you reach Milas, along the road to Bodrum, Route 525 skirts the southern shore of **Çamiçi Gölü** (Bafa Gölü or Lake Bafa). The lake is relatively small and largely undeveloped, especially away from the main road. For a real change of pace, hire a boat to take you across the lake, or drive the rough 10-kilometer (6-mile) road along the eastern shore, to the village of **Kapikiri** and the ancient ruins of **Heracleia.** Though a minor town in antiquity, Heracleia has a wonderful setting, surrounded by high mountains—and there's not a tour bus in sight. The villagers are Türkilometersen, descended from the Turkish tribes that settled Anatolia in the 13th and 14th century. The ruins, a Temple of Athena and some city walls, are also unusual: They are Carian rather than Greek. The Carians were a native Asian people who became Hellenized—that is, adopted Greek language and culture. On an islet facing the village are remains of a Byzantine monastery, and there are huge, volcanic boulders scattered about. The combination of elements is incredibly atmospheric.

Shopping

Shops and bazaars are usually open Monday–Saturday, 9:30–1 and 2–6.

Market Towns

The best include Ayvalık, Bergama, Bodrum, İzmir, and Kuşadası. All have traditional bazaar areas that make for entertaining exploring. In Bodrum, the main shopping street is Cevat Şakir Caddesi, where you will find the usual array of Turkish carpets, plus colorful baggy trousers, knock-off Lacoste shirts, and leather jackets.

Rugs

Everywhere you go, you will encounter carpets. It is frightfully difficult to rate the rug shops as most have at least something worthwhile—it just depends on what you like. In **Bodrum,** try Galeri Aikel (Kale Cad. 2); in **İzmir,** Dağtekin (1382 Sok., just off Atatürk Cad.); in **Kuşadası,** Lapis (Atatürk Bul. 12–14) and Uner Gallery (No. 6 on the harbor); and in **Selçuk,** Mercan Brothers (Kuşadası Cad. 4/A).

Sports and the Outdoors

Participant Sports

Boating Cruises
One of the most enjoyable ways to see the coast is from the water. Bodrum is the main harbor for chartering a yacht, either with crew or bare boat. You can take a one- or two-week **blue voyage cruise**—as the locals call almost every boat trip in the area. Many of these are on gulets, converted wooden fishing craft with full crew.

Cost is about $600 a day for a boat with six double berths and crew. Agencies in Bodrum can provide information and make arrangements in advance: **Era Travel** (tel. 252/316–2054, fax 252/316–5338), **Halikarnas Turizm** (tel. 252/316–2397), **Karya Tur** (tel. 252/316–1535), and **Motif Travel** (tel. 252/316–2309, fax 252/316–3522).

Alternatively, you can arrange a cruise on the spot and do your own negotiating at the docks and save up to 25% depending on the season.

Day Trips
You can join a group sailing or motorboat excursion from many of the seaside towns. It's also possible to hire a boat for a day and have a trip put together to suit you; inquire either at the local tourist office (*see* Important Addresses and Numbers in Essential Information, *above*) or, better still, ask around at the harbor.

In Bodrum, the prime cruising ground is the mountain-rimmed **Gökova Körfezi** (Gökova Gulf), the body of water between the Bodrum peninsula and the Datça peninsula, 30 kilometers (18 miles) or so to the south. This densely pine-forested region is punctuated by tiny farming and fishing settlements. Although there are many classical and Byzantine remains along the Datça peninsula, **Cnidos,** at its tip, is the only major site (*see* Tour 1 in Chapter 6, The Mediterranean Coast). **Sedir Island** (and the ancient city called Cedreae), due north of Marmaris, is delightful when not overrun with day-trippers attracted by the golden sands of the lovely "Cleopatra Beach," so called because Mark Antony is said to have sent for sand from the Sahara to please his love.

Diving and Snorkeling
The warm, placid bays along the coast are ideal for snorkeling, and many of the big beach resorts have gear. However, Turkish authorities frown on exploring near archaeological ruins without a permit.

To learn about local conditions and obtain permits required to snorkel or dive in areas near archaeological sites, contact the local tourist information office or one of the following dive centers: Motif Diving (Neyzen Tevfik Cad. 80, tel. 252/316–2309) or Bodrum Spor (Yeni Çarşi 4, tel. 252/316–3847) in **Bodrum,** or Altay Spor Klübü in **İzmir** (tel. 232/421–0626).

Specialized three-night mini blue-voyage trips are available for scuba divers and snorkelers.

Windsurfing
Steady breezes off the Aegean and the many sheltered coves and harbors make windsurfing popular. Either stay at one of the many beach resorts along the water (*see* Dining and Lodging, *below*) or call the nearest resort with facilities and inquire about rentals, which are widely available.

Beaches

Alluring white sand *plaji* (beaches) are one of the coast's big draws. The most notable are the one at **Akçay** (on the Gulf of Edremit), which stretches for 7 kilometers (about 4½ miles); the fine white sand **Sarmısaklı,** outside Ayvalık; those along **Akburun** (the White Cape) and **Ilıca** beach, 5 kilometers (3 miles) south and north of Çeşme respectively; deserted **Gümüssu,** down the hill from the ancient city of Colophon; the long strand at **Pamucak,** 2 kilometers (1 mile) west of Selçuk.

The town beach at Bodrum is not one of the reasons people flock to the town. You'll find better in the outlying villages on the peninsula—**Torba,** backed by a big holiday village and casino; **Türkbükü,** quiet and family-oriented; popular **Turgutreis,** more of a scene; **Akyarlar,** which is rarely crowded; **Ortakent,** backed by old wooden town houses; **Bitez,** on a small bay; **Gümbet,** popular for windsurfing and diving; and **Gümüşük,** rimming a perfect bay with the half-submerged ruins of ancient Mindos. At all of these, the water is clear and outdoor restaurants abound; all are easy to reach from Bodrum by minibus or dolmuş. **Sedir Island,** in the Gökova Gulf, is delightful when not overrun with day-trippers.

Dining and Lodging

For details and price-category definitions, *see* Staying in Turkey in Chapter 1, Essential Information. Highly recommended establishments are indicated by a star ★.

Dining Eating along the coast is a pleasure, especially if you like seafood. The main course is generally whatever was caught that day, though there are always beef and lamb kebabs. Regional specialties generally begin with the sea—mussels stuffed with rice, pine nuts, and currants (one of the many stuffed dishes that fall under the general heading of *dolma*); *ahtapot salatası*, a cold octopus salad, often with shrimps thrown in, tossed in olive oil, vinegar, and parsley; and grilled fish, including *palamut* (baby tuna), *lüfer* (bluefish), *levrek* (sea bass), and *kalkan* (turbot). As in other parts of Turkey, the main difference between good inexpensive restaurants and good expensive restaurants is the details—in the pricier places, you'll find linen or cotton tablecloths and napkins rather than paper, crystal rather than basic glass. Your standard Aegean coast eatery might have sturdy wood tables and chairs, paper napkins on the tables, and maybe a fishnet draped on the wall. Because the Aegean is the most heavily visited region of the country, prices are higher than in the interior or on the Mediterranean but are still reasonable.

Dress and Unless otherwise noted, dress is casual at all establishments de-
Reservations scribed below, and reservations are not required.

Lodging If you want something fancy and upscale, you'll have to stay in İzmir or Bodrum. Elsewhere, accommodations are much more modest. Expect clean, simply furnished rooms, with low wood beds, industrial carpeting or Turkish rugs, maybe a print on the wall. As many hotels are near the water, don't forget to ask for a room with a view; you'll rarely pay much more, if anything extra at all.

Assos **Assos Kervansaray.** The best-situated of the trio of Assos hotels,
Dining and right at the farthest edge of the harbor, the Assos Kervansaray has
Lodging an aura of antiquity, probably because of the gray lava stone of
★ which it was built just a few years ago. The rooms are small and functional, and most have terrific views of the Aegean. There is a large, comforting fireplace in the lobby, and the restaurant serves dressed-up versions of traditional Turkish dishes. There is a swimming pier, though the beach itself is rocky. *Behramkale, Ayvacık, tel. 286/721–7093 or 286/721–7199, fax 286/721–7200. 48 rooms with*

bath. Facilities: restaurant, swimming pier, windsurfing. AE, MC, V. $$

Hotel Assos. This blocky hotel between the Kervansaray and the Behram draws a decidedly international crowd. Built in Mediterranean style gray lava stone, it has burnished wood paneling inside and a refined Turkish restaurant that opens up to the bay in good weather. Rooms are done in the same minimalist style as those of its neighbors. *Behramkale, Ayvacık, tel. 286/721–7017 or 286/721–7034, fax 286/721–7249. 36 rooms with bath. Facilities: restaurant. AE, MC, V. $$*

Hotel Behram. This is the third in the line of hotels in Assos, the first one you reach when driving into town, and the one to book if the other two are full. The rooms are tidy and simple, with whitewashed walls and Scandinavian-style furniture; not all have a view, however, so ask for one when you book. The restaurant has a cozy fireplace and stone walls, and turns out standard Turkish fare. *Behramkale, Ayvacık, tel. 286/721–7016 or 286/721–7328, fax 286/721–7044. 17 rooms with bath. Facilities: restaurant. AE, MC, V. $$*

Ayvalık
Dining
★

Canlı Balık. This fish restaurant at the end of the pier around the small harbor is a cut above most other small-town dining options. It delivers excellent food in a romantic setting—with local fishing boats swaying in the water a few feet away and the Aegean stretching to the horizon. Mezes range from fried squid to mussel salad in local olive oil. Then move on to fresh, grilled local fish, perhaps *barbunya* (red mullet). You may not be served any alcohol here, due to a disputed ban by the governor in 1994, but check first. *2nd bldg. n. of İnönü Cad., on harbor, no phone. No credit cards. $$*

Lodging

Büyük Berk. This modern hotel is on Ayvalık's best beach, about 3½ kilometers (2 miles) from the center of town. All rooms have balconies, most looking out over the Aegean. Rooms are functional, with low wooden beds and whitewashed walls. *Sarmısaklı Plaj, tel. 266/324–1045, fax 266/324–1194. 189 rooms with bath. Facilities: restaurant, disco, outdoor swimming pool, exercise room, tennis court. AE, DC, MC, V. $$*

Grand Hotel Temizel. Set away from the other hotels along Sarmısaklı beach, the Temizel is a fairly plush luxury hotel, with its private beach, casino, diminutive Turkish spa, and elegant lobby, all cool marble and gleaming brass. The guest rooms are also a cut above the usual, with bigger beds, wooden dressers, and a minibar. Most have Aegean views. *Sarmısaklı Plaj, tel. 266/324–2000, fax 266/324–1274. 164 rooms with bath. Facilities: restaurant, bar, disco, casino, outdoor swimming pool, tennis court, football field, windsurfing, exercise room, sauna, Turkish bath. AE, DC, MC, V. $$*

Ankara Oteli. Another hotel with a great location on Sarmısaklı beach, just a few feet from the surf, this is the least expensive option. Although rooms are nondescript, they do have balconies; book ahead to get one facing the beach. *Sarmısaklı Plaj, tel. 266/324–1195 or 266/324–1048, fax 266/324–0022. 108 rooms with bath. Facilities: café, bar, games room. No credit cards. Closed Nov.–Mar. $*

Bergama
Dining

Bergama Restaurant. The food at this spot, on the main street and not far from the Archaeological Museum, is basic Turkish—nothing fancy. The kebabs are good, as is the spicy, cold eggplant salad. The interior is airy and simple; if the weather's nice, you can sit outside under the awning. *Cumhuriyet Cad. 13, tel. 232/632–0601. No credit cards. $*

Lodging

Hotel Iskender. Open since 1990, this is a plain-looking building located in the center of town. Rooms are comfortable and air-conditioned for the hot summers. An outdoor restaurant offers typical Turkish food. *Izmir Cad. Ilıca Önü Mevkii, P.K. 35, tel. 232/633-2123, fax 232/633-1245. 60 rooms with bath. Facilities: 2 restaurants, bar. No credit cards. $$*

Tusan Bergama Moteli. If you can't get to someplace more picturesque, like Ayvalık or Foça, this serviceable, two-story motel is a good bet. The rooms are simple and well maintained. The location on the main route leading into Bergama, a short drive from town, means that it's quiet, though not terribly convenient if you don't have a car. *İzmir Yolu, Yolaçtı Mev., tel. 232/633-1938, fax 232/633-1938. 44 rooms with bath. Facilities: restaurant, outdoor swimming pool. No credit cards. $$*

Bodrum **Restaurant Han.** This restaurant benefits from a fine location, in an
Dining old 18th-century caravansary with a tree-shaded courtyard a block from the harbor. The decor is minimal—you eat at trestle tables in the open air. But the kebabs, *köfte* (grilled, ground lamb patties), and grilled fresh prawns are crowd pleasers. So is the belly dancer who performs most nights. *Kale Cad. 29, tel. 252/316-2156. Reservations advised in summer. No credit cards. $$$*

Amphora. The options are dazzling: 20 or so mezes (would you like your eggplant pureed, sautéed with garlic, or in tomato sauce?) and two dozen kinds of kebabs (will you have lamb grilled or baked, or ground and made into patties, or served plain or with yogurt, grilled vegetables, or spicy peppers?). Another plus is the setting, opposite the marina at the edge of town in an old stone building decorated with kilims and boating and fishing gear. *Neyzen Tevfik Cad. 172, tel. 252/316-2368. Reservations advised in summer. MC, V. $$*

Club Pirinç. This restaurant is notable for its Turkish–French cuisine and pleasant bar. *Yenicarsi 8, tel. 252/316-1454. No credit cards. $$*

★ **Kortan Restaurant.** This seaside fish house has outdoor seating with views of Bodrum Castle and Chios. The better dishes include fish kebabs and octopus salad plus whatever the catch of the day happens to be, usually served grilled. *Cumhuriyet Cad. 32, tel. 252/316-1241. Reservations advised in summer. AE, V. $$*

Lodging **Çömça-Manzara Hotel.** Each of the 30 small, whitewashed two-story apartments in this group has a living room, kitchen, and terrace. The location on a hill facing Bodrum Castle across the bay makes the complex look like a little Mediterranean village. But don't expect high style in the furnishings—the interiors recall American motels of the 1950s. In peak season, half-board may be required. *Kumbahçe Mah. Meteoroloji Yanı, tel. 252/316-2012, or 252/316-1719, fax 252/316-1720. 30 units with bath. Facilities: restaurant, outdoor pool. AE, DC, MC, V. $$$*

Ayaz Hotel. This hotel is on a small bay just east of the Bodrum harbor, away from the noise and bustle of town yet less than five minutes' drive from the center. It has pleasant gardens and its own beach, with a bar where you can listen to the waves and while away the hours. The guest rooms are contemporary and have balconies and sea views. *On Gümbet Bay, tel. 252/316-1174 or 252/316-2956, fax 252/316-4751. 96 rooms with bath. Facilities: restaurant, bar, pool, playground, water sports. V. $$*

Manastir Hotel Bodrum. The bar in this comfortable, whitewashed stucco Mediterranean-style hotel was once the site of a monastery. Front rooms have balconies and look out on views of Bodrum Castle. *Baris Sitesi Mevkii, Kumbahçe, tel. 252/316-2854, fax 252/316-2772. 59 rooms with bath. Facilities: 2 restaurants, bar, 2 pools, tennis, sauna fitness center. AE, V. $$*

Maya Hotel and Pansiyon. Though in the center of town, this hotel feels secluded, with its appealing private garden and swimming pool bordered by bright flowers. The rooms, in low white-stucco buildings, are utilitarian and nondescript, with Scandinavian-style furniture. In the associated pansiyon, on a tiny side street behind the marina, rooms are smaller, and you have to walk over to the hotel for a dip in the pool—but the prices are lower. *Gerence Sok. 32, Gümbet, tel. 252/316–4741, fax 252/316–4745. Hotel: 72 rooms with bath. Hotel facilities: restaurant, bar, pool, sauna, exercise room. MC, V. Closed mid-Nov.–Apr. $$*

★ **Herodot Pansiyon.** Rooms on the marina side of this popular pansiyon have a fine view of the castle. All guest quarters are quite simple, but the staff is eminently cheerful. Because of the large number of repeat guests, you'll have to book ahead to get a room during the summer. *Neyzen Tevfik Cad. 118, tel. 252/316–1093, or 252/316–2423. 15 rooms, 8 with bath. No credit cards. $*

Mylasa Pansiyon. An Australian archaeologist who found it hard to leave Bodrum runs this pansiyon in an attractive white-stucco building in the center of town. There is a comfortable lounge, and the pleasant roof deck has a view of the Aegean. Rooms are just what you find in most pansiyons: The beds are low, with wooden frames, and there's no decor to speak of. *Cumhuriyet Cad. 34, tel. 252/316–1846, fax 252/316–1254. 16 rooms with bath. Facilities: bar, breakfast area, terrace. MC, V. $*

Çanakkale and Troy
Dining

Sehir Restaurant. This waterside eatery has spacious indoor seating dominated by a painting of the siege of Troy, wooden horse and all, though you might prefer the terrace out front, if it's not windy. Try the octopus salad followed by a grilled version of whatever looks freshest. Top it off with a sample of the local dessert, *höşmerim* (a pastry made with semolina and cheese). *Yalı Cad. 24, tel. 286/217–1070. Reservations advised in summer. No credit cards. $–$$*

Trakya Restaurant. Run by six brothers who prepare the food daily, this popular restaurant has three branches in the main square. The oldest branch is where you'll find the traditional Turkish stewed foods, such as Orman Kebab, Tas Kebab, Patlican Musakka, and the ever-present *kuru fasulye & pilav*, (rice and beans), while the other two specialize in doner kebabs and grilled meats. Neither the landlocked setting nor the decor is remarkable, but the food is worth the trip. *Cumhuriyet Meydanı 32, tel. 286/217–3152. Reservations necessary for large groups. No credit cards. $*

Yalova Liman. This waterfront restaurant near the ferry docks is one locals prefer as well. The menu includes a good variety of appetizers and grilled fish or meat served on white starched tablecloths. Ask the chef which fish is in season and order it grilled or fried. The best part of eating here, however, is the evocative setting of the Dardanelles with the hum of locals discussing the latest soccer match. *Gümrük Sok. 7, tel. 286/217–1045. Reservations advised in summer. No credit cards. $*

Lodging

Akol. In this modern hotel on the Çanakkale waterfront, the lobby is bright, full of cool white marble and brass fixtures. The rooms resemble the better roadside motels in the United States with their green carpeting, wooden café table and two chairs, and the TV on the low wooden dresser. But if you've been staying in pansiyons, what you will appreciate most is the good water pressure in the showers. Ask for a room with a terrace overlooking the Dardanelles; you'll be able to see the memorials to World Wars I and II in the distance. *Kordonboyu, tel. 286/217–9456, fax 286/217–2897. 137 rooms with bath. Facilities: restaurant, bar, outdoor pool. AE, MC, V. $$*

Grand Truva Oteli. This establishment is a training school for aspiring young hotel professionals, and the students in charge are solicitous, only partly because their grades depend on it. Otherwise, the style is very similar to that of the Akol. The older section has views of the Dardanelles; the modern section in back, which lacks the views, is quite a bit spiffier, with newer carpeting and a more recent paint job. The location near Çanakkale's center makes the hotel an excellent base for sightseeing. *Kayserili Ahmet Paşa Cad., Yalıboyu, tel. 286/217–1024, fax 286/217–0903. 69 rooms with bath. Facilities: restaurant, bar. MC, V. $$*

Hotel Bakır. This small hotel near the clock tower in Çanakkale is acceptable if you're on a tight budget. While accommodations are highly unexceptional, those on the waterside have great views—and the prices are low. Request a room overlooking the water when booking. *Rıhtım Cad. 12, tel. 286/217–2908, fax 286/217–4090. 35 rooms with bath. Facilities: restaurant, bar. MC, V. $*

Tusan Güzelyalı. Surrounded by a pine forest on a beach at Intepe, 14 kilometers (8½ miles) south of Çanakkale (on the road to Troy), the Tusan Güzelyalı is one of the most popular hotels in the area. The draw is the setting, as the two-story, stucco and brick structure holds the usual nondescript rooms: low wooden beds, no real decor. Be certain to reserve well in advance. *Güzelyalı tel. 286/232–8210 or 232–0646, fax 286/232–8226. 64 rooms with bath. Facilities: 2 restaurants, bar, disco, beach. MC, V. Closed Oct.–Feb. $*

Çeşme
Dining

Körfez. With its chic terrace restaurant, upbeat pizza section, and indoor disco, this popular waterfront restaurant fills with vacationers in summer. At white-linen-covered tables on the terrace you can sample appetizers and order grilled or stewed (*buğulama*) fish—or allow the chef to send you his specialty, *sütlü balık* (baked fish in a special sauce topped with mushrooms and cheese). *Yalı Caddesi 12, tel. 232/712–6718 or 232/712–0901. Reservations required in summer. V. $$*

Sahil. A waterfront eatery across from the Ertan Hotel, it serves fresh, tasty appetizers like eggplant salad and typical Turkish dishes such as lamb şiş kebab, as well as grilled fish of the season, though servings seem a bit dainty. Seating is indoors or outdoors on a terrace, with red tablecloths. For scenery, you have the pretty but unremarkable bay of Çeşme as well as holidaymakers out for a promenade. *Cumhuriyet Meydanı 12, tel. 232/712–8294. Reservations advised in summer. No credit cards. $*

Sevim Café. Despite its location on an awkward corner at the edge of the main square by the sea, this café and restaurant is charming and serves its dishes in a style that you won't find elsewhere. During the day, it's more of a café, and tables find customers who want to sip coffee and read the paper. The owner, Ms. Zehra, hand-prepares the main dish the café is famous for: *mantı* (meat-filled raviolis topped with garlicky yogurt and served with a speckle of hot pepper and saffron). The chef, whose expertise is enhanced by international experience, also juggles meats on the grill, and arranges beautiful salads on the side. *Hal Binası 5 (opposite Kervansaray Hotel), no phone. Come early for a good seat. No credit cards. $*

Dining and Lodging
★

Kervansaray. Built in 1528 during the reign of Süleyman the Magnificent, this old property in the town center, next to Çeşme's medieval castle, is somewhat run-down and largely decorated in traditional Turkish style with kilims, low wooden furniture, and brass fittings. The bathrooms are tiled, motel-modern affairs. The restaurant is excellent. Good choices for lunch or dinner include lamb kebabs with yogurt, cold eggplant salad, and *börek* (deep-fried pastry shells, here filled with goat cheese). In pleasant weather, you can dine out-

So, you're getting away from it all.

Just make sure you can get back.

AT&T Access Numbers
Dial the number of the country you're in to reach AT&T.

*AUSTRIA†††	022-903-011	*GREECE	00-800-1311	NORWAY	800-190-11
*BELGIUM	078-11-0010	*HUNGARY	00◊-800-01111	POLAND†♦²	0◊010-480-0111
BULGARIA	00-1800-0010	*ICELAND	999-001	PORTUGAL†	05017-1-288
CANADA	1-800-575-2222	IRELAND	1-800-550-000	ROMANIA	01-800-4288
CROATIA†♦	99-38-0011	ISRAEL	177-100-2727	*RUSSIA† (MOSCOW)	155-5042
*CYPRUS	080-90010	*ITALY	172-1011	SLOVAKIA	00-420-00101
CZECH REPUBLIC	00-420-00101	KENYA†	0800-10	S. AFRICA	0-800-99-0123
*DENMARK	8001-0010	*LIECHTENSTEIN	155-00-11	SPAIN•	900-99-00-11
*EGYPT¹ (CAIRO)	510-0200	LITHUANIA♦	8◊196	*SWEDEN	020-795-611
*FINLAND	9800-100-10	LUXEMBOURG	0-800-0111	*SWITZERLAND	155-00-11
FRANCE	19◊-0011	F.Y.R. MACEDONIA	99-800-4288	*TURKEY	00-800-12277
*GAMBIA	00111	*MALTA	0800-890-110	UKRAINE†	8◊100-11
GERMANY	0130-0010	*NETHERLANDS	06-022-9111	UK	0500-89-0011

Countries in bold face permit country-to-country calling in addition to calls to the U.S. **World Connect**℠ prices consist of **USADirect**® rates plus an additional charge based on the country you are calling. Collect calling available to the U.S. only. *Public phones require deposit of coin or phone card. ◊Await second dial tone. †May not be available from every phone. †††Public phones require local coin payment through the call duration. ♦Not available from public phones. • Calling available to most European countries. ¹Dial "02" first, outside Cairo. ²Dial 010-480-0111 from major Warsaw hotels. ©1994 AT&T.

Here's a travel tip that will make it easy to call back to the States. Dial the access number for the country you're visiting and connect right to AT&T. It's the quick way to get English-speaking AT&T operators and can minimize hotel telephone surcharges.

If all the countries you're visiting aren't listed above, call **1 800 241-5555** for a free wallet card with all AT&T access numbers. Easy international calling from AT&T. **TrueWorld Connections.**

AT&T

American Express offers Travelers Cheques built for two.

Cheques *for Two*[SM] from American Express are the Travelers Cheques that allow either of you to use them because both of you have signed them. And only one of you needs to be present to purchase them.

Cheques *for Two* are accepted anywhere regular American Express Travelers Cheques are, which is just about everywhere. So stop by your bank, AAA* or any American Express Travel Service Office and ask for Cheques *for Two*.

doors in a courtyard surrounded by the ancient stone walls of the Kervansaray. *Kale Yanı, tel. 232/712–7177 or 232/712–6491, fax 232/712–2906. 34 rooms with bath. Facilities: restaurant, bar. AE, DC, MC, V. Closed Nov.–Mar. $$$*

Lodging **Altın Yunus Tatilköyü.** The low, bright white cuboid buildings of
★ this big resort—whose name translates as "golden dolphin"—curve along an attractive white sand beach edging a cove dotted with sailboats. The rooms are done in Mediterranean style, with lots of white and pale ocean blue, thicker carpets, and bigger beds, and, a more plush feel than you usually find in Turkey. Completely renovated in 1991 and offering almost every imaginable recreational facility, the resort is essentially a destination unto itself. *Kalemburnu Boyalık Mev., Ilıca, tel. 232/723–1250, fax 232/723–2252. 526 rooms with bath. Facilities: 4 restaurants, 2 bars, nightclub, disco, 2 indoor and 2 outdoor pools, Turkish bath, 2 tennis courts, exercise room, water-sports equipment (diving, windsurfing, sailing), playground, hairdresser. AE, MC, V. $$$*

Turban Çeşme. A hot spring feeds the thermal baths of this pleasant, likable hotel on a nice stretch of beach in Ilıca, 5 kilometers (3 miles) north of Çesme. The main building is a white stucco mid-rise, and the rooms are modern—expect the comforts and style of a typical stateside Holiday Inn. *Ilıca Mev., tel. 232/723–1240 or 232/723–1249, fax 232/723–1388. 214 rooms with bath. Facilities: restaurant, bar, disco, pool, thermal baths, tennis courts. AE, MC, V. $$$*

Ertan Oteli. The five-story, white stucco Ertan, on the water on the north side of the main square, is modern and efficient. Many rooms have views of the Aegean, as does the pleasant terrace restaurant. *Cumhuriyet Meyd. 12, tel. 232/712–6795, telex 51980. 60 rooms with bath. Facilities: restaurant, bar. MC, V. $$*

Tani Pansiyon. This is a sweet but very modest pansiyon, run by a friendly retired couple. The rooms are simple, with low wooden beds, and have views of the bay through crochet lace curtains made by the wife. Be sure to ask for a room facing the bay. Bathrooms and showers are shared, as is a lace-decked kitchen upstairs on the terrace, where breakfast is served. *Musalla Mahallesi, Çarşı Sok. 5, tel. 232/712–6238. 6 rooms. Facilities: terrace, kitchen. No credit cards. $*

Foça **Restaurant Foça.** Foça is a fishing village, and the restaurants along
Dining the little harbor usually offer an appropriately dizzying array of fresh fish. In this one, the best of a good bunch, you can have your palamut, lüfer, or levrek grilled to perfection. *Küçükdeniz, Belediye Altı, tel. 232/812–1307. No credit cards. $*

Lodging **Club Mediterranée.** This fishing village seems an unlikely spot for one of these all-inclusive vacation resorts, but the French vacation operation does a creditable job here. Red-tile-roofed bungalows are grouped into two small hamlets, one atop a hill overlooking the Aegean, the other in an olive grove. As at all Club Meds, everything's included in the price you pay to stay. *In Eski Foça, on unnumbered rd., 12 km (7 mi) n. of Foça, tel. 232/812–1607, or 232/812–2176, fax 232/812–2175; in U.S., 212/750–1687. 376 rooms with bath. Facilities: restaurant, bar, pool, water-sports equipment (diving, waterskiing, windsurfing), tennis court. AE, DC, MC, V. $$$$*

Hanedan. This unassuming four-story hotel in what looks like a town house is at the opposite end of the spectrum from the Club Med. It is in town, on the harbor, and quite pleasant. Public areas are scattered with Turkish rugs and kilims; guest rooms are small and simple. *Büyükdeniz Sahil Cad. 1, tel. 232/812–1515, fax 232/812–1609. 27 rooms with bath. Facilities: restaurant. No credit cards. $$*

İzmir
Dining

Deniz. Befitting the bayside location, the main event in this attractive spot on the ground floor of the İzmir Palas hotel is the seafood. Options range from sole to sea bass, mussels to mullet, and *kılıç şiş* (grilled swordfish kebab) is a house specialty. *Vasıf Çınar Bul. 2, tel. 232/422–0601. MC, V. $$*

Mangal. A waterfront seafood spot, the Mangal is just a short stroll south from Cumhuriyet Square. The fried calamari is tasty, and there are some kebabs to balance the fish. While most tables are in the long, narrow dining room, there are some out on the sidewalk under umbrellas—go early to claim a seat in good weather. *Atatürk Cad. 110, tel. 232/425–2860. No credit cards. $$*

Park Restaurant. The best of the Kültürpark restaurants, this is a change of pace from your Aegean diet of waterfront seafood places. The setting amid the park's greenery is lovely, the grilled meats and mezes—eggplant salad, börek filled with white cheese, stuffed vine leaves, and stuffed peppers—are a notch above the usual. *Kültürpark, tel. 232/489–3590. No credit cards. $$*

Ilif İskender. Everybody in İzmir has a favorite kebab place, and this one is on a lot of lists. It's a lively sidewalk café in the center of the city, a block in from the water, with tasty döner kebabs—and budgetwise prices. *Cumhuriyet Bul. 194, no phone. No credit cards. $*

Lodging

İzmir Hilton. At 34 stories, the Hilton is one of the tallest buildings on the Aegean coast. Striking and modern, new in 1992, it looms over the center of the city. From the 10-story atrium to the elegant rooftop restaurant, the public spaces are suitably grand. Guest rooms are plush, with their thick floral comforters and matching drapes. And the facilities are more impressive than the competition's. About the only complaint that can be leveled is that there is nothing particularly Turkish about the place. *Gazi Osman Paşa Bul. 7, tel. 232/441–6060, fax 232/441–2277. 381 rooms with bath. Facilities: 4 restaurants, 2 bars, casino, 2 tennis courts, 2 squash courts, pool, health club, business center, shopping mall. AE, DC, MC, V. $$$$*

Pullman Etap Konak. Of İzmir's two hotels in France's Pullman chain, this is the better situated—right on the water. There's lots of cool marble and greenery, and the guest rooms are quite pleasant, with full-size beds, plush carpet, and big windows with views. The city's museums are within easy walking distance. *Mithatpasa Cad. 128, tel. 232/289–1500, fax 232/289–1709. 76 rooms with bath. Facilities: restaurant, bar, conference room. AE, MC, V. $$$*

Hotel Kilim. In this tastefully renovated hotel dating from the 1950s, rooms are comfortable, and some have bay views. Those close to the street can be noisy, so ask for one higher up. The hotel's nondescript restaurant serves seafood and traditional Turkish lamb dishes—in good weather at tables set up on the sidewalk to take advantage of harbor views. *Kazim Dirik Cad. 1, tel. 232/484–5340, fax 232/489–5070. 90 rooms with bath. Facilities: restaurant, bar. MC, V. $$*

Karaca Otel. This newish mid-rise hotel is on a little side street, and some rooms have a view of the gardens; some rooms have terraces. The decor is contemporary, with wall-to-wall carpeting and some Turkish touches, the location is convenient, and the rates are lower than at larger, neighboring properties. *Necati Bey Bul., 1379 Sok. 55, tel. 232/489–1940, fax 232/483–1498. 73 rooms with bath. Facilities: restaurant, meeting room, bar, hairdresser. AE, MC, V. $$*

Kısmet. The guest rooms and public spaces at the friendly, comfortable, and tastefully decorated Kısmet are comparable to those at the Karaca, but as it doesn't have the view and is a few years older, you'll pay less. The side-street location makes it quieter than places on the main drag. *1377 Sok. 9, tel. 232/463–3853, fax 232/421–4856. 68 rooms with bath. Facilities: restaurant. AE, DC, MC, V. $–$$*

Hotel Baylan. It's hard to beat the Baylan for value. This four-story property dating from the 1950s has been totally redone. Behind the shiny marble facade, the rooms are bright and pleasant if on the small side, with unprepossessing Scandinavian-style furniture—but then, few budget hotels in Turkey are known for high style. *Anafartalar Cad., Basmane, 1299 Sok. 8, tel. 232/483–1426, fax 232/483–3844. 33 rooms with bath. Facilities: restaurant, bar. No credit cards. $*

Kuşadası
Dining

Sultan Han. Full of atmosphere, and with excellent food, Sultan Han is in an old house built around a courtyard whose focal point is a stately, gigantic palm tree. You can dine in the open-air courtyard or upstairs in small rooms piled with kilims, where you sit on cushions at low brass tables. Either way, you'll want to start by stopping at the kitchen to select your meal from platters piled high with fish and shellfish of every possible variety. Much of it is grilled; mussels, prawns, and squid can be quite good fried. Fish baked in salt is a local specialty. It's in the heart of town, just off Barbaros Hayrettin Caddesi, the main shopping street. *Bahar Sok. 8, tel. 256/614–6380. Reservations required. No credit cards. $$$*

Ada Restaurant. This spacious open-air restaurant is beautifully located on Pigeon Island. Choices from the menu, such as local fish, appetizers, and kebabs, are conveniently displayed at the entrance along with their prices. *Güvercin Adası. tel. 256/614–1725. AE, MC, V. $$*

Ali Baba Restaurant. An appetizing and colorful mound of the day's catch meets you at the entrance to this waterside fish restaurant. The decor and the style are simple, but the view over the bay is soothing and the food fabulous. For starters, try the cold black-eyed bean salad, marinated octopus salad, or the fried calamari, and follow it with a grilled meat dish or whatever fish is in season. It's worth reserving in advance at this spot, which fills up by 8 PM. *Belediye Turistik Çarşısı 5, tel. 256/614–1551. Reservations advised. MC, V. $$*

★ **Nil Restaurant.** Under new management, the former Ibrahim Ustanin Yeri still serves some of the best food in town. You can make your selection from the appetizers on display and choose the barbecued shrimp or chicken—or try the dishes the cook prides himself on: fish baked in salt or *bugulama* (stewed fish with spices). The atmosphere, not as scenic as the seaside eateries, is nautical, with shells, fish, and garlics suspended with a ceiling fishnet. *Türkmen Mah., 50. Yıl Caddesi 3, tel. 256/614–8063. Reservations advised. AE, V. $$*

Çamtepe Restaurant. This new and modest terrace restaurant centrally located across from the Kervansaray Hotel and the central market has views of the sea as well as the bustling pedestrian street below. The *pirzola* (grilled lamb chops) are particularly good here, as are the appetizers. The seafood, as ever, is exhibited at the entrance in an artistic heap. *Cephane Sokak 3, tel. 256/614–8348. Reservations advised in summer. MC, V. $*

Özurfa. Özurfa is a good spot for Turkish fast food. The focus is on kebabs; the Urfa kebab—spicy, grilled slices of lamb on pita bread—is the house specialty, and the fish kebabs are tasty. The location just off Barbaros Hayrettin Caddesi is convenient to the market. *Cephane Sok. 7, tel. 256/612–6070. No credit cards. $*

Lodging

Club Kervansaray. A refurbished, 300-year-old inn that was once a way station for camel caravans, this hotel decorated in the Ottoman style is loaded with charm and atmosphere. The main entrance has massive, armor-plated doors; the central courtyard—where the camels once were kept—is paved with marble and planted with palm trees; and the rooms are decorated with kilims and Turkish folk art. The hotel, in the center of town, has a dressy Turkish restaurant with live entertainment: singers, perhaps a belly dancer, and, later, a pop band. *Atatürk Bul. 1, tel. 256/614-4115, fax 256/614-2423. 40 rooms with bath. Facilities: restaurant, bar, nightclub. AE, D, MC, V. $$$*

★ **Kismet.** Although small, Kismet is run on a grand scale by a descendant of the last Ottoman sultan and is surrounded by beautifully maintained gardens. Located on a promontory overlooking the marina on one side and the Aegean on the other, it feels almost like a private Mediterranean villa with its low, white stucco cubes stepped up a hillside. Each room has a private balcony, most with sea views. Kismet's popularity makes reservations a must. *Akyar Mev., Türkmen Mah., tel. 256/614-2005, fax 256/614-4914. 96 rooms with bath. Facilities: restaurant, tennis court, private beach. MC, V. Closed Nov.-Mar. $$$*

Atınç Otel. The Atınç, a mid-rise built in the late 1980s, has a good location: a walk from the center of town, but not so close that you're bothered by the noise. Other pluses include the Aegean views from the front rooms, and the rooftop pool with a panorama of town. Guest rooms have balconies, but not much style. *Atatürk Bul., tel. 256/614-7608, fax 256/614-4967. 75 rooms with bath. Facilities: 2 restaurants, 2 bars, pool, exercise room. MC, V. $$*

Efe Otel. This pleasant mid-priced hotel sits on the waterfront a little beyond the path to Pigeon Island. It's small—a four-story whitewashed box with dark wood trim—but the staff is pleasantly personal. Rooms are nondescript—the carpeting drab, the walls bare, and the beds low, with wooden frames—but many have balconies and views of Pigeon Island. *Güvercin Ada Cad. 37, tel. 256/614-3660, fax 256/614-3662. 44 rooms with bath. Facilities: restaurant, bar. MC, V. $$*

Bahar Pansiyon. There are whitewashed walls and dark wood beams throughout this cozy, small hotel. Front rooms have balconies; and all are quiet, easily affordable, and a block from Hayrettin Barbaros Caddesi. *Cephane Sok. 12, tel. 256/614-1191, fax 256/614-1099. 20 rooms with bath. Facilities: restaurant, bar. No credit cards. $*

Liman Hotel. Opened in 1993, this is a quaint, whitewashed, narrow building with contrasting black cast iron balconies located very close to the port, as its name denotes. The air-conditioned rooms, which are carpeted and clean, have basic but comfortable furniture, and the service is attentive and sincere. Don't forget to ask for a room in the front of the building, facing the sea. *Kıbrıs Cad. Buyral Sok. 4, tel. and fax 256/612-3149. 16 rooms with bath. Facilities: cafe, terrace restaurant. No credit cards. $*

Pamukkale
Dining and
Lodging
Though there are numerous pansiyons in Pamukkale village, the best bet are those clustered in one short strip at the top of the slope, overlooking the hot pools. Though they cost more than places down below, they take advantage of Turkey's most famous spa waters and offer wonderful views over the calcified cliffs—and that, after all, is the reason for coming here.

Tusan Motel. The pool, this white stucco hostelry's best feature, is one of the most enticing in the area, thanks to incredible views of the so-called cotton cliffs. Rooms are comfortable, if basic—with the usual bare walls and small, low wooden beds. The rectangular, one-story block of a building is at the top of a steep hill, with expansive views. *Tel. 258/272-2010, fax 258/272-2059. 47 rooms with bath. Fa-*

cilities: restaurant, outdoor swimming pool. AE, DC, MC, V.
$$–$$$

Hotel Koru. The rooms here are virtually indistinguishable from those at the Tusan. The differences are that this white stucco box is larger, with two stories rather than one; attracts tour groups; delivers slightly less personal service; and costs less. *Tel. 258/272–2429, fax 258/272–2023. 132 rooms with bath. Facilities: restaurant, disco, indoor and outdoor swimming pools. MC, V. $$*

Pamukkale Motel. This otherwise unexceptional motel is celebrated for its pool, which has pieces of marble columns and statuary from Roman times scattered about. The rooms are fresh and pleasant. *Tel. 258/272–2024, fax 258/272–2026. 45 rooms with bath. Facilities: restaurant, outdoor swimming pool, 2 tennis courts. No credit cards. $$*

Selçuk/ Ephesus Dining

Günhan Restaurant. One of the few places to eat at the Ephesus ruins, it offers a variety of foods, from sandwiches to traditional stewed Turkish dishes, while a chef in white gear juggles shish kebabs, lamb chops, and steaks on a grill. Shaded with red and white awnings, it's the perfect spot for a rest and cool drink before, or after, a trip to the ruins. *Efes Ruins, tel. 252/892–2291. No credit cards. $*

Meryemana Restaurant. This restaurant, which has sprawling outdoor seating under towering trees, is located on the grounds of Meryemana, the House of the Virgin Mary, just 5 kilometers (3 miles) from Ephesus. Meat dishes, in particular, *çöp şiş*, a smaller version of shish kebab cooked on thin wooden skewers, are the specialty here. In high season, it gets quite touristy, with busloads of visitors filling the seats and the shops nearby. *Meryemana, Selçuk, tel. 232/892–1422. Reservations necessary for groups. No credit cards. $*

Seçil Restaurant. Located centrally on Cengiz Topel Caddesi, this is a sidewalk restaurant in the summer. The appetizers are usually fresh, because there's a quick turnover in high season. Grilled meats are a better choice in summer, when there's a fishing ban and the price of fish goes up considerably. *Atatürk Mah. Cengiz Topel Cad. 63, tel. 232/891–5384. No credit cards. $*

Lodging

Hotel Pinar. The Pinar, a four-story concrete block, is the only hotel in town with a government three-star rating. But don't expect more than a modern motel, and a basic one at that, with small beds and industrial carpeting. On the other hand, the management is efficient and the location central, and there is always plenty of hot water—and good pressure in the showers, which you don't always find in a pansiyon. *Sehabettin Dede Cad., Selçuk, tel. 232/892–2561, fax 232/892–3033. 40 rooms with bath. Facilities: restaurant, bar. MC, V. $$*

Kale Han. A small hotel in an old, refurbished stone inn, Kale Han is run by a warm, welcoming family. The rooms are simple, with bare, whitewashed walls and dark timber beams. Off the lobby is a sitting area with kilim-covered couches and an old TV, and the dining area has stone walls and a big fireplace. A recently renovated building in the courtyard has been turned into private suites. The restaurant, which serves some of the best food in town, is open 24 hours. Ask for a room facing the castle behind the hotel. *Atatürk Cad. 49, Selçuk, tel. 232/892–6154, fax 232/892–2169. 52 rooms with shower. Facilities: restaurant, outdoor pool. V. $$*

Hotel Akay. The Akay has a nice alternative location, up in a quiet residential neighborhood by the İsa Bey Cami. A relatively new hotel, it at least has touches of old Ottoman style—whitewashed walls inside and out, latticed balconies, arched windows and doors, kilims on the floor, copper and brass pots here and there. *İsa Bey Camii*

Kar., Serin Sok. 3, Selçuk, tel. 232/892–3172, fax 232/892–3009. 16 rooms with bath. Facilities: restaurant. D, MC, V. $

Hülya. This pleasant pansiyon, painted lavender and pastel green, looks like a small apartment building and has lemon and tangerine trees in its courtyard. The rooms are simple, but the place does come with one special amenity: One member of the family who runs the place is a fisherman, and occasionally his day's catch is cooked to order for guests. This is probably the cheapest option in Selçuk. *Atatürk Cad., Özgür Sok. 15, Selçuk, tel. 232/892–2120. 8 rooms with bath. Facilities: restaurant. No credit cards. $*

Tusan Efes Motel. This pleasant, white stucco compound next to the Ephesus archaeological site feels removed from the action, as it's surrounded by eucalyptus trees and next to a campground. Though the rooms are bare and unimpressive, the location is great: Without taxing yourself unduly, you can get to the site well ahead of the bus tours. The restaurant offers a delicious array of Turkish foods. *Ephesus, tel. 232/892–6060. 12 rooms with bath. Facilities: restaurant, outdoor pool. No credit cards. $*

Victoria Hotel. The name of this recently expanded four-story hostelry in the heart of town recalls the owners' time in England. It's a tidy, cheerful little place with marble floors in the lobby and white-washed walls set off by honey-colored wood trim throughout. The restaurant is a good bet for traditional Turkish fare. Rooms have delightful views of storks nesting on the ancient columns of an aqueduct. *Cengiz Topel Cad. 4, Selçuk, tel. 232/892–3203, fax 232/892–3204. 24 rooms with bath. Facilities: restaurant. V. $*

The Arts and Nightlife

The English-language *Turkish Daily News*, available at most newsstands, carries dates and times for most events.

The Arts

The ancient theater at Ephesus is used now and again for concerts and other performances. The main event is the **International Ephesus Festival** held each May. The annual camel wrestling tournaments, held throughout the Aegean in January and February, pit specially trained animals against one another while townspeople watch. To find out more, contact the local tourist information office.

Nightlife

Dominating the after-dark scene are hotel nightclubs and restaurants with a Turkish pop singer or sultry female torch singer often followed by a belly dancer. In summer, the bigger towns also have open-air discos, which get rolling by about 10 PM and go well into the early morning hours.

Bodrum The scene here is more sophisticated than anywhere else along the Aegean. The **Halikarnas Disco** (Cumhuriyet Cad. 178, tel. 252/316–8000) bills itself as "probably the most amazing nightclub in the world." It is, in fact, rather like discos more commonly found in western Mediterranean resorts, complete with fog machines and laser lights. The **Mavi Bar** (tel. 252/316–3932) and **Hadigari** (tel. 252/316–7179) are venerable meccas in Bodrum drinking circles, attracting Turkish artists, writers, and their numerous hangers-on. The **Jazz Cafe** (Kumbahçe Mevkii, tel. 252/316–6340) near the marina is a pleasant place to while away the night hours.

İzmir   Three open-air restaurant/nightclubs, **Kubana** (Kulturpark, tel. 232/425–4773), **Mogambo** 232/425–5488), and **Bonsai** (opposite the tennis club, tel. 232/425–1447) are in the Kültürpark. At the **Grand Korfez II** (tel. 232/368–8082), in the Karsiyaka ferry terminal, Turkish musicians perform for diners. **Charlie's Cocktail Bar** (1386 Sok. 8/B, Alsancak, tel. 232/422–6658) is popular with the expatriate crowd. The **Epsilon Disco Bar** (Ataturk Cad. 390, tel. 232/421–4981) attracts a young crowd. Meanwhile, if you're into bar-hopping, 1469 Sokak is known as the bar strip.

Kuşadası   The **Club Kervansaray** (Atatürk Bul. 2, tel. 256/614–4115) has dining, dancing, and a show on most nights. In the market area are two decent bars, the **Beebop** (Cephane Sok 20, tel. 256/614–7070) and the **Orient Bar**, (Kişla Sok. 8, tel. 256/614–2249), usually with pop or jazz music and a younger crowd. You can also walk across the causeway to **Pigeon Island,** where today's Young Turks dress up to mingle with the more energetic tourists at a boisterous disco—there's no name beyond the "Disco" on the sign, and you can hear it almost all over this minuscule landfall. Several British-style pubs punctuate the street called **Eski Pazaryeri Sokak.** On **Barlar Sokak,** Kuşadası's bar strip, the spacious, popular **Queen Victoria** (tel. 256/614–1511) has live music in summer.

6 The Mediterranean Coast

Mention the Mediterranean, and the first images that usually come to mind are of the villas along the French Riviera, chic Italian resorts, or perhaps the white cuboid houses of the Greek Islands. Turkey's slice of the Med has elements of these and more. It has Turkey's best beaches, endless stretches of fine white sand, most of them seldom crowded. And, if you believe the endless references, Cleopatra and Mark Antony swam on most every one while carrying on their torrid affair. The Turkish Mediterranean has ancient cities of Greek, Roman, Arab, Seljuk, Armenian, crusader, and Byzantine vintage. There is Termessos, known as the Eagle's Nest, the one fortress Alexander the Great deemed too strong to take. There is Aspendos, whose Roman theater rivals the Colosseum. Here Saint Paul came, spreading the Gospel to the Seven Churches of Asia, and here as well the might of Islam overcame the Byzantines, setting the foundation for a great Muslim empire.

The modern Mediterranean is as noteworthy as the ancient. On the one hand, there are unspoiled fishing villages, such as Üçağiz on Kekova sound, and, on the other, ultrasmart seaports such as Marmaris. Along the coast you will find bustling bazaars stocked with piles of halvah; bright, baggy trousers; and exotic homemade jams—eggplant and rose among them. Turkish tourist brochures like to brag that the coast compares to the Greek Islands of 20 or 30 years ago. In a sense they're right. Tourism has not yet developed here to the point that restaurants serve up mainly fish-and-chips, or that the natives think of you only in terms of the trinkets you might buy. Here, if you ask a young man directions to the main highway, he is apt to jump onto his motorcycle and lead you the 5 kilometers (3 miles) or so to find it.

And yet Turkey's Mediterranean coast is not virgin territory. Though the big tour buses that ply the Aegean are much less common here, British and German travelers discovered the region long ago, and the requisite services have been developed. The roads are mostly paved, there are gas stations when you need them, and you can always find a clean, comfortable place to stay.

Essential Information

Important Addresses and Numbers

Tourist Information Tourist offices are in most of the coast's bigger towns, including **Adana** (Atatürk Cad. 13, tel. 322/359–1994); **Alanya** (Çarşi Mah. at Kalearkasi Cad., Damlatas Yani, tel. 242/513–5436); **Antakya** (Vali Orgen Alani 147, tel. 326/216–0610, fax 326/213–5740); **Antalya,** next to the Turkish Airlines office (Cumhuriyet Cad. 91, tel. 242/241–1747) and in the old town (Selçuk Mah., Mermerli Sok., tel. 242/247–5042, fax 242/247–6298); **Dalaman,** at the airport (tel. 252/692–5220); **Datça,** opposite the Ziraat Bank (İskele Mah. Hükümet Binasi, tel. 252/712–3163 or 252/712–3546); **Fethiye,** next to the Hotel Dedeoglu (İskele Meyd. 1, tel./fax 252/614–1527); **Kaş,** in the main square (Cumhuriyet Meyd. 5, tel. 242/836–1238); **Marmaris** (İskele Meyd. 2, tel. 252/412–7277), by the ferry dock; **Mersin,** near the docks (Ismet Inönü Bul., Liman Girişi, tel. 324/231–2710, fax 324/231–6358); **Side,** on the main highway (tel. 242/753–2657); and **Silifke** (Veli Gürten Bozbey Cad. 6, Gazi Mah, tel. 324/714–1151, fax 324/714–5328).

Travel Agencies The better establishments include **Tantur** (K Evren Bulvari, Emre Oteli, tel. 252/412–4616, fax 252/412–6921) in Marmaris, **Sardes**

Tourism (Kordon Cad. 26, Dalyan, tel. 252/284–2050, fax 252/284–2189) in Dalyan, **Kahramanlar Turizm** (Cumhuriyet Mey 9, tel. 242/836–1062 or 242/836–2400, fax 242/836–2422) in Kaş, and **Pamphylia Travel** (Istiklal Cad., tel. 242/243–1500, fax 242/242–1400) in Antalya.

Arriving and Departing by Plane

Airports and Airlines
The main airports for flights between the coast and Istanbul, İzmir, or Ankara are in **Dalaman** and **Antalya.** Service to far eastern Turkey is from **Adana.** Charter flights, some direct from Europe, predominate in Dalaman, which also has summer service by **Turkish Airlines** (tel. 212/663–6363 in Istanbul, 242/242–6272 or 242/241–2830 in Antalya) from Istanbul and Ankara. Antalya has several daily flights from Istanbul by Turkish Airlines and **Istanbul Airlines** (tel. 212/231–7526 in Istanbul, 242/243–3893 in Antalya), and less frequent service from Ankara and İzmir. Turkish Airlines also offers one direct flight each week from London, two from Zurich, and three from Tel Aviv.

Between the Airports and Town
There is frequent bus service between Antalya's airport and the city center, 10 kilometers (6 miles) away; the cost is $2. Taking a taxi to the city bus station (Kazım Özalp Cad., tel. 242/241–6231) should cost about $5.

From Dalaman Airport, buses travel frequently between Fethiye and Marmaris, 50 kilometers (31 miles) east and 60 kilometers (37 miles) west, respectively; the trip costs about $5. In Marmaris the city *otogar* (bus station, tel. 252/412–3037) is two blocks north of İskele Meydanı, the main square. In Fethiye, it is just off Atatürk Caddesi, about 1 kilometer (⅗ mile) east of the town center (tel. 252/614–3531).

Arriving and Departing by Car, Train, and Bus

By Car
The main coast road from the Aegean becomes Route 330 at Milas and continues through Mugla toward Marmaris. From Marmaris, the coast road going east is Route 400, which continues all the way to Mersin. The drive to Marmaris is 287 kilometers (177 miles) from İzmir, 178 kilometers (110 miles) from Bodrum.

To Antalya, the inland routes are the E87 from Pamukkale (296 kilometers, or 178 miles) and the E90 to Polatli, joining up with Route 695 heading south to Aksehir and Route 330 from Ankara (552 kilometers, or 341 miles).

By Train
There is no service along the Mediterranean coast. To reach Mersin or Adana in the east, the nearest trains leave from Ankara.

By Bus
Service is plentiful. Routes are between Bodrum or İzmir and Marmaris; between Pamukkale's station in Denizli and Antalya; between Ankara and Antalya or Mersin. The trip from Ankara is a long, slow 12 hours, but fares are only $10–$15.

Getting Around

By Car
Although the highways between towns are well maintained, the smaller roads are usually unpaved and very rough, and the twisty coast roads take concentration. Just don't try to rush or cover too much ground. Some sample distances: Marmaris to Fethiye, 168 kilometers (104 miles); Fethiye to Antalya, 318 kilometers (196 miles);

Antalya to Alanya, 115 kilometers (71 miles). To estimate drive times, figure on about 70 kilometers (42 miles) per hour.

By Bus Service here is not as frequent or convenient as that along the Aegean, but you can still get around easily enough. Every city has an intercity bus terminal—this is where you buy tickets and check schedules. Routes connect Antalya (bus station tel. 242/241–6231) with Marmaris (bus station tel. 252/412–3037) and Mersin (bus station tel. 324/233–7825), and Adana (bus station, tel. 322/234–1968), with stops in between.

By Boat This is the best way to see the many otherwise inaccessible coves and picnic areas. Local fishermen will transport you for a small fee, or you can hop on one of the many water taxis. You will see both types of transport lined up along the harbor in every seaside town. Many people charter boats and join the small flotillas that leave the Bodrum and Marmaris marinas daily for sightseeing in the summer.

Perhaps the most romantic way to tour the coast is to cruise for several days in a *gulet*, the traditional wood sailboat that looks so graceful on the turquoise water. In this dreamy, private world, timbers creak, brass fittings glint in the sun, hidden bays beckon off the bow, and beaches and ancient cities not on landlubbers' maps become your personal hideaways. The best time to go is on the edge of summer, in May, September, and October, when the weather is cooler and the number of fellow travelers is low. Though not for the bargain-minded, chartering a yacht or gulet is not as expensive as you might think—off-season rates start at about $300 per day, including crew. And the price becomes more reasonable still if you travel with a family or another couple or two, which is definitely a possibility since the boats typically offer from three to six double cabins. **Alkor Yachting** (tel. 252/412–4385, fax 252/412–4384) and **Yeşil Marmaris** (tel. 252/412–6486, fax 252/412–4470) are just two of the chartering agencies in Marmaris. In 1994, rates were about $500 a day for a boat with six double berths and crew, but the exact fare is a direct reflection of your ability to haggle. Except in summer, which is high season here, you can simply present yourself on the quay and strike a deal on the spot; you'll get a far better price than if you book your cruise stateside and end up paying commissions on top of the fare.

Exploring the Mediterranean Coast

Until the mid-1970s, Turkey's southwest coast was inaccessible to all but the most determined travelers—those intrepid souls in four-wheel-drive vehicles or on the backs of donkeys. Today well-maintained highways wind through the area. The following tours start at Marmaris and work their way east. The beaten track peters out after Antalya and Side, although those with plenty of time) can continue all the way to Antakya, near the Syrian border. Another option is to fly into Antalya and work your way west by car or bus. This approach leaves you in a good position to tackle the Aegean coast or to take the ferry from Marmaris to Rhodes and the Greek Islands.

Highlight for First-Time Visitors

Cnidos, Tour 1
Dalyan's cliff tombs, Tour 2

Hatay Müzesi, Antakya, Off the Beaten Track
İztuzu, Tour 2
Kaş, Tour 2
Keci Buku, Tour 1
Mountain aerie at Termessos, Tour 3
Ölü Deniz's beaches, Tour 2
Patara beach, Tour 2
Preserved theater at Aspendos, Tour 3

Tour 1: Marmaris and the Datça Peninsula

Numbers in the margin correspond to points of interest on the West-ern and Eastern Mediterranean Coast maps.

Ranging from the smart, international crowd partying in Marmaris to the wild, windswept ancient ruins of Cnidos, this tour does not cover a great deal of mileage. But it does encompass a vast span of time. You will also have the chance to explore the scenic Datça Pen-insula.

The 178-kilometer (111-mile) drive along Route 400 from Bodrum to Marmaris climbs over steep, winding mountain passes, with cliffs that drop straight into the sea. This dramatic introduction to the re-gion ends in the tame, broad boulevard lined with eucalyptus trees that runs the final 30 kilometers (19 miles) into town.

❶ **Marmaris,** like Bodrum, is a fashionable resort area situated be-tween two bays and backed by an old castle. The jumping-off point for some of the best sailing on the Mediterranean, it is a favorite stop for yachting parties from around the world and has sprouted the sorts of boutiques, restaurants, and nightlife that seem to be a re-quirement for this set. The result is an attractive ensemble that is a far cry from anything in rural Turkey. Because of this, some will say it is not authentically "Turkish" and push on into the hinterland; others will be mesmerized and settle in for a long stay.

Until the growth of tourism, Marmaris was a sleepy little fishing vil-lage, but its origins go back over 2,500 years. The modern town is built on the site of the ancient Greek city of Phryscus, the remains of which can still be seen on Asar Tepe, a hill 1.5 kilometers (1 mile) to the north of the modern town. Its fine natural harbor once attracted warships rather than today's yachts and pleasure boats. It was from Marmaris that Suleyman the Magnificent launched his successful seaborne assault on the island of Rhodes in 1522 and here too that the fleet of the British admiral Horatio Nelson sheltered before set-ting forth to defeat the fleet of Napoleon Bonaparte at the battle of Aboukir in Egypt in 1798.

Modern Marmaris could hardly appear more peaceful, with its pleasing palm-lined waterfront promenade, the boats bobbing on the gentle offshore swells, and a well-stocked bazaar where you can pick up delicious local honey and rose jam, frankincense, and other exotica. You can also strike out for nearby beaches at **İçmeler, Turunç,** and **Kumlubük** (*see* Beaches in Sports and Outdoor Activi-ties, *below*).

Time Out At the **Turunç Bar Yacht Club,** you can dine on traditional Turkish dishes on a small terrace built into a hill above a sandy cove, sur-rounded by mountains and pine forests. It's on the road toward Kumlubük beach, about a five-minute walk from the harbor, and is closed from November through mid-May.

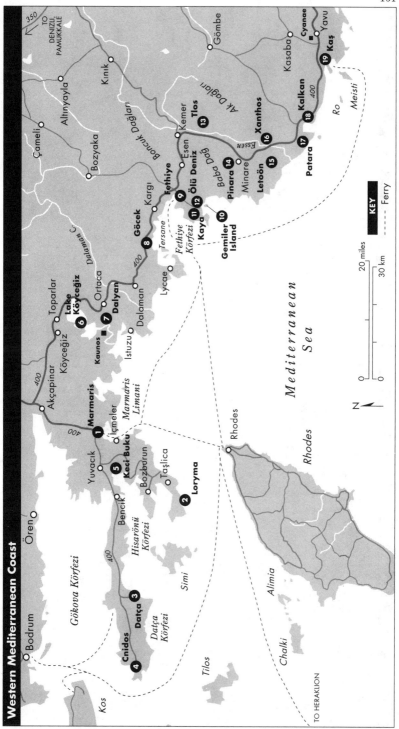

Western Mediterranean Coast

TO
DENIZLI,
PAMUKKALE

KEY

– – – Ferry

20 miles

30 km

Mediterranean Sea

Rhodes

TO HERAKLION

Bodrum • Ören • *Gökova Körfezi* • Yuvacık • Bencik • *Hisarönü Körfezi* • *Datça Körfezi* • Datça ③ • Cnidos ④ • *Simi* • İçmeler • Marmaris ① • *Marmaris Limanı* • Keçi Bükü ⑤ • Bozburun • Taşlıca • Loryma ② • *Tilos* • *Kos* • *Chalki* • *Alimia*

Akçapınar • Köyceğiz • Toparlar • Lake Köyceğiz ⑥ • Dalyan ⑦ • Kaunos • İstuzu • Dalaman • Ortaca • *Dalaman Ç* • Göcek ⑧ • *Tersane* • *Lycae* • Rhodes

Çameli • Bozyaka • Altınyayla • Kınık • *Boncuk Dağları* • Kargı • Fethiye • Ölü Deniz ⑨ ⑪ ⑫ • Kaya • Gemiler Island ⑩ • *Fethiye Körfezi*

Gömbe • Kasaba • Kemer • Tlos ⑬ • *Ak Dağları* • Esen • *Esen* • *Baba Dağı* • Pınara ⑭ • Minare • Letoön ⑮ • Xanthos ⑯ • Patara ⑰ • Kalkan ⑱ • Kaş ⑲ • Cyanae ■ • Yavu • *Ro* • *Meisti*

N

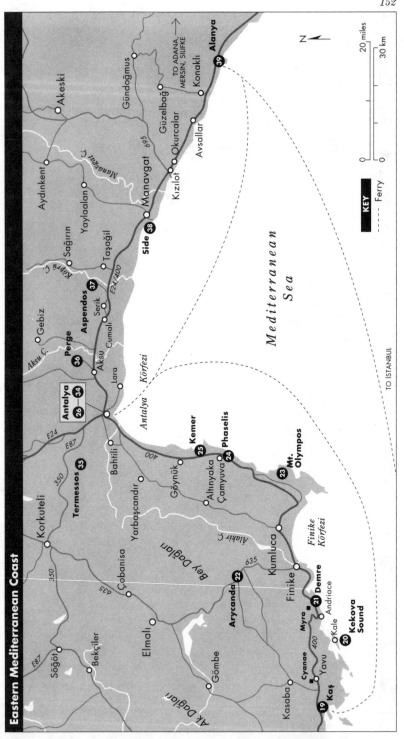

Eastern Mediterranean Coast

Akeski

Aydınkent

Gebiz

Sağırın

Yaylaalan

Gündoğmus

Güzelbağ

Okurcalar

Konaklı

TO ADANA,
MERSIN, SILIFKE →

Alanya 39

Serik

Taşağıl

Köprü Ç.

Manavgat Ç.

Manavgat

Kızılot

Avsallar

Aspendos 37

E24/400

Side 38

Perge 36

Aksu Ç.

Cumalı

Aksu

Lara

*Antalya
Körfezi*

Mediterranean
Sea

Antalya 26—34

E24

E87

Bahtılı

Kemer 25

Phaselis 24

**Mt.
Olympos** 23

Korkuteli

350

Termessos 35

400

Göynük

Altınyaka

Çamyuva

Yarbaşcandır

Alakır Ç.

Kumluca

*Finike
Körfezi*

TO ISTANBUL

Çobanisa

350

Bey Dağları

635

635

Arycanda 22

Finike

Demre 21

Andriace

Myra

Elmalı

Söğüt

Bekçiler

E87

Gömbe

Kasaba

400

Cyanae

Yavu

Kaş 19

O Kale

Myra 20

**Kekova
Sound**

Ak Dağları

KEY
- - - Ferry

N

0   20 miles
0   30 km

You don't have to go far to escape the crowds that gather in Marmaris in season. The Marmaris and Datça peninsulas, which together form a sort of lobster claw at the far southwestern edge of the country, are blissfully untrammeled. The best way to see them is by boat; inquire at the docks. Some have daily cruises and post signs indicating their routes, and others can be hired for individual trips—ask their captain.

② An essential excursion is to ancient **Loryma,** one of the most beautiful spots on the coast. Here, a vast citadel stands guard over lonely Bozuk Bay. It dates from Hellenistic times—that is, the late 3rd through 1st centuries BC. Also along the coast are **Amos,** with its heavily fortified towers and gates, and **Gerbekse,** with the romantic ruins of several Byzantine churches. Approaching each of these cities from the sea is all the more dramatic.

③ Getting to **Datça** is easiest and quickest by sea: By land, the trip from Marmaris on Route 400 is startlingly beautiful but a rough 108 kilometers (67 miles) and could take about two hours. The peninsula is heavily forested and lightly populated, and the city is charming, more than the fishing village it once was though not yet a real resort. There are a couple of nice antiques shops, simple restaurants, and even a bar or two for the boating crowd.

④ Half an hour farther along the same road lies the real goal of your journey west: **Cnidos,** a windswept headland at the very end of the peninsula, where the Aegean meets the Mediterranean. It is a very primitive site, its extensive ruins strewn amid olive groves and few hints of modern civilization. The city was founded in the 7th century BC by Dorian Greeks; because of its prime location on shipping routes between Egypt, Rhodes, Ephesus, the Greek mainland, and other major ports, it later served as the meeting place for a federation of Dorian cities—including Rhodes, Kos, and Halicarnassus. Its main claim to fame was a temple to Aphrodite that housed a 4th-century BC statue of the goddess by Praxiteles, a realistic nude that the historian Pliny called the finest statue in the world. Said to be modeled after an Athenian courtesan named Phyrne, the sculptor's mistress, it was so lifelike that it had to be locked up at night to protect it from its admirers. Even so, legend has it one love-struck fellow managed to hide away in the temple after dark in order to clench the goddess in passionate embrace. The statue became a tourist attraction, drawing travelers from afar, among them the likes of Cicero and Julius Caesar; eventually, it vanished. Some believe the Byzantine emperor Constantine had it brought to Constantinople, where it perished in a fire. Others say it remains buried in the rubble at Cnidos or lost at sea. A copy, made for the Roman emperor Hadrian and placed in Rome's Tivoli Gardens, is in the Louvre in Paris.

Though Cnidos is pretty much a do-it-yourself site, with few descriptive markers, the site custodian may be willing to show you around if the day is not too hot. As you approach, you will see the original stairway that led to the upper portion of the city to your right. Climb up and you will find the excavations of a **sanctuary to the goddess Demeter.** The British archaeologist Sir Charles Newton found a statue of her here in the 1850s and duly had it shipped to the British Museum.

To see the foundations of the unusual circular **temple** that housed the statue of Aphrodite, make your way to the trio of primitive restaurants by the harbor and pick up the path leading uphill to the right. In 1970, a fragment of what may have been the original statue, inscribed *Prax*(iteles) and *Aph*(rodite), was found at the top of the hill. Back by the harbor, there is a small **odeon**, or concert hall. On the promontory with the lighthouse is the rectangular, stone **Lion Tomb**—the lion, however, has been removed and now resides in the British Museum. You can swim in the bay here, or in the nice cove about 10 minutes north.

5 En route back to Marmaris, you might stop at **Keci Buku**, a tiny village surrounded by pine-covered mountains. Byzantine fortifications guard its idyllic bay, and the overall effect is one of great harmony.

Tour 2: The Turquoise Coast

From Marmaris, we head east through the mountains, stopping just short of Antalya. The countryside here is delightfully uncrowded, and the ruins are unlike anything on the Aegean coast. The best way to explore is by car, following the yellow signs that lead to archaeological sites both major and minor, lazing on empty beaches, and dining in seaside restaurants. Allow at least two days—you could easily be lulled into staying much longer.

Just east of Köyceğiz (40 kilometers, or 24 miles, east of Marmaris) begins the region known as Lycia, a compact, mountainous, and isolated area that extends all the way to Antalya. The first mention of the Lycians appears in Hittite records dating from the 14th century BC. Egyptian documents written a century later tell of a troublesome sea people called the Lukki, whom some historians believe to be the Lycians. The historian Herodotus, writing in the 5th century BC, said that the Lycians were descended from Sarpedon, who was exiled by his brother, King Minos of Crete, sometime around 1400 BC. Homer places them on the side of Troy in the Trojan War. The Lycians were considered an extradorinarily independent people, with their own language (even now not completely deciphered) and a fierce determination not to be conquered.

Like the rest of Anatolia, Lycia was ruled by a succession of overlords, starting with the Persians in the 6th century BC. It was the last region on the Mediterranean coast to be incorporated into the Roman Empire (at the end of the 2nd century BC). The six major cities in the Lycian Union—Xanthos, Patara, Pinara, Tlos, Myra, and Olympus—grew wealthy from sea trade. Its citizens made an art of building monumental tombs. There were regal rock tombs carved directly into cliff walls, resembling everything from Ionic temples to rustic houses; pillar tombs, such as the one at Xanthos, with a massive, rectangular grave chamber 26 feet high; and sarcophagi, giant treasure boxes with arched lids.

6 The first important stop on the eastward journey is **Lake Köyceğiz**, about an hour's drive east of Marmaris and 20 minutes west of Dalaman Airport on Route 400. This entire area is a wildlife preserve, inhabited by kingfishers, kestrels, egrets, and cranes. Peaceful Köyceğiz has a lakeside promenade and broad, shady trees. The lion statues displayed in the town square, dredged out of nearby marshes, hint at the buried riches yet to be found in the region. Dotting the lake's eastern shore are sulfurous hot springs said to have medicinal value; although the smell can be off-putting, the hot, muddy pools make for a bathing experience many pay good money for at posh spas. There are no public facilities, so bring your own towels.

7 Continue on Route 400 from Köyceğiz for 12 kilometers (7 miles), and then follow the sign pointing out the local road to **Dalyan**. Proceed another 10 kilometers (7 miles) and you will see rock tombs across the meandering river that connects Lake Köyceğiz with the sea. The site is the ancient city of **Kaunos**: the tombs, although evocative and beautiful, are not strictly Lycian, as they appear to be. Instead it was the Carians, whose kingdom bordered Lycia, who carved these tombs in the 4th century BC in the Lycian style. To reach the site and the exceptional **İztuzu Beach,** one of the most spectacular strands in Turkey, just downstream from Dalyan at Ekincik, rent a boat with a boatsman at the harbor in Dalyan (they'll be lined up waiting for you; expect to pay about $20). The beach stretches for 5 unspoiled kilometers (3 miles), with the Mediterranean on one side and a freshwater lagoon on the other.

In his *Metamorphosis,* Ovid immortalized Kaunos, who fled from the amorous advances of his sister Byblis and founded the city that now bears his name; nymphs turned Byblis, who wept inconsolably at the loss, into a fountain. The remains at Kaunos's city include a crumbling **Byzantine basilica,** a massive **Roman bath,** being restored as a site museum, and a well-preserved semicircular 4th-century BC **theater,** cut into the hillside in the Greek style.

⑧ **Göcek,** 40 kilometers (24 miles) east of Dalyan on Route 400, is another port where you can hire yachts and gulets. Though more ramshackle than fashionable Marmaris, it offers a quick way to get seaborne, being just 12 kilometers, or 7 miles, east of Dalaman Airport. From here you can take a water taxi to any of the Twelve Islands. Though lacking exceptional ruins, these tiny dots of land all do offer coves with beaches. The most popular anchorages include Tersane, Kapi Creek, Cleopatra's Bay, and Tomb Bay. You can also take the water taxi to **Kizilkuyruk Koyu,** a village on a small, remote bay near ancient **Lydae.** Though little is known about this site's history, it is a lovely and often deserted place with bits of ruined walls, foundations of ancient buildings, and fragments of decorative, carved marble.

Katranci, in a rocky headland about halfway between Göcek and Fethiye, is a secluded cove and one of the prettiest spots in the area for a swim.

⑨ **Fethiye,** 168 kilometers (104 miles) from Marmaris, was rebuilt after the original town was destroyed in an earthquake in 1957. Although it looks modern as a result, it's still an old-fashioned agricultural community where goats and sheep are herded along the main roads on their way to market. At night, residents promenade along the lighted harbor or relax, sipping tea, in their gardens. Daytimes lack charm, except for the spirited produce market where herbs, dried fruits, frankincense, and saffron are displayed and bartered. Saffron goes for a fraction of its price abroad.

Fethiye was known in antiquity as Telmessus (not to be confused with Termessos near Antalya) and was the principal port of Lycia from the Roman period onward. In front of the town hall is the finest of several scattered tombs, representing a two-story Lycian house, with reliefs of warriors on both sides of its lid. The local **museum** has some fine statues and jewelry from the glory days of Telmessus. *Off Atatürk Cad. (look for signs). Admission: $1. Open daily 8–5.*

Fethiye's most impressive site is the group of **rock tombs** carved into the cliff that looms above the town. To reach them you'll have to climb a lot of steps—the stairway starts at Kaya Caddesi, near the bus station—but your effort will be well rewarded, particularly at dusk, when the cliffs take on a reddish glow. The largest is the **Tomb of Amyntas,** presumably a 4th-century BC ruler or nobleman. The portico imitates an Ionic temple; the door to the main grave chamber even has faux iron studs. Inside are the slabs where corpses were laid out. In the hills above the town, west via Kaya Caddesi from the tombs, Fethiye also has a requisite **Crusader Castle,** probably dating from the 12th century and attributed to the Knights of St. John.

The boats and water taxis in Fethiye's harbors offer a variety of tours, some including meals, to Göcek, the Twelve Islands, Gemiler Island, and Ölü Deniz. Itineraries are posted, and there are people on hand to answer questions. Be sure to shop around, as packages vary widely. Cost ranges from $5 to $15 per person.

⑩ **Gemiler Island** is a scenic must, surrounded by an amphitheater of mountains and scattered with Byzantine remains, dating from the 7th to 9th centuries, though there are some Lycian tombs from the 2nd century BC, as well as a 19th-century Greek church with some intact mosaics dedicated to Demre's Saint Nicholas (*see below*).

From Fethiye, take the local road to Ölü Deniz; as you head east, look for the signs on the right side at the eastern edge of town. A well-marked trail about 5 kilometers (3 miles) after the turnoff to
⑪ Ölü Deniz detours through woodland to highly atmospheric **Kaya,** a ruin of an entirely different order from those you've been seeing. Turks assiduously avoid the place, a thriving Greek community until 1923, when all of the village's residents were repatriated to Greece after it unsuccessfully invaded Turkey in World War I; and the town, spread across three hills, is eerily quiet and slowly crumbling. You can wander through small cuboid houses reminiscent of those in the Greek islands, some with a touch of bright Mediterranean blue or red on the walls. In the two basilicas, the murals have all been defaced, although Christ and the Apostles are visible in one.

⑫ **Ölü Deniz** is one of Turkey's great natural wonders, an azure lagoon rimmed by white sand and pebble beaches. The area, a national park, is about 15 kilometers (9 miles) from Fethiye and can be reached by ferry, car, or dolmuş. The water is warm and the setting entirely delightful, even with occasional crowds. There's a single beachfront hotel, and you can rent one of the handful of chalets in the lagoon's-edge campgrounds. Opposite the beach, you'll find small restaurants with rooftop bars, many with live music.

Time Out One of the nicer waterside restaurants, **Ada Kamp,** serves excellent lobster and barbecued jumbo shrimp. It's on the one road that edges the beach; it doesn't have a phone or accept reservations or credit cards.

---

⑬ On the north side of the Xanthos valley lies **Tlos,** an old and important Lycian city, called Tlawa in Lycian, that archaeologists believe to be the Dalawa mentioned in 14th-century BC Hittite records. It is less arduous to tour but harder to find than Pinara, the next site you'll visit. About 20 kilometers (12 miles) east of Fethiye, exit Route 400 and follow the local road north to Kemer, where a yellow sign marks the right turn that leads, after 15 kilometers, or 9 miles, to Tlos.

Park, pay your admission to the site custodian, and climb up to the **acropolis** for a stunning view of the Xanthos valley to the west and mountains—holding a Roman **theater**—to the east. The **fortress** at the summit is Turkish, from the 18th century, and was a popular haunt of the pirate Kanli ("Bloody") Ali Aga. Below the fortress, off a narrow track, is a cluster of **rock tombs.** Note the relief here of Bellerophon, son of King Glaucus of Corinth, mounted on Pegasus, the winged horse. The monster he faces is the dread Chimera—a fire-breathing creature with a lion's head, goat's body, and serpent's tail. (According to legend, Bellerophon won.) If you have time, hike over to the theater you saw from the fortress; among the ruins are carved blocks depicting actors' masks. This is a do-it-yourself type of site, but though there are no descriptive signs or maps, you should have little trouble finding the main sights. *Admission: $1. Open daily 8:30–sunset.*

Route 400 leads south to several other ancient sites. The first, 40 kilometers (24 miles) east of Fethiye, atop a steep and strenuous dirt road and backed by high cliffs, is **Pinara,** probably founded as early as the 5th century BC, and eventually one of Lycia's most important cities. Today it is an exceptionally romantic ruin. You need time and determination to explore, as it is widely scattered, largely unexcavated, and overgrown with plane, fig, and olive trees.

Park down in the village of Minare and make the half-hour hike up the clearly marked trail. At the top, sitting on a chair in the shade, you will find the site steward, who will collect your admission and point you in the right direction—again there are no descriptive signs or good site maps. The spectacular **Greek theater,** which has overlooked these peaceful hills and fields for thousands of years, is one of the finest in Turkey. It is perfectly proportioned, and unlike that of most other theaters in Turkey, its stage building is still standing, so you can get a clear picture of what it actually looked like in use. The site also contains groups of rock tombs with unusual reliefs, one showing a cityscape, and a cliff wall honeycombed with hundreds of crude rectangular "pigeonhole" tombs. (It's not a bad idea to tour the site in the company of one of the villagers who may volunteer their services, as they know the highlights. A tip is customary.) *Admission: $1. Open daily 8:30–sunset.*

About 14 kilometers (8 miles) south of Pinara on Highway 400 is the next stop of interest—**Letoön**—a religious sanctuary, less grandiose than Pinara or Tlos. Excavations here have revealed three temples. The first, closest to the parking area, was dedicated to Leto, the mother of Apollo and Artemis, and dates from the 2nd century BC. The middle temple, the oldest, is dedicated to Artemis and dates to the 5th or 4th century BC. The last, dating from the 1st century BC, belongs to Apollo and contains a rare Lycian mosaic depicting a bow and arrow (a symbol of Artemis) and a sun and lyre (Apollo's emblems). If you want a quick refresher on the fine points of ancient architectural styles, compare the first and last temples: The former is Ionic, topped by a simple, triangular pediment and columns with scroll-shaped capitals. The latter is Doric, with an ornate pediment with scenic friezes and detailing, and its columns have undecorated capitals. *Admission: $1. Open daily 8:30–sunset.*

Return to Route 400 and head south toward Kınık, where you leave the highway and follow the bumpy signposted route for a mile to the right, to **Xanthos,** perhaps the greatest city of ancient Lycia. It was Xanthos that earned Lycia its reputation for fierceness in battle. Determined not to be subjugated by superior forces, the men of Xanthos twice set fire to their own city, with their women and children inside, and fought to the death. The first occasion was against the Persians in 542 BC, the second against Brutus and the Romans in the 1st century BC. Though the site was excavated and stripped by the British in 1838 and most finds are now in London's British Museum, the remains are worth your time. Largely undeveloped, with no snack shop, no detailed signage, and no paved walk, Xanthos is nonetheless easily explored on your own, scrambling along the dusty paths around the ruins. Allow at least two hours, and expect some company: Unlike the other Lycian cities, Xanthos is on the main tour bus route.

Start across from the parking area at the 2nd-century BC **theater,** built by Lycians in the Roman style. Inscriptions tell us that it was a gift from a wealthy Lycian named Opromoas of Rhodiapolis. Alongside are two much-photographed **pillar tombs.** The more famous of the pair is called the Harpies tomb after the half-bird, half-woman figures carved onto the north and south sides. Other reliefs show a seated figure receiving various gifts, including a bird, a pomegranate, and a helmet. The tomb has been dated to 470 BC, although the reliefs are plaster casts of originals in the British Museum. The other tomb consists of a sarcophagus atop a pillar, an unusual arrangement; the pillar section is probably as old as the Harpies tomb, the sarcophagus added later. On the side of the theater opposite the Harpies tomb, past the agora, is the **Inscribed Pillar of Xanthos,** a pillar tomb dating from about 400 BC, etched with a 250-line inscription that recounts the heroic deeds of a champion wrestler and celebrated soldier named Kerei. Cross the road and walk past the parking area to see the large **Byzantine basilica** and its abstract mosaics. Along a path up the hill, you will find several sarcophagus tombs and a good collection of rock-cut house tombs, as well as a spot of shade. Xanthos's center was up on the **acropolis** behind the theater, accessible by a trail. It was here that, when the battle turned against them, the Xanthian warriors rounded up their women and children, locked them into the fortress, set it aflame, and charged off to meet their death on the battlefield. *Admission: $1. Open daily 8:30–sunset.*

⑰ **Patara,** a 10-minute drive south of Xanthos, was once Lycia's principal port. Cosmopolitan in its heyday—Hannibal, Saint Paul, and the emperor Hadrian all visited, and Saint Nicholas, the man who would be Santa Claus, was born here—the port eventually silted up, and the ruins you'll find today are scattered among marshes and sand dunes. The city was famous for a time for its oracle and its temple of Apollo, still lost beneath the sands. Herodotus wrote that the oracle worked only part time, as Apollo spent summers away in Delos (probably to escape the heat!). While the sight of the 2,000-year-old theater half-buried in sand is unique, the real reason to come here is the beach, a superb 11-kilometer (7-mile) sweep of sand dunes popular with Turkish families yet never so crowded you need to walk far to find solitude. The ramshackle village at the southern end of the beach is the place to park your car as well as grab a bite to eat in an inexpensive restaurant.

⑱ The nearest place to stay is at **Kalkan,** a fishing village about 20 minutes east by car on Route 400. Kalkan has plenty of small hotels, guest houses, restaurants with roof terraces where you can watch sunsets over the water, and, lining the waterfront, pleasant seafood restaurants. To some it is the perfect Mediterranean hideaway, with its century-old houses topped by red-tile roofs, and blue waters lapping at the harbor. While some bemoan rapid development, its major negative now is the lack of a beach. Most take a water taxi to **Kapitaş,** a small strand of white sand dramatically set at the foot of a sheer cliff wall.

⑲ **Kaş,** another 30 kilometers (18 miles) down Route 400, is Kalkan's rival in the seaside resort category. Each town has its boosters: While Kalkan is more intimate and closer to Patara and the Xanthos valley, Kaş is livelier and has the prettier harbor. A few luxury hotels have replaced some of the tiny, traditional houses on the hills above the water, yet there are still plenty of inexpensive, old-fashioned pansiyons in town. It also has a few ruins, including a monumental **sarcophagus** under a massive plane tree, up the sloping street to the left of the tourist information office. The tomb has four regal lion heads carved onto the lid. In 1842, a British naval officer counted more than 100 sarcophagi in Kaş—then called Antiphellus—but most have been destroyed over the years as locals nabbed the solid, flat side pieces to use in construction of new buildings. This practice appears to have been stopped. A few hundred yards west of the main square, along Hastane Caddesi, is a small, well-preserved **theater,** with a lovely view of the Greek island of Kaştellorizon (called Meis in Turkish).

Kaş is another good base for boat excursions. Make the hour-long boat ride to **Kaştellorizon** for a taste of Greece. Although immigration regulations limit your stay to a day, it's a good trip: The island is completely undeveloped and holds an impressive 12th- to 16th-century crusader castle with crenellated gray stone walls. Or travel to magnificent **Kekova Sound,** the 5th- to 14th-century Byzantine fortress at **Kale,** or **Demre,** site of St. Nicholas Basilica (*see below*). Or head back toward Patara and Kapitaş beach. To hire a boat, stop at the quay, survey the vessels and their posted itineraries, and strike a deal. Trips start at about $10 per person; boats with crew can be chartered for less than $100. One important tip: Find out if lunch is included, and if so, what it will be. If it is not offered, too expensive, or uninteresting, pack your own.

⓴ The hearty few who venture to **Kekova Sound** for more than a mere day trip are richly rewarded; a visit here is among the high points of a Turkish adventure. Until recently, there was no road to this unusual part of the coast, and even now, most local transportation is by water—the overland journey, laborious yet magnificent, takes you southward over a rutted dirt track signed from Route 400, about halfway between Kaş and Demre. Kekova Island, 8 kilometers (5 miles) long, lies close by the notched shore, whose many inlets create a series of lagoons. Anchoring each is a little fishing community. **Tersane,** whose bay, a favorite swimming spot, is backed by the apse of a Byzantine church (with a kebab hut alongside). Delightfully unspoiled, **Üçağiz** has basic pansiyons, waterside restaurants, and, right on the water, one of the better rug shops on the coast, called Old St. Nicholas. **Kale,** the jewel of the sound, is a pleasing jumble of boxy vernacular houses—with white stucco walls and red-tile roofs—built up a steep rocky crag alongside layers of history: Lycian tombs, a tiny Greek amphitheater, and a crown of medieval battlements. As you cruise the waters between the villages, you can look overboard to see ancient Roman and Greek columns, buildings, stairways, and ubiquitous Lycian tombs, the last up to their lids in water—the sunken remains of a succession of ancient cities. Divers need permits here (*see* Diving and Snorkeling in Sports and Outdoor Activities, *below*), but you don't need official papers to swim in the crystal-clear water of perfect, private little bays while your boatman grabs a nap. The whole place is still fairly primitive—at least for the moment—and accommodations are clean but very basic, with plumbing and hot water in addition to some of most incredible views $20 or so a night can buy.

Without the side trip to Kekova, the drive from Kaş to Demre on Route 400 takes about an hour. But before you reach Demre, there is another detour to consider. Yellow signs on the highway and in town mark the turnoff for Yavu, a short drive beyond the road to Kekova, where you can park and hike up to uncrowded ancient **Cyaneae** and perhaps the greatest concentration of tombs on the coast. The 45-minute trek to reach them—along a rough trail about 2 kilometers (1 mile) long—takes in a theater, bath, and library, all from the Roman era, all heavily overgrown. The tombs vary in age, a few dating from as far back as the 3rd or 2nd century BC, most from the 2nd or 3rd century AD.

It's hard to say when Santa Claus moved to the North Pole, but we do know that the legend of jolly old Saint Nick started here, in what **㉑** is now **Demre**, 37 kilometers (22 miles) east of Kaş. Born up the coast at Patara and made bishop of Myra in the first half of the 4th century, he was said to have made nocturnal visits to the houses of local children to leave gifts, including gold coins as dowries for poor village girls; if a window was closed, said the storytellers, he would drop the gifts down the chimney. After the bishop's death, such legends grew, and he was officially canonized and eventually became the patron saint of children, poverty-stricken virgins, innocent prisoners, lost travelers, and sailors. A church was built around his tomb in the 6th century but was later destroyed in an Arab raid. In 1043, the **St. Nicholas Basilica** was rebuilt with the aid of the Byzantine emperor Constantine IX and the empress Zoe near the center of town, a couple of blocks from the square. St. Nicholas's remains, however, were stolen and taken to Bari, Italy, in 1087, where the church of San Nicola di Bari was built to house them. The church that can be seen in Demre today is mainly the result of restoration work financed by 19th-century Russian noblemen (whose patron saint St. Nicholas was also). It is very difficult to distinguish between the original church, parts of which may go back to the 5th century, and the restorations, although the bell tower and upper story are clearly late additions. A service is held in the church every year on December 6, the feast day of St. Nicholas. *Admission: $1. Open daily 8:30–5:30 (times vary according to whim of guardian).*

About 2 kilometers (1 mile) north of Demre, well marked by local signs, are the older monuments of ancient **Myra**: a striking Roman theater and a cliff face full of Lycian rock tombs. The theater dates from the 2nd century BC and was used, for a time, for gladiator spectacles involving wild animals. There are some fine reliefs on the tombs (a stairway leads to a raised viewing platform so you can see them up close) and on the bits of pediments and statuary scattered about the grounds of the site. *Admission: $2.*

Andriace, Myra's old port, has a decent beach (Çayagzi) but is hard to find. Coming from Kaş, at the intersection marked by a huge Roman tomb just before Demre, follow the signs for unremarkable Finike rather than Demre, go 2 kilometers (1 mile), and, opposite the main road's sharp left, bear right on a tarmac road, which travels 3 or 4 kilometers (about 2 miles) south through a flat, marshy plain to the sea.

㉒ By virtue of location, **Arycanda** remains one of Mediterranean Turkey's best undiscovered archaeological sites. The city first appeared in historical records in the 5th century BC, although it is probably considerably older. It passed through Persian hands, fell to Alexander, joined the Lycian League, and became a Roman province under the emperor Claudius in AD 43. To find it, abandon coast-hugging Route 400 just past Finike and go north on the Finike–Elmalí road, local Route 635, for 35 kilometers (20 miles). Arycanda's setting is in an alluring valley punctuated by gorges, pine forests, and waterfalls, the first of which is right by the yellow sign, about 1 kilometer (½ mile) from the site. There is a parking area and an easy-to-follow but unsigned trail up to the acropolis and across the little stream, which is dry in summer. It leads first to the monumental **Roman baths,** perhaps Turkey's best-preserved bathhouse with its intact mosaic floors, standing walls, and windows framing the valley. The **tombs,** farther east along the trail, are Roman rather than Lycian. North of the baths, toward the cliff face, you will come to a sunken **agora,** a market with arcades on three sides; the middle gate leads into an intimate **odeon,** a small concert hall topped by a Greek-style **theater** with a breathtaking view of the valley and the snow-covered mountains. Paved streets, mosaics, and an old church are scattered among these structures.

㉓ Continuing east past the town of Kumluca, Route 400 ascends to dizzying heights, where, just past the summit, a sign points to **Mt. Olympos,** 9 kilometers (5½ miles) south of the coast road. One of the 20 mountains to bear the name Olympos in antiquity, this one, known as Tahtali Dağ in Turkish, is the one where the hero Bellerophon is said to have defeated the legendary, fire-breathing Chimera. This is wild, undeveloped country—the first spot of civilization you reach is Çavus, where a fragment of wall here and there among the pink oleander and a crumbling temple to Marcus Aurelius mark the unexcavated remains of the ancient ciy of Olympos. Here, where a cool river reaches the sea, there is a pretty stretch of pebble beach, a coffeehouse, and little else.

You have to hike for about an hour from here up a dusty, rock-strewn mountain trail to discover the secret of the Chimera. From a gash in the rock, at a site known as the **Sanctuary of Hephaistos,** a natural gas produces a flickering flame, barely visible during the day but seen clearly by sailors far out at sea after dark since ancient times.

㉔ For romantic ruins, it would be hard to beat **Phaselis,** 1 kilometer (½ mile) off Route 400 about ½ hour past the Olympos turnoff, about 55 kilometers (33 miles) east of Finike on the way to Kemer. Follow the yellow sign down along a winding road through the pine forest. There are substantial remains of the town founded in the 7th century BC by settlers from Rhodes, a successful trading post through the Roman era; but many of them lie buried under thick gorse on a knoll overlooking the sea. A broad, grassy lane cuts through the half-walls of the Roman agora; a small theater sits just behind that; and fine sarcophagi are scattered throughout a necropolis in the pine woods that surround the three bays. Overgrown streets descend to the translucent water, which is ideal for swimming. This is not so much an important place as a poetic one, ideal for a picnic or a day at the beach. *Admission: $1. Open daily 8–6.*

㉕ **Kemer,** 7 kilometers (4 miles) farther on Route 400, is a center of intensive tourist development, with hotels and restaurants, a well-equipped marina, and all-inclusive holiday villages that make you forget you're in Turkey. The 35 kilometers (26 miles) between Kemer and Antalya are increasingly occupied by villas and motels alongside the smooth-pebbled Konyalti Beach. All told, there is perhaps a bit too much concrete in places, and the future only promises more. A single plus is that the big resorts rent horses for rides along the beach.

Tour 3: Antalya to Alanya

As you head toward Antalya, the wild, mountainous terrain of Lycia gives way to the broad plains of Pamphylia ("land of all tribes" in Greek). Alexander snapped up the region without much of a fight, although he simply passed around Termessos and its fortress stronghold high atop a mountain rather than wage a lengthy siege.

Under the Romans, the major cities of Pamphylia—Attaleia (Antalya), Perge, Aspendos, Sillyon, and Side—were considered backwaters and left relatively free to run their own affairs. In about 67 BC, after Rome launched a naval campaign against pirates who had been raiding the coast, the cities prospered under the *pax romana*.

㉖ The latecomer among Pamphylian cities, Attaleia, modern **Antalya,** was founded in about 160 BC by Attalus II, king of Pergamum, as his port on the southern coast. It has been the coast's major port ever since. Christian armies used it en route to the Holy Land during the Crusades, the Seljuk Turks held it for most of the 13th century, and the Ottomans kept a fleet here from the 1390s to the fall of their empire in the 20th century. Today the city is a booming resort center and a good base for excursions to the region's major archaeological sites: Perge, Aspendos, Side, and Termessos.

Numbers in the margin correspond to points of interest on the Antalya map.

A big city, downright ugly on the outskirts, it nonetheless has a beautifully restored harbor area whose narrow streets are lined with small houses, restaurants, and pansiyons. On the hilltop above the harbor are tea gardens where the brew comes from old-fashioned samovars, and the view extends beyond the bay to the Taurus Mountains, which parallel the coast.

Time Out The **Hisar Café, Tophane** tea garden, and **Mermerli** tea garden along Cumhuriyet Caddesi all overlook Antalya's harbor and serve inexpensive snacks along with their priceless views. Stop for kebabs, sticky-sweet baklava, or any of the several varieties of pistachio-filled, honey-soaked shredded wheat. All three are along the old city's walls, which surround the harbor in the section of town called Kaleiçi.

㉗ The **old harbor,** filled with yachts, fishing boats, and tourist-excursion boats, is the place to begin any visit. To the left of the harbor as
㉘ you face the water is the **İskele Cami,** a mosque set on pillars above the water. Heading up any of the lanes leading north and east out of the harbor will bring you into the heart of old Keleiçi ("Within the Citadel"), where you will find one of the purest examples of a traditional Ottoman neighborhood in Turkey. A restoration project launched in the 1980s has saved hundreds of Ottoman houses here, most dating from the 19th century and now being converted into pansiyons and rug shops, restaurants, and art galleries. As you wander the winding streets, note the use of timber, brick, and stone, and the ornate bay windows. Behind each house is the center of traditional Turkish family life, a shady garden punctuated with orange, fig, or palm trees and usually a little fountain.

Several of the old town's cobbled lanes lead north to the old stone
㉙ **Clock Tower** (circa 1244) at Kalekapısı Square, the border between the old town and new. On the south side of the square rises the graceful cylinder decorated with dark blue and turquoise tiles
㉚ known as the **Yivli Minare** (Fluted Minaret), a 13th-century minaret commissioned by the Seljuk sultan Alaeddin Keykubat. The adjoining **mosque,** named for the sultan, was originally a Byzantine church. Within the complex are two attractive **türbes,** or tombs, and an 18th-century **tekke,** or monastery, which once housed a community of whirling dervishes. Of late, the monastery has been used as an art gallery. On the far side of the square, across Cumhuriyet
㉛ Caddesi, is a delightful **covered bazaar.** This is the real thing, not a collection of mere tourist trinkets. Tiny stalls offer saddles, baggy

163

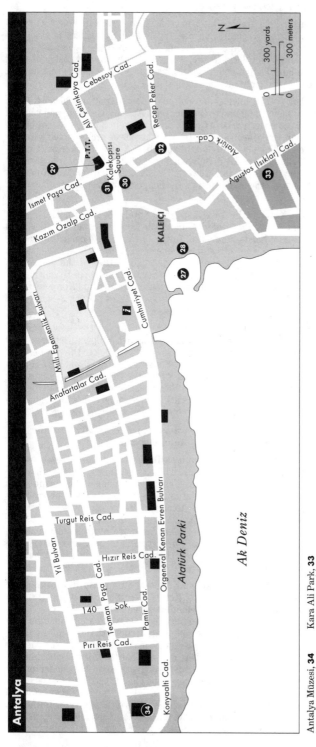

Antalya

Ak Deniz

Antalya Müzesi, **34**
Clock Tower, **29**
Covered Bazaar, **31**
Hadrian's Gate, **32**
İskele Cami, **28**

Kara Ali Park, **33**
Old Harbor, **27**
Yivli Minare, **30**

trousers, old jewelry, kitchen utensils, and fragrant spices. A row of men work old sewing machines by an ancient wall; a one-stool barbershop is painted bright green. Back across the street is a row of shops offering local honey, a Turkish delight, and pistachios and rose jam. People who say Antalya is lacking in charm just haven't been to the right places.

In the rest of town there are just a few attractions of note. Turn right from Cumhuriyet Caddesi onto Atatürk Caddesi, and you will **32** soon come to **Hadrian's Gate.** Constructed in honor of a visit by the Roman emperor in AD 130, the gate has three arches, each with coffered ceilings decorated with rosettes. A little farther on is pleas- **33** ant, shady **Kara Ali Park**, with a view of the Mediterranean and, at the north end, a stone tower 49 feet tall, called Hıdırlık Kulesi. It dates from the 2nd century AD, though no one really knows what it is—lighthouse, fortification, tomb?

34 The last stop is the **Antalya Müzesi** (Antalya Museum), 2 kilometers (1 mile) from the Fluted Minaret on Konyaalti Caddesi, the main road, as it heads west out of town. The first-rate collection encompasses Turkish crafts and costumes and artifacts from the classical and Roman eras (including the notable statues of the gods, from Aphrodite to Zeus, in the Gods Gallery), with bits of Byzantine iconography and some prehistoric fossils thrown in. *Konyaalti, tel. 242/241–4528. Admission: $1. Open Tues.–Sun. 9–noon and 1:30–6.*

Antalya's beaches—the pebbly **Konyaalti,** to the west, and the sandy **Lara,** to the east—are something of a letdown. Better to head to Phaselis (*see above*) or Side (*see below*) or stick to the tiny beach at the Talya Hotel (*see* Dining and Lodging, *below*). From Lara you can follow the signs to **Düden Falls,** where the Düden River plunges over a sheer cliff wall to pour into the sea. A tunnel behind the cascade (it's hard to find, so ask the locals for directions) leads to perhaps the coolest, and certainly one of the wettest, spots in Antalya.

Numbers in the margin correspond to points of interest on the Western and Eastern Mediterranean Coast maps.

35 Writers in antiquity referred to **Termessos** as the "Eagle's Nest," and it is not hard to see why. The city is impregnable, high in the mountains behind Antalya. The warlike people who made their home here launched frequent raids on their coastal neighbors. They were not Greek but a native Asian people who called themselves the Solymians, after ancient Mt. Solymus, which rises above the city. Termessos remained independent for much of its history and was quite wealthy by the 2nd century AD, and most of its remains date from this period. A massive earthquake in 567 fairly leveled the city, however, and it never recovered.

To reach Termessos, take the E87 north toward Burdur, bear left at the fork in the road onto Route 350, and follow the signs to Korkuteli; it's about 33 kilometers (21 miles) from Antalya. The attractions start right by the parking area, with a monumental **gate** dedicated to Hadrian. The steepness of the path that leads up to the craggy remains of the city walls soon makes it clear just why Alexander declined to attack. It is from here that the Termessans dumped boulders onto Alexander's soldiers. Next come a **gymnasium** and **bath** complex built of dark gray stone blocks, and the 5,000-seat **theater,** whose perch at the edge of a sheer cliff garners many votes as the most spectacular setting in Turkey. From this staggering height you can view the Pamphylian plain, Mt. Solymus, and the occasional mountain goat or ibex. Termessos has one more wonder: a vast necropolis, with nearly 1,000 tombs scattered willy-nilly on a rocky hill. To get there, head back to the main trail and make a left. There is no restaurant at the site, so pack a picnic lunch. And wear your sturdy shoes! *Admission: $1. Open daily 8–7.*

36 **Perge,** 13 kilometers (8 miles) east of Antalya via Route 400, suffers from comparison with more dramatic Termessos, and its 14,000-seat **theater,** though in good shape, is no match for its counterpart at nearby Aspendos. But a climb to the top of the theater rewards you with a panoramic view of the Perge ruins, including a **stadium** that is one of the best-preserved in the ancient world, once the site of athletic competitions, just to the north, and beyond it, the city's sturdy, 3rd-century BC **garrison towers.** The vaulted chambers under the stadium bleachers held shops; marble inscriptions record the proprietors' names and businesses.

The rest of the site is about 1 kilometer (½ mile) north. You enter through the old gates, having parked just outside the old city walls. Directly ahead is a fine **colonnaded avenue.** The slender, sun-bleached columns that line the street once supported a covered porch filled with shops. You can still see floor mosaics in places, and delicate reliefs of gods and famous citizens decorate the entablatures between some columns. The long grooves in the paving are ruts worn by chariot wheels; the channel running down the center carried water from a fountain at the far end. Saint Paul, who sailed here from Cyprus, preached at the ruined **basilica** near the end of the street, on the left. To get there, follow Route 400 to the turnoff for Aksu and continue 2 kilometers (1 mile) north to the site, following the yellow signs. *No phone. Admission: $1. Open daily 8–7.*

37 By now you have seen a fair share of ancient theaters. And while each has its boosters, most experts agree that the one in **Aspendos** is Turkey's best-preserved. Its quality rivals that of the Colosseum in Rome. From Perge, return to Route 400, drive 32 kilometers (19 miles) east and then 4 kilometers (2½ miles) north after the turnoff, marked by a yellow sign, past the tiny town of Belkis; at the fork, just before the acropolis, bear left to the splendid Roman **aqueduct,** which traverses the valley north of the acropolis. Another superior example of Roman engineering, it utilized the pressure of the water flowing from the mountains to supply the summit of the acropolis. The water tower here dates from the 2nd century AD; its stairway is still intact.

Return to the fork, make a left to reach the parking area for the main site, then pay your admission at what was once the actors' entrance to the theater. Built during the reign of Emperor Marcus Aurelius (ruled AD 161–AD 180) by a local architect called Xenon, it is striking for the broad curve of seats, perfectly proportioned porticoes, and rich decoration. While the Greeks liked open vistas behind their stages, the Romans preferred enclosed spaces; so the stage building you see today was once covered in marble tiles, and its niches were filled with statues, some now on view in the Antalya Museum (*see above*). The only extant relief depicts Dionysus (Bacchus) watching over the theater. The acoustics are splendid and the theater is still in use—though for music festivals and grease-wrestling matches rather than the wild-animal spectacles of ancient times.

Seeing the remainder of the site requires a hike up the zigzagging trail behind the theater, a trek of perhaps an hour or more. The rewards are a tall **Nymphaion**—a sanctuary to the nymphs built around a fountain decorated with a marble dolphin—and the remains of a Byzantine **basilica** and **market hall.** *Admission: $1. Open daily 8–7.*

③⑧ Will you like **Side?** On the positive side, this peninsular Pamphylian city has ancient ruins, some tumbled about by the water's edge; an excellent museum; and two beautiful, long, sandy beaches. The flip side is too much development and garish souvenir shops. Thousands *love* it, love its jumbled mix of old and new, its energy and spirit, its fun-in-the-sun hedonism. A vocal minority find it honky-tonk and less deserving of their time than less discovered Turkish destinations. It's 65 kilometers (40 miles) east of Antalya on Route 400—see for yourself.

The name means "pomegranate" in some mysterious, pre-Greek language. The town's known history starts with Greeks fleeing Troy after its fall. Following Alexander's reign, the city was dominated by the Seleucids of Syria and the Ptolemies of Egypt; after the demise of the Seleucids in 129 BC, pirates overran the coast and Side became a major slave-trading center. A naval expedition in 67 BC cleaned things up, and for the next couple of centuries, Side was a thriving Roman provincial town. By the 10th century it had been abandoned, most likely as a result of earthquakes and Christian and Arab raids.

Its beaches need little explanation: The one on the west side of the peninsula runs for miles; the one on the east is smaller but usually emptier. Ruins are all around: a lovely **theater** in the dead center of town, with splendid city and sea views from the top row, and 2nd-century AD **temples** to Apollo and Athena, a few blocks south, on the very tip of the peninsula.

Opposite the theater in reconstructed Roman baths is the **Side Müzesi** (Side Museum), with a small but rich collection of Roman statues: the Three Graces, various cherubs, a brilliant satyr, and a bust of Emperor Hadrian. *Selimiye Köyü, tel. 242/753–1006. Admission: $1. Open Tues.–Sun. 8:30–7.*

③⑨ Ancient sources had a hard time deciding exactly where on their maps to place **Alanya,** known to the Greeks as Korakesion. The rocky peninsula on which it is set, 60 kilometers (36 miles) east of Side via Route 400, forms a natural boundary between Pamphylia to the west and Cilicia, to the east, which Mark Antony gave to Cleopatra as a gift. Though the lovers are said to have enjoyed the fine beaches, it was Cilicia's forests that Cleopatra was after; lumber was one of Egypt's major imports, and the queen had a mind to build a navy. The city of Alanya, which Mark Antony included in the package, was fairly insignificant until the arrival of the Seljuk Turks in 1220. Several amusing stories explain the Seljuk sultan Alaeddin Keykubat's conquest: One says he married the commander's daughter, another that he tied torches to the horns of thousands of goats and drove them up the hill in the dark of night, suggesting that a great army was attacking. Most likely, he simply cut a deal; once settled, he renamed the place and built defensive walls to ensure that he would never be dislodged.

The road into Alanya passes through an area of modern resorts and affords splendid views of Keykubat's **Kale** (citadel). The outer wall is 8 kilometers (5 miles) long and took 12 years to build; through the battlement crenels and 150 towers, arrows could be sent down on attackers. Up the hill, past another wall, is the **İç Kale** (Inner Fortress), where you can park and strike out on foot along tree-shaded lanes into the old city's residential area, where many a crumbling building dates from Seljuk times. At its center are the simple, square, and single-domed **Süleymaniye Cami,** and the remains of the original **bedestan** (bazaar) and **caravansary.** A path leading west from these buildings takes you to the attractive tomb of Sultan Akşabe, the **Akşabe Sultan Tekke,** now the quarters of the local order of whirling dervishes. The exterior is stone; the interior, the dome, and truncated minaret red brick. Continue up the path to the top of the promontory, where you will find a third wall, around the **İç Kale** (Keep). Inside lie the foundations of Keykubat's palace and the ruins of a Byzantine church, with some 6th-century frescoes of the evangelists. Steps ascend to the battlement on the summit: from there, the panorama takes in the Mediterranean's technicolor blue-green, the two beaches, and a seemingly unending succession of cliffs jutting into the sea from the foothills of the Taurus Mountains. This, apparently, was the spot where condemned prisoners and unfaithful wives were tossed to their death.

Drive back down the hill, exit the old town, and head toward the eastern harbor. Make a right onto İskele Caddesi and continue to the end of the street and the **Kızıl Kule** (Red Tower), built in 1225 by an architect known as Abu Ali and patterned on other Mediterranean-coast crusader castles. Bricks are used inside, and there are loopholes just about everywhere for archers to shoot through and troughs to convey boiling tar and melted lead to be dumped on foolish attackers. A short walk south along the water, a second defensive tower rises above a 13th-century shipyard; a guardroom is to the left of the entrance, a mosque to the right.

Having explored the old harbor, head over to the other side of the promontory to stop at the **Alanya Müzesi** (Alanya Museum). The museum has some Greek and Roman pieces, including a noble bronze statue of Hercules and a big collection of Seljuk and Ottoman artifacts—beautiful old kilims, illustrated Korans and other religious books, silver and gold jewelry. *Müze Meyd., tel. 242/513–1228. Admission: $1. Open daily 9–noon and 1:30–6:30.*

From the museum, walk a few blocks south to **Damlataş Mağarasi** (Weeping Cave), named for the dazzling, multihued stalactites and stalagmites inside. Many Turks while away the hours here, in the belief that the high humidity and cool temperature alleviate asthma and respiratory illnesses. *Admission: $1. Open daily 10–5.*

As for the beaches, look over both sides and take your pick. Other beaches, coves, and caves can be reached by boat. Legend has it that buccaneers kept their most fetching maidens at **Korsanlar Mağarası** (Pirates' Cave) and **Aşıklar Mağarası** (Lovers' Grotto), two favorite destinations. Tour boats charge $5 to $10 per person; hiring a private boat, which you can do at the dock near the Red Tower, should cost less than $20—don't be afraid to haggle.

What to See and Do with Children

In **Demre,** kids can learn a bit about history while visiting the church of Father Christmas himself, Saint Nicholas—just don't point out the tomb. From there, head to **Myra** and its Lycian tombs, which kids can scrabble over to their hearts' content. The protected bays at **Ölü Deniz** and **Dalyan** are good for young swimmers.

Off the Beaten Track

Because of the distances involved and the declining caliber of accommodations, few tourists venture east of Alanya. But if you have time and an adventurous spirit, the trip can be rewarding.

The coastal plain narrows as you travel the 55 kilometers (34 miles) on Route 400 to Gazipaşa, where you come to a fine beach, then a long stretch reminiscent of the Amalfi coast or the French Riviera. For most of the 267 kilometers (165 miles) to Mersin, precipitous pine-forested slopes march down to red cliffs or to long stretches of powdery white sand bordering the turquoise sea; now and then, coastal plains break up stretches of luxuriant banana plantations and orange groves. Everywhere there are mighty medieval castles—Byzantine, Armenian, crusader, Seljuk. The occasional Hellenistic or Roman ruin adds to the spectacle.

Silifke boasts a basilica and tomb dedicated to Saint Thecla, Saint Paul's first convert and the first female Christian martyr, and a decent museum with Hittite artifacts. Cicero resided in **Korykos** when he was governor of Cilicia, from 52 to 50 BC. The fallen temples, palace, theater, and aqueduct and the vast necropolis are overshadowed by the imposing Armenian twin castles dating from the 13th century. On the outskirts of Mersin, bear right at the fork to **Viranşehir,** a colony settled by Rhodes and later a pirate stronghold. There you will find a long row of Corinthian columns and, in winter, the goatskin tents of Turkoman nomads known as the *yörük.* **Mersin,** a commercial center, is none too attractive but has good hotels. Saint Paul was born in **Tarsus,** 28 kilometers (17 miles) east, some 2,000 years ago. From **Adana,** Turkey's fourth-largest city, you cross the plain of Issos, where Alexander the Great defeated Darius III of Persia in 333 BC. Alexander founded a city that still bears his name, though translated now into Turkish: **İskenderun.**

If you've come all this way, it's probably to see **Antakya,** better known by its old name, Antioch. Founded around 300 BC by Seleucus Nikator, one of Alexander's generals, the city grew quickly, thanks to its strategic location on the trade routes between Asia, the Middle East, and the Mediterranean. After the Roman occupation began in AD 64, Antioch became the empire's third most important city, after Rome and Alexandria. Famed for its luxury and notorious for its depravity, it was chosen by Saint Paul as the objective of his first mission to the Gentiles. After enduring earthquakes and Byzantine and Arab raids, it fell to the crusaders in 1098; Egyptian raiders nearly leveled it in 1268, and it declined. A late addition to the Turkish Republic, it was occupied by France after 1920 as part of her mandate over Syria. Though it reverted to Turkey just before World War II, it still maintains a distinctive character. The people of Antakya are all bilingual, speaking both Turkish and a local dialect of Arabic. In the cobbled streets of the old quarter, on the east bank of the River Orontes, one can also hear Syriac (Aramaic), the language spoken by many of Turkey's Christians.

At the northern edge of town, off Kurtuluş Caddesi, is **Senpiyer Kilisesi** (the Church of Saint Peter), a tiny cave high up on a cliff, blackened by centuries of candle smoke and dripping with water seeping out of the rock. It is here that the apostle preached to his converts and where they first came to be called Christians. The present facade to the cave dates from the 11th and 12th centuries. Mass is celebrated here on the first Sunday of every month.

The River Orontes (Asi in Turkish) splits the town in two. In the old town you will find the 17th-century **Habib Neccar Cami,** a mosque on Kurtuluş Caddesi, due south of Saint Peter's, and just north, the **bazaar quarter,** a real change of pace: The feel here is more Syrian and Arab than Turkish. On Hürriyet Caddesi, several winding blocks southwest of the mosque opposite the Atahan Hotel, is the fine loggia of a derelict **Latin monastery**; enter its cloister from the side street.

In the central square on the right bank of the Orontes, at the intersection of Atatürk Caddesi, Cumhuriyet Caddesi, and Gündüz Caddesi, is Antakya's star attraction: the **Hatay Müzesi** (Hatay Museum). Experts consider its exceptional Roman mosaics—portraying scenes from mythology and figures such as Dionysus, Orpheus, Oceanus, and Thetis—among the highest achievements of Roman art. *Gündüz Cad. 1, tel. 326/214–6167. Admission: $1. Open Tues.–Sun. 8:30–noon and 1:30–5, Mon. 1–5.*

Most of the mosaics come from villas at **Harbiye,** originally called Daphne, a beautiful gorge of laurel trees and tumbling waterfalls, which was said to have been chosen by the gods for the Judgment of Paris and which contained one of the ancient world's most important shrines to the god Apollo. Mark Antony chose it as the venue for his ill-fated marriage to Cleopatra in 40 BC. Daphne was also a favorite resort for wealthy Antiochenes and developed such a reputation for licentiousness that it was put off limits to the Roman army.

You will find a beach at **Samandag,** 28 kilometers (18 miles) south of Antakya, as well as ruins of Antioch's old port, **Seleuceia ad Pieria,** which includes a 1,400-meter- (1,526-yard-) long underground water channel built entirely by hand and some rock tombs, which are still used by the local villagers to stable their donkeys.

Shopping

Shops pop up in the oddest places, places with no town for miles and sometimes no electricity. Such a spot is **Al-Dor,** on a bay in Kekova town. Run by a gentleman named Ümit Iris, it serves the yacht trade and offers an incredible selection of carpets and kilims, including rare pieces from the Caucasus. Amazingly, he accepts credit cards!

There are some finds in the bazaars at Antalya and Marmaris. Look for old jewelry, leather goods and sandals, local jams, honey, and spices. The smaller towns have outdoor markets, usually only once a week. Visiting on the right day is hard to plan, so accept fate and shop when the timing is right.

For clothes, stop at Antalya's branch of **Vakko,** a Turkish department store (Cumhuriyet Cad., tel. 242/241–1190), or **Beymen,** an upmarket Turkish outfitter (Konyaalti Cad. 64, tel. 242/248–7683), or the **Benetton** outlet (Kenan Evren Bul. 22/B, tel. 242/242–7518). Alanya's **Levi's** outlet (Atatürk Cad. 75/A, tel. 242/513–1034) offers better prices than you will find at home.

Antalya's **Kaleiçi Art Center** (Kılçarslan Mah., Hamam Sok. 2, tel. 242/242–2739) is a good source of local art.

Sports and the Outdoors

Participant Sports

Boating Inquire either at the local tourist office (*see* Important Addresses
Day Trips and Numbers in Essential Information, *above*) or ask around at the harbor in any of the seaside towns—even during the height of the season, there are excursion boats available. Most follow a regular

itinerary day in and day out; a few are for hire and will put together a trip to suit you.

Cruises Marmaris is the main harbor for chartering a boat, both with crew and bare; in 1994 rates were about $500 a day for craft with six double berths and crew. **Alkor Yachting** (tel. 252/412–4385, fax 252/412–4384) and **Yeşil Marmaris** (tel. 252/412–6486, fax 252/412–4470) are good sources.

Diving and Snorkeling The warm, placid bays along the coast are ideal, and many of the big beach resorts have snorkeling and diving gear.

Sunken archaeological sites, where the ocean floor is littered with ancient columns and bits of stairways and tombs, put Turkey's Mediterranean coast among the world's top diving experiences. Dive centers such as **Antbirlik Spor** (Antbirlik Genel Müdürlüğü, Antalya, tel. 242/321–2974), **Med Diving** (İskele Meydani, opposite the Yacht Marina, Fethiye, tel. 252/614–2587), and **Hotel Likya** (Hastane Cad., Kaş, tel. 252/614–2234, fax 252/614–3100) can provide information about local conditions and necessary permits. Permits to dive in Kekova Sound, one especially popular destination, must be obtained in advance from the Ministry of Tourism or the **Turkish Diving Federation** (Gençlik ve Spor Genel Mürdürlüğü, Sualtı Sporları, Cankurtarma ve Sukayağı Federasyonu, Ulus İşhane, A. Blok, No. 303–304, Ulus, Ankara, tel./fax 312/310–4136).

Horseback Riding Look into the **Sheraton Voyager Hotel** in Antalya (*see* Dining and Lodging, *below*) and the **Ozcan Riding School,** 2 kilometers (1 mile) west of Side, near the Turtel Hotel. The **Erendiz Ranch** in Kemer (tel. 242/814–2504, fax 242/814–3742) organizes tours of various lengths, from an hour to a day. Expect to pay about $3–$4 per hour, guide included.

Skiing On the Mediterranean coast, you can ski in the morning and spend the afternoon swimming at the beach when the weather is right, usually in March. The beaches are everywhere; the skiing (fairly basic skiing, but skiing nonetheless) is at **Saklıkent,** in the Beydağ Mountains, 50 kilometers (30 miles) northwest of Antalya. The lift runs from October through March. There are minibuses every day from Antalya bus station, leaving at 8:30 and returning from Salikent at 4. The small pansiyon in the resort has limited facilities, and it is usually easier to return to Antalya for the night. You can rent ski equipment at several places in Saklıkent. Expect to pay about $10 per day. Antalya's tourist office (Cumhuriyet Cad. 91, tel. 242/241–1747) is the best source for more information.

Windsurfing Steady breezes make windsurfing quite popular here. Most beach resorts (*see* Dining and Lodging, *below*) rent equipment to visitors.

Beaches

İztuzu beach, near Dalyan, and **Patara,** a bit farther east, are two of the most exceptional beaches in all Turkey. **Phaselis** is the nicest place to swim west of Antalya; east of the city are the splendid beaches at **Side** and, even better, **Alanya.** Near Marmaris, head for **İçmeler, Turunç,** or **Kumlubük.** All are blissfully clean and uncrowded; most have fine white sand, though the azure lagoon at **Ölü Deniz** and the beach by the ruins of **Olympos** are pebbled. Beach umbrellas, lifeguards, and changing rooms have yet to arrive—one or two ramshackle restaurants are the extent of the amenities.

Dining and Lodging

Dining   Eating along the coast is a pleasure, especially if you like seafood. The main course is generally whatever was caught that day, though there are always beef and lamb kebabs. Regional specialties are similar to the Aegean's: mussels stuffed with rice, pine nuts, and currants (one of the many stuffed dishes that fall under the general heading of *dolma*); *ahtopot salatası*, a cold octopus salad, tossed in olive oil, vinegar, and parsley; and grilled fish, including *palamut* (baby tuna), *lüfer* (bluefish), *levrek* (sea bass), and *kalkan* (turbot).

Dress and   As in other parts of Turkey, the main difference between good inex-
Reservations   pensive restaurants and good expensive restaurants is the setting: Higher tabs get you linen or cotton tablecloths and napkins rather than paper mats, crystal rather than glass.

Unless otherwise noted, dress is casual at all restaurants described below, and reservations are not required.

Lodging   As for lodging, most of the fancy, upscale places are in Marmaris, Kemer, and Antalya, and accommodations elsewhere are more modest. As a rule, expect clean, simply furnished rooms, with low, wood beds, industrial carpeting or Turkish rugs, and maybe a print on the wall. As many establishments are near the water, be sure to ask for a room with a view. The rare surcharges are insignificant.

For details and price-category definitions, *see* Staying in Turkey in Chapter 1, Essential Information. Highly recommended establishments are indicated by a star ★.

Alanya   **Canus Restaurant.** Close to the harbor, it is famous for excellent fish
Dining   dishes; the menu varies depending on what is available, but ask for *levrek* (sea bass) or *barbunya* (red mullet). *Rihtim Meydani, tel. 242/513–2694. No credit cards. $–$$*

Iskele Restaurant. As the name suggests (*iskele* means "quay" in Turkish), this restaurant is close to the harbor; it has an agreeable view. As well as fish, it serves a good range of *mezes* (starters). *Iskele Cad., no phone. No credit cards. $–$$*

Dincayi Mangal Tesisleri. This tree-shaded open-air restaurant near the water makes a pleasant lunch stop on your way east from Alanya. You choose your meat (chops, shish kebab, or kofte) and then grill it yourself over a barbecue while the waiters bring salads and drinks. *Mersin Yolu, Dincayi (3 km/2 mi east of Alanya on Rt. 400), no phone. No credit cards. $*

Lodging   **Club Hotel Alantur.** Like most of the other big seaside resorts here, this is a bright, white mid-rise hotel complex on the water, stocked with every facility. The beach itself is exceptional, and the comfortable rooms recall Holiday Inns. The garden is cool and well tended. The price, however, is a bit high for Turkey. *20 Dimçayı Mev., Çamyolu Köyü, tel. 242/518–1740, fax 242/518–1756. 350 rooms with bath. Facilities: restaurant, 4 bars, disco, 4 tennis courts, 3 pools, gym, minigolf, windsurfing and jet-ski equipment, beach. MC, V. $$$$*

Kaptan Hotel. If you want to stay in town rather than on the beach, this is the place. The building is small and modern, in a minimalist vein. It's well located near the Red Tower and has a lively poolside café. The view from the rooftop restaurant—which serves good, traditional Turkish dishes—is delightful. And the rooms are comfortable (and air-conditioned). *İskele Cad. 70, tel. 242/513–4900, fax 242/513–2000. 48 rooms with shower. Facilities: restaurant, 3 bars, 2 pools. MC, V. $$*

Alaiye Hotel. The low-budget version of the Alantur is smaller and more personal but less polished and with fewer facilities. Expect the familiar, white Mediterranean cube of a building; rooms are carpeted, though plain. There is an attractive flower garden, and the beach is just a short walk away. *Atatürk Cad. 228, tel. 242/513–4018, fax 242/512–1508. 50 rooms with shower. Facilities: restaurant, 2 bars, pool, parasailing, water skiing. No credit cards. $*

Antakya   **Büyük Antakya.** If you've made it this far, almost to the Syrian bor-
Lodging   der, you deserve the best hotel available, and this is it: a giant, white pyramid of a building with lots of cool marble in the lobby, and bright rooms with big windows and nonstop sun. *Atatürk Cad. 8, tel. 326/213–5860. 72 rooms with shower. Facilities: restaurant, bar, disco, air conditioning, satellite TV. No credit cards. $$*

Antalya   The fanciest places in town are the restaurants at the Talya and
Dining   Sheraton Voyager hotels (*see below*). The recently restored Marina Hotel (*see below*) in the heart of the old town is another option, with nouvelle Turkish fare.

Hisar. Built into the 700-year-old retaining walls of an old fortress, with its wood paneling and superb view over the harbor, this restaurant is hard to beat for atmosphere. Start with the above-average mezes—try the eggplant salad, hummus, and the stuffed vine leaves. Then consider a fish kebab, swordfish, or one of Hisar's specialities, such as the *cordon bleu* (tenderized steak, rolled with cheese, mushrooms, and ham). In summer meals are served on the terrace. *Cumhuriyet Meyd., tel. 242/241–5281. AE, V. $–$$*

Yat. Tables are usually set up outside this restaurant in an old stone building on the harbor, and the yachts bobbing in the gentle breeze and the soft light of dusk make a soothing backdrop to your meal. Lamb kebabs are particularly good, and there are other grilled and skewered meats in addition to the usual grilled fresh fish. *Yat Limanı, tel. 242/242–4855. Reservations advised in summer. AE, DC, MC, V. $$*

Blue Parrot Cafe. Located in the heart of Kaleiçi, whose winding streets can make it difficult to find, the café has tables set out beneath orange trees in the courtyard of a restored Ottoman house. The menu offers international and Turkish dishes and a variety of drinks. *Izmirli Ali Efendi Sok. 10, tel. 242/247–0349. No credit cards. $*

Eski Sebzeciler Sokak. The misleadingly named "Old Greengrocer's Street," just before the crossroads where Cumhuriyet Caddesi intersects with Atatürk Caddesi, is now almost completely given over to inexpensive kebab restaurants. There are more than 20 of them, their tables spread out under plastic awnings closing off the alley to all but pedestrian traffic. There is little to choose between them although a few offer a break from kebabs, such as the **Andaç**, which adds grilled chicken, and **Hüseyinin Yeri** (Huseyin's Place), which has a *guvec* (tomatoes, green pepper, onions, and lamb or fish, baked on a clay plate). *No credit cards. $*

Marina Bar. This intimate little yacht harbor restaurant attracts more locals than tourists. There's an open fire inside in winter, while in the summer tables are set along the waterfront. The menu includes both seafood and meat, with good squid and a very tasty *kiremit* (lamb casserole cooked in individual clay pots). *İskele Cad., Yat Limanı, tel. 242/247–2745 or 242/242–8987. V. $*

Dining and   **Sheraton Voyager Antalya.** This bright, shiny new resort, which
Lodging   looks something like a sleek cruise ship, is certainly up to international standards, with the potted palms in the lobby and the glass elevators bouncing up and down through the 10-story atrium. The

rooms are as plush as you'd expect, with thick carpeting, minibars, and terraces. The restaurants—where Turks go to impress business associates and dates—are among the best in town; offerings are Turkish and international cuisine with some flair. *100 Yil Bulvari, tel. 242/243–2432, fax 242/243–2462. 409 rooms with bath. Facilities: 2 indoor and 1 outdoor restaurant, 4 bars, disco, casino, 2 pools, health club, horseback riding, Turkish bath, tennis court, windsurfing, waterskiing, sailing, air-conditioning, satellite TV. AE, DC, MC, V. $$$$*

★ **Talya.** This luxurious eight-story resort curves around its own beach, which is accessible via an elevator that runs up and down the side of the cliff. The public areas seem like acres of cool, sand-colored marble, with a view of the sea from every window. Rooms are spacious, with big beds (very rare in Turkey) and private terraces. Restaurants offer the same views and high standards as the rest of the hotel: One serves international cuisine, and the others traditional Turkish fare. Reserve early in high season, as this hotel is often completely full. *Fevzi Cakmak Cad. 30, tel. 242/248–6800, fax 242/ 241–5400. 204 rooms with bath. Facilities: 3 restaurants, 3 bars, pool, casino, game room, health club, Turkish bath, tennis court. AE, DC, MC, V. $$$*

Hotel Kişlahan. The Kişlahan, next to the bazaar and a short walk from the old town, is a bit plainer and less expensive than the Turban and Talya. The boxy exterior makes you think of Mondrian: It's bright white and blue accented by thin red bands. The rooms have twin beds—common in Turkey but a nuisance for couples. *Kazim Özalp Cad. 55, tel. 242/248–3870, fax 242/248–4297. 104 rooms with bath. Facilities: indoor and outdoor restaurants, 2 bars, pool. AE, DC, MC, V. $$*

Marina Hotel. Three vintage Ottoman houses, white stucco with bay windows and dark wood trim, were restored and connected to make this attractive hotel in the historic heart of Antalya. The staff is attentive, and the restaurant turns out imaginative nouvelle Turkish dishes. Inside, there are old carpets and kilims, which always warm up a place, and the rooms, though on the small side, are attractively done in the same white and dark wood as the facade. *Mermeli Sok. 15, tel. 242/247–5490, fax 242/241–1765. 42 rooms with bath. Facilities: restaurant, 2 bars, pool. AE, DC, MC, V. $$*

Tutav-Turkevleri. Like the Marina (*see above*), the Tutav is formed from a row of painstakingly restored 120-year-old houses, just inside the old wall of the citadel. Rooms at the back look out over a pretty little garden, and there is a very good restaurant. *Mermerli Sok. 2, tel. 242/248–6591 or 242/248–6478, fax 242/241–9419. 20 rooms with bath. Facilities: 3 restaurants, 3 bars, pool, sauna. MC, V. $$*

Dedekonak Pansiyon. This pansiyon, in a traditional Old Antalya house in the old town, has evocative Ottoman woodwork and a marble fountain in the courtyard. The only modern touch is in the plumbing—just where you'd want it. Rooms are small. *Kilinçarslan Mah., Hidirlik Sok. 13, tel. 242/247–5170. 15 rooms with bath. No credit cards. $*

Natali Pansiyon. Run by the ponytailed Sahin Keskin and his German wife, the Natali is clean and simple. Breakfast is served on a terrace overlooking the street. Each room is a little different. If it's not taken, ask for the room with the huge tiled bathroom. There is parking close to the pansiyon but, as elsewhere in Kaleici, the problem is first negotiating the maze of narrow, one-way streets. *Izmirli Ali Efendi Sok. 13, Kaleici, tel. 242/247–7821. 7 rooms, 3 with bath. No credit cards. $*

Ottoman House Pansiyon. The facilities are well maintained and the staff highly accommodating at this establishment, one of the nicer pansiyons in the old town. The building is trimmed in honey-colored wood and Turkish tiles are everywhere, from the facade to the garden restaurant. *Mermerli Banyo Sok. 8, tel. 242/242–6630, fax 242/ 247–6258. 14 rooms with shower. Facilities: restaurant, bar. MC, V. $*

Dalyan/ **Denizatı.** This is probably the best of Dalyan's riverside restau-
Köycegiz rants. The putter of caïques out on the water and the chirp of crick-
Dining ets in the evening set the tone. The service is thoroughly pleasant, and the gray mullet are caught locally and usually grilled to perfection. *S. of main sq. and statue of Atatürk, tel. 252/284–2268. No credit cards. $–$$*

Şahil. Plain and simple is the style in this hole-in-the-wall, which serves kebabs, pilaf, and *köfte* (ground lamb) at very reasonable prices. It's by the mosque, directly behind the statue of Atatürk in Dalyan's main square. *No phone. No credit cards. $*

Yalı Restaurant. The tombs in the distance pass for decor at this restaurant just a walk from the Kaunos ruins, and you'll find traditional Turkish grub—kebabs, grilled fish, decent mezes. More to the point, the place is right on the water, on the far bank of Dalyan's river, and the trip takes only a few minutes by boat, which you can hire at the quay by Dalyan's main square for not more than a few dollars. *Tel. 252/284–1150. No credit cards. $*

Lodging **Antik Hotel.** It lacks the setting of the Dalyan, but the hotel is comfortable and well run, with air-conditioning in most of the rooms. It's 1 kilometer (½ mile) from the center of town. *48840, Dalyan, Mugla, tel. 252/284–2136, fax 252/284–2138. 42 rooms. Facilities: 2 restaurants, bar, pool with children's section. V. $$*

Dalyan Hotel. Comfortable, clean, and with wonderful views across Lake Koycegiz to the tombs, the Dalyan is set among trees on the shore of the lake. It has an excellent restaurant and a friendly, attentive staff. *Yali Sokak, Maras Mahalli, tel. 252/284–2239, fax 252/284–2240. 20 rooms with shower. Facilities: 2 restaurants, 2 bars, swimming pool. V. $$*

Binlik Hotel. Run by the ebullient Mehmet Binlik and his family, the Binlik is clean, comfortable, and only a few hundred yards from the center of town. *Sulungur Cad. 16, tel. 252/284–2148, fax 252/284– 2149. 82 rooms with shower. Facilities: restaurant, 2 bars, pool. V. $*

Hotel Ozay. On the shore of Lake Koycegiz with views across to the mountains beyond, this family-run hotel is quiet, modern, and efficiently run. There is an outdoor café in a charming garden draped with vines, bougainvillea, and jasmine, and the restaurant is above average. The hotel also organizes daily boat trips to nearby sites. *Kordon Boyu 11, Koycegiz, tel. 252/262–4300 or 252/262–4361, fax 252/262–2000. 32 rooms with bath. Facilities: restaurant, bar, pool, garden café. No credit cards. $*

Kaunos Hotel. This is one of several agreeable, inexpensive hotels overlooking the Dalyan River. The guest rooms and lobby recall budget roadside motels in the States. Only here, some of the rooms come with views of the ancient tombs across the water. The hotel also has a good outdoor restaurant that serves traditional Turkish dishes. *Topel Cad. 37, Dalyan, tel. 252/284–2057. 15 rooms with bath. Facilities: restaurant. $*

Olimpos Hotel. Opened in 1991, the Olimpos is airy and clean and beautifully decorated with old kilims and wooden furniture, in both rooms and lobby. The staff are very accommodating, and the restaurant is good. *Koru Mahalesi, Data, tel. 252/712–2001 fax 252/712– 2653. 30 rooms with bath. Facilities: indoor and outdoor restaurants, bar. V. $*

Datça **Hotel Mare.** Though the bright white building looks like a suburban
Lodging corporate headquarters, this is the quintessential spot for getting
away from it all, out on Datça's western beach, about 2 kilometers (1
mile) from town. The rooms have balconies but are otherwise simple, with low twin beds, and the lawns and flower gardens are well
manicured and quite pleasant. *Tel. 252/712–3397, fax 252/712–3396.
50 rooms with shower. Facilities: restaurant, bar, pool. V. $$*

Demre **Topçu Hotel.** On Route 400 at the turn to Demre, the Topçu is a typi-
Lodging cal clean, whitewash-and-wood provincial hotel. The staff is very
keen to be of assistance and serves an excellent breakfast of fresh
bread, eggs, and cheese. *Şehir Merkez Giriş, Kale, tel. 242/871–
2200, fax 242/871–2201. 42 rooms with shower. No credit cards. $*

Fethiye **Yat.** As its name suggests, this waterfront restaurant at the marina
Dining is where you will find the international yachting crowd. Fish (usual-
ly grilled), lamb (in stew and kebabs), and *bonfile* (steaks) are the
specialties. *Yat Limanı (yacht harbor), near Hotel Likya, tel. 252/
614–7014 or 252/614–9272. MC, V. $$*
Megris Restaurant. Away from the waterfront, this simple place has
a good selection of typical local food. *Çarşi Cad., tel. 252/614–3642.
No credit cards. $*
Tepsi Restaurant. On a street parallel to the main thoroughfare, this
restaurant offers standard Turkish dishes. *Çarşi Cad., tel. 252/614–
2233. No credit cards. $*

Lodging **Robinson Club Likya.** The real plus of this self-contained resort village is a full array of water-sports equipment and facilities. The hotel's low, red-tile-roofed buildings cluster along a private beach and
among green lawns and shady trees. The comfortable rooms are a
step above those in town—about the equivalent of rooms in a modern motel in the United States. *Ölü Deniz Kıdırak Mev., 15 km (9
mi) from downtown Fethiye, tel. 252/616–6010 or 212/253–6200 in
Istanbul; fax 252/616–6011. 550 rooms with bath. Facilities: 4 restaurants, 4 bars, nightclub, 2 pools, private beach, 21 tennis courts,
health club, windsurfing, sailing, diving, children's recreation cen-
ter with 6 pools and entertainment facilities. AE, DC, MC, V. $$$*
Hotel Likya. If you've stayed in other small Turkish towns, you know
what to expect—small rooms, small beds, simple wooden furniture.
But the grounds and location compensate: The gardens are attrac-
tively planted with flower beds, and rooms look out across them and
toward the bay. And the hotel's restaurant is one of the best in town,
if quite modest compared to those in Turkey's bigger cities. *Yat
Limanı, tel. 252/614–2234, fax 252/614–3100. 40 rooms with bath.
Facilities: 2 restaurants, 2 bars, pool. MC, V. $$*
Otel Dedeoglu. This old, reliable hotel is the budget traveler's alter-
native to the Likya. While the rooms are basic and have views over
the bay, as at the Likya, the lobby and grounds are somewhat plainer. The location is convenient, near the yacht harbor, near the tourist information office. *İskele Meyd., tel. 252/614–4010, fax 252/614–
1707. 44 rooms with bath. Facilities: terrace restaurant, bar. MC, V.
$*

Kalkan **Kalkan.** The panoramic view from the restaurant's perch partway
Dining up a hillside makes up for its distance from the water. Fish dishes,
varying according to the season, dominate the menu, but you can
also order kebabs, kofte, and a selection of salads and starters.
Kalkan Limanı, no phone. No credit cards. $–$$
Palanin Yeri. As in most small seaside towns, the restaurant scene is
down by the harbor. Palanin Yeri (Pala's Place) is on the waterfront
with a pleasant, vine-covered terrace and a good selection of fish and

meat dishes with salads and starters. *Kalkan Limani, no phone. No credit cards. $–$$*

Lodging **Hotel Pirat.** Some complain that this five-story property, the first really modern addition to this resort full of old Greek houses, doesn't suit Kalkan. But the location is good, right on the harbor and a short walk from the swimming platform, and rooms are bigger than in local pansiyons, with individual terraces. Be sure to ask for accommodations that overlook the water rather than the town. *Kalkan Marina, tel. 242/844–3178, fax 242/844–3183. 136 rooms with bath. Facilities: 2 restaurants, 2 bars, pool. MC, V. $$*

Kalkan Han. A rambling old house in the back part of the village, the Kalkan Han stands out for its roof terrace. With its sweeping bay views, it's splendid at breakfast and perfect after dark, when the rooftop becomes the Star Bar. An old kilim decorates the small lobby, and dark wood accents add character inside and out. *Köyiçi Mev., tel. 242/844–3151, fax 242/844–2048. 16 rooms with bath. Facilities: restaurant (daytime), bar (evening). V. Closed Nov.–Apr. $$*

Balıkçı Han. This delightful pansiyon, the only hotel on the small street edging the waterfront, is in a converted 19th-century inn. The faded, Ottoman Victorian–style café-bar in the lobby is open to the sea, and some rooms have old brass beds, a nice change from the usual wood platforms. This place is tiny and extremely popular, so book ahead. *Tel. 242/844–1075. 7 rooms with bath. No credit cards. $*

Kaş **Eris.** In a recently restored Ottoman house 50 yards north of the *Dining* square, the Eris specializes in seafood, with excellent squid, lobster, and prawns, in addition to the usual range of Turkish grilled meats and appetizers. *Uzuncarsi Cad., Ara Sokak, Orta Sokak, tel. 242/836–2134 or 242/836–1057. AE, DC, MC, V. $$*

Mercan. On the eastern side of the harbor, the Mercan serves good, basic Turkish food in an attractive open-air setting. Prawns, sautéed in garlic or served cold tossed with lemon juice and olive oil, are usually on the menu, as well as grilled palamut, lüfer, levrek, and kalkan. The water is so close you can actually hear fish jumping. *Hükümet Cad., tel. 242/836–1209, fax 242/836–1138. MC, V. $$*

Derya. In the row known as Restaurant Alley near the governor's office (Kaymakamlik) northwest of the main square, make like the locals and head for the Derya. With the waiters bustling about, it's lively—perhaps even too lively—but the activity makes for a great floor show. The options are more usual: kebabs, grilled fish, stuffed eggplant. *Orta Okul Cad. 7, tel. 242/836–1093. No credit cards. $*

Lodging **Hotel Club Phellos.** If you're looking for a break from simple pansiyons and are willing to pay a bit more, this could be the answer. The building is modern, but the old-fashioned wooden balconies add a nice touch, as do the marble floors and Turkish carpets in the public spaces. Rooms are decent in size, though most have the usual pair of single or twin beds. *Doğru Yol Sok., tel. 242/836–1953 or 242/836–1326, fax 242/836–1890. 81 rooms with bath. Facilities: 1 restaurant, 2 bars, 2 pools (1 children's). MC, V. $$–$$$*

Kaş Oteli. There's good swimming off the rocks in front of this basic motel-style place, or you can laze in the sun with drinks and snacks from the bar or restaurant and enjoy the wonderful views of the Greek island of Kaştellorizon. Rooms are comfortable, if not particularly memorable. *Hastane Cad. 15, tel. 242/836–1271, fax 242/836–2170. No credit cards. Closed Nov.–Apr. $$*

Mimosa. This motel-modern property, conveniently located on a hill near the otogar, has a basement pub/bar with darts and pool tables. Rooms, plain but adequate, have small balconies and water views.

*Elmalı Cad., tel. 242/836–1272 or 242/836–1472, fax 242/836–1368.
26 rooms with bath. Facilities: restaurant, bar, pool. No credit
cards. $–$$*

Kemer **Club Méditerranée.** The French holiday-makers are old hands at cre-
Lodging ating pleasing vacation villages, and this all-inclusive resort land-
scaped with thick groves of pines is no exception. With its white,
cube-shaped buildings set along a curve of beach and climbing up a
hillside, it recalls a small town in Greece. As at other Club Meds,
there are plenty of facilities; windsurfing is something of a specialty.
Menus at the restaurants offer both traditional Turkish and Continental cuisine. Advance reservations are essential. *Tel. 242/814–
1009 or 212/246–1030 in Istanbul or in U.S.; fax 242/814–1018. 450
rooms with bath. Facilities: 3 restaurants, 3 bars, pool, water-
sports equipment, 8 tennis courts. AE, DC, MC, V. $$$$*
Renaissance. With its 150 acres of gardens, pools, and sandy beach,
and its nightclub, restaurants, and host of sports facilities, this resort is a world unto itself. However, it's more international than
Turkish, and its reddish, seven-story buildings would be equally at
home in Orlando or Phoenix. That could be a negative or a plus, depending on how you look at it. If you're tired of the same old low,
wooden beds, you'll welcome the bigger, cushier mattresses, the
hair dryers, the room service, and all the other amenities that the
hotel's international standards mandate. *Beldibi, tel. 242/824–8431,
fax 242/824–8430. 338 rooms with bath. Facilities: 3 restaurants, 2
bars, disco, casino, pool, waterskiing, sailing, diving, windsurfing,
2 tennis courts, health club. AE, DC, MC, V. $$$*

Marmaris **Çağlayan Pınarbası.** This pleasing little restaurant is in a grove of
Dining trees, surrounded by flowers and the sound of running water from a
natural spring. The specialty is trout, fresh from the spring's pools.
Rte. 400, 15 km (9 mi) n. of Marmaris, no phone. No credit cards. $$
Birtat. This is one of the best restaurants along the atmospheric wa-
terfront promenade at the yacht harbor. It specializes in fish dishes
and a good selection of starters. *Barbaros Cad. 19, tel. 252/412–
1076. No credit cards. $–$$*
Ayyıldız Restaurant. It lies just north of the harbor and serves a substantial range of kebabs and salads. *Eski Carsi Sok., tel. 252/412–
2158. No credit cards. $*
Özyalçın Restaurant. Here you can eat grilled meats and salads in
the midst of the town's small bazaar. *Gözpinar Sok., no phone. No
credit cards. $*

Lodging **Hotel Elegance.** At this beach resort just outside town, the two six-
story buildings are bright white. Rooms are done in pastels, with
floral-print curtains and bedspreads; most have terraces and sea
views. The grounds are dotted with palm trees, and the beach is a
long strip of white sand. There are also more amenities here than in
most Turkish hotels. *Uzunyali Cad. 130, tel. 252/412–2369, fax 252/
412–2005. 208 rooms with bath. Facilities: 2 restaurants, 4 bars,
disco, room service, Turkish bath, 2 pools, sailing, windsurfing,
waterskiing, baby-sitting, in-room minibars and hair dryers. No
credit cards. $$–$$$*
Turban Marmaris Holiday Village. One of the nicer all-inclusive resorts along the coast, the Turban Marmaris is on enchanting Turunç
Bay, well away from the action of Marmaris itself—that can be good
or bad, depending on your perspective. Families, for a start, will like
the place, because accommodations are mostly in individual chalets
in the pines. Guest rooms and public spaces alike are very plain; the
beauty of the surroundings is the dominant feature. There's a good
beach and plenty of water sports. *Boynuzbuku, Marmaris, tel. 252/*

412–1843, fax 252/412–3576. 234 bungalows with bath. Facilities: 2 restaurants, 2 bars, disco, beach, windsurfing, diving, waterskiing, sailing. DC, MC, V. $$–$$$

Hotel Halici. That Halici is off Marmaris's waterfront promenade means it doesn't have a view. What it does have is something more unusual here—quiet—which you won't find right on the main drag; the extensive gardens filled with eucalyptus trees add to the sense of peace. Public areas and guest rooms are decorated with Turkish antiques and kilims, though the rooms could otherwise have come straight out of a 1950s roadside motel. *66 Sok. No. 5, tel. 252/412–1683 or 252/412–3626, fax 252/412–9200. 131 rooms with bath. Facilities: restaurant, bar, pool. MC, V. $$*

Hotel Lidya. You will find the often elusive double bed in many rooms here. Though it's in no way intimate, it has pretty gardens filled with jasmine and bougainvillea and a full range of amenities, rather like a small-town Holiday Inn. It is also one of the few hotels in town with a private beach. The disco and casino draw the nightlife crowd. *Siteler Mah. 130, Uzunyalı, tel. 252/412–2940, fax 252/412–1478. 343 rooms with bath. Facilities: 2 restaurants, 5 bars, disco, casino, private beach, indoor and outdoor pools, sailing, windsurfing. AE, DC, MC, V. $$*

Otel 47. This modern hotel on the waterfront has very comfortable rooms, many with double beds and wooden balconies overlooking the sea. It's smaller and more personal than the Lidya but with fewer amenities. *Atatürk Cad. 10, tel. 252/412–4747, fax 252/412–4151. 51 rooms with bath. Facilities: restaurant, bar. DC, MC, V. $$*

Mersin **Mersin Hilton.** Sometimes when you head off the beaten track, it's
Lodging nice to see a familiar name, and that may be the case here. Hilton has a good reputation in Turkey, and this new hotel delivers what you expect: It's thoroughly modern, efficient, more luxurious than the competition, and well equipped. At 14 stories, it's one of the taller buildings on the coast. The rooms are good-sized, and most offer views of the Mediterranean. *Adnan Menderes Bul. 3310, tel. 324/326–5000, fax 324/326–5050. 188 rooms with bath. Facilities: restaurant, bar, casino, shopping arcade, pool, health club, sauna, tennis courts. AE, DC, MC, V. $$$*

Mersin Oteli. The Mersin, which rates four stars on the rating system devised by the Turkish government, aspires to be the Hilton but doesn't quite succeed. Though it, too, is a big, white, modern box of a hotel, it's older and its public and private spaces are less grand. Of course, it costs less, too. *Gümrük Meyd. 112, tel. 324/238–1040, fax 324/231–2625. 105 rooms with shower. Facilities: restaurant, bar, casino, sauna, fitness center, nightclub. AE, DC, MC, V. $$*

Ölü Deniz **Beyaz Yunus.** Wicker chairs and wooden floors are set beneath a
Dining domed ceiling here at the so-called White Dolphin, probably the nicest place in the area. It's on the adjacent bay of Belcekiz rather than on Ölü Deniz itself, on a promontory near Padirali, a spot with fine views of the placid turquoise waters. Continental and Turkish dishes are imaginatively prepared and presented. *Tel. 252/616–6036. No credit cards. $$*

Asmali Restaurant. On the road to the Meri Hotel, this family-run restaurant offers a range of homemade dishes, which vary from day to day, together with cold mezes, kofte, grilled meats, and fish. It has a beautiful garden terrace with overhanging vines. *No phone. No credit cards. $*

Lodging **Meri Oteli.** Here, a series of one-room bungalows cluster on a steep incline above the lagoon, alongside terraced gardens; this setting, on a hillside overlooking one of Turkey's most beautiful bays, is a delight. Rooms are another story: Although perfectly clean, they're a bit down-at-the-heel and overpriced. But the area is short on accommodations, other than a few small pansiyons. To get here, look for signs for Meri; this is the only hotel on its bay. *Tel. 252/616–6060, fax 252/616–6456. 79 rooms with bath. Facilities: restaurant, bar, private beach. AE, V. $$*

Side
Dining

Aphrodite Restaurant. On the square next to the waterfront, this restaurant is quiet. You can sample the good range of fish and meat dishes in the pleasant terrace garden. Ask for *kuzu baligi* (mutton fish), a local specialty, which tastes something like swordfish. *Iskele Cad., tel. 242/753–1171. No credit cards. $-$$*

Nergis Restaurant and Bar. On the waterfront just to the east of the square, it is both convenient and far enough away from the throng on the main street to allow the enjoyment of a quiet drink or meal at sunset. Fish and meat are both on the menu. *Iskele Meyd., no phone. No credit cards. $-$$*

Sur Restaurant. Close to the waterfront, it has a pleasant first-floor terrace overlooking the square and a panoramic view. Fish dominates the menu, which varies according to what is in season. You can also choose from a selection of kebabs and good salads. *Iskele Cad., tel. 242/753–1087. No credit cards. $-$$*

Lodging

Hotel Acanthus. There are a lot of huge, ugly modern resorts on Side's outskirts, but the Acanthus is not one of them. The modest four-story building is done in Mediterranean style, with white-washed walls, dark wood trim and terraces, and a red tile roof. Rooms are comfortable if unimpressive. They are also air-conditioned—a rarity here. *Side Köyü, Box 55, tel. 242/753–3050, fax 242/753–1913. 104 rooms with bath. Facilities: 2 restaurants, bar, tennis court, horseback riding, windsurfing, waterskiing, sailing, private beach. MC, V. $$-$$$*

Subaşi Motel. You'll be hard-pressed to decide which view here you prefer: the sunrise over the eastern beach and the ruins or the sunset behind the western beach and the rolling hills. The motel itself is less impressive, as its rooms have twin beds and cheap wooden furniture. Still, the place is on the beach and only a short walk from town. *Side, tel. 242/753–1215, fax 242/753–1855. 20 rooms with shower. Facilities: bar. V. $-$$*

Nightlife

Nightlife barely exists in the small Mediterranean-coast towns and villages. However, you will find disco and bar action in the main resort areas, typically within hotels and beach resorts, and in Kemer, for example, it's hard to find a place without a disco. Elsewhere, do as the locals do and let dinner in a waterfront setting be the evening's entertainment. Sometimes your meal will be accompanied by music; it will always be accompanied by raki—Turkey's distinctive anise–grape seed schnapps. It shouldn't be hard to strike up a conversation with residents and vacationing Turks, as the coast is not so heavily visited that they have lost interest in visitors. If you are headed for a disco, the action usually starts around 10 PM and ends around 2 AM.

Antalya

Antalya's late-night scene runs to belly-dancing shows at the big hotels and gypsy bands and more belly dancers—some quite enticing—at a line of smoky clubs along Atatürk Caddesi, below Cumhuriyet Caddesi. Meals at these are overpriced, so come around midnight and stick to drinks. The restaurant **Club 29** (on the marina, tel. 242/241–6260) is a disco in the late evening. **Karpiç** (Cumhuriyet Cad. 59, Sok. 6/A, tel. 242/242–5662) is a bar with live pop music.

Marmaris Marmaris has the major nightlife scene on the coast, with several bars and even a disco—the **Joy Club** at Içmeler beach. In town, try the **Daily News** and **Sultan** bars, both on a little square by the caravansary in the historic district. **Physkos,** a bar at the yacht harbor, is big with the boating crowd.

Side In Side, the **Ambience Bar,** beside the post office, has a disco; its main competitor, the **Deniz-ati,** is a few yards away. Alanya also has a German beer hall, **Ali Bey's Biergaste** (Keykubat Cad. 16, tel. 242/512–0819), with German food and live music.

7 Ankara and Central Anatolia

History has a way of coming full circle over long stretches of time. In the 2nd millennium BC, Central Anatolia was the center of one of the earliest empires—that of the Hittites. In the 13th century AD, long after the Hittites had disappeared, the Seljuks built a new empire in the center of Asia Minor. By the turn of the 19th century, the region had become a backwater province in a failing Ottoman Empire, but after founding the modern Turkish Republic in 1923, Kemal Atatürk chose Ankara to be the seat of his government. In answer to his call, tens of thousands of Turks streamed into the town, mostly on foot, to undertake the building of the new capital. The population has swelled to well over 3 million today, and Central Anatolia is once again a political center.

Ankara is the natural base for exploring the ancient Hittite cities of Hattuşaş, Alacahöyük, and Yazılıkaya; the wild lunar landscapes of Cappadocia; and the old Seljuk capital at Konya, home of the whirling dervishes (members of a Muslim religious order known for their mystic dance). But while Ankara may be physically close to these regions, in spirit it belongs to a totally different world. Atatürk was determined to westernize Turkey, and nowhere has that objective been more fully realized than in Ankara. In the 1930s, the neo-Ottoman architectural style popular in Turkey was scrapped in favor of a symbolic and stark modernism heavily influenced by Walter Gropius and the German Bauhaus school. A master plan for the city was devised by Hermann Jansen, Berlin's city architect. Today's city is thoroughly modern, very much imbued with the spirit that Atatürk envisioned. It is the haunt of politicians and civil servants, and its social calendar is studded with cocktail parties and diplomatic receptions. Ankara is also the home of Turkey's finest museum, the Museum of Anatolian Civilizations.

The historic towns of Central Anatolia are dramatically different. Çatal Höyük, settled around 7000 BC, quickly grew to become one of the world's first towns. Since then, Central Anatolia has been the homeland of numerous tribes and nations and has served as a historical battleground as well as a melting pot of East and West. There were Hattis and Hittites, Luwians, Phrygians, Cimmerians, Lydians, Persians, Macedonians, Bithynians, Galatians, Romans, Byzantines, Seljuks, and Ottomans. Frontiers remained nebulous, as even the Taurus mountain chain, to the south, and higher chains to the southeast proved ineffective as natural boundaries on the interminable Anatolian plateau.

The layers of history left by these civilizations provide a richly textured background for travelers. Many of the sites—and sights—are utterly unique: churches carved into volcanic rock, underground cities inhabited by thousands of people, and the whirling dance of the Mevlana dervishes.

If you are coming from the temperate Aegean or Mediterranean coasts, Central Anatolia provides a change of pace. The climate is harsh and full of temperature extremes, especially in the north. Much of the plateau is an arid plain, slashed by ravines, centered on a huge salt lake, and scattered with mountains (often extinct volcanoes) and, nearby, rivers dammed up into artificial lakes. In Cappadocia, volcanic eruptions long ago covered the ground with tuff, a thick layer of mud and ash, over which lava spread. Erosion by rain, snow, and wind created "fairy chimneys"—surrealistic cones, needles, pillars, and pyramids. To the infinite variety of forms oxidation added an improbable range of colors, from the off-white of Göreme through yellow, pink, red, and russet to the violet-gray of Ihlara.

Essential Information

Important Addresses and Numbers

Tourist Information In **Ankara,** the main source is at the Ministry of Tourism (Gazi Mustafa Kemal Bul. 33, tel. 312/230–1911 or 312/231–7380), 10 minutes from Kizilay. There are also offices at the airport (tel. 312/398–0348) and in **Ulus** (Istanbul Cad. 4, tel. 312/311–2247 or 312/310–6818).

In Cappadocia, there are information offices in **Nevşehir** (Atatürk Cad., Hastane Yani, tel. 384/213–3659, fax 384/213–1137), **Ürgüp** (Kayseri Cad. 37, tel. 384/341–1059), and **Kayseri** (Kagni Pazari Hunat Cami Yani 61, tel./fax 352/222–3903). The tourist office in **Konya** is by the Mevlana Museum (Mevlana Cad. 21, tel. 332/351–1074, fax 332/350–6461).

Emergencies **Police** (tel. 155). **Emergency** (tel. 112). **Directory Inquiries** (tel. 118). **Hospitals:** In Ankara, the **Balgat Amerikan Tesisleri** (American Hospital, tel. 312/425–9945). Your hotel is the best source of information on good local hospitals elsewhere as well as on doctors and dentists.

Late-Night Pharmacies Pharmacies stay open late on a rotating basis. Ask at your hotel to find an *eczane* (drugstore) that's open.

Travel Agencies In Ankara, **Setur Ankara** (Kavaklıdere Sok. 5/B, tel. 312/467–1165, fax 312/467–8775), **VIP Turizm** (Halici Sok. 8/3, Gaziosmanpasa, tel. 312/467–0210), and **Türk Ekspres** (Cinnah Cad. 9, Çankaya, 312/467–7334 or 312/467–7335), the local American Express representative, are the major operations.

Arriving and Departing by Plane

Airports and Airlines Central Turkey is well served by Ankara's **Esenboga Airport,** 30 kilometers (19 miles) north of the city. There are direct flights from Europe and New York, as well as a heavy schedule of domestic flights. Carriers include **THY Turkish Airlines** (tel. 312/312–4900 or 312/309–0400), **Delta Airlines** (tel. 312/468–2808 or in U.S., 800/221–1212). THY also offers daily direct flights from Istanbul to the airport at **Kayseri,** in the heart of Cappadocia.

Between the Airport and Downtown A taxi into Ankara can cost as much as $20. Shuttle buses operated by **Havas,** less comfortable, cost $1. They board in front of the terminal shortly after flight arrivals and call at the THY office in Kavaklidere on their way to the train station.

Arriving and Departing by Car, Train, and Bus

By Car There are good roads between Istanbul and the main cities of Anatolia: Ankara, Konya, and Kayseri. The highways are generally well maintained and lead to all the major sights, though truck traffic on the E5 from Istanbul to Ankara can be heavy. At press time the toll road (*Ucretli gecis* in Turkish) linking Istanbul and Ankara had yet to be completed although two long stretches (E80 from Istanbul to Duzce and E89 from Dortdivan to the outskirts of Ankara) provide at least a temporary relief from the rigors of the E5. Minor roads are rough and full of potholes. On narrow, winding roads, look out for oncoming trucks—their drivers often don't seem to believe in staying on their side of the road. From Ankara, the E23 leads southwest to Afyon, where you can pick up highways going south to Antalya or west to İzmir. To the east is Route 200, from which you can pick up highways heading northeast to Amasya or to Samsun, on the Black Sea coast.

By Train Regular rail service connects Ankara to both Istanbul and İzmir. On the Ankara–Istanbul route, the **Ankara Express** and **Anatolia Express** have sleeper compartments (about $30); the overnight trip takes about 11 hours in romantic, two-person compartments. The **Mavi Tren** (Blue Train) has no sleepers but takes only about eight hours ($12). The newly introduced **Fatih Ekspres** costs a little more and is slightly faster at 7½ hours, but it runs only in the daytime, leaving at 10 AM, and is often airless and overheated. A Blue Train from İzmir ($12) leaves in the evening and arrives in Ankara early the next morning. There is also Blue Train service from Ankara to Lake Van and the east, but whether it is of any real use is another question. When on time, and that's rarely, the trip can take 30–35 hours. For details contact the *gar* (train station, Hipodrom Cad. at Cumhuriyet Bul., tel. 312/311–0620 for information, 312/310–0615 for reservations).

By Bus It's hard to imagine a major town or city not connected to Ankara by bus. The nine-hour trip from Istanbul costs a mere $10 or so, the 14-hour trip to Trabzon around $15. There are many bus lines, and, though there should always be seats available to major destinations, you may certainly buy tickets in advance. The standard of buses is generally good, although inevitably some companies are better than others and cost a little more. The most comfortable is probably **Varan** (Ankara, tel. 312/417–2525; Istanbul, tel. 212/251–7474), followed by **Ulusoy** (Ankara, tel. 312/418–3636; Istanbul, tel. 212/547–7022) and **Bosfor Turizm** (Ankara, tel. 312/425–7203; Istanbul, tel. 212/251–7000). To get information, go to Ankara's *otogar* (bus station; Hipodrom Cad. at Talat Paşa Bul., tel. 312/310–4747).

Getting Around

By Car Ankara is a big city with chaotic traffic, so you'll save yourself a lot of grief if you park your car and get around by public transportation. Unlike İstanbul, the center of the city is also relatively compact, and it is possible to walk to most places. A car is useful for excursions to the Hittite cities and to Cappadocia. Boğazkale and Hattuşaş are about 125 kilometers (78 miles) east of Ankara, Konya is 261 kilometers (162 miles) to the south, and Kayseri is 312 kilometers (194 miles) southeast.

Car Rental Major agencies in Ankara include **Avis** (at the airport, tel. 312/398–0315; at the Ankara Hilton Hotel, Tahran Cad. 12, Kavaklıdere, tel. 312/467–2313), **Hertz** (at the airport, tel. 312/398–0535), and **Budget** (at the airport, tel. 312/398–0372; Tunus Cad. 39, Kavaklıdere, tel. 312/417–5952).

By Train Though there is Blue Train service between the region's main cities—Ankara, Konya, and Kayseri—trains are almost nonexistent between small towns. The one route that may be of use to tourists is Ankara–Kayseri, but it's generally much quicker to take a bus. For information, contact the train station (Hipodrom Cad. at Cumhuriyet Bul., tel. 312/311–0620 for information, 312/310–0615 for reservations).

By Bus Buses link most towns and cities, and fares are reasonable (less than $10 from Ankara to most anywhere in Central Anatolia, for instance). The Ankara bus station (Hipodrom Cad. at Talat Paşa Bul., tel. 312/310–4747) is next to the train station and near the Ministry of Transportation.

By Taxi The cost of traveling by taxi to historic sites outside Ankara is usually reasonable ($10–$30), but always agree on the fare in advance. Cabs can be hailed, or ask at your hotel.

Guided Tours

Since Cappadocia is so vast, you'll need at least two days to see the main sights. If you are driving, consider hiring a guide (about $15 to $30 a day). Local tourist offices and hotels can make recommendations. Ankara travel agencies can arrange bus tours to Cappadocia and Konya as well as day trips within the city (*see* Travel Agencies in Important Addresses and Numbers, *above*).

Exploring Ankara and Central Anatolia

With proper respect for the capital city, the first tour will guide you through Ankara. From here, the Hittite cities of Tour 2, to the east, can easily be done as a day trip. Ankara, Cappadocia (Tour 3), and Konya (Tour 4) form something of a triangle; base your decision as to what to see first on where you are headed next or where you are coming from. Konya is en route to Antalya and the Mediterranean coast, or, if you stay inland, to Pamukkale and then to İzmir on the Aegean. Cappadocia, southeast, is on the way to Diyarbakır and the far east. Tours 3 and 4 require at least two days each.

Highlights for First-Time Visitors

Anit Kabir, Tour 1
Ankara Anadolu Medeniyetieri Müzesi, Tour 1
Göreme Açik Hava Müzesi, Tour 3
Hattuşaş, Tour 2
Kaymaklı, Tour 3
Mevlana Türbesi, Tour 4

Tour 1: Ankara

Numbers in the margin correspond to points of interest on the Central Anatolia and Ankara maps.

❶ Although **Ankara** is a young city, it has an ancient heart. It was here, at the dawn of the 15th century, that the Ottoman sultan Beyazıt I came face to face with the dread warrior Tamerlane, a descendant of Genghis Khan. Tamerlane came to Anatolia with an impressive record. He had subjugated all of Asia east of the Caspian Sea, invaded Persia, laid waste the Kirghiz plain, marched on Russia, turned south and attacked India, driven the Egyptians from Syria, and destroyed Baghdad, all in the course of 30 years. Beyazıt, called Yıldırım ("the Thunderbolt"), had not done badly himself. He had wrested Bulgaria, Macedonia, and Thessaly from their Christian rulers and had slaughtered an army of crusaders at the battle of Nicopolis.

The clash took place in July 1402, in the plain below the small town that was then called Ancyra. Beyazıt lost, decisively, providing much useful material for future poets. The Thunderbolt was taken prisoner, and some say the ruthless Tamerlane took pleasure in humiliating and torturing him. Most authorities, however, agree that the prisoner was treated with the regard due his rank. Beyazıt died

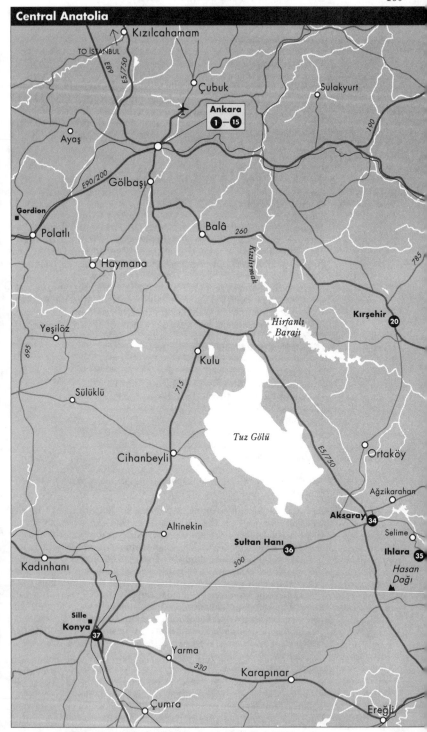

Central Anatolia

TO İSTANBUL

Kızılcahamam

Çubuk

Sulakyurt

Ankara
1 — 15

Ayaş

E90/200

Gölbaşı

Gordion

Polatlı

Balâ

Kızılırmak

Haymana

Hirfanlı
Barajı

Kırşehir 20

Yeşilöz

Kulu

Sülüklü

Tuz Gölü

Cihanbeyli

Ortaköy

Ağzikarahan

Altinekin

Aksaray 34

Selime

Sultan Hanı 36

Ihlara 35

Kadınhanı

Hasan
Dağı

Sille
Konya 37

Yarma

Karapınar

Çumra

Ereğli

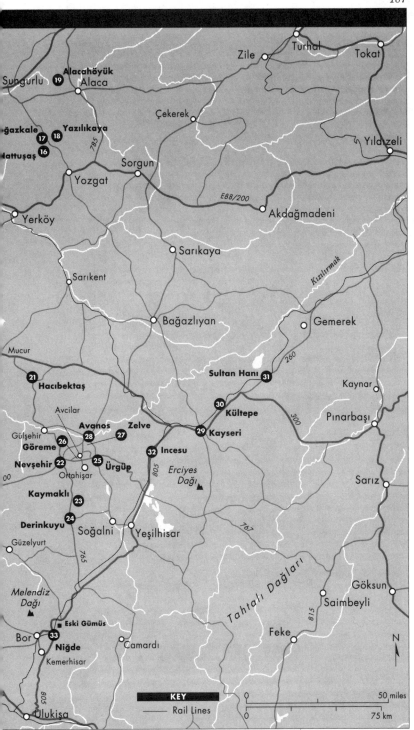

Sungurlu • **Alacahöyük** ⑲
Alaca ○

○ Çekerek

Zile ○ Turhal ○ Tokat ○

Yazılıkaya
⁊azkale ⑰ ⑱
⑯ ᴴattuşaş

78.5

○ Yıldızeli

Sorgun ○

Yozgat ○

E88/200

Yerköy ○

○ Akdağmadeni

○ Sarıkaya

Kızılırmak

Sarıkent ○

○ Bağazlıyan ○ Gemerek

Mucur ○

260

⑳ **Hacıbektaş**

Sultan Hanı ㉛ Kaynar ○

Avcılar ○ ㉚ **Kültepe** Pınarbaşı ○

Avanos **Zelve**
Gülşehir ○ **Göreme** ㉖ ㉘ ㉗ ㉙ **Kayseri**
Nevşehir ㉒ ㉕ **Ürgüp**
Ortahisar ○ ㉜ **Incesu** 300

00 _Erciyes_
Dağı ▲

Kaymaklı ㉓

Derinkuyu ㉔
Güzelyurt ○ Soğanlı ○ Yeşilhisar ○ Sarız ○

805

765 767

Melendiz
Dağı ▲ _Tahtalı Dağları_

■ Eski Gümüş Göksun ○
Bor ○ ㉝ Saimbeyli ○
Niğde ○ Camardı
Kemerhisar ○ 815

Feke ○

N

805 ┌─────── **KEY** ───────┐ 0 _____ 50 miles
Ulukışa ○ ──── Rail Lines 0 _____ 75 km

Ankara

Anit Kabir, **14**

Ankara Anadolu
Medeniyetleri
Müzesi, **3**

Atatürk Orman
Çiftliği, **15**

Çankaya Köşkü, **13**

Cumhuriyet Müzesi, **5**

Etnoğrafya Müzesi, **11**

Gençlik Parkı, **10**

Hacı Bayram Cami, **8**

Hisar, **2**

Jülyanüs Sütunu, **7**

Kocatepe Cami, **12**

Roma Hamamları, **6**

Samanpazarı, **4**

Temple of Augustus, **9**

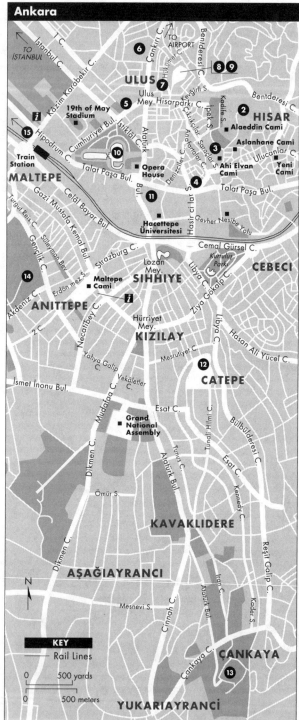

after eight months of captivity, probably of a stroke, and Tamerlane, instead of continuing his march into Europe, turned his horse around and led his men back to the Mongol plains. He died the following year.

Before that epic battle, Ankara suffered a succession of Lydian, Persian, and Macedonian conquerors. Legend attributes the city's foundation to the redoubtable Amazons, but many archaeologists have identified it with the Hittite city of Ankuwash, which is thought to have been founded in around 1,200 BC and taken over by the Phrygians in around 700 BC. It was later taken by Alexander the Great, the Seleucids, and the Galatians before being annexed to Rome by Augustus in 25 BC. Ankara retained its strategic significance through the Byzantine empire—as evidenced by the battle mentioned above—but under the Ottomans its importance gradually declined. By the early 20th century it was little more than a dusty provincial town with an illustrious pedigree, the perfect site for Ataturk to build his new capital.

Today, Ankara is an energetic, modern city. Traffic moves smoothly along the wide, tree-lined avenues—except in the old town, the Ulus district, where narrow lanes surround the main sights of Ancyra, some untidy Roman remains, several mosques, and the citadel. Reminders of Atatürk are everywhere, from statues in his likeness to streets bearing the honorific name bestowed by his countrymen: Atatürk, the Father of the Turks; and Gazi, the Conqueror.

To understand the city's layout, it's best to start at the top; walk up Hisarparkı Caddesi to the **Hisar** (citadel). Fortified by the Galatians, strengthened by the Romans, rebuilt by the Byzantines, and maintained by the Seljuks and Ottomans, the Hisar and its double walls are now crumbling away. Of the 20 towers that once guarded the structure, 15 are still standing to various heights. The citadel gates are fairly well intact; the best-preserved sections of the fortifications are near the Parmak Kapısı (inner gate). The Hisar Kapısı (outer gate) is topped by an inscription. Within the walls is a rambling, old-fashioned Turkish town. The picturesque, ramshackle houses in the warren of narrow, cobbled lanes gain a touch of elegance from incorporated bits of broken marble columns and slabs taken from Roman ruins. The city's oldest *cami* (mosque) is also here, the small **Alaeddin Cami**, originally built in 1178, although much of what you see today is later additions. The view from the citadel walls is splendid. To the south and west rise the skyscrapers of modern Ankara; the plains on which Tamerlane defeated Beyazıt stretch to the northeast; and the neighborhoods of Ankara's urban immigrants sprawl to the east.

At the end of the garden terrace below the Hisar's outer gate, on Kadife Sokak, is the superb **Ankara Anadolu Medeniyetleri Müzesi** (Museum of Anatolian Civilizations), housed in a restored 15th-century *bedestan* (covered bazaar) and *han* (inn). Though the museum itself is relatively small, the collection is world-class. Masterpieces from the Neolithic and Bronze ages and the Assyrian, Phrygian, Urartu, Hellenistic, and Roman eras are carefully displayed, all with explanations in English. (The freelance "guides" who offer their services tend to overcharge and add little to your visit.) The heart of the museum is its comprehensive collection of Hatti and Hittite art and crafts, dating back to the dawn of the 2nd millennium BC. Here you will find the graceful, stylized deer statues that pop up on postcards throughout Turkey, as well as a bronze statuette of a bull (circa 2400 BC), a limestone Cappadocian idol with two heads (3rd millennium BC), a ram's-head vase (19th century BC), and a large bull's-head cauldron. Another huge cauldron, with clean, precise lines, is held up by four figures; it was found in Gordion, where a prophecy predicted Alexander the Great's rise to glory. There are small statues, jewels worked in gold and iron, combs, and needles as well as wonderful bas-relief carvings in stone, which display an incredible mastery of movement. This is best shown in a small bas-relief whose warriors, brandishing lances under cover of their shields, still bear faint traces of color. Another bas-relief depicts the Gilgamesh legend, which includes the Babylonian version of the Flood. *Kadife Sok., tel. 312/324–3160. Admission: $1. Open daily 8:30–5:30.*

Outside the outer citadel walls is the neighborhood known as **Samanpazarı.** Along Kadife Sokak is the city's **bedestan,** where wide canvas tarps offer shade over piles of fruit, vegetables, and rice. Also in the neighborhood are the 13th-century **Aslanhane Cami** (Lionhouse Mosque), which took its name from the lion relief on a wall in front; the **Ahi Elvan Cami,** dating from the early 1400s, with Roman columns and a fine *mimber* (pulpit); and the 16th-century **Yeni Cami** (New Mosque). The Yeni Cami was built by Süleyman's grand vizier, Çenabi Ahmet Paşa, supposedly after plans by the master architect Sinan, and executed by one of the great architect's pupils. The dark red porphyry of its walls is enhanced by the white marble mimber and *mihrab* (prayer niche). *Mosques: on or near Ulucanlar Cad., e. of Çıkrıkçılar Sok.*

From here, head west on Ulucanlar Caddesi to Talat Paşa Bulvari; turn right on Atatürk Bulvari and follow it to **Ulus Meydanı** (Nation Square), where Atatürk Bulvari ends (or starts, depending on your perspective) below the great man's equestrian statue. Just off the square is the **Cumhuriyet Müzesi** (Republic Museum), the birthplace of the Turkish Republic. It was here in 1920 that Atatürk was elected chairman of the Grand National Assembly, which would organize the new nation and galvanize the counterattack against the Greek troops occupying the Aegean. The early history of the parliament is given in photographs and documents. Most of the labels are in Turkish only. *Cumhuriyet Cad., tel. 312/310–5361. Admission: 50 cents. Open Tues.–Sun. 9–noon and 1–5:30.*

Head north on Çankırı Caddesi to the heart of the old town and the entrance to the 3rd-century **Roma Hamamları** (Roman baths). You can still see the oval soaking pool as well as the *frigidarium* and *caldarium* (cold and hot rooms). The steam rooms have raised floors; hot air once circulated below them from the furnace. A colonnaded palaestra, for sports and exercise, is part of the site. *Çankırı Cad. 43, no phone. Admission: $1. Open Tues.–Sun. 8:30–12:30 and 1:30–5:30.*

A few blocks farther south, on Hükümet Meydanı, rises the **Jülyanüs Sütunu** (Column of Julian). It was erected in honor of the Roman Emperor Julian the Apostate (AD 361–363), so-called because he attempted to reverse his father's decision to make Christianity the Empire's official religion. The column has 15 fluted drums topped by a Corinthian capital and commemorates a visit by the emperor in AD 362, when he was headed for battle with the Persians. Unfortunately, Julian didn't get to enjoy it; he died a year later. Storks often build their nests here now, gallantly withstanding the pollution. Facing the column across a fountain is the former **Ministry of Finance;** it is white with pointed arches and blue glazed tiles above big windows.

Walk east up the hill, turn right, and make the next left onto Bayram Caddesi, a street lined with religious bookshops and stalls selling

❽ prayer beads. At the end of the block is the **Hacı Bayram Cami,** built in the early 15th century of yellow stone and brick, with lavish touches of marble from the nearby Roman ruins and an unusual tiled roof. The glazed Kütahya tiles on the interior walls were added 300 years later. Hacı Bayram was a founder of an order of dervishes, and his tomb is near the entrance to the mosque. *Bayram Cad. Tomb open Tues. 3–5, Wed.–Sun. 8–11 and 3–5.*

❾ Behind the mosque are the remains of the **Temple of Augustus.** Built in the 2nd century BC as a shrine to Cybele, nature goddess of Asia Minor, it was dedicated to Augustus after a Roman law deified dead emperors. Augustus, who was rather opposed to this concept, nonetheless requested that a summary of the achievements of his rule (known today by its Latin title *Res Gestae* or "Things Done") be carved into the walls of all his temples. The inscription discovered here in 1555 by a Flemish diplomat named Ghislain de Busbecq is the longest Latin inscription ever found and the only complete version of Augustus's text in the world. Fortunately Busbecq copied it down, as time has crumbled the stone and worn away most of the writing. Today you can make out only a few words here and there and only occasionally an entire line.

A walk through Ankara's new town also starts at Ulus Meydanı. A few blocks south on Atatürk Bulvarı, near Itfaiye Meydanı (Opera Square) and the city's opera house, is the entrance to the welcome

❿ green expanse of **Gençlik Parkı.** Known as the Youth Park, it is filled with shady walks, tea gardens, and band shells, and has a small amusement park with a Ferris wheel and rides for children as well as a small lake where rowboats can be rented. *Entrance west of İtfaiye Meydanı. Admission: 25¢. Open daily 8 AM–10 PM.*

Across Atatürk Bulvarı from the park entrance, south of the inter-

⓫ section with Talat Paşa Bulvarı, is the **Etnoğrafya Müzesi** (Ethnographic Museum), which houses a rich collection of Turkish carpets, folk costumes, Anatolian handcrafts, and weapons. The building is done in Ottoman Revival style and includes a big oriental dome and marble decoration. Atatürk lay in state here from 1938 to 1955, when his mausoleum was finished. *Talat Paşa Bul., Opera, tel. 312/311–3007. Admission: $1. Open Tues.–Sun. 8:30–12:30 and 1:30–5:30.*

Next door is the **Resim ve Heykel Müzesi** (Painting and Sculpture Museum), with works by contemporary Turkish artists. *Talat Paşa Bul. at Ocağı Sok. Admission: $1. Open Tues.–Sun. 8:30–12:30 and 1:30–5:30.*

Farther south on Atatürk Bulvarı is the huge campus of **Hacettepe University,** modern Turkey's educational showpiece. Above the small campus park is the **Karacabey Cami,** built in 1428 on a T-shaped plan; it has a rather thick minaret striped with colored, glazed tiles.

After you pass the railway viaduct, Atatürk Bulvarı becomes the principal shopping street of the Sihhiye district and contains many of the better hotels. To the right is a monumental replica of a **Hatti Sun Disk;** the radial lobes surrounding the disk represent the planets, a rather impressive notion for 2000 BC. In the distance, on Gazi Mustafa Kemal Bulvarı, is the **Maltepe Cami,** a handsome building whose large brass-plated dome is topped by two slender minarets. To the left is the small **Kurtulus Park** (bordered by Ziya Gökalp

Caddesi and Cemal Gürsel Caddesi), with a pond, and a Turkish Airlines ticket office.

Continuing along Atatürk Bulvari, you will come to Hürriyet Meydanı, recognizable by the high-rise Gima department store, once the city's tallest building. The neighborhood is known as **Kizilay** (Crescent), after the curving intersection here, and is the heart of the new town.

⑫ Visible to the south (and just a bit to the left), is the vast **Kocatepe Cami**, opened to the faithful in 1982. Walk uphill on Esat Caddesi, and turn left at the end of the block. The city's largest mosque, it was funded by the Saudi government; one has to wonder what Atatürk would have thought of such a gift in his secular capital city. Aside from its political significance, the mosque is lovely, built in a classical Ottoman style reminiscent of the grand old mosques in Istanbul. *Near intersection of Tunalı Hilmi Cad. and Bülbüldere Cad.*

Another half mile south of the mosque on Atatürk Bulvari is the governmental district, Bakanliklar, beginning with the **Grand National Assembly Hall**, the parliament building, at the intersection with Ismet Inönü Bulvari. Farther still is **Embassy Row**, with its pleasant gardens, in the neighborhood known as Kavaklıdere.

Atatürk Bulvari finally ends at the fashionable suburb of Çankaya.
⑬ Here you'll find **Çankaya Köşkü** (Çankaya Pavilion), built for the president after he moved the capital to Ankara. The little house is within the grounds of the **Cumhurbaskanlığı Köşk** (Presidential Mansion), which also has formal flower gardens and a fine view, though you can't visit the mansion itself. *Atatürk Bul. Admission free, but you may need to show your passport. Open Sun. 1:30–5:30.*

⑭ The last but in no way the least of Ankara's attractions is the **Anit Kabir** (Monumental Tomb), which is the Atatürk mausoleum. Perched on a hilltop, it is reached by a marble-paved path lined with Hittite-style lions. To each side are pavilions with remarkable bas-relief carvings. At the far end is a square hemmed in by a colonnade, and in the middle, a towering mast with the Turkish flag floating in the breeze. At the entrance to the mausoleum are carved the words "Beyond all doubt, government belongs to the people." Sailors in white ducks and soldiers in olive drab mount the guard. The mausoleum itself is a vast, soaring hall lined with brilliant gold mosaics and marble, pierced by seven tall windows looking out over the city Atatürk built. The immensely impressive solitary marble sarcophagus is symbolic, as Atatürk's actual remains rest in the vault below. The **Atatürk Museum,** with personal belongings, objects associated with his life, and mementos from the War of Liberation (1919–22), is housed in an arcaded wing. *Southern end of Anit Cad. tel. 312/310–7140 (museum). Admission free. Open daily 9–4 (mausoleum); 9–12:30 and 1:30–6 (museum).*

⑮ When Turks want to get away from the heat of the city, many head for **Atatürk Orman Çiftliği**, a model farm Atatürk had built on the city's western outskirts. In 1981, for the centenary of Atatürk's birth, a replica of his family home, the comfortable pink house of a merchant in Thessaloniki, was opened to visitors in the large park at the site. Pack a picnic lunch or try the pleasant on-site restaurant.

Tour 2: The Hittite Cities

From Ankara, take the Samsun Yolu (Samsun Highway), Route 200, to the E88 heading east out of the city. After about 123 kilometers

(76 miles), bear left, or northeast, on Route 190 and follow the signs for Sungurlu and Corum. Just past Sungurlu, look for the sign identifying the road to Boğazkale and Hattuşaş. The great sites of the Hittite Empire are contained within a triangle bounded by Hattuşaş, Yazılıkaya, and Alacahöyük. The three sites can easily be seen in a day.

There is old and then there is *old*. The Greek and Roman ruins you may have seen elsewhere in the country are mere yearlings compared to **Hattuşaş**. The city dates to the Bronze Age and the sophisticated culture of a people called the Hatti, who were thriving here by 2300 BC. From about 2000 BC on, the Hatti princes ruling the main city-states of Hattuşaş, Kaneş, Kushara, and Zalpa were doing brisk trade with the great Mesopotamian towns, from which they derived considerable wealth. Around 1800 BC, Anitta, king of the lost city of Kushara, formed an Anatolian confederacy and took for himself the title *Rabum Rabum* (King of Kings). His glory was short-lived.

At about that time, a mysterious people known as the Hittites came to dominate the Hatti. The Hittites, of Indo-European origin, apparently entered Anatolia after crossing the Caucasus and the steppes beyond the Black Sea. They claimed Hattuşaş as their capital and soon built an empire of their own. Labarna, who ascended to the throne in 1680 BC, is considered the founder of the Old Kingdom. Royal intrigue and invasions by new tribes from the east sent the empire into decline, and the Old Kingdom was followed by the New Kingdom. A series of battles with the Egyptians in about 1296 BC appears to have favored the Hittites, but a familiar pattern of family strife reemerged. In decline for a second time, the reign of the Hittites finally came to an end in 1200 BC, when Hattuşaş was sacked and burned by tribes from the north.

As mysteriously as they arrived, the Hittites suddenly dispersed, disappearing from history for almost three millennia. Then, in 1812, a German traveler named Burckhardt found at Hamath, in Syria, a stone tablet bearing hieroglyphics different from the Egyptian ones previously encountered. In subsequent years ruins of some of the cities were discovered, but it wasn't until 1879 that Englishman Henry Sayce suggested that the Hittites of the Bible had at last been located. Some 30,000 cuneiform tablets, incised into soft clay, have since been dug up and deciphered, covering everything from marriage contracts to treaties between ancient nations. From an unknown people, the Hittites have emerged as one of the best-documented cultures of early antiquity.

Though of small physical stature (probably under 5 feet), the Hittites were muscular and strongly built. Society was sharply divided into free people and serfs, and the sovereign who ruled over the federation of principalities was also its high priest, becoming a god after death. Their religion was a tolerant polytheism, and subsequent cultures may well have borrowed from the Hittite creed. For example, many of the Hittites' gods bear striking similarities to Etruscan, Greek, and Anatolian gods.

The first thing to notice is the city's location—an excellent defensive position in a valley framed on both sides by rivers. The second item of note is the city's incredible size. Its walls, made of brick on stone foundations, reinforced by large cut stones, and surmounted by towers, were 6 kilometers (4 miles) in circumference.

After investigating the ramparts of the lower city, walk in the direction of the citadel. The first ruins to the right as you ascend are those of the **Temple of the Storm God** (Temple I). Hattuşaş had five temples, all patterned on the same model. Like Babylonian temples, they consisted of small rooms arranged around a paved courtyard roughly 700 feet by 1,700 feet. Near the entrance to this temple complex are pieces of a ceremonial basin made from limestone and carved with trademark Hittite lions. Within the temple, you should be able to make out the main courtyard and two large rooms, which housed statues of the storm god and a sun goddess. The rooms opening out from the courtyard were probably administrative offices and archives. The temple stands on a terrace overlooking some of the public buildings; to the north and east once lay private residential buildings, parts of which have been excavated.

The ruins of the **Büyükkale** (great fortress), the second most important ruins at the site, are reached by a modern stairway that has replaced the ancient ramp. On the terrace atop the sheer cliff stood the royal palace, probably several stories high. The citadel's outbuildings include the **State Archive,** where, in 1906, thousands of stone tablets were found, mute but eloquent survivors of the plundering Phrygians. Among them was a copy of the Treaty of Kadesh, signed in 1279 BC after the war with the Egyptians. Continuing up the hill, you come first to the eastern side of the upper city's fortified wall. The ramparts here are the most impressive. They consist of two parallel walls connected by two main gates (one of which is the **Kral Kapısı,** or Royal Gate), which are themselves formidable bastions.

Follow along the ramparts. The ruins of **Temples II, III,** and **V** lie to your left. Beyond is the entrance to the **Yerkapı** (Earth Gate). Though only its foundations remain, it is still impressive, set on a man-made ridge some 30 feet high. In its day, the gate was decorated with finely carved sphinxes; to see one, you'd have to visit museums in either Istanbul or Berlin. Directly underneath the gate is an odd tunnel, 200 feet long and paved. No one is really sure of its purpose, although it may have led to a postern gate for sallies against besieging forces. The ruins of **Temple IV** are to the north. Beyond, at the end of the pathway that runs the length of the ramparts, rises the well-preserved **Gate of the Lions.** The lions themselves are reproductions. *Admission: $1. Open daily 8–5.*

17 In 1839, a Frenchman, Charles Texier, stumbled on the ruins of **Boğazkale,** which included stone carvings and bas-reliefs. (A *Guide to Boğazköy*, in English, is helpful; it's available at the archaeological museums in Ankara, Alacahöyük, and the nearby village of Boğazkale as Boğazköy is also known.) Today there is a museum here, but if you've been to the Museum of Anatolian Civilizations in Ankara, you've already seen the best finds from the Hittite sites. *Less than 5 km (3 mi) n. of Hattuşaş. Admission: 75¢. Open daily 8–noon and 1:30–5:30.*

18 **Yazılıkaya,** northeast of Hattuşaş, is thought to have served the capital city as a religious sanctuary or temple complex. The name means "rock with writing," a fitting title, as the natural rock walls here are covered with the carvings of Hittite artists dating to about 1300 BC. At the site, a large entrance portal opens onto a natural crevice that forms a narrow passageway through the rocks and ends at a small, circular open space—the **shrine** proper. The rocky walls of the passageway are decorated with bas-reliefs illustrating various Hittite gods and kings. Within the large shrine are depicted 42 gods marching from the left to meet 21 goddesses coming from the right. The largest section portrays the most important figures, including the carved figures of Teshub, the weather god (the fellow with the most horns on his cap), and his consort, the goddess Hepatu, astride a leopard. Her son Sharruma, also riding a leopard, is directly behind her. Sharruma is believed to be a god of death and rebirth, like the Egyptian Osiris. On the opposite wall is a king with a major ego, Tudhaliya IV. Not only did he have his likeness placed among the gods, he also ordered that it be larger than any of them. If size alone is not enough to pick him out, look for a man with a rounded skullcap, earring, and curved scepter.

Next to the main shrine, a second, smaller passageway leads to a small **gallery.** Here again is King Tudhaliya, this time alongside a particularly fine and well-preserved image of Sharruma. The frieze of the twelve gods opposite is another exceptional work. Another gallery figure is the so-called Sword God, shown with the head of a god attached to a body made up of four lions; he carries a sword with its point aimed downward. Funeral rites for recently departed kings were probably held here. There are no official guides, but pamphlets are available at the ticket kiosk. *2 km (1 mi) northeast of Hattuşaş. Admission: $1. Open daily 8–5.*

⑲ The site of **Alacahöyük,** was settled as early as 4000 BC and not discovered until the 19th century AD by Englishman John Hamilton. Some scholars assert that it might be King Anitta's lost city of Kushara. Continuing excavations have brought to light 15 levels of four different cultures, beginning with 13 rectangular **burial chambers** belonging to Hatti kings. In the tombs were golden diadems, belts, necklaces and other jewelry, silver combs, mirrors, drinking vessels, and other funerary artifacts, all now in the Ankara museum. A later **Hittite temple** was entered through the **Gate of Sphinxes,** likewise now in Ankara, with concrete replicas in situ, and a pamphlet is available at the ticket kiosk. The double-headed eagle, an emblem of the Hittites as well as many succeeding empires, appears on the inside wall. Concrete casts of original bas-reliefs depict a royal couple before an altar with a bull on it, the sun goddess Arima, two musicians playing odd instruments, and a procession of animals. A modern tower provides a view of the entire site. *14 km (9 mi) n. of Boğazkale. Admission: $1. Open daily 8:30–5:30.*

Though there are other Hittite sites in the region, they are minor and not really worth the time. **Gavur Kalesi** (Fortress of the Infidels), 40 kilometers (25 miles) south of Ankara on the Haymana Road, has some bas-reliefs. **Hasanoğlan,** to Ankara's east, has little if anything; the early Bronze Age figure found here was quickly dispatched to the museum in Ankara.

Tour 3: Cappadocia

Cappadocia forms a rough triangle, starting about 272 kilometers (169 miles) southeast of Ankara, between Nevşehir, Kayseri, and Niğde. The main sights are within an even smaller triangle, marked by Ürgüp, Göreme, and Avanos. Ürgüp is the center from which to explore the monastic villages of Cappadocia and the best place to shop and to arrange tours; Nevşehir is a good base for exploring the underground cities of Kaymaklı and Derinkuyu.

⑳ The quickest route is to take the E5 south out of Ankara and turn left (southeast) on Route 260. You will pass through **Kiirşehir,** an important agricultural center with a scattering of Seljuk monuments. These include the **Alaeddin Cami,** one of many mosques in the region of the same name, after the great Seljuk sultan Alaeddin Keykubat (ruled 1219–1236); the **Caca Bey Cami** on Ankara Bulvari, built in 1272 as an astronomical observatory; and the **Ahi Evran Cami,** which has the *türbe* (tomb) of the founder of the Ahi brotherhood, a religious sect that exercised considerable influence in Anatolia for several centuries. Its precepts had much to do with hospitality and good fellowship, a likely reason for the group's popularity. Just before the junction with Route 280 stands the *türbe* of the poet Aşık Paşa, built during the Mongol occupation of the region.

Beyond Mucur, turn right (south) on Route 765, the shortest road, at 68 kilometers (42 miles), to Nevşehir. After 20 kilometers (12 miles), you arrive at **Hacıbektaş**, where a religious sect was founded by Hacı Bektaş Veli in the 13th century. His teachings were based on a synthesis of Sunnism and Shiism, two branches of Islam, blended with a touch of Christianity. Hacı Bektaş became the spiritual leader of the newly founded Janissary Corps, the fierce warriors of the Ottoman Empire, which gave him tremendous political as well as religious influence. The monastery that belonged to his disciples is now the **Hacıbektaş Müzesi.** He is buried in a türbe behind a gilded door here. *Center of town, tel. 384/441-1022. Admission: 75¢.*

Continue south through **Gülşehir,** where Grand Vizir Kara Mehmet Paşa constructed a rare Ottoman Baroque complex with a mosque, *medrese* (mosque compound), *hamam* (Turkish bath), and six fountains next to some Byzantine ruins. Soon the scenery starts to change. Pink-and-white mushroom-shaped rocks are scattered along the 19 kilometers (12 miles) to **Nevşehir.** Known in ancient times as Nissa, this is the region's largest town. It clings to the slopes below a ruined **Seljuk fortress** and boasts a 13th-century Seljuk mosque, the **Kaya Cami.** The town owes its prosperity to Grand Vizir Damat Ibrahim Paşa, who endowed his birthplace with the **Kurşunlu Cami** (Lead-domed Mosque) and its medrese, hospice, and library in 1726. The setting is pleasant; solid square houses of light local stone often stand amid pleasant gardens.

Now it's time to get on to the whole point of this particular tour: the incredible kingdom of Cappadocia. The story begins over 10 million years ago, when the three peaks that dominate the region—Erciyes Dağ, Hasan Dağ, and Melendiz Dağ (Mts. Erciyes, Hasan, and Melendiz)—were active volcanoes. Aeons' worth of eruptions dumped layers of mud, ash, and lava on the area. Eventually the ground turned to tuff, a soft, porous rock. Rain, snow, and wind created a fantasyland of rock formations resembling chimneys, cones, needles, pillars, and pyramids, often topped by perfectly balanced, gigantic slabs of rock. Then came earthquakes to add vast valleys and oxidation to give the area the final artistic touch: rocks "painted" yellow, pink, red, russet, and gray-violet.

No one is really sure when people came to inhabit Cappadocia. There are signs of Hittite occupation, and by 600 BC, there are references to the Kingdom of Cappadocia, a loose confederacy of neighboring states. Its first capital was at Nissa; later it was moved to Mazaca (modern Kayseri). Alexander the Great never bothered with the region, and it wasn't annexed by Rome until Emperor Tiberius claimed it in AD 17 and changed the capital's name to Caesarea. Still a backwater, albeit now a Roman one, Cappadocia never gained much in the way of theaters and temples. It did, however, go over to Christianity with great zeal following a visit from Saint Paul. In 370, a local son named Basilius became bishop of Caesarea. A believer in spiritual perfection through monasticism, he was also noted for his good works. His considerable inheritance was spent on the establishment of a charitable institution that cared for the poor and the sick. Though himself in bad health, he personally looked after the poorest of the poor, the lepers, and still found time to preach and write doctrinal treatises. The Eucharist Liturgy of the Greek Church bears his name, and he is one its Four Doctors. He died on January 1, 379, and, as Saint Basil, entered Christian tradition as a bringer of joy and gifts. His foundation became the nucleus of Byzantine Caesarea, and his rules for Orthodox monks are still followed today.

From the 7th through the 10th century, the Christian Cappadocians were under siege from Arab raiders. During this time they took refuge in about 40 **underground cities.** These were cities in the truest sense, some stretching as deep as 20 stories below the surface and able to house as many as 20,000 people. Each had dormitories, dining halls, sewage disposal systems, and ventilation chimneys, as well as a cemetery and a prison. Large millstones sealed off the entrances from enemies. Who actually built these cities is a mystery. Some exhibit traces of Hittite settlements. The Greek historian Xenophon mentions Cappadocian underground dwellings as early as 401 BC. The Christians probably expanded what they found; certainly the cities took centuries to complete. Two of these cities are nearby, one at Kaymaklı, 21 kilometers (13 miles) south of Nevşehir, and the other at Derinkuyu, a bit farther south.

㉓ The narrow entrance to **Kaymaklı** was only uncovered in the 1950s. A central airshaft assures perfect ventilation throughout the 394 feet that have been opened up so far. Sloping corridors and steps connect the floors, self-contained but for cemeteries and kitchens, which are spaced on every second level. Smoke was not allowed to escape for fear of betraying the hideout. Huge stone doors could be rolled across the tunnel entrances to cut off invaders. In some cases a hole is cut above the doorway; through it defenders could pour boiling oil down on their attackers. The impermeable tuff kept the stone dry, and interior wells provided water. Little arrows enable you to take a self-guided tour. A flashlight is helpful, and you'll want a sweater (it's about 50°F inside both in summer and winter). *21 km (13 mi) s. of Nevşehir on road to Niğde. Admission: $2. Open daily 8–sunset.*

㉔ Kaymaklı is believed to be connected by a 10-kilometer (6-mile) tunnel to **Derinkuyu,** though this has not yet been unblocked. Continue south by car or dolmuş. The layout here is similar to that of the other hideaway, though there is an unusual Greek church about halfway down. Some carvings and paintings are visible, but they are fading fast. *30 km (19 mi) south of Nevşehir on road to Niğde. Admission: $2. Open daily 8–sunset.*

The underground cities are far from Cappadocia's only wonders. Long before the Arab raids, ascetics inspired by Saint Basil carved cave dwellings into the soft tuff. This quickly led to the formation of religious colonies that combined the individuality of meditation with communal work on fertile volcanic soil wherever there was a patch of level ground. Rock chapels proliferated, especially in the Göreme Valley. Later, churches were designed in contemporary Byzantine architectural styles and decorated with geometric paintings and increasingly ambitious frescoes. Ironically, ecclesiastical art climaxed in the 11th century, just when the Christian era in Turkey was drawing to a close. Yet Christian communities persisted here, under tolerant Seljuk and Ottoman rulers, up until an exchange of Greek (Christian) and Turkish (Muslim) populations following World War I.

Cappadocia has changed little over the centuries. People travel between their farms and villages in horse-drawn carts, women drape their houses with strings of apricots and paprika for drying in the sun, and nomads pitch their black tents beside sunflower fields and cook on tiny fires that send smoke billowing through the tent tops. In the distance, a minaret pierces the sky. Recently, however, the spellbinding tuff rocks have been revealed to be no less dangerous to their inhabitants than the most ruthless invaders of old. For generations, villagers at Karain have suffered painful deaths, known throughout the area as "the Karain agony." These have finally been diagnosed as cancer, caused by prolonged exposure to the pale yellow rock. Karain and a similarly affected village nearby have been declared natural disaster areas, and the villagers have been evacuated, a fate that seems to them no less an evil than the disease. Only a few improbable villages carved from the rocks are still inhabited, while the holes that riddle the nearby cliff bases shelter the occasional anachronistic troglodyte.

㉕ The logical base for exploring is **Ürgüp.** (Be warned, however: Hotels might be booked up by tours—not a problem, of course, if you sign up for one, which is not a bad idea.) Independent travelers should consider hiring a guide through the local tourist office (*see* Tourist Information in Essential Information, *above*). Expert advice, in fluent if slightly overenthusiastic English, helps you plan your sightseeing according to the time available.

Ürgüp is a green city, full of flowers and parks deep in vines. The town has some fine, old, white, cube-shaped, Greek-style houses, converted now into hotels and carpet shops. In summer, its streets are filled with tourists from around the world, haggling in myriad languages for antique copper and old kilims. Hotel windows open on breathtaking scenery. A serrated white cliff is riddled with manmade holes, filled with fragile masonry walls; some of the walls have crumbled away, revealing the interior of a house. These caves, as well as some giant cones and chimneys in nearby villages, are still inhabited by troglodytes, who simply remove any fallen walls and dig deeper into the rock.

To the south, on the Yeşilhisar road, there are several towns with cave churches, including **Mustafapaşa** and **Soğanlı.** The citadel of **Ortahisar** is hewn out of a gigantic serrated heap of stone; you can climb to the top for a panoramic view.

㉖ The main sights, however, are 7 kilometers (4 miles) to the northwest, in the vineyard-filled valley of **Göreme.** The **Göreme Açik Hava Müzesi** (Göreme Open-Air Museum), 1 kilometer (½ mile) southeast of Göreme village, contains a wealth of rock churches. Signs provide good information on what there is to see, but bring a flashlight, since the churches are only illuminated by the natural light that seeps in.

The oldest rock church here dates from the 4th century. Frescoes first appeared around the 8th century, when the geometric designs applied directly to the rock face gradually gave way to scenes from the New Testament and the lives of the more popular saints painted on plaster. The steep rock to the left of the entrance of the site housed a six-story **convent,** which had a kitchen and refectory on the lower levels and a cruciform chapel on the third; large millstones lay ready to block the narrow passages in time of danger. Opposite is a **monastery** on the same plan, close to the **Elmalı Kilise** (Church with the Apple), probably named after a now vanished orchard. This church is relatively new, only 12th-century. Like those in other main churches, its polychrome scenes from the life of Christ on a dark blue background have been restored under the auspices of UNESCO. To protect the frescoes, all the churches are kept locked and are opened only to groups or by special permission.

The **Barbara Kilise** (Church of Saint Barbara) is decorated with early red designs from the Iconoclastic period (726–842) and 11th-century frescoes of Saint Barbara above the baptistry font. The **Yılanı Kilise** (Serpent Church) might be named after Saint George's dragon, pictured here. A bevy of saints adorns the two sections of this church, one barrel-vaulted, the other flat-roofed. In one mural, Saint Thomas and Saint Basil flank a rather unusual half-female, half-male figure—probably an ancient image of the Anatolian mother goddess, transformed under Christianity into a saint. The 11th-century **Karanlık Kilise** (Dark Church) is lit only through a small orifice in the narthex, reached by a spiral staircase from a refectory. The frescoes are exceptionally fine, especially the Christ, who appears in vivid colors on a dark blue background in the center of the main apse. The **Çarıklı Kilise** (Church of the Sandal) was named after the footprint below the Ascension fresco, which some experts believe to be a cast of Jesus's own footprint. *Open Air Museum: Ürgüp rd. Admission: $2. Open daily 8:30–5:30.*

Outside the fenced-in site, down the hill from the parking lot, is the largest of the area's churches, the 10th-century **Tokalı Kilise** (Church of the Buckle), which contains scenes from the life of Saint Basil. Inside, you might be in any Byzantine church, as sunlight streams in from the barrel entry and turns the underground vaults into gold. A path to the right leads to the **Madonna Kilise** (Church of the Madonna), and the 11th-century **El Nazar Kilise** stands in a nearby orchard. The aptly named **Saklı Kilise** (Hidden Church), a 12th-century work, has fine frescoes if you can find it. Follow the road past the Tokalı Kilise for 1 kilometer (½ mile); the church is 600 feet to the left. These churches have the same admission and hours as the ones above.

In the vicinity of the troglodyte village of **Avcılar**, a long walk or short drive away, are five more rock churches. At **Çavuşin** the church is guarded by frescoes of the angels Michael and Gabriel; inside are scenes from the life of Christ.

㉗ **Zelve,** 6 kilometers (4 miles) northeast of the Göreme museum, is another canyon filled with fairy chimneys and churches; this time the stone is a deep red rather than white. At the mouth of the canyon rises a small minaret. The central ridge divided the valley into Christian and Muslim sectors, with a mosque and church hewn back to back out of the same rock. Rockfalls in the 1960s caused the town to be evacuated. At the far end of the left-hand valley is a narrow tunnel in the rocks; it leads to a lovely canyon with a stream, a peaceful place to rest awhile.

㉘ **Avanos,** on the north bank of the Kızılırmak (Red River), is an attractive old town filled with shops selling onyx jewelry and pottery. The river is named for the local red clay, from which the pottery is made. Off a dirt road 20 kilometers (12 miles) to the north of town is the latest of the region's underground cities to be discovered: **Özkonak.** Potentially the largest of all, this hidden city may have been able to shelter up to 60,000 people, although as yet only a small portion of it has been excavated. Since it is somewhat off the main circuit and still needs a good bit of cleaning up, it is omitted by most guided tours. About 5 kilometers (3 miles) east of Avanos is the **Sari Han,** a 13th-century Seljuk caravansary from the time of Sultan Alaeddin Keykubat. Caravansaries were major outposts on trade routes. They had stables, sleeping quarters, a mosque, and baths, and within their sturdy walls, the goods carried by merchants were kept safe from highway robbers.

㉙ The last of the major cities of Cappadocia is **Kayseri,** a conservative, historic town that is unfortunately now being rebuilt in International Concrete Modern. Still, there are some engaging Seljuk monuments here. On Cumhuriyet Meydanı, where Sivas Caddesi and Istanbul Caddesi meet at the center of town, are not one but two statues of Atatürk. The black basalt walls of the old **citadel** still watch over the square; inside is a modern Turkish shopping mall. The citadel was built by the Byzantines and patched up by Sultan Alaeddin Keykubat in 1224 and again by the Ottomans after the conquest by Sultan Selim I in 1515. Two Seljuk lions guard the gate in the 10-foot-thick ramparts. The fortress walls, sufficiently intact for a trip around the catwalk, offer a fine view of the city.

On the west side of the square is **Atatürk Parkı.** Within this park is the **Kurşunlu Cami,** which has a fine, lead-covered cupola. It was completed in 1585 by Ahmet Paşa after a design by the 16th-century architect Sinan who was born in a nearby village and designed many of Istanbul's greatest landmarks. Facing the citadel on the north side of the square is the **Sahabiye Medrese,** established by the Seljuk vizir Sahipata in 1267. Set around an open courtyard, the seminary has some of the finest carvings of the late Seljuk period. *Cumhuriyet Meydanı.*

To the north, in the maze of back streets, is the **Giyasiye Medrese,** the first medical school in Anatolia (and older than any in Europe). A passage joined it to the **Şifahiye Medrese,** a hospital. Both were built in 1206 from legacies left by the daughter of Sultan Giyassedin Keyhusrev I. Much restored, they are now museums of Islamic medicine. *Mimar Sinan Parkı. Buildings usually locked; ask for watchman.*

North again, just off İstasyon Caddesi, is the **Hacı Kılıç Cami and Medrese,** built in 1249 by the Seljuk vizir Abdül Gazi. The architectural detail of the complex is quite good, especially the handsomely wrought portals. *Admission free. Open daylight hrs.*

Return to the square, pass the PTT (post office) and tourist office on Talas Caddesi, and keep walking until you reach the complex containing the **Huant Hatun Cami, Medrese, and Türbe.** This outstanding group of buildings demonstrates the influence of Huant Hatun, the wife of the greatest Seljuk sultan, Alaeddin Keykubat. The title Noble Lady given to this Georgian princess refers, clearly, to birth rather than character, as it is suspected that she poisoned the sultan when he was about to disinherit their son. In 1237, once the lad was safely enthroned, the queen mother had the religious complex constructed, perhaps by way of atonement. The mosque has a finely decorated main gate and double arches. The first instructor at the medrese, now an **ethnographical museum,** was Burhaneddin Tirmizi, teacher of Mevlana Celaleddin (*see* Tour 4: Konya, *below*). The octagonal türbe is encircled by a double band of elegant geometric designs. The austere interior is distinguished by a rare Seljuk stone mihrab and holds three sarcophagi; Hunad Hatun's is of white marble, decorated with fine calligraphy. The main hamam, next door, is still in use. *Cumhuriyet Meydanı. Museum admission: $1. Open 8–noon and 1–5:30.*

Just west of the citadel is Kayseri's jumble of a **bazaar.** The centuries-old covered market is noted, as you might expect, for its carpets—and there are plenty of exceptional pieces to choose from—though it also stocks all the other necessities of Turkish life. A word on Kayseri and its carpet salesmen: In Turkish folklore, the people of Kayseri are renowned for being crafty dealers. Freelance touts pick up commissions for each tourist they convince to stop in a shop. So keep your wits about you and remember: If you don't want to shop or buy, make it absolutely clear from the outset. If all else fails, use the Turkish word *yok*, the ultimate, highly effective, don't-argue-with-me version of no!

From the bazaar, you should be able to see the double domes of the **Ulu Cami** (Great Mosque). It was begun in 1135 and completed in 1205 and contains a finely carved wooden mimber. A tile mosaic is the outstanding feature of its cylindrical minaret. *Near Düvenönü Meydanı.*

South of the citadel, scattered along Cumhuriyet Bulvari, are numerous Seljuk *kümbets* (mausoleums). In 1247, three rival vizirs prepared for the uncertain future by constructing the cylindrical **Sırçalı Kümbet** (Crystal Mausoleum), named for decorative tiles that have since vanished; the **Çifte Kümbet** (Twin Vault Mausoleum), octagonal under a cone-shaped roof; and the **Ali Kafer Kümbet** (Ali Kafer Mausoleum). The **Kasbek Kümbet** (Kasbek Mausoleum) is the oldest, but the best known is the **Doner Kümbet** (Turning Mausoleum) of Sultan Shah Cihan, built in 1276. The name is derived not from the popular kebab but from the tomb's conical roof, which fits upon the 12-sided structure so lightly that it might be turned by any breeze. All its panels are decorated with bas-reliefs, among others the Tree of Life and a double-headed eagle above lions. Unfortunately, signs are only in Turkish. *Open daylight hrs.*

The local **Arkeoloji Müzesi** (Archaeological Museum) is farther up Cumhuriyet Bulvari. The best pieces are finds from Kültepe, site of the ancient Hittite city of Kaneş, including many cuneiform tablets. There is some Greek and Roman statuary as well. *Kışla Cad., tel. 352/331–1131 or 352/331–4941. Admission: $1. Open 8–noon and 1–5:30.*

After the museum, the boulevard narrows and climbs into the foothills of Mt. Erciyes. A pleasant villa suburb has risen over the site of ancient Eusebeia, followed by barren slopes dotted with beehives, which supply the excellent honey sold along the roadside.

There are a few sites to see in the vicinity of Kayseri. On the road toward Sivas northeast on 260, 20 kilometers (12 miles) will take you to **Kültepe** (Hill of Ashes). This is the site of Kaneş, an important Hittite city. Inhabited from the 4th millennium BC, Kaneş became powerful around 2500 BC. Five hundred years later, Assyrian trade caravans passed through Anatolia, and the trade colony of Kaneş flourished behind its single wall, attached to the double fortifications of an upper town. Only the foundations are left, and most of the 15,000 cuneiform tablets, alabaster idols, statuettes, and painted pottery found here are now in Ankara and Kayseri museums.

Two remarkable caravansaries and hans are also nearby. About 30 kilometers (18 miles) farther along the Sivas road, Alaeddin Keykubat built the **Sultan Hanı,** one of the most handsome in Anatolia. Behind the thick, rectangular walls (138 by 95 feet), travelers and their beasts found ample space for a rest. For a good view of the surroundings, take the stairway to the right of the main gate up to the roof. The han was built in 1236. *Admission: 50¢. Open daily 9–1 and 2–5.*

At **Incesu**, 35 kilometers (22 miles) southwest of Kayseri on Route 805 heading toward Niğde, Kara Mustafa Paşa had another caravansary built. It contains a bazaar as well as the usual mosque and baths.

33 From here, continue on Route 805 to **Niğde.** (Alternatively, if you are coming from Nevşehir or the underground city of Derinkuyu, take Route 765 south.) This quiet provincial town has Hittite roots, though it really flourished in the 13th century, when Sultan Keykubat built the **Alaeddin Cami.** The mosque proudly bears three domes, exquisitely pure in line. A century later, the Mongol Sungur Bay constructed a **mosque** of his own, with portals distinguished by unusual Gothic features. The inevitable **fortress** looks down from the heights; dating from the end of the 11th century, it's the town's earliest Seljuk monument. Subtle, lacy stone carvings adorn the **Hudavent Hatun Türbe** (1312) and the charming white **Akmedrese** (1409), which is now a small regional museum with a Byzantine mummy that is something of a scene stealer. A 16th-century **bedestan** adds to the list of distinguished architecture here.

About 9 kilometers (6 miles) northwest of Niğde is the 10th-century church of **Eski Gumus** (Old Silver), featuring exceptionally well-preserved frescoes of Christ, Mary, and the saints. The adjoining monastery is hollowed out of the rock. **Bor,** 14 kilometers (9 miles) southwest of Niğde along Route 330, has yet another Alaeddin Cami as well as a 16th-century covered bazaar and bath. More interesting are the Roman aqueduct, pool, and hot springs at nearby **Kemerhisar,** another 5 kilometers (3 miles) south on the same road; in Hittite days the town was called Tuvana. *All sites: Admission free or nominal charge. Open daylight hrs.*

If you want to head for the Mediterranean, now would be a good time. In short order, you can take Route 805 south to the E5 heading for Tarsus. From there, head east to Adana or west to Mersin.

34 If you're heading for Konya, you might consider a detour to **Aksaray.** (It's just off the E90, or take one of the local roads out of Niğde or the 300 from Nevşehir.) Thanks to the **Melendiz Çayı** (Melendiz River), Aksaray is surrounded by an oasis in the baked plain. Though not quite up to the standards of Pisa's Leaning Tower, the **Egri Minare** (Crooked Minaret), a reddish brick structure, has leaned alarmingly over the low houses on the riverbanks for almost as long, since 1236. The main monuments date from the 15th century: the **Ulu Cami,** which dominates the main square, and the **Ibrahim Bey** and **Zinciriye medreses.**

Another old caravansary built under the aegis of Alaeddin Keykubat, **Ağzıkarahan,** 15 kilometers (9 miles) east of Aksaray on Route 300, has been restored to a semblance of the splendor it had when opened in 1239. On your way back to Aksaray, take a left onto the road leading south to **Selime,** just after the Mamasın Reservoir. Once again, you're back in the fairyland of Cappadocia.

The first violet-gray fairy chimneys appear at Selime, where Sultan Selim is buried in an octagonal türbe. The frescoes in the three-naved, barrel-vaulted basilica are late Byzantine.

Continuing on, bear left at the next fork in the road to reach **Güzelyurt,** where yet another large concentration of rock needles
35 and pillars is being opened up. Return to the fork and take the right-hand road to **Ihlara,** where the Melendiz River has carved a rift into the sheer tuff cliffs, which rise up to 492 feet. They are pierced by thousands of churches, chapels, and caves. The best view can be obtained from the hilltop restaurant, from which 285 steps descend the wall-like rock to the bottom of the canyon, a green gash in the barren

highland below Mt. Melendiz (9,627 feet). Byzantine Peristrema, the ancient name for Ihlara, is still idyllic; poplars and wild olive trees shade the slow-moving water, along which the 20 main churches are slowly crumbling away.

It is hard to tell the difference between steppe and desert, at least in summer, on the remaining 142 kilometers (88 miles) of Route 300 southwest to Konya. Most travelers welcome a stop along the way: **36** **Sultan Hanı,** 95 kilometers (59 miles) northeast of Konya, is Anatolia's largest and best-preserved caravansary and in ancient times was a place of rest and shelter for travelers and their camels plying the trade routes. Hans were constructed every 30 kilometers (19 miles) or so, so there are two others on this route, the **Agizkara Han** (Dark-mouthed Inn), dating from 1231, and the **Sari Han** (Yellow Inn), from 1249.

Tour 4: Konya

37 **Konya,** at an altitude of 3,336 feet in a large, well-watered oasis, is the home of the whirling dervishes and one of the largest and fastest-growing cities in the country. Many travelers arrive from Cappadocia, but you can also get here from Ankara, 262 kilometers (163 miles) to the north via Route 715 to E90, and from Antalya on the Mediterranean coast, 427 kilometers (265 miles) southwest. As befits what was the capital of the Seljuk Empire for two centuries, it has the largest concentration of Seljuk architecture in Turkey. The Seljuks chose their capital wisely; the combination of altitude and setting provides Konya with cool breezes from the surrounding mountain chains and a much more moderate climate than in the rest of Anatolia.

Konya was hardly new when the Seljuks arrived in 1076. Earlier there had been a Hittite settlement here and, later, an important Phrygian town. Saint Paul and Saint Barnabas delivered sermons in the years 47, 50, and 53. Konya was prosperous under the Romans and hosted one of the first ecumenical councils, in 235. After suffering at the hands of Arab raiders from the 7th to 10th centuries, the city flourished again in the early 13th century, during the reign of Alaeddin Keykubat. It was a golden era that would last until the city fell to Mongol invaders in the early 1400s.

The most-visited site in Konya is the **Mevlana Türbesi** (Tomb of Mevlana Celaleddin), the 13th-century poet and philosopher who founded the mystic order of the Mevlana dervishes. The tomb, as well as the *tekke* (monastery) of Mevlana, is situated at the eastern end of Konya's main avenue, Mevlana Caddesi. Born in present-day Afghanistan in 1207, Mevlana Celaleddin was the son of a renowned theologian who fled with his family before Genghis Khan's hordes. Celaleddin came to Konya at the age of 22, during the reign of Sultan Alaeddin Keykubat. He studied philosophy and religion and, like his father, became famous as a teacher of canonical law. In 1244, he came under the influence of a Persian dervish named Şemseddin (or Sems), abandoned his profession, and devoted himself to philosophical discussions with his new mentor. When Sems disappeared, most likely murdered by Celaleddin's jealous followers, Celaleddin in his grief turned to Sufic mysticism and to poetry. His greatest work, *The Mesnevi*, consists of 25,000 poems that were read and taught in the countless tekkes of the order he founded. *The Mesnevi* is the only philosophical system formulated in poetry that ranks close to the Koran in Islamic literature, and it earned the great mystic the Persian title of Mevlana (Grand Master). Mevlana died on December

17, 1273, and was succeeded by Hüsamed-din Çelebi, followed in turn by Mevlana's son, Sultan Veled.

Mevlana was a firm believer in the virtues of music and of its corollary, dance, as a means of abandoning oneself to God's love and freeing oneself from earthly bondage. He considered the whirling pattern of motion to be representative of the soul's state of agitation. In the early years of the republic all religious orders were banned and forced to go underground, although they have gradually been re-emerging since the 1980s. Until recently very few read Mevlana's works, but the authorities did preserve the *sema* (the whirling dance of his order) as a folklore spectacle. The sema is still held in Konya once a year, during the weeklong festival to mark the anniversary of Mevlana's death on December 17. When it came to communicating with God, Mevlana made no distinction between social class, race, or even religion; the sema was open to all. The dancers one sees today are men of ordinary trades and, despite 60 years pretending to be merely a dance, the sema retains all its religious symbolism. The dancers' accelerated turning and position—right arm pointing up and left down—suggest their openness to divine grace. Their conical hats represent tombstones, their jackets the tombs themselves, and their skirts the funerary shrouds. Removing their jackets signifies their shedding of earthly ties and their escape from their graves. As they whirl, they also rotate around the room, as the universe rotates in the presence of God. Thus, in whirling away his earthly ties, the dervish effects a union with God. Several travel agencies operate tours to the Mevlana festival; they are often fully booked weeks in advance. If you want to join a tour, book before you leave home. The Tourism Information Office in Konya will help individuals find tickets and make hotel reservations for the festival. Several of the staff speak English and are invariably delighted by foreign interest in what is a considerable source of local pride, but it as well to call or fax them several weeks in advance. *Konya Tourism Information, tel. 332/351–1074, fax 332/350–6461.*

The tekke of Mevlana became the **Mevlana Müzesi** (Mevlana Museum) in 1927. Small, lead-topped domes set over the dervishes' cubicles form an honor guard around the garden leading up to the entrance. Inside, vivid reconstructions illustrate the dervishes' way of life in their former cells. The square room that you enter first is the Koran reading room. On the walls hang framed examples of distinguished calligraphy, including one specimen executed by a great devotee of this art, Sultan Mahmut. The translation of the quotation above the silver door is "He who enters incomplete here will leave complete." One showcase contains the first 18 verses of *The Mesnevi*, written in Mevlana's own hand. To the right and left of the reading room lie the tombs of the most illustrious disciples, 65 in all.

Continue on into the room where Mevlana's enormous tomb rests on a pedestal. At its head are his black turban and the curious cylindrical headgear of the sect. Two silver steps lead up to the platform; they are the sacred stairway. Believers press their faces against it as a sign of devotion. A brocade cover, embroidered with gold thread and weighing almost 110 pounds, covers the biers of Mevlana and his eldest son; it was a gift from the Ottoman sultan Mehmet II (1451–81). At the foot of the tomb, the coffin of Mevlana's father stands vertically, his white funerary turban on top. Quotations from the Koran are embedded in the sarcophagus with the exquisite precision and mastery of technique that characterize Seljuk art at its best. The mausoleum itself dates from the 13th century; the rest of the monastery was built later. *Mevlana Meydanı (eastern end of*

Mevlana Cad.). Admission: $1.50. Open daily 9–noon and 1–5; occasionally closed Mon. during the winter.

The **Selimiye Cami** (Selim Mosque), opposite the Mevlana Museum on Mevlana Meydanı, was started by the heir to the throne in 1558, when he was governor of Konya, and finished after he had become Sultan Selim II. The style is reminiscent of that of the Fatih Cami in Istanbul, with soaring arches and windows surrounding the base of the dome. The surrounding streets have a lot of character and some shops, if you have spare time for wandering.

There is more to see in the direction of the ancient acropolis, now called Alaeddin Tepe (Alaeddin Hill), about 1 kilometer (½ mile) from the Mevlana Museum. The main street leading there is called Alaeddin Caddesi. At the beginning of the street, on the right side, is the **Şerefettin Cami,** built in 1636. It was started by the Seljuks and completed by the Ottomans. To the north of the mosque, off Hükümet Alanı, is the **Şemsi Tebrizi Cami and Türbe,** dedicated to Mevlana's mentor and friend. Almost across Alaeddin Caddesi stands Konya's oldest mosque, the **İplikçi Cami** (Thread Mosque), dating from 1202.

The beautiful **Alaeddin Cami,** completed in 1220 and recently restored, crowns the acropolis hill. Designed by an architect from Damascus, the mosque is of the Syrian style, unusual for Anatolia. Its pulpit stands in a forest of 42 columns taken from Roman temples. Most of the hill is devoted to a park, which contains a pleasant café, with good views over the town. Below are the scanty remains of a Seljuk palace, two venerable stumps of walls. The city has for some reason deemed it expedient to throw an unsightly concrete shelter over them.

On the north side of the hill is the **Büyük Karatay Medrese,** a theological seminary founded by Emir Celaleddin Karatay in 1251. (His tomb is in a small room to the left of the main hall.) It is now a ceramics museum, the Karatay Müzesi (Karatay Museum), and it is easy to understand why this particular building was selected for that purpose. Its dome is lined with tiles, blue predominating on white, and the effect is dazzling. The frieze beneath the dome is in terrific shape, and the hunting scenes on the rare figurative tiles from the Kubadabat Palace at Beyşehir show the influence of Persia on Seljuk art. The soothing sound of a fountain spilling into a basin in the middle of the main hall sets just the right mood for meditation and study. The spectacular ceramics collection includes figures of almond-eyed women, animals, and vine leaves highlighted in shades of cobalt blue and turquoise. *Alaeddin Cad., at intersection with Ankara-Istanbul Yolu. Admission: $1. Open daily 8:30–noon and 1:30–5:30.*

If you walk along Alaeddin Caddesi to the right after exiting the Karatay, you will soon come to the 13th-century **İnce Minare Medrese** (Medrese of the Slender Minaret). The minaret in question, bejeweled with glazed blue tiles, is now only half its original size, thanks to an ill-placed bolt of lightning. Like the other medrese, the İnce Minare now serves as a museum, this one with a fine collection of stone and wood carvings. Be sure to note the ornate decoration of the building's entry portal. *Alaeddin Cad., on w. side of Alaeddin Tepe. Admission: 50¢. Open daily 8:30–noon and 1:30–5:30.*

Farther along Alaeddin Caddesi is the **Sırçalı Medrese** (Crystalline Seminary), opened in 1242 as a school for Islamic jurisprudence. The lavish tile decoration provides a dignified home for the Museum of Funerary Monuments. The small Catholic Church of Saint Paul next door proves that Konya has remained as tolerant as it was in its Seljuk heyday. On the opposite side of the Sırçalı are Roman catacombs and a mosaic.

Continue due south to Larende Caddesi, where another magnificent portal marks the remains of the **Sahip Ata** complex, a group of buildings dating from 1283. The mosque complex here has been converted into an **Arkeoloji Müzesi** (Archaeological Museum). Though the collection begins with items from the Bronze Age, its most important artifacts are Greek and Roman; the 3rd-century BC marble depicting the 12 labors of Hercules is outstanding. *Ressam Sami Sok., off Larende Cad. Admission: $1. Open daily 8:30–noon and 1:30–5:30.*

Two blocks to the right (facing the Sahip Ata complex) is the **Etnoğrafya Müzesi** (Ethnographic Museum). It contains Islamic art, embroidery, carpets, and weapons. *Larende Cad. Admission: 50¢. Open daily 8:30–noon and 1:30–5:30.*

Carpets and rugs still provide the main interest in the **bazaar,** off lower Hukumet Caddesi (back toward Mevlana Meydanı); turn left off Selimiye Caddesi. Though the rugs sold here today hardly justify Marco Polo's judgment as "the most beautiful carpets in the world," their colors and designs are pleasing enough. The bazaar is flanked by the **Aziziye Cami** (Sultan Abdül Aziz Mosque), dating from 1676, which has two short minarets topped off by a kind of loggia with a Florentine flavor. *Market district, near intersection of Selimiye Cad. and Karaman Cad.*

If you're heading out of town in the direction of Ankara, look for yet another of those fabulous Seljuk portals at the entrance to the ruined **Horozlu Han,** near the four-lane beginning of Route 715. At **Sille,** 8 kilometers (5 miles) northwest, Saint Helena, mother of Constantine the Great, built a small church in AD 327. Nearby, frescoed rock chapels overlook the shores of a tiny artificial lake.

What to See and Do with Children

In this area, Ankara is the best bet for children. Its green **Gençlik Park** offers shady walks, a small amusement park with a Ferris wheel and other rides, and a small lake where rowboats can be rented (*see* Tour 1: Ankara, *above*). The green countryside around the **Bayındır Dam,** 16 kilometers (10 miles) east of Ankara, off the Samsun road, is nice for picnics. **Gölbaşı,** 25 kilometers (16 miles) south of Ankara on E90, is the only natural lake in the area; it has a beach for swimming.

Off the Beaten Track

You might want to leave a day in your schedule for a trip from Ankara to the city made famous by King Midas, he of the golden touch. Though only about 100 kilometers (62 miles) southwest of Ankara, **Gordion** lies in the opposite direction from the main tourist routes to Cappadocia and Konya. Take the E90 to Polatlı; then look for the road to Gordion branching off to the right, approximately 12 kilometers (8 miles) west of Polatli. This was the capital of Phrygia, whose population most likely emigrated from Macedonia and Thrace about 3,000 years ago. Legend has it that the city was founded by a poor farmer named Gordios, who fulfilled an oracle predicting that the first man to enter the gates of the ancient city would become its ruler. After the town was named for him, the new king dedicated a chariot to the gods, tying the yoke and shaft together with a knot so stout that another oracle declared that whoever was to rule Asia would first have to untie it. Alexander the Great found the challenge irresistible and, deviating from his march of conquest in 334 BC, resolutely sliced through the Gordian knot with his sword.

The city's other celebrity is rather a hard-luck story. Midas, son of Gordios, succeeded in 738 BC. According to Herodotus, he was asked to judge a music contest and picked Pan's flute over the other contestant's lyre, not realizing that the loser was Apollo. Considerably put out, the god caused donkey's ears to sprout from Midas's head. Having learned nothing from his first encounter with the Olympians, Midas later entertained Dionysus, who promised to grant the king a wish in return for his hospitality. Midas rashly asked that everything he touched be transformed into gold. No sooner said than done, but though Midas was then richer than Croesus, he was starving, as even his food turned to gold. Dionysus prescribed a plunge into the Paktolos River to get rid of this over-generous gift. Forever after, the story goes, the river was full of gold, to the joy of the Lydians downstream. Midas had yet more bad luck to come, this time in the form of marauding Cimmerians. After a crushing defeat in 695 BC, Midas apparently committed suicide.

There is not terribly much to see at Gordion these days. Where once the royal palace stood on the low hill, with the town spread below the fortified terrace to the banks of the Sakarya, there are few remains. More interesting is the **Great Tumulus** on the edge of town, including what is believed to be the tomb of King Midas. A well-lit tunnel, some 230 feet long, has been cut through the mound to the burial chamber, which is framed with cedar and juniper beams. When the tomb was opened, the skeleton of a rather short man, about age 60, lay on a large table. The funeral artifacts and bronze fibulae were taken to the Museum of Anatolian Civilizations in Ankara; the small local museum displays only a minor miscellany of pottery and copper objects.

Shopping

The best bazaars can be found in Ankara, Kayseri, and Konya (*see* Tours 1, 3, and 4, *above*). **Rugs** and **kilims,** of course, are everywhere. In Ankara, look for products made from **angora,** a local specialty (which may have been named after the city); but check where it has come from, as much of the angora now on sale in the city has been imported. A wide variety of reasonably priced yarns and sweaters is available.

Dining and Lodging

Restaurants in this region serve food that's almost the same as what you'll find throughout Turkey: kebabs, kebabs, and more kebabs. Other common dishes include *mezes* (appetizers), grilled fish and meat (especially lamb), and vegetarian dishes. Most restaurants serve wine, beer, and *raki* (a Turkish brandy). Dress is casual, and unless otherwise noted, reservations are not necessary—in fact, you will seldom need them except in Ankara, where dining is more sophisticated. Similarly, outside Ankara hotels are mostly unexceptional. For details and price-category definitions for both restaurants and hotels, *see* Dining and Lodging in Staying in Turkey in Chapter 1, Essential Information. Ankara costs are in the Major Cities column, costs elsewhere in the Other Areas column.

Highly recommended establishments are indicated by a star ★

Ankara
Dining

RV. As befits a restaurant in the embassy quarter, RV is both elegant and pricey. It's one of the few places men will feel more comfortable in a jacket. The menu covers both traditional Turkish specialties and European dishes, a boon for homesick diplomats. *İlbank Bloklari 243, Atatürk Bulvari, Kavaklıdere, tel. 312/427–4344. Reservations advised. MC, V. $$$*

Kale Washington. One of the two offspring of the former Washington Restaurant in Kizilay, the Kale Washington is situated in the Kale, the ancient heart of the city, and serves a superb selection of grilled fish, various kebabs, and Imam bayildi (eggplant stuffed with ground lamb). *Doyran Sok. 5, Kaleiçi, Ulus. Ankara, tel. 312/311–4344 or 312/324–5959. Reservations advised. MC, V. $$–$$$*

Nenehatun Washington. The other offspring of the Washington, the Nenehatun, is located in the upmarket residential area of Gaziosmanpasa. The menu is similar to its sibling's but it also offers a range of Russian dishes and very fine crepes. *Nenehatun Caddesi 97, Gaziosmanpaşa, tel. 312/445–0212 or 312/436–4353. MC, V. $$–$$$*

Göksu. Opened in 1992, the Göksu specializes in Black Sea cuisine, even importing all its fish and cheese from the region, thus making it a popular hangout for exiled Black Sea businessmen and their families. Rather incongruously, the walls are decorated with Hittite reliefs, but the food is excellent. *Bayindir Sok 22/A, Kizilay, tel. 312/431–2219 or 312/431–4727. Reservations advised. MC. $$*

Mest. Ankara may seem an unlikely place to find a restaurant serving northern Italian cuisine, but here it is. The Mest also has a fine selection of Turkish and continental dishes. Situated in a restored two-story villa, it has an upstairs terrace for cocktails together with a summer garden and a bar. *Attar Sok. 10, Gaziosmanpasa, tel. 312/468–0743 or 312/468–6028. V. $$*

★ **Zenger Paşa Konaği.** The Mansion of Zenger Paşa, a traditional old house within the citadel, has been restored and is now a fine restaurant. The food is traditional, too, from the *mantı* (Turkish ravioli) to the *saç kavurma* (sautéed lamb). The fine view of the city is an added attraction. *Doyran Sok. 13, Ankara Kalesi, tel. 312/311–7070 or 312/311–4060. Reservations advised. AE, MC, V. $$*

Akman Boza. This spot has been serving tasty breakfasts, sandwiches, desserts, and snacks since the 1930s. Tables are set out in a pleasant courtyard with a small fountain. *Atatürk Bul. 3, Ulus, no phone. No credit cards. $*

Lodging

★ **Ankara Hilton.** This luxurious 16-story hotel in Embassy Row, in the quiet, hilly neighborhood called Kavaklıdere, provides all the amenities and a fine view to boot. *Tahran Cad. 12, Kavaklıdere, tel. 312/468–2888, fax 312/468–0909. 325 rooms with bath. Facilities: 2 restaurants, bar, casino, indoor pool, health club, business center. AE, DC, MC, V. $$$*

Büyük Ankara. This high rise across from the Grand National Assembly was long Ankara's poshest hotel. Now competition from the international chains has relegated it to second place. Then again, it's less expensive than the Hilton or Sheraton and has Turkish, rather than international, charm. *Atatürk Bul. 183, Kavaklıdere, tel. 312/425–6655, fax 312/425–5070. 192 rooms with bath. Facilities: 3 restaurants, bar, casino, pool. AE, DC, MC, V. $$$*

Dedeman Oteli. The Dedeman is the best bargain among the upper-echelon hotels. It has a gleaming marble lobby, a rooftop nightclub, and other nice facilities. The hotel has two wings: one more modern (and expensive), the other with older, smaller rooms. *Büklüm Sok. 1, Akay, tel. 312/417–6200, fax 312/417–6214. 292 rooms with bath.*

Facilities: 4 restaurants, bar, nightclub, swimming pool, health club. AE, DC, MC, V. $$$

Sheraton Ankara. The newest and splashiest of Ankara's luxury hotels is hard to miss; it's tall, white, and round. It is also well run, fashionable, and thoroughly international in style. Atatürk would have approved. *Noktali Sok., Kavaklıdere, tel. 312/468-5454, fax 312/467-1136. 311 rooms with bath. Facilities: 3 restaurants, bar, swimming pool, health club, 4 squash courts. AE, MC, V. $$$*

Kent. A very pleasant, helpful staff distinguishes this hotel in the heart of the city literally a couple of minutes' walk from the main shopping and business areas. The restaurant is above average for a hotel. *Mithatpaşa Cad. 4, tel. 312/435-5050, fax 312/434-4657. 117 rooms with bath. Facilities: restaurant, bar. AE, MC, V. $$*

Seğmen Hotel. Near the Dedeman, the Seğmen is relatively new; interiors are done up in natural wood. The hotel is well located and reasonably priced. *Büklüm Sok. 13, Kavaklıdere, tel. 312/417-5374, fax 312/417-2859. 98 rooms with bath. Facilities: restaurants, bar. AE, MC, V. $$*

Tunali. In the center just across from the Kuglu Park, the Tunali is unspectacular and clean; the staff is very friendly. *Tunali Hilmi Cad. 119, Kavaklıdere, tel. 312/467-4410 or 312/427-8100, fax 312/427-4082. 52 rooms with shower. Facilities: restaurant, bar. AE, MC, V. $-$$*

Hotel Sultan. This hotel is not fancy, but it's a perfectly acceptable place to stay and very inexpensive. Though there's no decor to speak of, the hotel does have clean sheets, hot water, and a friendly staff. The location is near Kızılay, though on a pleasantly quiet side street in a residential area. *Bayındır Sok. 35, tel. 312/431-5980, fax 312/431-1083. 40 rooms with bath. Facilities: parking garage. MC, V. $*

Otel Karyağdi. Good hotels on the Ulus side of town are rare; this is the exception. The exterior is a purplish gray and looks a bit like a fortress. The interior is well furnished, though in a no-nonsense style. It is not far from Itfaiye Meydanı (Opera Square). *Sanayi Cad., Kuruçeşme Sok. 4, Ulus, tel. 312/310-2440, fax 312/312-6712. 40 rooms with bath. Facilities: 2 bars, game room, playground, parking. No credit cards. $*

Avanos
Lodging
Zelve. This is one of the several perfectly decent small hotels and pensions in town. Built in the 1980s, it has a modern, minimalist decor. Rooms have tile baths. *Hükümet Meydanı tel. 384/511-4524, fax 384/511-4687. 29 rooms with bath. Facilities: restaurant, bar. AE, MC, V. $$*

Sofa Motel. A charming hotel with lots of character, it was built from a row of restored old stone houses that Ferit, the manager, estimates to be at least 200 years old. The excellent restaurant serves local cuisine. *Orta Mah, Avanos, tel./fax 384/511-4489. 34 rooms with shower. Facilities: restaurant, bar. MC, V. $*

Göreme
Dining
★
Ataman. Run by tourist guide Abbas and his wife, Şermin, this restaurant is built into the face of a rock. It is decorated with kilims and handicrafts and serves a good selection of Turkish and international cuisine. *On main st., tel. 384/271-2310, fax 384/271-2313. No credit cards. $*

Harmandali. This cavernous restaurant prides itself on being able to offer more kinds of meze (30) than anyone else in the region. It also serves a wide variety of main dishes, all for one price. The house specialty is chicken *güveç* (chicken, peppers and tomatoes, baked in a clay pot). The floor show that follows the meal has made it a popular spot with tour groups. *Uçhisar, near Göreme, tel. 384/219-2364, fax 384/219-2394. $*

Lodging **Cave Hotel Melek.** Though decidedly basic, the Melek is special for one reason: Like most other buildings here, it's partially carved out of the rock. *On the main street, tel. 384/271–2463 fax 384/271–2463. 20 rooms, 12 with bath. Facilities: restaurant, terrace. No credit cards. $*

Kayseri The Hattat and Turan hotels have the best restaurants in town.
Dining **Cumhuriyet Lokantasi.** Similar to the Iskender (*above*) and only two doors away, it serves the same type of good basic food but specializes in roasted chicken. Tables are set out on the street in good weather. *27 Mayis Caddesi 9, tel. 352/231–4911. No credit cards. $*

Iskender Kebab Salonu. Here, near the citadel, you can try a good range of standard Turkish fare. *Iskender kebab* (slices of lamb grilled on a spit served with yogurt and a tomato sauce) is the specialty. The main dining area is on the first floor with views over the street, but there is a quieter, more pleasant *aile salonu* (family room) on the next floor up. *27 Mayis Caddesi 5, tel. 352/231–2769. No credit cards. $*

Dining and **Hattat Hotel.** A business-type establishment, the Hattat is more
Lodging modern, both in style and facilities, than the Turan. It has a good restaurant, which serves kebabs and the usual mezes. *Park Cad. 21, tel. 352/222–6620, fax 352/232–6503. 72 rooms with bath. Facilities: restaurant. No credit cards. $$*

Hotel Turan. This reliable, old-fashioned hotel is right in the center of town. Though it is a bit worn, it has the advantages of a roof terrace, a decent restaurant with traditional Turkish food, and a Turkish bath. *Turan Cad. 8, tel. 352/231–8214 or 352/231–1029, fax 352/231–1153. 40 rooms with bath. Facilities: restaurant, roof terrace, Turkish bath. No credit cards. $–$$*

Konya **Hanedan.** Kebabs are the order of the day at Hanedan, particularly
Dining the *tandir* (lamb baked in a bread oven and served with thick pita bread) or the *inegol kofte* (ground lamb with garlic, onion, pepper, and tomatoes). *Mevlana Cad. 2/B, tel. 332/311–4546. No credit cards. $–$$*

Horozlu Han Kervansaray. In a restored 700-year-old Seljuk caravansary on the old Silk Road 7 kilometers (4½ miles) from the Mevlana Museum on the road to Ankara, the Horozlu has a huge, cavernous interior where the old stone offers a cool refuge from the summer heat. There are often floor shows in the evening. Specialties include *ezo gelin* (lentil soup), *etli ekmek* (flat bread with ground lamb), and some excellent fish, which vary according to the season. *Konya-Ankara Yolu Üzeri 4 km, TNP Yani, Konya, tel. 332/248–3115 or 332/248–3130, fax 332/248–3130. V. $–$$*

Konya Fuar. Pleasant outdoor dining is provided in the city's Luna Park. The food is much the same as elsewhere: kebabs. *Luna Park, no phone. No credit cards. $–$$*

Damla Restaurant. Damla is owned and run by a woman who is famous for her kitchen wizardry, especially when it comes to her *piliç* (chicken, cheese, peas, and potatoes baked in a small clay pot) and *saç kavurma* (sautéed lamb). *Hükümet Alanı, near Sahin Oteli, tel. 332/351–3705. No credit cards. $*

Şifa 1, Şifa 2. Opposite one another, both self-service restaurants offer a good range of basic Turkish fare. No alcohol is served. *Mevlana Cad. tel. 332/352–0519 (Şifa 1) and 332/353–3666 (Şifa 2), fax 332/351–9251. No credit cards. $*

Lodging **Hotel Balikçilar.** Some of the rooms in this relative newcomer have views of the Mevlana Museum that more than make up for the rather plain styling. *Mevlana Kar. 1, tel. 332/350–9470, fax 332/351–3259. 48 rooms with bath. Facilities: restaurant, 2 bars. V. $$*

Konya Oteli. The Konya is just a block from the Mevlana Museum. Its staff seems eager to please, and most guests give the place a strong endorsement. Though older than other hotels here, the building is well kept. *Mevlana Meydanı, Turizm Yanı 8 (near the Tourism Office), tel. 332/351-6677, fax 332/352-1003. 50 rooms with bath. Facilities: restaurant. V. $$*

Sema Oteli. Centrally located, this comfortable hotel is only a few minutes' walk from the Mevlana Museum. It looks like a five-story apartment house, but the rooms are clean and spacious. A pleasant, vine-hung terrace offers refuge from the bustle of the town, and the restaurant is excellent. *Mevlana Cad., tel. 332/322-1510, fax 332/321-1263. 64 rooms with shower. Facilities: restaurant, bar, terrace. MC, V. $-$$*

Başak Palas. The Başak Palas is an older but charming small hotel that is very conveniently located. Not all rooms have showers, so investigate before agreeing to a particular room. *Hükümet Alanı 3, tel. 332/351-1338. 35 rooms, most with bath. No credit cards. $*

Nevşehir **Aspava.** Centrally located, the Aspava offers a good-quality range of
Dining *hazır yemek* (food prepared earlier and kept hot) and kebabs. *Atatürk Bul., tel. 384/213-1051. No credit cards. $*

Park. In the park northwest of the post office, this restaurant has good views over the city and a more extensive range of food than the Aspava, with a selection of mezes, soup, and good fried chicken. *Atatürk Bul., next to Asgari gazino, tel. 384/213-4487. No credit cards. $*

Lodging **Altinoz Hotel.** This modern hotel lacks the character and charm of many smaller establishments in the region, but it is clean and comfortable, with a helpful staff and very passable restaurants. *Ragip Uner Cad. 23, tel. 384/213-5305 or 384/213-9961, fax 384/213-2817. 120 rooms with shower. Facilities: 3 restaurants, roof bar, sauna. V. $$*

Hotel Nevşehir Dedeman. This modern high rise offers the closest thing to luxury in the area. There are plenty of facilities, including a pool to cool off in. It's about 2 kilometers (1 mile) out of town along the road to Ürgüp. *Ürgüp Yolu, tel. 384/213-9900, fax 384/213-2158. 349 rooms with bath. Facilities: 2 restaurants, bars, disco, indoor and outdoor pools, sauna, Turkish bath, tennis court, billiards room. AE, DC, MC, V. $$*

Hotel Orsan Kapadokya. The Orsan is quite chic by Turkish provincial standards; it has fine Turkish carpets in the public areas, a smart bar, and, what's more, a pool. *Yeni Kayseri Cad. 15, tel. 384/213-2115 or 384/213-5329, fax 384/213-4223. 95 rooms with bath. Facilities: restaurant, bar, pool. AE, MC, V. $$*

Ürgüp **Hanedan.** Located in an old Greek-style house, the Hanedan is on a
Dining hill a short distance from town. You can sit on the terrace and watch the sun set across the plains toward the mountains. The traditional Turkish food, including fresh fish and meat, especially lamb, is very good and presented with flair. *Nevşehir Yolu Üzeri, tel. 384/341-4266, fax 384/341-8866. V. $$*

Çirağan. The setting within an old caravansary gives the Çirağan some charm. The menu usually offers *sac tava* (small pieces of fried beef, onion, pepper, tomato, and rice), *güveç* (a traditional lamb or beef stew in a jealously guarded secret sauce cooked in an earthenware pot), as well as *mantı*. *Cumhuriyet Meydanı (main sq.), tel. 384/341-2566, fax 383/341-8539. MC, V. $-$$*

Lodging **Perissia Hotel.** Probably the best of a string of good hotels along Kayseri Caddesi, the Perissia is clean and very comfortable, with a large outdoor pool and a terrace. *Kayseri Cad., tel. 384/341-2930,* *fax 384/341–4524. 230 rooms with bath. Facilities: 3 restaurants, roof bar, pool, tennis court. AE, MC, V. $$*

Turban Ürgüp Motel. Big rooms and good facilities make this state-run holiday village 1 kilometer (½ miles) from the center a popular overnight spot for tour groups. *Nevşehir Yolu, Esbeli Mah, tel. 384/341–2290, fax 384/341–2299. 234 rooms with bath. Facilities: restaurant, disco. DC, MC, V. $$*

★ **Hotel Alfina.** If you really want to experience Cappadocia, why not lodge troglodyte-style? In the Alfina, a hotel carved out of volcanic rock, you get the definite sensation of being in a cave—despite the small windows in every room. Bathrooms are modern, however, and the restaurant is quite good. *İstiklal Cad., Urgup Girisi 25, tel. 384/341–4822, fax 384/341–2424 (Ankara representative 312/417–8425, fax 312/418–6207). 27 rooms with bath. Facilities: restaurant, terrace. MC, V. Closed Nov.–Mar. $–$$*

Hitit. This family-run hotel is comfortable and small and has a restaurant that serves basic but enjoyable food. With simple wood furnishings, it's not fancy but a good value. However, do expect to hear the call of the muezzin from the nearby minaret five times a day. *Istiklal Cad. 46, tel. 384/341–4481, fax 384/341–3620. 16 rooms without bath. Facilities: restaurant. V. $*

Hotel Ozata. This hotel just outside the center of town is ideal if you're on a tight budget. It's family-run and perfectly clean. *Atatürk Bul. 56, tel. 384/341–4981, fax 384/341–4355. 30 rooms with bath. No credit cards. $*

Nightlife

Nightlife

In the provincial towns, you'll have to comb through the hotel listings for a place with a bar or disco if you're hungry for nightlife. Ankara, on the other hand, has discos and nightclubs with live bands and singers at the **Büyük Ankara, Hilton,** and **Dedeman** hotels. You can also head for the **Luna Park Aile Gazinosu** (Family Nightclub) in Gençlik Parkı. Here you'll find a stage where Turkey's top pop singers perform nightly. Though things start early, the best acts come on late—about 11 PM. Of course, the good seats go early. Tickets are available at the door.

8 The Black Sea Coast

Driving the twisty roads along the Black Sea coastline is not easy, but it is always dramatic. On the one hand lies a dark blue sea; on the other, surprisingly lush greens slowly give way to snowy white peaks. The course rolls over steep forested hills, dips down to dry plains, scuttles over rocky outcrops, skims past wheat fields, and plunges back into forest. Ancient stone bridges alternate with patches of road so narrow that car drivers must pull over and stop to allow an oncoming vehicle to pass. Sometimes you'll see a huddle of Turkish men pushing a bus up a steep incline rather than riding inside. There aren't many towns along the way, and the going is slow. Gas stations can be few and far between; if you're traveling by car, try to keep the gas tank well topped up.

Gone is the guaranteed sunshine you find elsewhere in Turkey. Though the coastal climate is temperate, skies are often overcast. It may rain for days on end, even in summer—especially in the eastern parts below the Giresun Dağları and the Karadeniz Dağları, a pair of gently curved massifs that link into the mighty Pontic Mountains, now called the Kusey Anadolu Sira Dağları (North Anatolian mountain chain), rising nearly 13,000 feet. Each mountain and valley along the chain seems to shelter a distinct culture. In some villages you will hear Greek spoken, while in others the locals speak Laz and a strong dialect of Turkish almost incomprehensible even to western Turks.

Although Greek colonists settled along the coast in the 8th century BC, the interior was dominated by feudal Persian nobility. In 302 BC, following the War of Succession sparked by the death of Alexander the Great, octogenarian Mithridates II Ktistes ("the Founder") established a dynasty in Amaseia, today's Amasya. During the next two centuries, his successors extended their rule over the petty Hellenistic and Anatolian states along the coast, making the kingdom of Pontus a power to reckon with in Asia Minor. Though superficially Hellenized, the Pontic kingdom preserved a Persian religious and social structure, and the monarchs even claimed a spurious descent from Persia's Great Kings. Mithridates V's forces occupied the lands of Phrygia and Cappadocia to the southwest, and his son, known as Mithridates the Great (132–63 BC), expelled the Roman armies from Asia Minor, advanced into Greece, and seriously contested Rome's influence. It took Rome's greatest generals—Sulla, Lucullus, and Pompey—30 years to drive Mithridates VI back to his homeland, where he committed suicide. Julius Caesar finally incorporated the kingdom into the Roman Empire in 63 BC.

Things settled down for a long time, but the region had another brief moment of glory before all was said and done. In 1204, after the armies of the Fourth Crusade sacked Constantinople, a group of Byzantine aristocrats led by Alexius Comnene created the Trebizond Empire of the Grand Comneni. A lone Christian outpost in the Islamic East, the empire became a thriving city-state, with its capital at what is now Trabzon, surviving for two centuries. Then came the Ottomans, and the Black Sea coast reverted to marginal status within a great empire.

Today this coast harbors some of Turkey's wildest and most primitive districts, undeveloped regions that are very far from the modern tourist resorts along the south and west coasts, in both distance and character. Tiny villages, unmarked on maps, seem to have been left in the 19th century with their old wooden Ottoman houses, cobblestone alleys filled with chickens and donkeys, and bare, plain mosques. Accommodations are still very simple, outside of a few modern hotels in the bigger towns, but roughing it seems a small price to pay for an unmediated glimpse of an ancient part of the world.

Essential Information

Important Addresses and Numbers

Tourist Information Tourist information offices are in **Amasya** (Pirinci Cad., tel. 358/218–7428, and Mustafa Kemal Bul. 27, Mehmetpasa Mah, tel. 358/218–7427, on the riverbank, just north of the main square), **Giresun** (H. Avni Ogutcu Sok. 11/2, Seyh Keramettin Mah., tel. 454/212–3190), **Kars** (Ortakapi Mah., Ordu Cad. 241, tel. 474/223–2300), **Ordu** (Vilayet Binasi, A Blok Kat 1, tel. 452/223–1607, fax 452/223–2922), **Samsun** (Talimhane Cad. 6, 19 Mayis Mah, tel. 362/431–1228, and **Trabzon** (Ataturk Alani, at Boztepe Cad., tel. 462/321–4659).

Travel Agencies Two agencies in Istanbul specialize in trekking and whitewater-rafting trips along the Black Sea coast: **Trek Travel** (main office in Istanbul, tel. 212/235–8230, fax 212/253–1509; branch office in Dogubeyazit, tel. 472/215–3271, fax 472/215–1981) and **Kosmos Travel** (Istanbul office tel. 212/241–5253).

Rental Cars **Avis** has an office in Trabzon (Gazipasa Cad. 20/b, tel. 462/322–3740). There are also several local companies around the main square in Trabzon (Ataturk Alani). As elsewhere in Turkey, local companies offer cheaper rates than international names, but not all companies include comprehensive insurance coverage in the price. Check the small print before agreeing on terms.

Arriving and Departing by Plane

The airports at **Istanbul** (*see* Essential Information in Chapter 3) and **Ankara** (*see* Essential Information in Chapter 7) are the jumping-off points for the western half of the coast. There are also daily flights from both airports to Trabzon via **Turkish Airlines** (tel. 212/663–6363 in Istanbul) or **Istanbul Airlines** (tel. 212/231–7526 in Istanbul). Fares are about $50 one way.

Arriving and Departing by Car, Bus, and Boat

By Car The quickest way to the east from Istanbul is to take the E80 toll road (Ucretli Gecis) to Düzce and then cut up north along Route 655 to Akçakoca to join Route 10, which follows the coast the rest of the way east. The slower, but more picturesque, Route 20 passes through Sile to join up with Route 10 at Karasu. From Ankara, you can take the E89 north to Dörtdivan and then Route 750 to join Route 10 at Zonguldak; to explore only the eastern section of the coast, take E88 east through Kırıkkale, then head northeast along Route 190 toward Çorum to join Route 795 to Samsun, where you join Route 10.

By Bus As is usual in Turkey, you can get anywhere you want along the coast by bus. There is a daily service from Istanbul (Esenler bus terminal, tel. 212/658–0505) to Samsun (bus terminal tel. 362/238–1706), which takes about 12 hours and costs around $10. From Istanbul to Trabzon (bus terminal tel. 462/325–2397), the daily bus service takes nearly 20 hours and costs $12. There is also daily bus service to these cities from Ankara (bus terminal tel. 312/310–4747).

By Boat **Turkish Maritime Lines** (Rihtim Cad. 1, Karaköy, tel. 212/244–0207, reservations 212/249–9222; in Trabzon, Trabzon Liman Isletmesi, tel. 462/321–2018 or 462/321–7096) operates two weekly ferries between Istanbul and the Black Sea ports of Giresun, Ordu, Samsum, Sinop, and Trabzon during the summer months. The trip from Istanbul to Trabzon takes a day and a half and costs from $10 for a Pullman seat to $25 for a bed and shower; cars cost $25. Sleeper cabins and car spaces sell out quickly in summer, so reserve in advance.

Getting Around

By Car   The coast road from Istanbul, Route 10, winds along cliffs, takes an occasional hairpin turn, and can be rough in spots. It is, however, passable, and once you get past Sinop the road improves significantly.

By Bus   Bus service between towns runs frequently and is inexpensive. You can get schedules at the local tourist information office or directly from the bus station in each town: **Amasya** (tel. 358/218–8012), **Erzurum** (tel. 442/212–3969), **Kars** (tel. 474/223–9992), **Ordu** (tel. 452/223–0672), **Sinop** (tel. 368/261–5415), and **Trabzon** (tel. 462/325–2397).

By Boat   *See* Arriving and Departing by Boat, *above.*

Exploring the Black Sea Coast

Traveling the length of the coast from Istanbul to the Georgian border, with a few inland detours to historic sights, the following route falls into three tours. The first tour covers 737 kilometers (457 miles) from Istanbul to the port of Samsun. Tour 2 swings inland to the ancient Pontic capital, Amasya, and the ruined Seljuk fortress at Tokat. Tour 3 completes the coastal stretch with a 363-kilometer (225-mile) run from Samsun to Trabzon, capital of the medieval Trebizond Empire.

Highlights for First-Time Visitors

Akçako's strand, Tour 1
Amasya, Tour 2
Haghia Sophia, Trabzon, Tour 3
Kastamonu, Tour 1
Monastery of the Virgin, Sumela, Tour 3
Safranbolu, Tour 1

Tour 1: Şile to Samsun

Numbers in the margin correspond to points of interest on the Black Sea Coast map.

Traveling east on Route 20 from Istanbul, some 71 kilometers (44 miles) northeast from the Bosphorus Bridge, you come first to the beach resort of **Şile,** dominated by a ruined Genoese castle (along this coast you'll see several such relics of medieval commerce between Italy and the Comnene kingdom based at Trebizond, today called Trabzon). With its picturesque harbor and lighthouse, this is a popular getaway for residents of Istanbul. Route 20 continues eastward, with some rough patches, 82 kilometers (49 miles) to the fishing village of **Kandira**; near here, Jason and the Argonauts sup-

The Black Sea Coast

*Kara Deniz
(Black Sea)*

*Kara Deniz
(Black Sea)*

KEY

Rail Lines
Ferry

N

0   100 miles

0   150 km

1 Şile
2 Akçako
3 Amasra / Bartın
4 Safranbolu
5 Kastamonu
6 Sinop
7 Samsun
8 Amasya
9 Zile
10 Tokat
11 Ünye
12 Ordu
13 Giresun
14 Trabzon
15 Sumela

İstanbul
Kandira
İzmit
Orhangazi
Bilecik
Bursa
İnegöl
Kütahya
Gediz
Afyon
Çifteler
Emirdağ
Sivrihisar
Eskişehir
Tavşanlı
Gordion
Polatlı
Kulu
Ankara
Gölbaşı
Balā
Elmadağ
Kaman
Mucur
Kirşehir
Kırıkkale
Sungurlu
Yozgat
Hattusas & Boğazkale
Yazılıkaya
Alaca
Çorum
Çankırı
Çubuk
Kızılcahamam
Gerede
Bolu
Düzce
Dörtdivan
Nallıhan
Mihalıçcık
Hacıbayram
Sorgun
Akdağmadeni
Sarıkaya
Sultanhanı
Kayseri
Gemerek
Şarkışla
Kangal
Gürün
Pınarbaşı
Sivas
Hafik
Zara
Yıldızeli
Almus Barajı
Niksar
Erbaa
Çarşamba
Havza
Alaçam
Bafra
Boyabat
Ayancik
Abana
İnebolu
Cide
Kurucaşile
Zonguldak
Ereğli
Karasu
Karadeniz Ereğli
Adapazarı
Kızılırmak
Göltürmak
Şebinkarahisar
Refahiye
Şiran Kelkit
Gümüşhane
Espiye
Tirebolu
Görele
Eynesil
Akçaabat
Vakfıkebir
Macka
Erzincan
Divriği
Arapgir
Keban
Keban Barajı
Tunceli
Elâziğ
Sincan
Kızılırmak
Yeşilırmak
Akkuş
Erzincan
Hirfanlı Barajı
E5
E80
E23
E96
E390
E391

Kızılırmak

posedly saw a vision of Apollo during their quest for the Golden Fleece.

Route 20 runs inland south to Adapazari (which can be reached more quickly on the E5 from Istanbul), then cuts back to the coast at Karasu, where you pick up Route 10. A short distance east of Karasu lies the beach resort of **Akçako** (240 kilometers, or 149 miles, from Istanbul), named after an Ottoman general who conquered Bithynia between 1326 and 1330. Under the ruins of yet another Genoese castle stretches a long sweep of sand beach, popular with Turkish families.

The next town along the coast, **Ereğli**, claims to have the largest steel mill in the Middle East, not something that will attract hordes of tourists. It is, however, a town with significant classical connections. It was believed in antiquity to have been the location of the grotto from which Hercules descended to the underworld to accomplish the most difficult of his labors—fetching Cerberus, the god Hades's three-headed, hundred-eyed watchdog; here, also, an ancient Greek philosopher named Herecleides concluded that the earth turns on its axis every 24 hours. Another 65 kilometers (40 miles) east is **Zonguldak,** with another huge iron foundry, vast underground coal mines, and Turkey's main port for shipping coal. If you're hankering after outdoor sports, you may want to take a detour south from Zonguldak. Go 90 kilometers (54 miles) on Route 750, then 40 kilometers (25 miles) west on Route E5 to Bolu; a clearly marked access road leads north from E5 to **Yedigöller National Park,** where there are seven lakes and forests of oak, elm, and beech. Continue west on E5 about 12 kilometers (7½ miles) past Bolu to Yolçaltı, where a local road runs south 20 kilometers (12 miles) to Lake Abant, a magnificent mountain resort area offering what is probably the best trout fishing in Turkey.

Along the coast past Zonguldak, **Amasra** (which has, yes, another Genoese castle) is named after Amastris, a nephew of the great Persian king Darius I. Recognizing the advantage presented by the town's two harbors divided by a rocky promontory, Amastris promptly built his fortress here. If you hunger after historic sights, you can wander around the tiny old quarter within the fortress walls, stopping to visit an old Byzantine church that has been converted into the Fatih Cami mosque.

From Amasra, you have a choice of two routes. The next 166 kilometers (103 miles) along the coast, to **Inebolu,** is a particularly untrammeled stretch of coastline, with ramshackle Mediterranean-style fishing villages and empty beaches. From Inebolu it's another 158 kilometers (100 miles) to Sinop—a rather difficult drive, with parts of the road still under construction and, at press time, no gas station along the route. The nearly deserted **Inceburun Peninsula,** extending into the Black Sea west of Sinop, offers a striking combination of forests, sand dunes, and lagoons. A detour inland from Amasra on Route 755, however, will allow you to explore some fine old villages. Along this route, note the traditional Ottoman houses: square, half-timbered buildings with tile roofs and overhanging second stories. A short distance south from Amasra in **Bartin,** you'll see the first of these. Drive on to **Safranbolu** to see a historic district full of perfect wattle-and-daub houses. Tucked away behind a modern town of the same name, old Safranbolu has preserved a slice of the past, with artisans sitting in open storefronts plying their crafts, and cars are banned from the center. Some of the buildings are open to the public, including the **Kaymakan Evi** (Governor's House), which has been restored with furnishings of 200 years ago. The lovely 17th-century *arasta* (market hall) once served the tanners' and cobblers' guilds. If you wander around long enough, residents may invite you in to see their homes.

As you head east from Safranbolu, Route 30 climbs over two passes through the densely wooded Küre Mountains. After 95 kilometers (59 miles), you'll reach the pleasant medieval city of **Kastamonu,** once the stronghold of Alexius Comnene, the founder of the Comnene dynasty in Constantinople (1081), who recaptured it from the Seljuk Turks during the First Crusade. The **Comnene fortress** has survived, thanks to Tamerlane and his hordes, who swept through in the early 15th century and for some reason decided to re-build the Comnene fortress rather than raze it. For an incredible view of the countryside, drive up to the castle past splendid 19th-century Ottoman mansions—run-down, but still occupied. The Seljuks are represented in Kastamonu by the 13th-century **Atabey Mosque**; the Isfeniyar Beys by the **Ibn Neccar Mosque** (1353); the Ottomans by the 16th-century **Yakup Ağa** mosque and seminary complex. The **Karanlık Bedestan,** a covered bazaar built in the 1470s, is still in use, bearing few signs of change through the intervening centuries. The **town museum** is housed in an attractive old building where Atatürk announced the abolition of the fez in 1926, though if you don't read Turkish, the exhibits in the museum may be incomprehensible to you. In the neighboring village of Kasaba, 15 kilometers (9 miles) north of town on the road to Daday, is the incredibly beautiful **Mahmut Bey Cami,** a 14th-century wooden mosque.

Heading northeast on Route 30, you'll cross an old stone bridge with five arches across the Gökırmak River at Taşköpru, which means Stone Bridge. Nearby, at **Ev Kaya,** is an interesting 6th-century BC rock tomb, with colonnades and a frieze. Just before the town of Boyabat, Route 785 branches northeast, rolling through tobacco fields and over the wild forests of the Damaz Pass, to return you to the coast at Sinop.

Known in ancient times as Sinope, **Sinop** is the oldest city on the Black Sea coast, reputedly founded by the Amazon queen Sinova. Legend has it that Sinova attracted the interest of Zeus, who, to get on her good side, offered to grant her one wish. Sinova requested everlasting virginity, thus foiling Zeus's amorous intentions. In the 7th century BC, this region was colonized by an Aegean kingdom called Miletus, who imported their Greek culture; ruins of a 2nd-century BC **Hellenistic temple** still stand near the Municipal Park in the center of town. The park also marks the birthplace of the Cynic philosopher Diogenes (about 400–325 BC), who reportedly lived in a large earthenware tub and preached an extravagantly simple way of life that included the disregard of conventions, even suggesting that people should feel free to make love in public like dogs—*kyon* in Greek, hence "cynic."

The first **citadel** at Sinop is believed to have been built by the Hittites, though the present layout dates from the Pontic King Mithridates IV, who ordered its reconstruction in the 2nd century BC. The **mosque** bearing the name of Alaeddin Keykubat, the prominent Seljuk sultan, was built in 1214; its splendid original *mihrab* (prayer niche) is displayed in Istanbul's Museum of Islamic Art. The **Alaiye Medrese** seminary, now a museum with some interesting tombs, was built in 1262 by the Grand Vizir of Keykubat, Süleyman Pervane. A walk through the town reveals many other small mosques, tombs, and fountains: the **Saray** and **Fetih Baba** mosques, both built in 1339; the **Çifte Hamam,** built in 1332; and a 7th-century Byzantine church, **Balat Kilise,** standing within the grounds of a ruined palace. The church retains some frescoes, though they are badly damaged; its fine icons are displayed now in the city museum. On a hilltop at the edge of town, the 14th-century **Sayid Bilal mausoleum** offers a good view over the town. Around Sinop, which is set on the neck of a narrow peninsula with the sea on either side, are some pleasant, usually empty beaches.

The road improves considerably as you drive the 168 kilometers (104 miles), most of it along the coast, to Samsun. But the countryside grows flatter and the scenery less impressive, given over mostly to tobacco fields. One stop you may want to make is at **Bafra,** near the mouth of the Kızırmak River, where thermal springs supply a 13th-century *hamam* (Turkish bath).

❼ Developed as a port under the Ottomans, **Samsun** is a booming commercial port and not particularly attractive still. It was here that Atatürk landed on May 19, 1919, after World War I, slipping away from the Allies occupying Constantinople to launch his campaign for Turkish independence (May 19 is now a national holiday). The Atatürk Monument opposite the government house is the largest dedicated to the great leader outside of Ankara; the **villa** he stayed in here, in the city park, is open to the public as a museum. *Luna Park, tel. 362/431–6828. Admission: $1. Open Tues.–Sun. 8:30–12:30 and 1:30–5:30.*

Tour 2: Inland to Amasya and Tokat

Departing from the coast to visit three historic inland towns, this tour could conceivably be done as a long day trip from Samsun.
❽ **Amasya,** 131 kilometers (81 miles) south of Samsun on Route 795, is one of Turkey's most attractive towns. Clustered around an ancient fortress hemmed in by sheer cliff walls, the city overlooks the valley of the Yeşilırmak (Green River). Old Ottoman houses line the riverside, with a break for a shady park with tea gardens. According to its most famous son, the geographer-historian Strabo (c 63 BC–AD 19). Amasya was founded by the Amazon queen Amasis, but its epoch of glory was as the first capital of the kingdom of Pontus, which lasted from the decline of Alexander the Great's empire until the Romans took the town in 47 BC. The Seljuks moved in after 1071, followed by the Mongols in the 13th century and the Ottomans in the beginning of the 15th.

The historic center of Amasya is on the right (southern) bank of the river. Start your walking tour in the central square, by the equestrian statue of Atatürk. Stroll westward along the tree-lined river (down Ziya Paşa Bulvari), past a row of overhanging houses and several old bridges. A banner on an old house on the north bank marks the restored 19th-century **Hazeran Mansion,** which houses an ethnology museum and a fine arts gallery (open weekday mornings). A 16th-century **bedestan** anchors the bazaar area that runs for several blocks between Ziya Paşa Bulvari and Atatürk Caddesi. Behind the bedestan, away from the river, is the **Burmaı Minare Cami** (Mosque with the Twisted Minaret), built in 1242; its extravagant fluted minaret is a striking architectural oddity. The **Fethiye Cami,** a mosque located a few blocks uphill, was first built as a Byzantine church in the 7th century and became a mosque in 1116.

A few blocks west of the bedestan, set on a shady terrace along the river, is the two-domed **Sultan Beyazıt Cami,** built in 1486. The imposing mosque features a fine *mimber* (pulpit) and *mihrab* (prayer niche) made of marble and blue tiles inscribed with quotations from the Koran. Across the street from the mosque, on Atatürk Caddesi, the **Amasya Museum** displays a broad collection covering the nine civilizations that have ruled over the city. Wood carvings, astronomy instruments, old coins, and tombs make this a worthwhile stop; the Tomb of Sultan Mesut is on the museum grounds, alongside several Mongol mummies. *Atatürk Cad., tel. 358/218–4513. Admission: $1. Open Tues.–Sun. 8:30–noon and 1:30–5:30.*

Just west of the museum is the **Gök Medrese** (Blue Seminary), built in 1276, now a museum containing among other things the mummies of its Seljuk founder, Seyfeddin Torumtay, and a few of the town's Mongol rulers. *Atatürk Cad. Admission: $1. Open Tues.–Sun. 8:30–noon and 1:30–5:30.*

As you go back toward the main square along Atatürk Caddesi, the town's main street is lined with tranquil little *türbes* (tombs) containing the mortal remains of such dignitaries as Prince Sehzad, Halifet Gazi, Mehmet Paşa, and Sultan Mesut.

You can either hike or drive most of the way up to the **citadel,** high above the north bank of the river. In the few bits of ruined tower and wall that remain upright, you can attempt to distinguish the different stones used by various builders, from the Greeks through the Romans to the Seljuks. Though it's a scramble to get up here, the view is worth it. While on this side of the river, make the short but steep climb north from the Alçak and Hükümet bridges up the cliff face. After you pass the remains of the Pontic palace, you'll reach the **Kral Kaya Mezarlaıri,** the well-preserved rock tombs of the first four Pontic kings, impressively floodlit at night. Fourteen in all, the earliest dating from the late 4th century BC, the tombs are entire buildings carved out of the stone; you can walk all the way around them.

As you drive southeast from Amasya on Route 795, toward Tokat, there's a brief but worthwhile side trip on Route E180 (turn south at Turhal and go 20 kilometers, or 12 miles) to **Zile.** From the fortress above the restored Uli Cami mosque, built in 1296, you can gaze out on the scene of Julius Caesar's victory over the Pontic king Pharnakes II. This battle inspired Caesar's celebrated terse message to the Roman Senate: *"Veni, vidi, vici"* ("I came, I saw, I conquered").

Back on Route 795, **Tokat** lies 115 kilometers (71 miles) southeast of Amasya. The Seljuk hilltop fortress, with 28 towers, is now a crumbling ruin, but still intact are the **Garipler Cami** mosque and the fine **Gök Medrese** seminary, built in 1275 and now a museum full of tiles and Byzantine frescoes. *Gazi Osman Paşa Bul., tel. 356/228–1509. Admission: $1. Open 8:30–5:30 (depends on mood of custodian).*

Tokat also contains several **mausoleums** of Seljuk origin—those of Elbukasim and Halef Gazi, Acikbas, Nurettin Sentimur, and Sumbul Bab—and the **Hatuniye** school and mosque, built in 1485 by Beyazıt II in honor of his mother. Another of those atmospheric Seljuk bridges spans the Yeşilırmak River here. To return to the coast, you can take Route 850 northeast from Tokat, which rejoins Route 10 at Ünye.

Tour 3: Ünye to Trabzon

Route 10 connects the sea, long stretches of empty beach, and plains covered with hazelnut bushes, fruit trees, and vast cornfields, as it winds east from Samsun about 95 kilometers (60 miles) to **Ünye.** This popular weekend spot for Samsun's moneyed classes offers splendid beaches around a crescent-shaped bay. In the Middle Ages this was the western border of the Trebizond Empire, but the only notable architecture standing today is an 18th-century town hall. Outside of town are caves where Mediterranean seals breed.

⓬ Another 75 kilometers (47 miles) east, outside the town of **Ordu,** a few ruins from the 5th-century BC Greek settlement of Kotyora survive on the beach at Bozzukale. Ordu itself is a port city dominated by a once resplendent 8th-century basilica. It is more famous today for being the venue for an annual bull-wrestling festival, which is held each May.

⓭ **Giresun,** known in ancient times as Kerasous, lies 45 kilometers (28 miles) east of Ordu. Reputedly, the Roman general Lucullus, who was something of a gourmand, introduced to Europe the cherry, a fruit he first tasted in Kerasous. Today the town spreads over a cape below a ruined Byzantine fortress, where there is now a pretty city park. Some ramparts still rise from the cliffs to guard the **tomb of Seyyit Vakkas,** who helped the Turks win Kerasous in battle in 1461. Jason and the Argonauts are reported to have stopped here and attributed the temple they found on the island (Buyuk Ada) facing the town to the Amazon god of war; a small teahouse stands here today, and you can take a swim in complete solitude. The **Şehir Müsezi,** the small city museum, displays some Byzantine relics, old carpets, and jewelry, housed in an old Orthodox church. *Eastern edge of town, 2 blocks from Rte. 10, tel. 454/212–1322. Admission: 50¢. Open 8:30– 5:30 (depends on mood of custodian).*

The next stretch of coastal road passes an enticing waterfall at Çağlayan, some ruined churches, and more inviting beaches, before coming to **Tirebolu,** ancient Tripolis or Triple Town. The name refers to the three 14th-century Genoese fortresses in the area: **Andos,** near Espiye; **St. John,** atop Tirebolu itself; and **Bedrama,** 15 kilometers inland on the Harşit River (with an exceptional panoramic view).

⓮ Between the pleasant fishing ports of Görele, Vakfıkebir, and Akçaabat, the road turns inland, up into densely wooded hills and narrow vales, before entering cosmopolitan **Trabzon,** the Trebizond of old. In its glory days, Trebizond was the sort of place that epitomized the exotic East for European travelers. Early in the 14th century, a Venetian friar named Odoric described the city as "a haven for the Persians, Medes, and all the people on the farther side of the sea." Built of golden towers and glittering mosaics, probably with family money diverted from the royal till before the fall of Constantinople, Trebizond was the capital of the empire founded in 1204 by Alexius Comnene, grandson of Andronikos I, emperor of Byzantium. Alexius's successors continued to live well while playing off their powerful Muslim neighbors against one another. Genoese and Venetian colonies at Trebizond ensured extensive cultural interaction with the West; Marco Polo, among others, came to visit, and Trebizond's own Cardinal Bessarion returned the favor by pursuing a successful career at the Medici court. The glory came to an end when the Turkish sultan Mehmet the Conqueror swept through in 1461.

At first glance the city may well disappoint you, with its squalid port area and far too much concrete strewn about. But if you push on, up İskele Caddesi, you'll reach a pleasing central square atop the promontory, **Atatürk Alani** (also called Taksim, or Park, Meydanı), full of trees and tea gardens and surrounded by most of the city's hotels and restaurants.

Maraş Caddesi leads west out of the square into the maze of the covered **bazaar** (just past Cumhuriyet Caddesi), which includes a 16th-century **bedestan** used by local jewelers. The city's largest mosque, the **Çarşi Cami** (built in 1839), is joined to the market by an archway. Farther along the street is the city's oldest church, the **Küçük Ayvasil,** or Aya Ann, built in the 7th century and restored in the 9th century.

Double back to Hükümet Caddesi and follow the Tabakhane Bridge over the gorge, turn left onto Kale Caddesi, and enter the **citadel.** Situated between two ravines, this Comnene fortress is still imposing, its ramparts restored after the Turkish conquest in 1461 (an effective job of saber rattling by Sultan Mehmet), although the remains of the Byzantine palace are insignificant. No army ever took Trabzon by force, though many tried. Within the citadel walls is the 10th-century **Church of Panaghia Chrysokephalos** (the Virgin of the Golden Head), which was the city's most important church for several centuries, until the Hagia Sophia (*see below*) was built. The Ottomans converted it into a mosque, the Ortahisar Cami, in the 16th century.

Follow Iç Kale Caddesi beyond the walls to the south for a good view of the city. You'll also be able to make out three other Byzantine monuments, all south of the Atatürk Alani: the **Yeni Cuma Cami** (New Friday Mosque), built as the Church of St. Eugene in the early 13th century; the 13th-century **Teokephastos Convent,** on the other side of the hill; and the **Kudrettin Cami,** consecrated as the Church of St. Philip in the 14th century. The best-known Byzantine monument is about 3 kilometers (2 miles) west of Atatürk Alani, set on a green hill overlooking the bay: the 13th-century **Hagia Sophia** (church of the Holy Wisdom), today a museum displaying some of the finest Byzantine frescoes and mosaics in existence. The ruined church, also known as Aya Sofya, stands open to the air—no doors, no windows, only roof and walls. In the west porch are the real masterpieces: frescoes of Christ preaching in the temple, the Annunciation, and the wedding at Cana, executed in a style that shows strong Italian influence. As at Istanbul's Hagia Sophia, the artworks here were not destroyed by the Ottomans, only hidden under a hard layer of plaster. *No phone. Admission: $1. Open June–Sept., daily 8–6; Oct.–May, Tues.–Sun. 8–5.*

On the southwest fringe of town, 7 kilometers (4 miles) from the central square, is the **Atatürk Köşkü,** Atatürk's summer villa, though he didn't actually spend much time here. Today a museum, this attractive white gingerbread house in its pretty garden makes for a pleasant outing. *Soğuksu Cad., no phone. Admission: $1. Open daily 9–5.*

Route E390, heading southwest from Trabzon inland toward Erzurum, follows a tunnel through the mountains. Somewhere around here in 401 BC, a ragtag army of Greek mercenaries wearily retreating from supporting a failed coup attempt against Artaxerxes, the king of Persia, first saw the Black Sea and knew they would get safely home. Their commander, a young Athenian officer named Xenophon, wrote the story of that march across Anatolia many years later in a famous book called the *Anabasis (The Ascent).* Follow this highway 31 kilometers (19 miles) from Trabzon and turn **⑮** left at Maçka to get to **Sumela** (Mereyemana in Turkish), site of the **Monastery of the Virgin.** It's not the easiest place to reach—it's 23 kilometers (14 miles) from Maçka, and the road isn't the best. From the parking lot, pick up a well-worn trail for the 40-minute hike to the monastery, which clings to the cliff face over 820 feet above the valley floor and disappears completely when the clouds come down.

The monks who founded the retreat in the 4th century carved their cells from sheer rock. Built to house a miraculous icon of the Virgin painted by St. Luke, this shrine was later rebuilt by Alexius III, who was crowned here in 1340—an event depicted in the frescoes of the main church in the grotto. Where chunks of the frescoes have fallen off—or been chipped away by over-enthusiastic souvenir hunters—three layers of plaster from repaintings in the 14th and 18th centuries are clearly visible. The frescoes themselves are not as well preserved as those at Trabzon's Hagia Sophia, but the setting—a labyrinth of courtyards, corridors, and chapels—is incredible. Tolerant Ottoman sultans left the retreat alone, but after the Greeks were expelled from Turkey in 1922, the Turkish government permitted monks to transfer the Virgin icon to a new monastery in Greek Macedonia.

From here, you could continue on to Erzurum (*see* Chapter 9), crossing the hair-raising **Zigana Pass,** a stunning rift some 2,025 meters (6,645 feet) high, and descending to the low brushwood and yellow dust of the vast, arid Anatolian plateau.

Off the Beaten Track

Perhaps the most scenic portion of the coastal Black Sea drive is the 189 kilometers (117 miles) northeast from Trabzon to Hopa. Densely wooded slopes sometimes tumble straight into the sea, but they are more often broken by rice paddies and intensely green tea plantations where women in bright-striped aprons pick tea from early May to the end of October. Occasional tea factories exude black smoke, the only pollution on the coast. **Rize,** the tea capital, rises steeply from the sea to a ruined Genoese castle. Beyond Rize, a 22-kilometer (13-mile) jog inland from Ardesen will bring you to the exceptionally attractive village of **Çamlıhemşin,** a good center for mountain hiking and trout fishing. The bustling frontier town of **Hopa** is journey's end for the Turkish Maritime Line boats as well as for cars; you'll need a special military permit to drive the remaining 22 kilometers (13 miles) to the Georgian border.

Shopping

The best bazaars are in **Trabzon, Amasya,** and **Kastamonu,** all with a very strong sense of history. In **Ünye,** hazelnuts are the thing to buy, and they will be almost everywhere you look. **Safronbolu** is named after the pricey spice saffron, which you can buy in this region for considerably less than what you'd pay at home. Since the collapse of the Soviet Union an influx of Georgian, Russian, and Ukrainian street traders has created a lively open market in Trabzon at the foot of Iskele Caddesi by the entrance to the docks, offering everything from car parts and vodka to samovars and Zenit cameras.

Several smaller towns clustered around Trabzon hold weekly markets where you can see mountain clanspeople coming down to trade, as they have for centuries. Markets are held in **Rize** and **Vakfıkebir** on Monday; **Akçaabat** and **Çaykara** on Tuesday; **Tonya** and **Çayeli** on Wednesday; **Maçka, Araklı,** and **Of** on Thursday; **Rize** again on Friday; and **Yomra** on Saturday.

Sports and the Outdoors

Participant Sports

Canoeing and Rafting Running parallel to the eastern portion of this coast, the churning waters of the **Çoruh River** are considered to be among the top canoe courses. Rubber-rafters prefer the **Fırtına River** (17 kilometers [10½ miles] north of the village of Çamlıhemşin), **Aksu River** (near Giresun), and **Kara Dere River** (near the village of Yağmurdere). The waters can be dangerous, so seek advice from local guides.

Mountain Climbing The **Kaçkar** mountain range, about 50 kilometers (30 miles) south of Rize, is 3,937 feet high and can be comfortably climbed by beginners in decent physical shape. Discuss your options on various base camps and routes with an experienced travel agent (*see* Travel Agencies in Essential Information, *above*) or local climbing guide.

Beaches

Şile and **Akçakoca** are beach resorts popular with Istanbulites. A number of fine beaches lie between **Amasra** and **Inebolu**; Kapısuyu beach near Kurucaşile is the nicest. Lovely Karakum beach at the tip of the **Sinop** peninsula is a good base for fishing trips or windsurfing. The **Ünye** bay area offers several fine beaches, particularly the one at Camlık. Güzelyali beach is 2 kilometers (1 mile) east of **Ordu.**

Dining and Lodging

The Black Sea supplies the seafood restaurants along this part of the coast with many varieties of fish. The specialty is *palamut*, which tastes like a cross between tuna and mackerel. For details and price-category definitions, *see* Dining and Lodging in Staying in Turkey in Chapter 1, Essential Information.

Abant Lodging **Abant Palace.** Perched on a sliver of land between the shore of the lake and the pine-clad hills, the hotel manages, despite its size, to remain fairly unobtrusive. Long and narrow, built parallel to the lake, it gives guests views across the water or into the forest. It is a favorite getaway for wealthy Istanbulites and offers perhaps more facilities than strictly necessary for a stopover on the way east. *Abant Gölü Kenari, tel. 374/224–5012, fax 374/224–5011. 157 rooms with bath. Facilities: restaurant, 7 bars, disco, nightclub, indoor pool, sauna. AE, DC, MC, V. $$–$$$*
Turban Abant Hotel. Surrounded by pine forests, this eminently peaceful hotel sits on the shores of Lake Abant. Rooms are motel quality, comfortable but drab—the star here is the setting. Rooms looking out over the lake cost 10% extra but are well worth it. *On Lake Abant, tel. 374/224–5033, fax 374/224–5031. 94 rooms with bath. Facilities: pool, sauna, restaurant. MC, V. $$*

Amasya Dining **Amasya Turban Restaurant.** The restaurant of the Turban Amasya Hotel serves good Turkish cuisine in a dining room overlooking the Yesilirmak. *Elmasiye Cad., tel. 358/218–4054. No credit cards. $–$$*
Çiçek Lokanta. On a market street near the square, this cozy restaurant serves basic Turkish fare. *No phone. No credit cards. $*
Sehir. On the north end of Hükümet Köprüsü (Government Bridge), just downstream from the Turban Amasya Hotel, the restaurant hangs over the river, offering great views. The decor is strictly

downscale, but the traditional Turkish grilled meat dishes are above average. *No phone. No credit cards.* $

Lodging **Turban Amasya Hotel.** The best bet in Amasya. Though unexceptional, it's well run, the restaurant is good, and the setting is nice, on the north bank of the river. *Elmasiye Cad., tel. 358/218–4054, fax 358/218–4056. 50 rooms with shower. No credit cards.* $–$$

Artvin   **Karahan Otel.** Functional and unprepossessing, the centrally lo-
Lodging   cated Karahan is nevertheless far and away the best hotel in the Artvin area. The staff are friendly and the restaurant more than adequate. *İnönü Cad. 6, tel. 466/212–1800, fax 466/212–2420. 57 rooms. Facilities: restaurant, bar. No credit cards.* $

Gerze   **Köşk Burnu Tesisleri.** Though not much to look at, this is a nice little
Lodging   beachside motel, in a nice little resort town. The restaurant is quite good, too. *On the waterfront, tel. 368/718–1081. 22 rooms with bath. No credit cards.* $

Rize   **Hotel Keles.** It's not much, but it's acceptable. And at least the res-
Lodging   taurant is good. *Palandöken Cad. 2, tel. 464/217–4612, fax 464/213–2230. 28 rooms with bath. No credit cards.* $–$$
Turist. Much like the Keles (*see above*), the Turist is at best another decent place to spend the night. *Atatürk Bul., tel. 464/511–3368, fax 466/211–2420. 30 rooms with bath. Facilities: restaurant, bar. No credit cards.* $

Safranbolu   **Havuzlu Konak.** The hotel has been restored to resemble a typical
Lodging   affluent Safranbolu house in Ottoman times. Painstaking attention has been given to detail—from the embroidered floral motifs on the blinds to the *havuz* (pool) in the breakfast room from which it takes its name. The excellent restaurant serves the Safranbolu kebap of grilled lamb, tomato sauce, and yogurt on pita bread and topped with cheese. On the same grounds is the **Küçük Konak,** a smaller version of the Havuzlu Konak with access to the same facilities but with no showers in the rooms. *Haci Halil Mah 18, tel. 372/725–2883, fax 372/712–3824. Havuzlu Konak: 11 rooms with shower; Küçük Konak: 7 rooms. Facilities: indoor and outdoor restaurants. No credit cards.* $–$$

Samsun   **Cumhuriyet Restaurant.** The best restaurant in town outside the ma-
Dining   jor hotels, the Cumhuriyet, just off Saat Hane Meydani, offers the normal range of cold mezes and grilled meats and prides itself on its *kuzu tandir* (baked lamb). *Atatürk Alani (Meydan), tel. 362/431–2165. No credit cards.* $
Divanrama Restaurant. On the first floor, overlooking the street, the Divanrama has a good selection of fish, seafood, kebabs, and mezes. *Istiklal Cad, Başoğlu İşhani, tel. 362/230–6219. No credit cards.* $

Lodging   **Turban Büyük Samsun.** The Grand Samsun hotel is hardly grand by
★   Istanbul standards, but for this undeveloped strip of coastline it's about as good as it gets. The restaurant here is the best in town. Stop for lunch and you can sample the *kebab 19 mayis,* a dish commemorating the day of Atatürk's arrival in Samsun. *Sahil Cad., tel. 362/431–0750, fax 362/431–0740. 114 rooms with bath. Facilities: pool, tennis court, nightclub, restaurant, bar. No credit cards.* $$

Dining and   **Hotel Burç.** Though this comfortable hotel is centrally located, the
Lodging   street is busy and thus a bit noisy. So it's clearly the third choice in town, after the Turban and the Yafeya. *Kazım Paşa Cad. 36, tel. 362/431–5480, fax 362/431–3788. 38 rooms. No credit cards.* $
Hotel Yafeya. Cheap, clean, and eminently acceptable, the Yafeya sits right on the main square. There is a fountain in the lobby and a

rooftop terrace with a nice view. The suites even have minibars. *Cumhuriyet Meyd., tel. 362/435–1131, fax 362/435–1135. 96 rooms with shower. Facilities: restaurant, lounge. MC, V.* $

Şile
Lodging

Değirmen Hotel. An old standby among vacationing Istanbulites, the Değirmen has a beach and a nightclub and a good sense of fun. *Plaj Yolu 24, tel. 216/711–5048, fax 216/711–5248. 69 rooms with bath. Facilities: bar, swimming pool, windsurfing. MC, V.* $–$$

Sinop
Lodging

Melia Kasım Hotel. Though hardly memorable, the Melia is generally regarded as the best lodging Sinop has to offer. *Gazi Cad. 41, tel. 368/261–4210, fax 368/261–1625. 57 rooms with bath. No credit cards.* $$

Karakum Motel. Just outside town, the Karakum offers the advantage of a private beach and bungalows with a sort of ramshackle charm. *On the waterfront, tel. 368/261–4210, fax 368/261–1625. 60 rooms with bath. Facilities: restaurant, bar. No credit cards.* $

Trabzon
Dining

Hotel Usta. The restaurant here is the pick of the hotel dining rooms in town. The large, mirrored room lacks character, but the menu offers a substantial range of traditional Turkish fare, and the service is good. *Telgrafhane Sok. 1, Iskele Cad., tel. 462/326–5704. No credit cards.* $–$$

Cosandere Restaurant. On the banks of a stream beside the road from Macka to Sumela, it's an ideal lunch spot for visitors to the monastery. The specialties are *sutlac* (rice pudding) and *ayran* (buttermilk), but the kofte, which you grill on an individual barbecue at your table, are excellent as well. *Mereyemana Yolu., no phone. No credit cards.* $

Kibris Restaurant. This kebab restaurant has a broad range of food, including a selection of *hazir yemek* (pre-cooked dishes kept hot). There is also a "family room" upstairs with views across the square. *Ataturk Alani, no phone. No credit cards.* $

Meydan Restaurant. One of a string of inexpensive kebab places around the central square, it has functional decor and plastic furniture. It is clean, the service quick, and the food very palatable. *Ataturk Alani, no phone. No credit cards.* $

Lodging

Horon Hotel. Partially renovated in 1994, the Horon has less character than the Özgur but is quieter, cleaner, and a little more expensive. At press time the restaurant had been closed for renovation but was due to be reopened in 1995. *Siramagazalar Cad. 125, tel. 462/321–1199, fax 462/321–6860. 42 rooms. Facilities: bar, breakfast room. No credit cards.* $

Hotel Özgur. For years the best hotel in Trabzon, the Özgur is in need of renovation. Its dim corridors, creaking lift, and shabby furniture nevertheless give it a faded charm. It overlooks the main square, and rooms at the front tend to be noisy. *Taksim Cad., tel. 462/321–1319, fax 462/321–3952. 45 rooms with shower. Facilities: rooftop restaurant. MC, V.* $

★ **Hotel Usta.** Renovated in 1993, the Usta has displaced the Özgur (*see above*) as the best hotel in Trabzon. It can be a little hard to find, as the entrance is in an alley off İskele Caddesi, to the north of the main square. The rooms are clean and well-furnished. The staff is friendly and courteous and the restaurant exceptional. *Telgrafhane Sok. 1, İskele Cad., tel. 462/326–5704, fax 462/322–3793. 76 rooms. Facilities: restaurant, bar. V.* $

Ünye
Lodging

Kumsal Hotel. Five kilometers (3 miles) outside Ünye on the road to Samsum, the Kumsal is clean and simple, with whitewashed walls, wooden shutters, and balconies overlooking a lush green garden. *Samsun Asfalti Üstü, Gölevi Köyü, tel. 452/323–4490, fax 452/323–*

4490. 27 rooms with shower. Facilities: restaurant, bar, sauna, private beach. $–$$

Belediye Çamlık. Set in a pine forest, this pleasant little seaside motel has its own beach. The rooms are rather bare, with low wooden single beds. The restaurant is good and inexpensive. *On the waterfront, tel. 452/323–1085. 13 rooms with bath. Facilities: restaurant, bar. No credit cards. $*

9 The Far East

The far east of Turkey is a harsh but beautiful region, with lonesome plains, alpine forests, and imposing black mountains—the kind of countryside for adventuring on an epic scale that has attracted a small but steady stream of hardy travelers who have come to see the ruins of the remarkable Armenian kingdom of Ani; Mt. Ararat, where, according to Genesis, Noah's Ark came to rest after the Great Flood; the wild, desolate landscape around immense Lake Van; the mighty, black basalt fortress at Diyarbakır; and the awe-inspiring temple atop Mt. Nimrod.

The population of Turkey's eastern provinces is primarily Kurdish. In recent years escalating clashes between the Turkish armed forces and Kurdish separatists trying to carve an independent state out of portions of Turkey, Iran, Syria, and Iraq, have severely restricted the movements of foreign visitors.

At press time (summer 1994) the United States Department of State strongly advises Americans not to travel to the area unless the journey is essential. If you must visit the region, try to minimize the risks by remaining in the larger towns (there are direct flights to Erzurum, Diyarbakır, Batman, Gaziantep, Sivas, Elaziğ, Kars, Erzincan, and Van); if you need to travel between them, do so only in daylight using a reputable bus company. Tour companies still offer coach tours of the region, particularly to Mt. Nemrut, but if you take one, be aware that you do so at your own risk.

Up-to-date information on the current security situation in the eastern provinces can be obtained from the State Department hot line (U.S. tel. 202/647–5225) or from the American Consulate in Istanbul (tel. 212/251–3602, fax 212/251–2554) and the American Embassy in Ankara (tel. 312/439–2740, fax 312/440–9222).

A drive from Istanbul to Lake Van takes some 25 grueling hours, and even if you fly directly to Erzurum, you still face long, hard outings from site to site within the region, with highways and facilities running a short gamut from basic to primitive.

Essential Information

Important Addresses and Numbers

Tourist Information Tourist information offices are in **Adiyaman** (Atatürk Bul. 184, tel. 416/216–1008, fax 416/216–3840); **Ağri** (Cumhuriyet İlkokul arkasi, Sağlik Eğitim Merkezi eski binasi, tel. 472/215–3730); **Diyarbakır** (Kultur Sanayi, tel. 412/221–7840); **Erzurum** (Cemal Gürsel Cad. 9/A, tel. 442/218–5697, fax 442/218–5443); **Kars,** in the Kultur ve Turizm Mudurlugu (Central office, Ordu Cad. 241, Ortakapi Mah, tel. 474/212–2300); and **Van** (Cumhuriyet Cad. 19, tel. 432/216–3675).

Even before the current troubles the number of tourists visiting the east was relatively low. While there will usually be someone in the tourism information office who knows at least a few words of English, callers would be advised to have a Turkish speaker on hand to help with any difficulties.

Arriving and Departing by Plane

Scheduled service from Istanbul and Ankara to Erzurum is via **Turkish Airlines** (tel. 212/663–6363) and **Istanbul Airlines** (tel. 212/231–7526). Fares are about $50 one way. Turkish Airlines also has daily flights from Istanbul to Erzurum, Diyarbakır, and Van and from Ankara to Erzurum, Gaziantep, Kars, Malatya, Van, Diyarbakır, and Batman, as well as less frequent flights from Istanbul to Gaziantep and from Ankara to Elaziğ, Erzincan, Sivas, and Şanlıurfa.

Arriving and Departing by Car, Bus, and Train

By Car From Trabzon, a twisty, mountainous road (E97 to Aşkale, then E80) covers the 322 kilometers (193 miles) to Erzurum. The drive from Ankara is a whopping 882 kilometers (530 miles) across much of Anatolia, first on Route E88, then on E80. From Adana, on the Mediterranean coast, take E90 to Sanliurfa and E99 to Diyarbakır, a distance of 536 kilometers (321 miles).

By Bus Erzurum, the main hub of the regional transportation system, is about 15 hours from Ankara (about $18), 20 hours from Istanbul (about $26), and nine hours from Trabzon (about $12). Many bus companies serve the region.

By Train The train ride from Ankara to Erzurum and Van seems to take forever—20 to 30 hours. Fares are $16 (first class) to $60 (sleeper bunk) per person.

Getting Around

By Car With fewer services and more heavy trucks than on the Mediterranean or Aegean coast, these are not Turkey's best roads. To make matters worse, a series of dams under construction in the region can make existing highways impassable. Some sample distances: Erzurum to Kars, 212 kilometers (131 miles); Erzurum to Van, 361 kilometers (223 miles); Van to Diyarbakır, 408 kilometers (252 miles).

By Bus Within the eastern region, buses take a long time—Erzurum is 11 hours from Diyarbakır, eight hours from Van, four hours from Kars—but you can get wherever you want to go without spending much money. There's an *octogar* (bus station) in each of the main towns.

By Train Train service is very limited.

Exploring the Far East

Odds are that you will start your tour in the north at Erzurum (if you're coming from Ankara or the Black Sea coast) or in the south at Diyarbakır (if you're coming from the Mediterranean). The region's two main airports are near these two cities. These tours start in the north and work down, though it's easy enough to do them the other way around.

Highlights for First-Time Visitors

Ani, Tour 1
Fortress city of Diyarbakır, Tour 3
İşak Paşa Saray, Doğubayazıt, Tour 2

Tour 1: Erzurum to Ani

Numbers in the margin correspond to points of interest on the Lake Van and the East map.

❶ Erzurum occupies a strategic spot along the old trade routes to Russia, India, and Persia, a fact quickly recognized by the Byzantines, who made this their eastern bastion. The city fell to the Seljuks in 1071, after the battle of Manzikert, and they built most of the sights that remain today. Still a strategic spot (as you can see from the military barracks), Erzurum has developed into a sprawling, rather somber modern city with a major university. The most interesting part is still the old town at the very center. Start at the massive portal of the **Çifte Minareli Medrese** (Seminary of the Twin Minarets), on the eastern end of Cumhuriyet Caddesi, the main downtown street. Built in 1253, the seminary was sponsored by Sultan Alaeddin Keykubat II during the height of the Seljuk Empire. Inside, past the surprisingly airy courtyard, under a shallow dome sits the Hatuniye Türbesi, the tomb of the sultan's daughter. *Open dawn–dusk.*

Just west of the seminary is the **Ulu Cami** (Great Mosque), also on Cumhuriyet Caddesi, built in 1179 with seven wide naves and a fine colonnaded courtyard. The exterior is plain, even severe. To the north lies the Byzantine **citadel,** notable for its precisely hewn blocks, started in about AD 400. Its curious vintage clock tower was originally a minaret. Notice the few cannons scattered about, some Ottoman and some left by the Russians, who invaded in 1882 and 1916. *Admission: $1. Open daily 8–noon and 1:30–7:30.*

Head back to Cumhuriyet Caddesi and turn west, passing two Ottoman mosques—on the right is the 17th-century **Caferiye Cami,** and across the way is the classical 16th-century **Lala Mustafa Paşa Cami,** built by the grand vizir of the same name during the golden age of the empire; it looks rather similar to the mosques designed by Sinan in Istanbul. To the north lies the maze of Erzurum's **bazaar,** where you will find brightly shining samovars, kilims and carpets, and Muslim prayer beads made from a lightweight, jet-black mineral called *oltutaş;* to the west is the **Yakutiye Medrese,** a seminary built in the early 14th century by a Mongol emir. (Mongol buildings are rarely finished and certainly less refined than Seljuk architecture; the Mongols were usually more interested in conquering the next town than in building monuments.) The tomb at the back was built for the emir, though he never used it. The interior of the medrese was not open to the public at press time.

Turn left at the Havuzbaşi, the pool and fountain at the center of a traffic circle bearing a large statue of Atatürk, and walk up the hill along a tree-lined boulevard to the **Erzurum Müzesi** (Erzurum Museum). Egyptian coins, Roman pottery, and the like are on display; the best pieces are the old Turkish kilims and carpets, home furnishings, and weapons. *Tel. 425/218–1406. Admission: $1. Open Tues.–Sun. 8–noon and 1:30–5:30.*

The best, shortest road from Erzurum to Kars, 211 kilometers (131 miles) to the northeast, is the E80 east through Pasinler to Horasan, then northeast on Route 80 to Karakurt, and north on Route 957. **Sarıkamış,** a 7-kilometer (4-mile) detour north from Route 957, may be a better place to stay overnight than Kars itself, some 50 kilometers (30 miles) farther on.

❷ Kars looks like the frontier town it is: forbidding, cold, and grayish, set high on a wide plateau at the mercy of the winds. Ever since the Byzantines forced the last Armenian prince to abdicate in 1064, Kars has been besieged by invaders: the Seljuks, the Mongol warriors of Tamerlane, and, three times in the 19th century, czarist armies from Russia. The Turks finally claimed Kars after the war of independence in 1921, but Russian influence is still obvious in many buildings, and a weekly train still runs from Kars to the former Soviet Union. The **old Georgian fort** that overhangs Kars from a high, rocky vantage point is more than a mere relic: Extensively rebuilt in the 1850s, it is the military headquarters for the region. Below, at the foot of the hill by the Kars River, is the **Kümbet Cami** (Drum-Dome Mosque). Obviously not Turkish, it was originally the Armenian Church of the Twelve Apostles, built in the 10th century: You can still make out the Apostles on the exterior of the drum-shaped cupola. Just to the northwest is the **Taş Köprü,** a bridge of Seljuk origin dating from the 1400s. On the eastern edge of town, on the road to Ani, the small local **museum** exhibits relics of all of Kars's many rulers: Roman, Greek, Seljuk, and Ottoman artifacts, along with bits of Armenian churches and a Russian church bell. *Cumhuriyet Cad., no phone. Admission: $1. Open daily 8–5:30.*

❸ The real reason to come to Kars is to get to the ruins at **Ani,** 49 kilometers (30 miles) east on Route 36–07. Ani stands within sight of the Armenian border—machine-gun towers keep a close watch on it—so to visit the site you must obtain a military permit in Kars. Bring your passport to the tourist office (Mon.–Sat., before 2:30 PM for same-day permits; 2:30–5:30 for next-day permits), then take your registration form to the security headquarters on Faik Bey Caddesi to have the form stamped.

Situated on a triangular promontory bounded on two sides by steep river gorges, Ani still has an impressive **great wall,** spanning two deep ravines, to defend the city. Until the devastating Mongol invasion of 1236, Ani was the chief town of a medieval Armenian kingdom, with 100,000 inhabitants and "a thousand and one churches," according to historical sources. Although it was occupied by the Mongols, Ani still had a large Armenian population well into the 14th century. In 1319 it was struck by a terrible earthquake, after which the townspeople began to leave. The latest inscription to be found in the city is dated 1348. Scarcely half a dozen churches remain today, and all are in ruins. After you enter Ani, through the **Lion's Gate,** the path to the left takes you to the **Church of the Redeemer,** a huge, quadrangular cathedral built at the end of the 10th century; its dome (1036) is now half-collapsed. There are three churches dedicated to **St. Gregory,** the Armenian prince who converted his people to Christianity. The best preserved is the one built by an Armenian nobleman, Tigran Honentz (1215), by the ravine; note the remarkable murals in the interior. The striking **Convent of the Three Virgins** stands on a rocky outcrop lower down the gorge. To the right of the gate, through the weeds and thistles, are the remnants of a **Georgian church** (1218); the unusual, round **Church of St. Gregory,** built by Gagik I in 998; the **Church of the Holy Apostles** (1013); and the 11th-century **Church of Gregory** built by Prince Aplgharib Pahlavuni. Clinging to the heights overlooking the Arpa River, the **Menucer Mosque** (1070s) was originally an Armenian building, perhaps even a palace. Climb up to the first citadel and continue on to the second at the far edge of town, where the two gorges converge. From here you have a good view of the many cave dwellings in the walls of the western gorge, which once housed the city's poor. *No phone. Admission: $1. Open daily 8:30–5.*

Tour 2: Mt. Ararat to Lake Van

Route E80/100 leads east from Erzurum 286 kilometers (177 miles)
❹ to **Doğubayazıt,** another rough frontier town, filled with farm equipment, sheep, and Iranian tourists. Use Doğubayazıt as a base for

Lake Van and the East

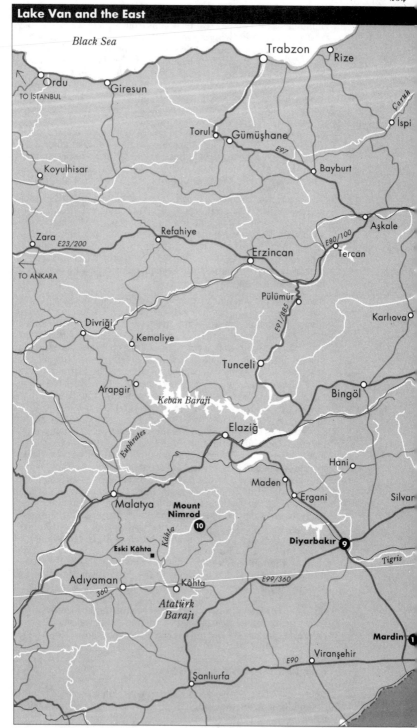

Black Sea

Trabzon
Rize

Ordu
Giresun
TO İSTANBUL

Çoruh
İspi

Torul
Gümüşhane
E97
Bayburt

Koyulhisar

Aşkale
Zara
E23/200
Refahiye
Erzincan
E80/100
Tercan

TO ANKARA

Pülümür
Karlıova

Divriği
Kemaliye
E91/885

Tunceli

Arapgir
Keban Barajı
Bingöl

Elazığ

Hani
Euphrates
Maden
Silvan
Malatya
Mount Nimrod
10
Ergani

Diyarbakır 9

Kâhta
Eski Kâhta
Tigris

Adıyaman
Kâhta
E99/360
360

Atatürk Barajı
Mardin 1

E90
Viranşehir
Şanlıurfa

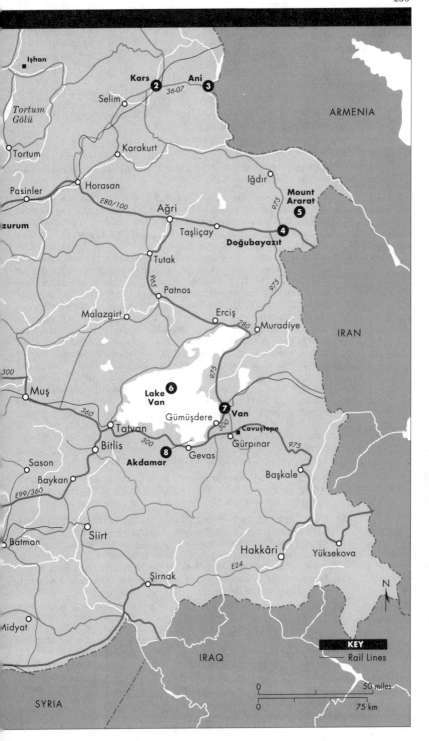

Işhan

Kars **2** Ani **3**

Selim *36-07*

Tortum Gölü

ARMENIA

Tortum

Karakurt

Pasinler

Horasan Iğdır

Mount Ararat **5**

zurum *E80/100*

Ağrı Taşlıçay Doğubayazıt **4**

975

Tutak

965 Patnos

Malazgirt Erciş *280* Muradiye

IRAN

300

Muş *975*

Lake Van **6**

7 Van

360 Gümüşdere

Tatvan Çavuştepe

Bitlis *300* Gürpınar *975*

Akdamar **8** Gevas

Sason Başkale

Baykan

E99/360

Batman Siirt

Hakkâri Yüksekova

E24

Midyat Şirnak

N

IRAQ

SYRIA

0   50 miles
0   75 km

visiting Turkey's highest mountain, the majestic Mt. Ararat; the only sight in the city itself is 6 kilometers (4 miles) up a hill to the east of town—the İşak Paşa Saray, a fortified palace built in the late 17th century by local potentate Çolak Abdi Paşa and his son İşak. This fairy-tale castle and mosque, set in a spacious courtyard, offer a magnificent view over the valley to the western spur of Ararat. The interior of the building is extremely ornate, a fantastic mixture of Georgian, Persian, and Ottoman styles. The gold-plated front doors, unfortunately, were carted off by Russian troops in 1917. *Admission: $1. Open Mon.–Sat. 9–5.*

From Doğubayazıt, Route 975 heads north across a broad, dusty ❺ plain to **Mt. Ararat** (in Turkish, Ağrı Dağı). An extinct volcano, snow-covered even in summer, Ararat soars up 16,945 feet, dominating the arid plateau.

According to Genesis, after the Great Flood "the waters were dried up from off the earth; and Noah removed the covering of the ark, and looked, and behold, the face of the ground was dry." The survivors, as the story goes, had just landed on top of Mt. Ararat. Many other ancient sources—Chaldean, Babylonian, Chinese, Assyrian—also tell of an all-destroying flood and of one man who heroically escaped its consequences. Scientists generally agree that sometime during the 4th millennium BC, a veritable cataclysm may have occurred, accompanied by rains and floods. But did Noah's Ark really exist? Since medieval times, the locals here have sold Christian pilgrims old planks reputedly from the ark; the modern ark hunt dates to 1876, when an Englishman named James Bryce discovered on the peaks "amid blocks of lava, a piece of wood about 4 feet long and 5 inches wide, which had obviously been shaped by means of a tool." Fragments of ancient timber, embedded in the ice, have been brought back by various ark-hunting expeditions since then, but radiocarbon dating tests proved inconclusive. Satellite photos showed a boat embedded in a glacier at 12,500 feet, similar to objects observed by pilots from low-flying aircraft, but on-the-spot examination of one of these "boats" proved it to be nothing more than a freak formation in the strata. Yet expeditions by Christian fundamentalist groups constantly make new claims, and the mystery continues, as compelling in its way as that of Scotland's Loch Ness monster.

Because the Armenian frontier is so close, mountain climbers must obtain permission from the Turkish military authorities, usually months in advance (*see* Sports and Outdoor Activities, *below*).

❻ **Lake Van** would not be terribly far from Doğubayazıt—if there were a straight road between the two. Alas, you must follow a huge U-shaped jog: Drive 95 kilometers (59 miles) on E80/100 back to Ağri, then south 80 kilometers (50 miles) on Route 965 to Patnos, and another 51 kilometers (32 miles) to the lakeshore, just past Ercis. When you finally reach the lake, you'll find a landscape that is forbiddingly barren and desolate, because of wintertime flash floods and the region's violent earthquakes. But it is Turkey's largest and most unusual lake, 3,738 square kilometers (1,443 square miles) of brackish water surrounded by mighty volcanic cones, so travelers continue to come. Lake Van was formed when a volcano blew its top and blocked the course of a river, so it has no natural outlet; the water is highly alkaline, full of sulfides and mineral salts, much like the Dead Sea. The only life within it is one small member of the carp family, the *darekh*, which has somehow adapted to the saline environment. Beaches along the rocky shores are few and far between, and swimming in the soft, soapy water is pleasant (although try not to swallow any—the taste is horrible!).

Route 280 continues another 39 kilometers (24 miles) around the lake's eastern tip, and then Route 975 takes you 96 kilometers (60 miles) to **Van,** the largest city in the area. Van first appears in history 3,000 years ago when it was the site of the Urartian capital of Tushpa, whose formidable fortress built on a steep cliff rising from the lake shore dominated the countryside. (The Urartians first appeared in this region in the 12th century BC, and by the mid-8th century BC ruled an empire extending from the Black Sea to the Caspian Sea, only to be wiped out over the next 150 years by various rivals, primarily the Assyrians.) Steps—considerably fewer than the 1,000 claimed in local tourist handouts—still ascend to the **citadel.** A path branches right to Urartian tombs in the sheer southern rock face; a cuneiform inscription here honors King Xerxes, whose Persian troops occupied the fortress early in the 5th century BC. The crumbling ramparts are still impressive, but as is true so often in these parts, it is the view from such a vantage point that makes the steep climb worthwhile.

The old city, nestled below the southern cliff, was totally destroyed in battles with the Armenians and Russians in 1917, during World War I. The melancholy jumble of foundations cannot be sorted out; only two vaguely restored mosques, one 13th-century, the other 16th-century, rise from the marshland. When it came time to rebuild the city after the war, the residents selected a higher, healthier spot, 5 kilometers (3 miles) from the fortress. The new city has little to recommend it, though, besides a large new mosque and the small but well-arranged archaeological and ethnographical **Van Müze** (Van Museum), which displays many Urartian artifacts: rich, golden jewelry; belts and plates engraved with lions, bulls, and sphinxes; and a carved relief of the god Teshup, for whom their capital was named. *1 block e. of Cumhuriyet Cad., tel. 432/216–1139. Admission: $1. Open Tues.–Sun. 9–noon and 1–6.*

One short excursion south from Van will take you to two historic sites. The first is 25 kilometers (15 miles) south of the city, at **Çavuştepe,** where you can clamber around the finely worked stone foundations of a ruined 8th-century BC Urartian fortress-city, Sardurihinli. A striking cuneiform inscription in the lower terrace credits King Sarduri with building the city in honor of Haldi, the war god. About a half hour's drive farther south leads you to **Hoşap Castle,** a compelling fortress looming over a river chasm. Built in 1643 by a Kurdish strongman, Sari Sulayman, who used it as a base to "protect" (i.e., ransack) caravans, its strong walls ascend a forbidding cliff, creating a safe haven for a palace, two mosques, three baths, and a dungeon. The great gate, with its carved lions and an inscription in the Farsi language of Persia, is quite a show of strength; a tunnel carved through bedrock leads inside from here. Bring a flashlight; there are no lights within the castle. *Admission: 50¢. Open daily 8–5, though the caretaker may close the place down when he has his lunch.*

A decidedly worthy excursion from Van follows the lakeshore south on Route 300. After 15 kilometers (9 miles), you'll reach **Gümüşdere,** locally called Edremit, the nearest beach and not much at that. Go 41 kilometers (25 miles) farther on to **Gevaş,** where motorboats wait at the landing stage to collect the required number of passengers—between 12 and 17—to chug over to the Islet of **Akdamar,** a lovely place for a picnic lunch (a 20-minute boat ride should cost $3–$5, depending on how many people are on the boat). On this tranquil, uninhabited islet, among wild olive trees stand the scant remains of a monastery, including a truly splendid **Church of the Holy Cross.**

Built in 921 AD by an Armenian king, Gagik Artzruni of Vaspurakan, it is very much a cousin to the Armenian churches at Ani in structure, but a series of incredible high-relief carvings makes this church a work of art. Nearly the entire story of the Bible is told here, from Adam and Eve to David and Goliath. Along the top is a frieze of running animals; another frieze shows a vineyard where laborers work the fields and women dance with bears; and, of course, King Gagik is depicted, offering his church to Christ. *Admission: $1. Open during daylight hours.*

Tour 3: To Diyarbakır and Mt. Nimrod

From Van follow Route 300 the length of the lake to Tatvan, where you turn southwest and drive away from the water west on Route E99 toward Diyarbakır. Twenty-five kilometers (16 miles) from Tatvan, you'll pass through **Bitlis,** a green oasis among towering mountains on a tributary of the Tigris. Its two principal landmarks are a sprawling castle built above the town by one of Alexander the Great's generals, and the odd 12th-century Ulu Cami (Grand Mosque)—apparently its sponsor ran out of money before its conical dome could be built.

Defended by a stretch of impregnable black basalt walls, three layers thick in places, **Diyarbakır** commands the rough, dusty plain 230 kilometers (143 miles) west of Tatvan. With its great walls, one would think this stronghold could survive any siege; in fact, it seems to have fallen to about every petty raider to pass this way. One of the oldest cities anywhere, set in what is widely accepted as the "cradle of civilization" (the area between the Tigris and Euphrates rivers), it has seen a lot of raiders in its 5,000 years. The Hurrians were probably first, founding a city called Hurri-Mitanni. The Assyrians absorbed it, renaming it Amida in the process. Next came a century of Urartian domination, followed by the familiar succession of Medes, Persians, Macedonians, Romans, Sassanids, and Byzantines. Then several Arab Muslim groups battled with one another for possession of the city. They gave the city its present name, Diyarbakır, "City of the Bakır tribes." Later came the Turkomans, the Ortokids, the eastern and western Seljuks, and the Mongolian hordes. Finally, Selim I took it for the Ottomans, the beginning of a long and relatively calm period.

Roman influence is evident in the layout of the old town within the citadel walls (the new town sprawls outside): a rough rectangle, with two main streets connecting the four gates, one at each of the compass points. Emperor Constantius reconstructed the walls in AD 349; further work was done by the Seljuks in 1088. On the whole, the walls are still in good shape along their entire length of 5½ kilometers (3 miles). Of the original 72 towers, 67 still stand, decorated with myriad inscriptions in the language of every conqueror and Seljuk reliefs of animals and men; you can explore their inner chambers and corridors. Make the circuit on foot or hire a *fayton,* an old-fashioned horse-drawn carriage. Start at the **Mardin Kapisi** gate on the south side and take the wall-top path west toward the **Urfa Kapisi** gate, also called the Bab El Rumi. About halfway, you will come to the twin bastions, **Beden Burcu** and **Yedi Kardeş Burcu,** added to the fortifications in 1208. From here, you can see the old Ottoman bridge over the Tigris, called Dicle Köprüsü. Continue inside the ramparts to the elevated northeast corner, where the sad remains of the Artakid palace surround a dry, octagonal pool known as the Lion's Fountain. Not long ago, there were two carved lions here; where the second one went is a mystery. In this corner, off Izzet

Paşa Caddesi, you will find **İç Kale,** the inner fortress, with its 16th-century **Hazreti Süleymaniye Cami** (also called the Citadel Mosque). The mosque, with its tall, graceful minaret, is striped with black basalt and pale sandstone, a favorite design of this city's medieval architects. Its courtyard fountain is fed by an underground spring that has probably supplied cold, clear water to the city for all its 5,000 years.

Though you will most likely get lost in the impenetrable maze of streets, try to make your way toward the center of the old city. Eventually, on Gazi Caddesi you will find the **Ulu Cami,** very possibly the oldest mosque in Turkey. Though its present form dates to the 12th century, in an older form it served as a Byzantine basilica; its colonnades and columns are made from bits and pieces of earlier Greek buildings. Note its Arabic courtyard plan, which contrasts with the covered and domed mosques common in Turkey. Around this venerable mosque is **Diyarbakır's bazaar,** starting across the street with the grand 16th-century **Hasan Paşa Han,** a caravansary now used mostly by carpet and souvenir dealers. Also adjoining the mosque are two former seminaries, the Mesudiye and Zinciriye Medreses, the latter converted into the local **Archaeological Museum,** where the exhibits cover a period of some 4,000 years. *Gazi Cad., tel. 412/221-2755. Admission: $1. Open Mon.–Sat. 8:30–noon and 1:30–5:30.*

By the Ulu Cami, Gazi Caddesi crosses Yenikapi Caddesi; head east on this street, and soon on the right you'll pass the **Kasım Padişah Cami** (1512), a mosque recognizable by its famed **Dört Ayaklı Minare** (Four-legged Minaret). Seemingly suspended in the air, this minaret balances upon four basalt columns right in the middle of the street. Legend has it that your wish will come true if you pass under it seven times.

❿ From Diyarbakır, a uniquely rewarding excursion climbs up the (8,205-foot) peak of **Mt. Nimrod** (in Turkish, Nemrut Dağ). Head west on E99/360 for 115 kilometers (71 miles), and then turn off on Route 360 and continue another 54 kilometers (33 miles) to Kahta. Minibuses run to the peak from Kahta ($45 and $100 depending on the length of the tour); if you drive to the summit yourself, the trip from Kahta takes a good two hours via the rough Route 02–03. Because of severe weather conditions, the trip should be undertaken only between May and October—even then, when it is baking down on the plain there is a stiff morning chill at the summit. Tour guides recommend setting out at 2 AM in order to reach the summit at sunrise and return before the fierce midday heat. The sunrise is lovely, but if you start later you'll avoid the sunrise tourist rush and the coldest part of the morning.

Cars must park 1 kilometer (½ mile) below the sepulchral mound that tops the ocher-pink, cone-shaped pinnacle of Mt. Nimrod. The hike up from there takes a good 20 minutes and can be tiring, given the altitude. When you finally reach the summit, though, you'll meet a stupendous spectacle. Temples stand on two terraces—one facing the rising sun, the other the setting sun—with a pyramid of small rocks, the **Tumulus of Antiochus,** between them. The man responsible for the fantastic project, King Antiochus I, is buried somewhere underneath (though they have tried, archaeologists have yet to find him—all attempts at excavation have caused cave-ins). From 64 to 32 BC, Antiochus was king of Commagene, a tiny Roman puppet state founded by his father, Mithridates the Great (it lasted until its annexation to Rome in AD 72). The kings of Commagene grandly claimed descent from Alexander the Great, and so young Antiochus reasoned that if

Alexander was a god, he must be one, too—and set a veritable army of slaves to work building a suitable monument to himself. Enthroned on the two terraces are massive white statues of gods, Antiochus seated among them as an equal. Originally 26 feet–30 feet high, the statues have been decapitated over the centuries by the forces of erosion and earthquakes; in 1926 a thunderstorm brought the last one—Tyche, goddess of fortune—crashing down. Their gigantic heads are nowadays set upright on the ground around the tumulus; note how they combine the Greek harmony of features with Oriental headgear and hairstyles. On the east terrace, left to right, they are: Apollo, Tyche, Zeus (at center, with his pointed cap and bushy whiskers), Antiochus, and Heracles. The west terrace is a mirror image of the east, with the addition of some fine relief carvings portraying Antiochus shaking hands with Apollo, Zeus, and Heracles, all with smiles and dignity. The inscriptions carved everywhere mostly describe the Commagenes and their religious practices; the message on the throne of Antiochus reads, "I, Antiochus, caused this monument to be erected in commemoration of my own glory and of that of the gods."

Along the road back from the mountain to Kahta, you can see some other remarkable relics of Commagene in **Eski Kahta** (Old Kahta). Cross the Kahta River on the Seljuk bridge to see, carved into the rock, a stunning relief of Antiochus I's father, Mithridates, being greeted by Heracles. Higher up on the rock face are copious inscriptions proclaiming the glory of the Commagene dynasty; on the top of this peak stand the foundations of an ancient acropolis with colored floor mosaics. Also in Eski Kahta, Yeni Kale (New Castle) was built by the Mameluks over a smaller Commagene fortress. Recross the Kahta via the Cendere Köprü, a single-span bridge with two tall columns on one end and one on the other, built by the Roman emperor Septimus Severus in the 3rd century AD.

A spate of dam building in this region will eventually submerge much of the vast Euphrates valley south of Adıyaman, and intensive excavations are going on now to save relics of this cradle of civilization, many of them at the Commagene capital of Samasota, now **Samsat,** 38 kilometers (24 miles) southeast of Adıyaman. At this time, these finds are not on public display, but if you're in the region, it can't hurt to make inquiries.

From Kahta, you can either return to Diyarbakır the way you came or follow another, longer route through new territory at the edge of the Syrian desert. Turn right on E99 and drive 68 kilometers (42 miles) south to **Şanlıurfa** (more commonly called Urfa), a sleepy, midsize town most famous as the birthplace of the biblical patriarch Abraham. Half a dozen mosques crowd around the cave where Abraham reputedly was born, and a sacred pool near the cave is filled with sacred carp (why they are sacred no one seems able to say).

⓫ East of Sanliurfa 162 kilometers (100 miles) on Route E90, **Mardin** is defended by a medieval pale sandstone citadel, so impregnable that neither the Seljuks in the 12th century nor the Mongols in the 13th managed to capture it. At the tail end of the 14th century, Tamerlane did conquer the city, but when he returned in 1401 to crush the revolt of his own brother, Isa, the citadel resisted even Tamerlane. *E. of main sq., tel. 482/212–7797. Admission 50¢. Open Mon.–Sat., 8:30–noon and 1:30–5.*

The other outstanding buildings here are Islamic: the **Lâtifiye Cami** (1371); the Seljuk **Ulu Cami,** dating from the 11th century, restored in the 15th century and disfigured in the 19th; and the **Sultan İsa Medrese** (1385), renowned for its exquisite stone carvings. The **local**

museum next door to the Sultan İsa Medrese is worth a visit: Its courtyard shelters tombstones inscribed with cuneiform writings. The 17th-century **covered bazaar** here has a very Arabic flavor. From Mardin it's a 94-kilometer (58-mile) drive northwest back to Diyarbakır on Route 950.

Off the Beaten Track

North from Erzurum on Route 950, the **Tortum and Çoruh River valleys** offer some interesting walks. About 23 kilometers (14 miles) beyond Tortum on Route 950, you will find the trail to **Haho** on the left side of the road, where you can visit a well-preserved mosque originally built in the 10th century as a Georgian monastery by an Armenian prince called David of Tayk (one of several by that name); allow two hours round-trip. At the northern end of long, narrow **Lake Tortum,** past a small but lively waterfall, go another 23 kilometers (14 miles) on Route 950 and, on the right side of the road, pick up another hiking trail, to the village of **Ishan.** Here you'll see the 10th-century Church of the Mother of God, built in the shape of a cross, with bas-reliefs carved on the exterior walls. The setting is spectacular, an oasis of tall green trees backed by barren peaks.

Shopping

Erzurum has a highly authentic Oriental bazaar, with particularly talented metalworkers; Şanlıurfa's is marvelously medieval. **Van** is noted for its weavings, especially its kilims and traditional Kurdish fabrics.

Sports and the Outdoors

Mountain Climbing Mt. Ararat requires a special permit to climb; contact the Turkish embassy in your home country before departing to join an organized climbing group. If you haven't made arrangements in advance, try Trek Turizm in Doğubayazıt (Emniyet Caddesi Otel, tel. 472/215–3271). On the way up the mountain, you must brave spiders, snakes, and bears, as well as suspicious military patrols, snowstorms, and avalanches. Horses and guides are for hire at Iğdır (to the north of the mountain) and Doğubayazıt.

You can also arrange to hike or climb Mt. Nimrod (*see* Tour 3). Better choices include the Sat and Cilo ranges, in the southeast spur of Turkey, between the borders of Iran and Iraq, where there are nearly 20 glaciers and more than 100 peaks of different heights, covered with snow most of the year. Guides are required. Overall, your best source of information is **Dagcılı Federasyonu** (Turkish Mountaineering Club, B.T.G.M., Ulus Işhanı, A Block, Ulus, Ankara).

Skiing In a delightful alpine setting, ski at Inis Boğazi, 6 kilometers (4 miles) from Erzurum. The Palandöken resort has a centrally heated lodge, a lift, ski instruction, and equipment rentals.

Dining and Lodging

For details and price-category definitions, *see* Dining and Lodging in Staying in Turkey in Chapter 1, Essential Information. Highly recommended establishments are indicated by a star ★ .

Diyarbakır **Babaman.** For solid Turkish fare at bargain prices, this is the place;
Dining kebabs are the best bet. *Kıbrıs Cad., tel. 412/223–5887. No reserva-*
★ *tions. No credit cards. $*

Güneydoğu. A newer and comparatively fancier dining spot, this
restaurant has both decent food and air-conditioning, a blessing in
the height of summer. *İnönü Cad. 32/A, tel. 412/221–2597. Reserva-*
tions not necessary. No credit cards. $

Kent. The Kent is another pleasant kebab house, with a touch of native decor. *Kıbrıs Cad. 31/A, tel. 412/223–10899. Reservations not*
necessary. No credit cards. $

Lodging **Demir Hotel.** The Demir is not luxurious, but it's very comfortable.
There is a swimming pool, a rooftop restaurant, and a terrace for
music and dancing. *İzzet Paşa Cad. 8, tel. 412/221–2315, fax 412/*
222–4300. 58 rooms with shower. Facilities: 3 restaurants, 2 bars,
swimming pool. No credit cards. $$–$$$

Aslan Hotel/Aslan Palace. These twins (located next door to each
other) are two of the better inexpensive hotels in town. *Kıbrıs Cad.*
23, tel. 412/221–3971, fax 412/224–1179. 36 rooms with bath. Facili-
ties: restaurant. No credit cards. $$

★ **Otel Büyük Kervansaray.** There's something particularly apt about
the Turkish concept of turning old caravansaries into fancy hotels.
This is an attractive newcomer, in a 16th-century building with
sandstone walls and traditional furnishings. *Gazi Cad., tel. 412/*
223–5019, fax 412/223–7731. 45 rooms with bath. Facilities: swim-
ming, pool, restaurant, bar. MC, V. $$

Turistik. If you're feeling nostalgic for a 1950s-style hotel, try the
Turistik. Guest rooms are larger than average and still comfortable,
and the garden restaurant, around a fountain, is quite pleasant.
Front rooms can be a bit noisy. *Ziya Gökalp Cad. 7, tel. 412/224–*
7550, fax 412/224–4274. 57 rooms with shower. Facilities: restau-
rant. MC, V. $$

Doğubayazıt The hotels typically have the best restaurants. The **Istanbul** (on the
Dining main street) and **Karadeniz** (across from the Ararat) are restaurants
where the local Turks eat.

Lodging **Hotel Isfahan.** There is a Turkish bath here, and the lobby and bar
are decorated in traditional kilims. A sightseeing room on the fifth
floor offers especially good views of Mt. Ararat. *Emniyet Cad. 26,*
tel. 278/1139, fax 278/2044. 73 rooms with shower. Facilities: restau-
rant, bar. No credit cards. $

Sim-Er Motel. This modern motel 5 kilometers (3 miles) east of town
is clean, fairly attractive, and, as a result, popular with tour groups
and truck drivers en route to Iran. It has magnificent views of Mt.
Ararat, another plus. *On Hwy. E3, tel. 278/1601, fax 278/3403. 130*
rooms with shower. Facilities: restaurant. No credit cards. $

Erzurum Again, the hotels are the best bets. Basic, inexpensive Turkish
Dining dishes can also be found along the main street, Cumhuriyet Caddesi,
at the **Tufan** (tel. 442/218–3107) and the **Guzelyurt** (tel. 442/218–
1514; V), which serves an excellent *mantarli guvec* (mushrooms,
lamb and vegetables baked in a clay pot and topped with melted
cheese).

Lodging **Büyük Erzurum.** This was the town's major hotel until the Dilaver
came along. Although the furniture is somewhat worn and the walls
bare, it's friendly, and you'll find a good bit of English spoken. The
top-floor restaurant is one of the best in town. Front rooms can be
rather noisy. *Ali Ravi Cad. 5, tel. 442/218–6528, fax 442/212–2898.*
50 rooms with bath. MC, V. $–$$

★ **Otel Oral.** The newest, most modern hotel in Erzurum, the Oral has one main drawback: it is on the outskirts of town. Still, the rooms are comfortable, with TVs and refrigerators; the staff is helpful and there's a good restaurant. *Terminal Cad. 3, tel. 442/218-9740, fax 442/218-9749. 90 rooms with bath. MC, V. $-$$*

Dilaver. Opened in summer 1993, the Dilaver is the plushest hotel in Erzurum. Comfortable, if somewhat lacking in character, it has satellite TV and a good restaurant. *Pelit Meydani, Asagi Mumcu Cad., tel. 442/235-0068, fax 442/218-1148. 75 rooms with shower. Facilities: restaurant, 2 bars. No credit cards. $*

Otel Polat. This centrally located, inexpensive spot is popular with Turkish business travelers and young couples. Despite an attempt to be modern and stylish, it is certainly nothing special, but you could pass a night comfortably here. *Kazim Karabekir Cad., tel. 442/218-1623 or 442/218-3370, fax 442/234-4598. 57 rooms with shower. No credit cards. $*

Kars
Dining

Kars is one of the few towns in the east where young men and women meet openly for a cup of coffee or a meal. Yet ironically there are very few good places to eat. The best is probably the **Manolya Restaurant and Pastry Shop** (Ataturk Cad.), although the nearby **Yeni Nil Kebab Salonu** also offers a passable range of kebabs.

Lodging

Yımaz. Though this is the best hotel in Kars, it's tired and worn, hardly anything to get excited about. Check a couple of rooms, as some are better than others. If you're not exhausted, push on to Sarıkamiş. *Küçük Kazımbey Cad. 14, tel. 474/223-1074, fax 474/223-2387. 50 rooms with shower. No credit cards. $*

Mt. Nimrod
Area
Lodging

Bozdoğan. This modern, relatively new hotel is the best place to stay in Adıyaman. Its restaurant is also the town's best. *Atatürk Bul., Adıyaman, tel. 416/216-2716, fax 416/216-3630. 54 rooms with shower. Facilities: restaurant. No credit cards. $$*

Hotel Euphrat. One of two places available on Mt. Nimrod itself, the Euphrat is a low stone building pleasantly situated near a waterfall. The location is special, the hotel is not; that's the trade-off. *Nemrut Yolu, 54 km (34 mi) from Kahta, tel. 8795/2428 (or 1/144-6583 in Istanbul for reservations). 55 rooms, 43 with shower. Facilities: restaurant, swimming pool, camping area. No credit cards. $$*

Zeus. Only a few kilometers from the summit, the Zeus is ideal for watching the peak at sunrise or sunset. An attractive mountain inn set in a secluded valley, it has fireplaces in most of the rooms and cool, clear air all around. *Nemrut Yolu, Karadat Köyü, tel. 8795/2427. 20 rooms with shower. No credit cards. $$*

Hotel Selçuk. Generally considered one of the better places to stay in the area, the Selçuk is often booked up by tour groups. Guest rooms are clean and comfortable; though the pool is small, the restaurant is nicely situated on a shady terrace. *Adıyaman Yolu, Kahta, tel. 8795/1835. 58 rooms with shower. Facilities: restaurant, swimming pool. No credit cards. $-$$*

Hotel Kommagene. This is really a *pansiyon* with pretensions of being a hotel, but there are old kilims decorating the lobby and a shady terrace, and the restaurant is quite decent. *Rte. 360, Kahta, tel. 416/715-1092, fax 416/725-5548. 24 rooms with shower. Facilities: restaurant. No credit cards. $*

Palandoken
Lodging

Palandoken Dedeman. A ski resort may seem a little incongruous so far east, but it is perfectly adequate, with a good restaurant and helpful staff. The season lasts from October to May. Another 98-room block is due to be completed for the 94/95 season; this should ease bookings on weekends when the hotel is inundated with wealthy students from Erzurum University and fugitive businessmen from Ankara. Ski equipment is available to rent, and the hotel also provides airport transfers from Erzurum. *Palandoken Dedeman Ski Center, Erzurum (1), tel. 442/316–2414, fax 442/316–3607. 17 rooms with bath. Facilities: restaurant, terrace, indoor pool. AE, DC, MC, V. $$–$$$*

Sarıkamış
Lodging

Turistik. "Simple" is the word, though you can comfortably pass the night here. You'll climb a marble stairway to the reception area; kilims decorate the lounge, and the restaurant is perfectly acceptable. *Halk Cad. 64, tel. 474/413–4176, fax 474/413–5151. 48 rooms with bath. Facilities: restaurant. No credit cards. $$*

Van
Lodging
★

Büyük Urartu. This is probably the best place in town—and the most educational, since the manager is a professor of archaeology. The decoration carries Urartian motifs. Guest rooms are small, though still pleasant; the restaurant is accommodating. *Hastane Cad. 60, tel. 432/212–0660, fax 432/212–1610. 82 rooms, 70 with shower. Facilities: restaurant. MC, V. $$*

Tekin. Clean, quiet, and recently refurbished, the Tekin has a rooftop terrace with a view of the lake. *Hacıosman Cami, Nur Sok., tel. 432/216–3010, fax 432/216–1366. 52 rooms with shower. No credit cards. $–$$*

Turkish Vocabulary

Words and Phrases

	English	Turkish	Pronunciation
Basics	Yes/no	Evet/hayir	**eh**-vet/**haw**-yer
	Please	Lütfen	**lewt**-fen
	Thank you	Tesekkür ederim	tay-shake-**cure** eh-day-**reem**
	You're welcome	Rica ederim	ree-**jaw** eh-ay-**reem**
		Bir sey değil	beer shay **day**-eel
	Excuse me, Sorry	Özür dilerim	oh-**zewr** deel-air-eem
	Sorry	Pardon	**pahr**-doan
	Good morning	Günaydin	goo-eye-**den**
	Good day	Iyi günler	ee-yee gewn-**lair**
	Good evening	Iyi akşamlar	ee-yee awk-shom-**lahr**
	Goodbye	Allahaismarladik	**allah**-aw-ees-mar-law-deck
		Güle güle	**gew**-leh-**gew**-leh
	Mr. (Sir)	Bay, or Bey	buy, bay
	Mrs.	Hanım	ha-nem
	Miss		
	Pleased to meet you	Tanıştığımıza	Tawnesh-tumu-**zah** **mam**-noon
		memnun oldum	ohl-doom
	How are you?	Nasıl sınız?	**Gnaw**-sull-suh-nuz
Numbers	one	bir	beer
	two	iki	ee-**kee**
	three	üc	ooch
	four	dört	doort
	five	beş	besh
	six	altı	awl-tuh
	seven	yedi	yed-dy
	eight	sekiz	sek-**kez**
	nine	dokuz	doh-**kooz**
	ten	on	own
	eleven	onbir	**own**-beer
	twelve	oniki	**own**-ee-kee
	thirteen	onüç	**own-ooch**
	fourteen	ondört	**own-doort**
	fifteen	onbeş	**own**-besh
	sixteen	onaltı	**own**-awl-tuh
	seventeen	onyedi	**own**-yed-dy
	eighteen	onsekiz	own-sek-**kez**
	nineteen	ondokuz	**own**-doh-**kooz**
	twenty	yirmi	yeer-mee
	twenty-one	yirmibir	**yeer**-mee-beer
	thirty	otuz	oh-**tooz**
	forty	kırk	kirk
	fifty	elli	el-leeh

sixty	altmış	**ought**-mush
seventy	yetmiş	**yet**-mish
eighty	seksen	sex-an
ninety	doksan	dohk-**san**
one hunred	yüz	yewz
one thousand	bin	bin

Colors	black	siyah	**see**-yah
	blue	mavi	**mah**-vee
	brown	kahverengi	**kah**-vay-**ren**-gee
	green	yeşil	yay-sheel
	orange	portakal rengi	pohr-tah-kawl ren-gee
	red	kırmızı	ker-muz-eh
	white	beyaz	**bay**oz
	yellow	sarı	sah-**reh**

Days of the Week	Sunday	Pazar	Poz-**ahr**
	Monday	Pazartesi	Poz-**ahr**-tes-sy
	Tuesday	Sali	Saul-luh
	Wednesday	Çarşamba	Char-shom-**bah**
	Thursday	Perşembe	Pair-shem-**beh**
	Friday	Cuma	**Joom**-ah
	Saturday	Cumartesi	Joom-**ahr**-tes-sy

Months	January	Ocak	oh-**jock**
	February	Şubat	shoo-**bought**
	March	Mart	mart
	April	Nisan	Nee-**sahn**
	May	Mayıs	My-us
	June	Haziran	Hah-zee-**rahn**
	July	Temmuz	**Tem**-mooz
	August	Ağustos	Ah-oos-tohs
	September	Eylül	Ay-**lewl**
	October	Ekim	Eh-**keem**
	November	Kasım	Kaw-sem
	December	Aralık	Ah-raw-**luk**

Useful Phrases	Do you speak English?	Ingilizce biliyormusunuz?	in-**gee-leez**-jay bee-lee-**your**-moo-soo-noose
	I don't speak Turkish	Turkçe bilmiyorum	**tewrk**-chah **beel**-mee-your-oom
	I don't understand	Anlamıyorum	On-**lah**-muh-your-oom
	I understand	Anlıyorum	on-**lew**-your-oom
	I don't know	Bilmiyorum	**beel**-meeh-your-oom
	I'm American/	Amerikalıyım	ahm-ay-**ree**-kah-lew-yum
	I'm British	Ingilizim	**een**-gee-leez-um
	What's your name?	Isminiz nedir?	ees-mee-niz nay-der
	My name is . . .	Benim adım . . .	bay-**neem** ah-dumb . . .
	What time is it?	Saat kaç?	sought **kawch**

How?	Nasıl?	**naw**-sill
When?	Ne zaman?	**Nay** zoh-mawn
Yesterday	Dün	dewn
Today	Bugün	**Boo**-gown
Tomorrow	Yarın	**Yaw**-run
This morning/ afternoon	Bu sabah/ ögleden sonra	**boo** saw-bah/ **ow-lay**-den sewn-rah
Tonight	Bu gece	**boo** ge-jeh
What?	Efendim?/Ne?	**eh**-fen-deem/neh
What is it?	Nedir?	**neh**-deer
Why?	Neden/Niçin?	**neh**-den/**nee**-chin
Who?	Kim?	kim
Where is . . .	. . . nerede?	. . . **nay**-ray-deh
the train station	tren istasyonu	tee-**rehn** ees-**taws**-yone-oo
the subway station	metro durağı	metro doo-**raw**-ugh
the bus stop	otobüs durağı	oh-tow-**bewse** doo-**raw**-ugh
the terminal (airport)	hava alanı	haw-**vah ah**-lawn-eh
the post office	postane	post-**ahn**-eh
the bank	banka	**bahn**-kah
the . . . hotel?	. . . oteli [nerede]	. . . oh-**tel-ly** [nay-ray-deh]
the . . . museum?	. . . müzesi [nerede]	. . . news-zay-**see**
the hospital	hastane	hoss-**taw**-neh
the elevator	asansör	aw-sahn-**seur**
the telephone	telefon	teh-leh-**fon**
Where are the restrooms?	Tuvalet nerede?	too-vah-**let** nay-ray-deh
Here/there	Burası/Orası	**boo**-rah-seh/ **oh**-rah-seh
Left/right	sağ/sol	saw/soul
Is it near/ far?	Yakın mı?/ Uzak mı?	**Yaw-kin** muh/ Ooz-**ahk**-muh
I'd like . . .	. . . istiyorum	. . . **ess**-tee-your-room
a room	bir oda	beer oh-**dah**
the key	anahtarı	**on**-ah-tahr-eh
a newspaper	bir gazete	beer **gauze**-eh-teh
a stamp	pul	pool
I'd like to buy . . .	. . . almak istiyorum	. . . ahl-**mock** ees-tee-your-room
cigarettes	sigara	see-**gahr**-rah

matches	kibrit	**keeb**-rit
city map	şehir planı	shay-**hear plah**-nuh
road map	karayolları haritası	**kah**-rah-yow-lahr-**uh** hah-ree-tah-**suh**
magazine	dergi	dair-gee
envelopes	zarf	zahrf
writing paper	mektup kağıdı	**make**-toop **kah**-uh-duh
postcard	kartpostal	cart-poh-stall
How much is it?	Fiyatı ne kadar?	fee-yacht-eh **neh** kah-dar
It's expensive/cheap	pahalı/ucuz	pah-hah-**luh**/oo-**jooz**
A little/a lot	Az/çok	ahz/choke
More/less	daha çok/daha az	da-ha choke/da-ha oz
Enough/too (much)	Yeter/çok fazla	**yay**-tehr/**choke** fahz-lah
I am ill/sick	Hastayım	**hahs**-tah-yum
Call a doctor	Doktor çağırın	dohk-tore **chah**-uh-run
Help!	İmdat!	eem-**dot**
Stop!	Durun!	Doo-**roon**
Dining Out A bottle of . . .	bir şişe . . .	**beer** she-shay
A cup of . . .	bir fincan . . .	beer **fin**-john
A glass of . . .	bir bardak . . .	beer **bar**-dock
Ashtray	kül tablası	kewl tahb-lah-**suh**
Bill/check	hesap	heh-**sop**
Bread	ekmek	ekmek
Breakfast	kahvaltı	**kah**-vaul-tuh
Butter	tereyağ	tay-**reh**-yah-uh
Cocktail/aperitif	kokteyl, içki	cocktail, **each**-key
Dinner	aksam yemeği	**ahk**-shom yem-ay-eeh
Fixed-price menu	fiks menü	fix menu
Fork	çatal	**cha**-tahl
I am a vegetarian/ I don't eat meat	vejeteryenim/ et yemem	vegeterian-**em**/ et yeh-**mem**
I cannot eat . . .	. . . yiyemem	**yee**-yay-mem
I'd like to order	. . . ısmarlamak isterim	us-mahr-lah-**muck** ee-stair-em
I'd like . . .	. . . isterim	ee-stair-**em**
I'm hungry/ thirsty	acıktım/ susadım	ah-**juck**-tum/ soo-saw-**dum**

Is service/the tip included?	Servis fiyata dahil mi?	service **fee**-yah-tah dah-heel-**mee**
It's good/bad	güzel/güzel değil	gew-**zell**/gew-**zell** **day**-eel
It's hot/cold	sıcak/soğuk	suh-**jock**/soh-**uk**
Knife	bıçak	buh-**chock**
Lunch	öğle yemeği	**ew**-leh **yem**-ey-ee
Menu	menü	
Napkin	Peçete	**peh**-che-teh
Pepper	Karabiber	kah-**rah**-bee-bear
Plate	tabak	tah-**bock**
Please give me . . .	Lutfen bana . . . verirmisiniz?	**loot**-fen bah-nah . . . vair-**eer**-mee-see-niz
Salt	tuz	tooz

Index

Abant, 225
Accident insurance, 13
Acropolis
Aspendos, 165
Pergamum, 115
Sardis, 120
Tlos, 156
Xanthos, 158
Adana, 168
Aegean Coast, 32, 103–145
arts, 144
consulates, 105
emergencies, 105
guided tours, 106
hotels, 134–144
nightlife, 144–145
restaurants, 134–144
shopping, 132
sports, 133
tourist information, 105
transportation, 105–106
Agizkara Han, 203
Agora, 117
Ağzıkarahan, 202
Ahi Elvan Cami, 190
Ahi Evran Cami, 195–196
Air travel
Aegean Coast, 105
Ankara and Central Anatolia, 183
Black Sea Coast, 215
Bursa, 93
children, 17
Far East, 230–231
Istanbul, 53–54
Mediterranean Coast, 148
in Turkey, 23
from United Kingdom, 22
from United States, 20–22
Akçako, 218
Akçay, 113
Akdamar, 237–238
Akmedrese, 202
Akşabe Sultan Tekke, 167
Aksaray, 202
Alacahöyük, 195

Alaeddin Cami (Ankara), 189
Alaeddin Cami (Kırşehir), 195
Alaeddin Cami (Konya), 205
Alaeddin Cami (Niğde), 202
Alaeddin Keykubat, 219
Alaiye Medrese, 219
Alanya, 166–167, 171–172
Alanya Müzesi, 167
Alexandria Troas, 112
Ali Bey Adasi, 114
Ali Kafer Kümbet, 201
Ali Paşa, 65
Ali Paşa Bazaar, 89
Alim Bey Caddesi, 131–132
Altar of Zeus, 115
Altınkum, 130
Amasra, 218
Amasya, 220–221, 225–226
Amasya Museum, 221
Amos, 153
Anadolu Hisar, 71
Anadolu Kavaği, 71
Anatolia. See Central Anatolia
Andos, 222
Andriace, 160
Ani, 233
Anit Kabir, 192
Ankara, 181–182, 185, 189–192
emergencies, 183
guided tours, 185
hotels, 208–209
nightlife, 212
pharmacies, 183
restaurants, 208
shopping, 207
tourist information, 183
transportation, 183–185
travel agencies, 183
Ankara Anadolu Medeniyetleri Müzesi, 189–190
Antakya, 168, 172

Antalya, 161–164, 172–174, 179–180
Antalya Müzesi, 164
Antioch, 168
Anzac Memorial, 110
Apartments, 31
Aphrodisias, 121–122
Apollo Smintheon, 112
Aqueduct, Roman, 165
Arcadian Way, 127
Archaeological Museum, 239
Arkeoloji Müsezi (Bergama), 116
Arkeoloji Müsezi (Bursa), 98
Arkeoloji Müzesi (İstanbul), 61
Arkeoloji Müsezi (İzmir), 119
Arkeoloji Müzesi (Kayseri), 201
Arkeoloji Müsezi (Konya), 206
Arnavutköy, 69
Artvin, 226
Arycanda, 160–161
Arz Odası, 61
Aşıklar Mağarası, 167
Askeri Ve Deniz Müzesi, 110
Asklepieion, 116
Aslanhane Cami, 190
Aspendos, 165–166
Assos, 112–113, 134–135
Atabey Mosque, 219
Atatürk Alanı, 222
Atatürk Caddesi, 119
Atatürk Köşkü, 223
Atatürk Kültür Merkezi, 67
Atatürk Monument, 220
Atatürk Museum (Ankara), 192
Atatürk Museum (Bursa), 98
Atatürk Müzesi (İzmir), 119
Atatürk Orman Çiftliği, 192
Atatürk Parkı, 200

Atatürk's Cottage, 94–95
Ava Irini, 57
Avanos, 199, 209
Avcılar, 199
Aydin, 48
Ayvalık, 106, 113–114, 135
Aziziye Cami, 206

Babakale, 112
Bab-ı Saadet, 61
Bab-ı-Selam, 57
Bafra, 220
Balat Kilise, 219–220
Balik Pazar, 67
Balikesir, 48
Baltalı Kapı, 130
Banking hours, 26
Barbara Kilise, 199
Bardiz, 49
Bartin, 218
Basilica Cistern, 64
Basilica of St. John, 124
Bat Pazar, 97
Baths, Roman, 94, 129–130, 155, 161, 166, 190
Bayburt, 49
Bayındır Dam, 206
Beaches, 28, 75, 87, 113, 114, 120, 128, 130, 133–134, 155, 164, 166, 169, 170, 225
Bebek, 69
Bedestan, 97
Bedrama, 222
Belediye Saray, 95
Bergama, 48, 116, 135–136
Beyazıt Cami, 89
Beyazıt Mosque, 65
Beyazıt Tower, 65
Beylerbeyi Palace, 69
Bitlis, 238
Black Sea Coast, 33–34, 213–228
hotels, 225–228
rental cars, 215
restaurants, 225–228
shopping, 224
sports, 225
tourist information,

215
transportation,
215–216
travel agencies, 215
Blue Mosque, 62–63
Boat travel, 24–25,
55–56, 86, 93–94,
106, 149, 215–216
Boating, 27, 133,
169–170
Bodrum, 122,
131–132, 136–137,
144
Boğazkale, 194
Bor, 202
Bosporus, 69–71
Bosporus Bridge, 69
Bouleterion (Priene),
128
Burmaı Minare Cami,
220
Bursa, 91–92, 96–99
emergencies, 93
guided tours, 94
nightlife, 102
hotels, 100–101
restaurants, 97, 100
shopping, 99
tourist information,
93
transportation,
93–94
Bursa Etnoğrafya
Müzesi, 97
Bus travel
Aegean Coast, 105,
106
Ankara and Central
Anatolia, 184
Black Sea Coast, 215,
216
Bursa, 93
Edirne, 88
Far East, 231
Istanbul, 54, 55
İznik, 93
Mediterranean Coast,
148, 149
in Turkey, 23–24
Business hours, 26
Büyük Karatay
Medrese, 205
Büyükada, 87
Büyükkale, 194
Byzantine basilica
(Kaunos), 155
Byzantine basilica
(Xanthos), 158
Byzantine church,
121

Caca Bey Cami, 195
Caferiye Cami, 232
Cağaloğlu Hamamı,
64, 75
Camcorders and
videotape, 11
Cameras and film, 11
Camping, 27–28
Canoeing and rafting,
225
Cape Helles, 110
Cappadocia, 195–203
Car rentals, 14–15,
106, 184, 215
Car travel
Aegean Coast, 105,
106
Ankara and Central
Anatolia, 183–184
Black Sea Coast, 215,
216
Bursa, 93
Edirne, 88
Far East, 231
Istanbul, 54
İznik, 93
Mediterranean Coast,
148–149
in Turkey, 24
from United
Kingdom, 23
Caravansaries, 128,
199–200, 201–202,
203
Carpets, kilims, 27,
42–49, 63, 74, 132
Cash machines, 8
Castle of St. Peter,
132
Castles, 69, 70, 71,
120, 131, 132, 156,
236, 237
Çamlıca, 72–73
Çamlıhemşin, 224
Çamiçi Gölü, 132
Çanak Kale, 110
Çanakkale, 107, 110,
137–138
Çankaya Köşkü, 192
Çarniçi Gölü, 130
Çarşi Cami, 223
Çarıklı Kilise, 199
Çavuşin, 199
Çavuştepe, 237
Çekirge, 99
Cemeteries, military,
110
Central Anatolia, 33,
181–182
emergencies, 183

guided tours, 185
kilims, 48
pharmacies, 183
tourist information,
183
transportation,
183–185
travel agencies, 183
Çesme, 120, 138–139
Cevat Şakir, 131–132
Children
apartments and villa
rentals, 31
attractions for, 72,
132, 167, 206
traveling with, 16–17
Chronology, 38–41
Church of Gregory,
233
Church of Panaghia
Chrysokephalos, 223
Church of St.
Gregory, 233
Church of the Holy
Apostles, 233
Church of the Holy
Cross, 237–238
Church of the Holy
Savior (Chora), 72
Church of the
Redeemer, 233
Churches
Aegean Coast, 114,
121, 124, 127
Ankara and Central
Anatolia, 198–199
Black Sea Coast,
219–220, 223
Far East, 233,
237–238
Istanbul, 57, 62, 67,
72
İznik, 95
Mediterranean Coast,
159, 160, 168
Çiçek Pasaji, 67
Çifte Hamam, 219
Çifte Kümbet, 201
Çifte Minareli
Medrese, 232
Çinarlı Cami, 114
Çınılı Kösku, 62
Çırağan Palace, 68
City Hall (Bursa), 97
Claros, 123
Climate, 3–4
Clock Tower
(Antalya), 162
Clock Tower
(Istanbul), 67

Cnidos, 153–154
Colophon, 122–123
Column of
Constantinos, 63
Comnene fortress, 219
Constantinian Walls,
72
Consulates, 105
Convent of the Three
Virgins, 233
Cost of traveling, 8–9
Court of the
Janissaries, 57
Credit cards, 32
Crusader Castle, 156
Cumhurbaskanlığı
Köşk, 192
Cumhuriyet Müzesi,
190
Currency, Turkish, 8
Currency exchange, 8
Customs, 10–11
Cyaneae, 159

Dalyan, 154–155, 174
Damlatas Magarasi,
167
Datça, 153, 175
Demeter, sanctuary to
the goddess, 153
Demre, 159, 160, 175
Deniz Kuvetler, 87
Deniz Müsezi, 68
Derinkuyu, 197
Didyma, 130
Dilek Peninsula
National Park, 128
Disabilities, hints for
travelers with, 18
Discounts
for children, 16
student, 16
travel clubs and
agencies, 21–22
Divan-ı-Humayun, 57,
60
Diving and
snorkeling, 133, 170
Diyarbakır, 238–239,
242
Doğubayazıt, 233,
236, 242
Dolmabahçe Mosque,
67
Dolmabahçe Palace,
67–68
Dolmuş, 55, 93–94
Doner Kümbet, 201
Dört Ayaklı Minare,
239

Duties, *10–11*
Düden Falls, *164*

Edirne, *88–90*
Edremit Körfezi, *113*
Educational travel, *19*
Egri Minare, *202*
Egyptian Bazaar, *65, 73*
Egyptian Obelisk, *63*
Electricity, *6–7*
El Nazar Kilise, *199*
Elmalı Kilise, *198–199*
Embassies, *53*
Embassy Row, *192*
Emergencies
Aegean Coast, *105*
Ankara and Central Anatolia, *183*
Bursa, *93*
Istanbul, *53*
Eminönü, *65*
Emir Sultan, *97*
Emirgan, *71*
Ephesus, *122, 123–124, 126–127, 143–144*
Ephesus Museum, *126*
Erzurum, *49, 232, 242–243*
Erzurum Müzesi, *232*
Eski Cami, *88–89*
Eski Gumus, *202*
Eski Kahta, *240*
Eskı Şark Eserlerı Müzesi, *61–62*
Etnoğrafya Müzesi (Ankara), *191*
Etnoğrafya Müzesi (Konya), *206*
Ev Kaya, *219*

Far East, *34–35, 229–244*
hotels, *241–244*
restaurants, *241–244*
shopping, *241*
sports, *241*
tourist information, *230*
transportation, *230–231*
Ferries. *See* Boat travel
Festivals and seasonal events, *5–6*
Fethiye, *155–156, 175*
Fethiye Cami, *220*
Fetih Baba mosque,

219
Foça, *116–117, 139*
Fortresses, *69, 98, 110, 117, 124, 156, 159, 194, 195, 196, 202, 219, 221, 222, 233*
French embassy, *114*

Galata Bridge, *66*
Galata Tower, *66*
Galatsaray Square, *67*
Gallipoli, *110*
Garipler Cami, *221*
Gate of Sphinxes, *195*
Gate of the Lions, *194*
Gavur Kalesi, *195*
Gay and lesbian travelers, hints for *19–20*
Gemiler Island, *156*
Gençlik Parkı, *191, 206*
Genoese castle (Çesme), *120*
Genoese castle (Kuşadası), *128*
Gerbekse, *153*
Gerze, *226*
Gevaş, *237*
Giresun, *222*
Giyasiye Medrese, *200*
Golf, *74*
Gordion, *206–207*
Göcek, *155*
Gök Medrese, *221*
Göreme, *198–199, 209–210*
Göreme Açık Hava Müzesi, *198*
Grand Bazaar, *64–65, 73*
Grand National Assembly Hall, *192*
Graves of the Seven Sleepers, *127*
Great Theater (Miletus), *129*
Great Theater (Pergamum), *115–116*
Great Tumulus, *207*
Greek Monastery of St. George, *87*
Greek theater, *157*
Green Mosque (Bursa), *96–97*
Green Mosque (İznik), *96*
Gülşehir, *196*
Gümüşdere, *237*

Gümüşsu, *123*

Habib Neccar Cami, *168*
Hacettepe University, *191*
Hacı Bayram Cami, *191*
Hacı Kılıe Cami and Medrese, *200*
Hacı Özbek Cami, *95*
Hacıbektaş, *196*
Hacıbektaş Müzesi, *196*
Hadrian's Gate, *164*
Haghia Sophia (Trabzon), *223*
Hagia Sophia (Istanbul), *62*
Haho, *241*
Halicarnassus, *131*
Hans, *203, 206*
Harbiye, *169*
Harem, *60*
Hasan Paşa Han, *239*
Hasanoğlan, *195*
Hatay Müzesi, *169*
Hatti Sun Disk, *191*
Hattuşaş, *193*
Hazeran Mansion, *220*
Hazreti Süleymaniye Cami, *239*
Health and fitness clubs, *74*
Health and medical services, *12–13*
Hellenistic temple, *219*
Heracleia, *132*
Heybeli, *87*
Heykel, *96*
Hıdıv Kasrı, *71*
Hierapolis, *121*
Hiking, *28, 74–75*
Hippodrome, *63*
Hisar, *98, 189*
Hittite cities, *192–195*
Holidays, public, *4–5*
Holy Road, *116*
Homer, *110*
Hopa, *224*
Horozlu Han, *206*
Horseback riding, *170*
Hoşap Castle, *237*
Hostelling, *16*
Hotels. *31–32. See also under specific areas*
discounts for children, *17*

Huant Hatun Cami, Medrese, and Türbe, *200*
Hudavent Hatun Türbe, *202*
Hünkar Kasri, *63*
Hürriyet Meydanı, *88*
Huzur, *72*

Ibn Neccar Mosque, *219*
Ibrahim Bey, *202*
Ibrahim Paşa Palace, *63*
Iç Kale, *166, 167, 239*
Iftariye, *61*
Ihlara, *202–203*
Ilıca beach, *120*
İlyas Bey Cami, *130*
Ince Minare Medrese, *205*
Inceburun Peninsula, *218*
Incesu, *201–202*
Inebolu, *218*
Inscribed Pillar of Xanthos, *158*
Insurance, *13–14, 15*
İsa Bey Cami, *124, 126*
İşak Paşa Saray, *236*
Ishan, *241*
İskele Cami, *162*
İskele Meydanı, *107*
İskenderun, *168*
Istanbul, *50–90*
arts, *84–85*
attractions for children, *72*
beaches, *75*
embassies, *53*
emergencies, *53*
English-language bookstores, *53*
free attractions, *72*
guided tours, *56*
hotels, *67, 80–84*
island excursions, *86–90*
nightlife, *85–86*
restaurants, *61, 65–66, 69, 72–73, 75–80*
shopping, *73–74*
sports, *74–75*
tourist information, *53*
transportation, *53–56*
travel agencies, *53*
Turkish baths, *75*

Istanbul University, 65
İstiklal Caddesi, 66–67
İzmir
environs, 117–120
hotels, 140–141
nightlife, 145
restaurants, 140
travel agency, 106
İzmir Etnoğrafya Müzesi, 119
İznik, 91–92, 95–96
guided tours, 94
hotels, 101
restaurant, 101
tourist information, 93
transportation, 93–94
İznik Museum, 96
Iztuzu Beach, 155

Jogging, 74–75
Jülyanüs Sütunu, 190

Kadifekâle, 117
Kahta, 239–240
Kale (Alanya), 166
Kale Caddesi, 131–132
Kale (Kekova Sound), 159
Kale (Üçağiz), 159
Kalkan, 158, 175–176
Kandira, 216
Kanes, 201
Kanlıca, 71
Kanuni Kervansaray, 120
Kapikiri, 132
Kapitas, 158
Kara Ali Park, 164
Karacabey Cami, 191
Karanlık Bedestan, 219
Karanlık Kilise, 199
Karatay Müzesi, 205
Kariye Museum, 72
Kars, 49, 232–233, 243
Kasbek Kümbet, 201
Kaş, 158–159, 176–177
Kaştellorizon, 159
Kastamonu, 219
Kasım Padişah Cami, 239
Katranci, 155
Kaunos, 155
Kaya, 156

Kaya Cami, 196
Kaymakan Evi, 218–219
Kaymaklı, 197
Kayserı, 48, 200–201, 210
Keci Buku, 154
Kekova Sound, 159
Kemer, 161, 177
Kemerhisar, 202
Kilims, 27, 42–49, 74, 132
carpet and kilim museums, 63
Kırşehir, 195–196
Kızıl Avlu, 116
Kızıl Kule, 167
Kizilay, 192
Kizilkuyruk Koyu, 155
Kocatepe Cami, 192
Konak Square, 119
Konya, 48, 203–206, 210–211
Konyaalti, 164
Kordonboyu, 119
Korsanlar Mağarası, 167
Korykos, 168
Köycegiz, 174
Kral Kapısı, 194
Küçük Ayvasil, 223
Kudrettin Cami, 223
Kültepe, 201
Kültür Park (Bursa), 98
Kültür Park (İzmir), 119
Kümbet Cami, 233
Kümbets, 201
Kurşunlu, 94
Kurşunlu Cami (Kayseri), 200
Kurşunlu Cami (Nevşehir), 196
Kurtulus Park, 191–192
Kuş Cenneti National Park, 99
Kuşadası, 106, 127–128, 141–142, 145

Lake Köyceğiz, 154
Lake Tortum, 241
Lake Van, 236
Lakes, 130, 154, 236, 241
Lala Mustafa Paşa Cami, 232

Language, 12
Laptops, 11–12
Lara, 164
Lâtifiye Cami, 240
Latin monastery, 169
Lefke Kapısı, 96
Letoön, 157
Library of Celsus, 127
Lion Tomb, 154
Lion's Gate, 233
Long-distance calling, 9
Loryma, 153
Luggage, 7, 13
Lycia, 154
Lydae, 155

Madonna Kilise, 198
Magnesian Gate, 127
Mail, 26
Maltepe Cami, 191
Manastir, 48
Marble Avenue, 127
Mardin, 240–241
Marmaris, 150, 153, 177–178, 180
Mausoleums, 131, 192, 201, 220, 221
Maylatya, 48
Medical services, 12–13
Mediterranean Coast, 32–33, 146–180
hotels, 171–179
nightlife, 179–180
restaurants, 150, 156, 162, 171–179
shopping, 169
sports, 169–170
tourist information, 147
travel agencies, 147–148
Medreses, 202, 205–206, 219, 221, 232, 240–241
Melendiz Cayı, 202
Menucer Mosque, 233
Mersin, 168, 178
Meryemana, 126
Mevlana Müzesi, 204
Mevlana Tübesi, 203
Milâs, 130
Miletus, 129–130
Ministry of Finance, 190
Mısır Çarşısı, 65
Monastery of the Virgin, 223–224
Money, 8

Mosques
Aegean Coast, 113, 114, 124, 126, 130
Ankara and Central Anatolia, 189, 190, 191, 192, 195–196, 200, 201, 202, 205, 206
Black Sea Coast, 219, 220, 221, 223
Bursa, 96–98
Edirne, 88–89
Far East, 232, 233, 239, 240
hours, 26
Istanbul, 62–64, 65, 67, 69
İznik, 95, 96
Mediterranean Coast, 162, 167, 168
Mountain climbing, 225, 241
Mt. Ararat, 236
Mt. Nimrod, 239–240, 243
Mt. Olympos, 161
Murad Hüdavendigâr Mosque, 113
Muradiye, 98
Museum of Ottoman Arms, 120
Museum of Underwater Archaeology, 131
Museums
Aegean Coast, 110, 114, 116, 119, 120, 121, 122, 126, 131
Ankara and Central Anatolia, 189–190, 191, 192, 194, 198, 200, 201, 202, 204–205, 206
Black Sea Coast, 219, 220, 221, 222
Bursa, 97, 98
Far East, 232, 233, 237, 239, 240–241
hours, 26
Istanbul, 61–62, 63, 68, 71, 72
İzmir, 119, 120
İznik, 96
Mediterranean Coast, 155, 164, 166, 167, 169
Termal, 94–95
Mustafapaşa, 198
Mut, 48
Myra, 160

NATO Southern Command Headquarters, *119*
Naval Museum, *68*
Nevşehir, *196, 211*
Neyzen Tevfik Caddesi, *131–132*
Niğde, *202*
Notion, *123*
Nuruosmaniye, *65*
Nymphaion (Aspendos), *165*
Nymphaion (Ephesus), *127*
Nymphaion (Miletus), *130*
Nymphaion (Pamukkale), *121*

Odeon, *122*
Old Stamboul, *57, 60–64*
Older travelers, hints for *19*
Ordu, *222*
Orhan Cami, *97*
Ortahisar, *198*
Ortaköy Mosque, *69*
Osman and Orhan, tombs of, *98*
Ölü Deniz, *156, 167, 178–179*
Ören, *113*
Ozkonak, *199*

Packing, *6–8*
Palaces, *57, 60–61, 63, 64, 67–69, 71, 236*
hours, *26*
Palandoken, *243–244*
Pamucak, *123*
Pamukkale, *120–121, 132, 142–143*
Pamukkale Museum, *121*
Pansiyons, *31*
Parks, *68–69, 98, 99, 119, 128, 164, 191–192, 200, 218, 222*
Passports, *9*
Patara, *158*
Pergamum, *114–116*
Perge, *165*
Petronion, *131*
Pharmacies, *183*
Phaselis, *161*
Pillar tombs, *158*
Pinara, *157*
Polonezköy, *71*

Priene, *128–129*
Princes Islands, *86–88*
Prytaneion, *127*
Publications
air travel, *22*
for disabled, *18*
English-language bookstores, *53*
for gay and lesbian travelers, *19–20*
for older travelers, *19*
on Turkey, *20*
traveling with children, *16–17*

Resim ve Heykel Müzesi, *191*
Restaurants, *28–30. See also under specific areas*
Rivan Köşk, *61*
Rize, *224, 226*
Roma Hamamları, *190*
Roman theater, *121*
Rugs (kilims), *27, 42–49, 63, 74, 132*
Rumeli Hisar, *69*
Rumeli Kavaği, *71*
Rustempaşa Kervansaray, *89*
Rüstem Paşa Cami, *65*

Saat Kulesi, *119*
Saatli Cami, *114*
Sacred Column, *62*
Sacred Stoa, *128*
Sadberk Hanim Museum, *71*
Safranbolu, *218, 226*
Sahabiye Medrese, *200*
Sahip Ata, *206*
Sailing, *27*
St. John, *222*
St. Nicholas Basilica, *159, 160*
St. Nicholas Church, *114*
Sakh Kilise, *199*
Salacak, *73*
Samandag, *169*
Samanpazarı, *190*
Samsat, *240*
Samsun, *220, 226–227*
Samsundağ National Park, *128*
San Antonio di

Padua, *67*
Sancta Sophia, *95*
Sanctuary of Demeter, *129*
Sanctuary of Hephaistos, *161*
Saray mosque, *219*
Sarayiçi, *89*
Sardis, *120*
Sari Han, *199, 203*
Sarmısaklı, *114*
Sarıkamuş, *232, 244*
Sarıyer, *71*
Sayid Bilal mausoleum, *220*
Şanliurfa, *240*
Schliemann, Heinrich, *110–111*
School of Philosophy, *122*
Şehir Müzesi, *222*
Selçuk, *123, 124, 126, 143–144*
Selçuk Yasar Müzesi, *119*
Seleuceia ad Piería, *169*
Selime, *202*
Selimiye Cami (Edirne), *89*
Selimiye Cami (Konya), *205*
Seljuk fortress, *196*
Seminaries, *202, 205–206, 219, 221, 232, 240–241*
Şemsi Tebrizi Cami and Türbe, *205*
Senpiyer Kilisesi, *168*
Şerefettin Cami, *205*
Serpentine Column, *63*
17th-Century House, *98*
Şeytan Sofrasi, *114*
Seyyit Vakkas, tomb of, *222*
Shopping, *26–27. See also under specific areas*
hours, *26*
Shrine of Artemis, *116*
Side, *166, 179, 180*
Side Müzesi, *166*
Şifahiye Medrese, *200*
Şile, *216, 227*
Silifke, *168*
Sinop, *219–220, 227*
Sırçalı Kümbet, *201*

Sırçalı Medrese, *205*
Sivas, *48–49*
Skiing, *28, 99, 170, 241*
Smyrna, *117, 119*
Soccer, *75*
Soğanlı, *198*
Sokollu Mehmet Paşa Cami, *63*
Spas, *94*
Spice Market, *65*
Sports and outdoor activities, *27–28, 74–75, 99, 133, 169–170, 225, 241*
Stadiums, ancient, *126, 165*
State Agora, *127*
State Archive, *194*
Street of Kuretes, *127*
Student and youth travel, *15–16*
Süleymaniye Cami (Alanya), *167*
Süleymaniye Cami (Istanbul), *65*
Sultan Ahmet Cami, *62–63*
Sultan Beyazıt Cami, *220*
Sultan Hanı (Anatolia), *201, 203*
Sultan İsa Medrese, *240*
Sultan Murat II Cami, *98*
Sumela, *223–224*
Sünnet Odası, *61*
Swedish consulate, *67*
Synagogue, *120*

Taksim Square, *67*
Tarabya, *71*
Tarsus, *168*
Taxes, *8, 27*
Taxiarchis Church, *114*
Taxis, *55, 185*
Telephones, *9, 25*
Temple of Aphrodite, *122*
Temple of Apollo (Claros), *123*
Temple of Apollo (Didyma), *130*
Temple of Apollo (Pamukkale), *121*
Temple of Artemis, *120*

Temple of Athena (Assos), *113*
Temple of Athena (Pergamum), *115*
Temple of Athena (Priene), *129*
Temple of Augustus, *191*
Temple of Domitian, *127*
Temple of Euromos, *130*
Temple of Hadrian, *127*
Temple of Telesphorus, *116*
Temple of the Storm God, *194*
Temple of Trayan, *115*
Temples II, III, IV, and V, *194*
Teokephastos Convent, *223*
Termal, *91–92, 94–95*
hotels, *101*
restaurants, *101*
tourist information, *93*
transportation, *93–94*
Termessos, *164–165*
Tersane Byzantine Church, *159*
Tetrapylon, *122*
Theaters, ancient, *115–116, 121, 126–127, 129, 131, 155, 156, 157, 158, 159, 160, 164, 165*
Thrace, *49*
Tipping, *26*
Tirebolu, *222*
Tlos, *156–157*

Tokalı Kilise, *199*
Tokat, *221*
Tomb of Amyntas, *155–156*
Tombs, *96, 97, 98, 155–157, 159, 160, 161, 203, 207*
Topkapı Saray, *57, 60–61*
Tortum and Çoruh river valleys, *241*
Tourist offices, government, *2*
Tour operators, *16*
Tours, guided
Aegean Coast, *106*
Ankara and Central Anatolia, *185*
Bursa, *94*
Istanbul, *56*
İznik, *94*
Trabzon, *222–223, 227*
Train travel
Aegean Coast, *105*
Ankara and Central Anatolia, *184*
Edirne, *88*
Far East, *231*
Istanbul, *54*
Mediterranean Coast, *148*
in Turkey, *23*
from United Kingdom, *22–23*
Tours and packages, *2–3*
Travel agencies, *15–16, 18, 53, 147–148, 183, 215*
Traveler's checks, *7*
Treasury, *61*

Trip cancellation insurance, *13–14*
Troy, *110–112, 137–138*
Tumulus of Antiochus, *239–240*
Tünel Square, *66*
Türk Ve Islâm Eserleri Müzesi, *63*
Turkish baths, *64, 75*
Turquoise Coast, *154–161*

Uç Horan Armenian Church, *67*
Uç Serefeli Cami, *88*
Üçağiz, *159*
Ulu Cami (Aksaray), *202*
Ulu Cami (Bitlis), *238*
Ulu Cami (Bursa), *97–98*
Ulu Cami (Diyarbakır), *239*
Ulu Cami (Erzurum), *232*
Ulu Cami (Kayseri), *201*
Uludağ, *99*
hotels, *101–102*
nightlife, *102*
restaurants, *101–102*
skiing, *99*
Ünye, *221–222, 227–228*
Ürgüp, *198, 211–212*

Valide baths, *94*
Value-added tax, *8, 27*
Van, *49, 237, 244*
Van Müze, *237*
Villa rentals, *31*

Viranşehir, *168*
Visas, *9*
Vocabulary, Turkish, *245–249*
Voyvoda Caddesi, *66*

Windsurfing, *133, 170*
Women traveling alone, *17–18*

Xanthos, *157–158*

Yakup Ağa, *219*
Yakutiye Medrese, *232*
Yazılıkaya, *194–195*
Yedigöller National Park, *218*
Yeni Cami (Ankara), *190*
Yeni Cami (Istanbul), *65*
Yeni Cuma Cami, *223*
Yeniköy, *71*
Yeralti Mezar, *96*
Yerebatan Saray, *64*
Yerkapı, *194*
Yeşil Cami (Bursa), *96–97*
Yeşil Cami (İznik), *96*
Yeşil Türbe, *96–97*
Yıldırım Beyazit, *97*
Yıldız Park, *68–69*
Yivli Minare, *162*
Yörük Ali Plaj, *87*

Zelve, *199*
Zigana Pass, *224*
Zinciriye medreses, *202*
Zonguldak, *218*

Personal Itinerary

Departure *Date*

Time

Transportation

Arrival *Date* *Time*

Departure *Date* *Time*

Transportation

Accommodations

Arrival *Date* *Time*

Departure *Date* *Time*

Transportation

Accommodations

Arrival *Date* *Time*

Departure *Date* *Time*

Transportation

Accommodations

Personal Itinerary

Arrival *Date*   *Time*

Departure *Date*   *Time*

Transportation

Accommodations

Arrival *Date*   *Time*

Departure *Date*   *Time*

Transportation

Accommodations

Arrival *Date*   *Time*

Departure *Date*   *Time*

Transportation

Accommodations

Arrival *Date*   *Time*

Departure *Date*   *Time*

Transportation

Accommodations

Personal Itinerary

Arrival *Date*   *Time*

Departure *Date*   *Time*

Transportation

Accommodations

Arrival *Date*   *Time*

Departure *Date*   *Time*

Transportation

Accommodations

Arrival *Date*   *Time*

Departure *Date*   *Time*

Transportation

Accommodations

Arrival *Date*   *Time*

Departure *Date*   *Time*

Transportation

Accommodations

Personal Itinerary

Arrival *Date*   *Time*

Departure *Date*   *Time*

Transportation

Accommodations

Arrival *Date*   *Time*

Departure *Date*   *Time*

Transportation

Accommodations

Arrival *Date*   *Time*

Departure *Date*   *Time*

Transportation

Accommodations

Arrival *Date*   *Time*

Departure *Date*   *Time*

Transportation

Accommodations

Personal Itinerary

Arrival *Date*   *Time*

Departure *Date*   *Time*

Transportation

Accommodations

Arrival *Date*   *Time*

Departure *Date*   *Time*

Transportation

Accommodations

Arrival *Date*   *Time*

Departure *Date*   *Time*

Transportation

Accommodations

Arrival *Date*   *Time*

Departure *Date*   *Time*

Transportation

Accommodations

Addresses

Name	*Name*
Address	*Address*
Telephone	*Telephone*
Name	*Name*
Address	*Address*
Telephone	*Telephone*
Name	*Name*
Address	*Address*
Telephone	*Telephone*
Name	*Name*
Address	*Address*
Telephone	*Telephone*
Name	*Name*
Address	*Address*
Telephone	*Telephone*
Name	*Name*
Address	*Address*
Telephone	*Telephone*
Name	*Name*
Address	*Address*
Telephone	*Telephone*
Name	*Name*
Address	*Address*
Telephone	*Telephone*

Addresses

Name	*Name*
Address	*Address*
Telephone	*Telephone*
Name	*Name*
Address	*Address*
Telephone	*Telephone*
Name	*Name*
Address	*Address*
Telephone	*Telephone*
Name	*Name*
Address	*Address*
Telephone	*Telephone*
Name	*Name*
Address	*Address*
Telephone	*Telephone*
Name	*Name*
Address	*Address*
Telephone	*Telephone*
Name	*Name*
Address	*Address*
Telephone	*Telephone*

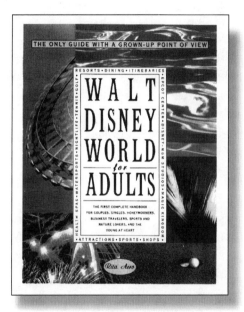

Fodor's Travel Guides

Available at bookstores everywhere, or call 1–800–533–6478, 24 hours a day.

U.S. Guides

Alaska

Arizona

Boston

California

Cape Cod, Martha's Vineyard, Nantucket

The Carolinas & the Georgia Coast

Chicago

Colorado

Florida

Hawaii

Las Vegas, Reno, Tahoe

Los Angeles

Maine, Vermont, New Hampshire

Maui

Miami & the Keys

New England

New Orleans

New York City

Pacific North Coast

Philadelphia & the Pennsylvania Dutch Country

The Rockies

San Diego

San Francisco

Santa Fe, Taos, Albuquerque

Seattle & Vancouver

The South

The U.S. & British Virgin Islands

USA

The Upper Great Lakes Region

Virginia & Maryland

Waikiki

Walt Disney World and the Orlando Area

Washington, D.C.

Foreign Guides

Acapulco, Ixtapa, Zihuatanejo

Australia & New Zealand

Austria

The Bahamas

Baja & Mexico's Pacific Coast Resorts

Barbados

Berlin

Bermuda

Brittany & Normandy

Budapest

Canada

Cancún, Cozumel, Yucatán Peninsula

Caribbean

China

Costa Rica, Belize, Guatemala

The Czech Republic & Slovakia

Eastern Europe

Egypt

Euro Disney

Europe

Florence, Tuscany & Umbria

France

Germany

Great Britain

Greece

Hong Kong

India

Ireland

Israel

Italy

Japan

Kenya & Tanzania

Korea

London

Madrid & Barcelona

Mexico

Montréal & Québec City

Morocco

Moscow & St. Petersburg

The Netherlands, Belgium & Luxembourg

New Zealand

Norway

Nova Scotia, Prince Edward Island & New Brunswick

Paris

Portugal

Provence & the Riviera

Rome

Russia & the Baltic Countries

Scandinavia

Scotland

Singapore

South America

Southeast Asia

Spain

Sweden

Switzerland

Thailand

Tokyo

Toronto

Turkey

Vienna & the Danube Valley

Special Series

Fodor's Affordables

Caribbean

Europe

Florida

France

Germany

Great Britain

Italy

London

Paris

**Fodor's Bed &
Breakfast and
Country Inns Guides**

America's Best B&Bs

California

Canada's Great
Country Inns

Cottages, B&Bs and
Country Inns of
England and Wales

Mid-Atlantic Region

New England

The Pacific
Northwest

The South

The Southwest

The Upper Great
Lakes Region

The Berkeley Guides

California

Central America

Eastern Europe

Europe

France

Germany & Austria

Great Britain &
Ireland

Italy

London

Mexico

Pacific Northwest &
Alaska

Paris

San Francisco

**Fodor's Exploring
Guides**

Australia

Boston &
New England

Britain

California

The Caribbean

Florence & Tuscany

Florida

France

Germany

Ireland

Italy

London

Mexico

New York City

Paris

Prague

Rome

Scotland

Singapore & Malaysia

Spain

Thailand

Turkey

Fodor's Flashmaps

Boston

New York

Washington, D.C.

Fodor's Pocket Guides

Acapulco

Bahamas

Barbados

Jamaica

London

New York City

Paris

Puerto Rico

San Francisco

Washington, D.C.

Fodor's Sports

Cycling

Golf Digest's Best
Places to Play

Hiking

The Insider's Guide
to the Best Canadian
Skiing

Running

Sailing

Skiing in the USA &
Canada

USA Today's Complete
Four Sports Stadium
Guide

**Fodor's Three-In-Ones
(guidebook, language
cassette, and phrase
book)**

France

Germany

Italy

Mexico

Spain

**Fodor's
Special-Interest
Guides**

Complete Guide to
America's National
Parks

Condé Nast Traveler
Caribbean Resort and
Cruise Ship Finder

Cruises and Ports
of Call

Euro Disney

France by Train

Halliday's New
England Food
Explorer

Healthy Escapes

Italy by Train

London Companion

Shadow Traffic's New
York Shortcuts and
Traffic Tips

Sunday in New York

Sunday in San
Francisco

Touring Europe

Touring USA:
Eastern Edition

Walt Disney World and
the Orlando Area

Walt Disney World
for Adults

**Fodor's Vacation
Planners**

Great American
Learning Vacations

Great American
Sports & Adventure
Vacations

Great American
Vacations

Great American
Vacations for Travelers
with Disabilities

National Parks and
Seashores of the East

National Parks
of the West

**The Wall Street
Journal Guides to
Business Travel**

At last — a guide for Americans with disabilities that makes traveling a delight

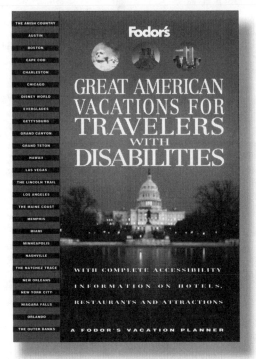

0-679-02591-X $18.00 ($24.00 Can)

This is the first and only complete guide to great American vacations for the 35 million North Americans with disabilities, as well as for those who care for them or for aging parents and relatives. Provides:

- Essential trip-planning information for travelers with mobility, vision, and hearing impairments

- Specific details on a huge array of facilities, along with solid descriptions of attractions, hotels, restaurants, and other destinations

- Up-to-date information on ISA-designated parking, level entranceways, and accessibility to pools, lounges, and bathrooms